WINGS
OF FAME™

Aerospace Publishing Ltd
AIRtime Publishing Inc.

Published quarterly by
Aerospace Publishing Ltd
179 Dalling Road
London W6 0ES
UK

Copyright © Aerospace Publishing Ltd
1997

ISSN 1361-2034

Aerospace ISBN 1 86184 008 X
                (softback)
                1 86184 009 8
                (hardback)
AIRtime ISBN   1-880588-23-4

Published under licence in USA and
Canada by AIRtime Publishing Inc.,
10 Bay Street, Westport,
CT 06880, USA

Editorial Offices:
WINGS OF FAME™
Aerospace Publishing Ltd
3A Brackenbury Road
London W6 0BE UK

Publisher: Stan Morse
Managing Editor: David Donald
Editors: Jim Winchester
         David Donald

Sub Editor: Karen Leverington
Editorial Assistant: Tim Senior
US Correspondent: Robert F. Dorr

Artists: Mike Badrocke
         Chris Davey
         Keith Fretwell
         Mark Rolfe
         Kata Vida
         John Weal
Origination by
  Chroma Graphics, Singapore
Printed by
  Officine Grafiche DeAgostini,
  Novara, Italy

The editors of WINGS OF FAME™
welcome photographs for possible
publication, but cannot accept any
responsibility for loss or damage to
unsolicited material.

The publishers gratefully acknowledge
the assistance given by the following
people:

Lt Mario and Peggy de Luca USN,
National Museum of Naval History,
Peter M. Bowers, William Swisher,
Nick Williams, Al Hansen, Ken
Wilson, Dave Scheuer, Bob Lawson, Al
Lloyd, Hal Andrews, Roger Seybel of
the Grumman History Center,
Paul Bowers of the Vought Aircraft
Co., Bill Ahlstrom of McDonnell
Douglas and PH1 Casey Atkins of the
'Blue Angels' for all their assistance
with the 'Blue Angels' feature

James C. Goodall, 'Blackbird' historian
and Crew Chief of preserved A-12
60-6931 for his invaluable assistance
with the A-12/YF-12/SR-71 article

XF8B-1 pilots Don Lopez and Barney
Turner, Tom Lubbemeyer at Boeing
and Hal Andrews, Warren M. Bodie,
Wayne Mutza and Nick Veronico for
their help with the F8B article

Tranh Dinh Kiem, Nguyen Van Dinh,
Emá Bohár, Vietnamese Embassy,
Budapest, Ministry of Foreign Affairs,
Hanoi, VPAF Museum, Hanoi, Hanoi
Air Base, Da Nang Air Base and Nha
Trang Air Base for their assistance with
the VPAF MiG-17 article

The author of the Lockheed A-12/
YF-12/SR-71 article, Paul F.
Crickmore, would like to thank, first
and foremost, his wife, Alison, for all of
her hardwork in the preparation of this
article, and for her unstinting interest
and support. Thanks are also due to
dear and long-standing friend Jay Miller
for access to additional information in
his superb book Lockheed Skunk Works:
the First Fifty Years (Aerofax Inc. 1993,
ISBN: 1-85780-037-0)

During the production of this
volume the editorial team was
shocked to learn of the tragic
death of aviation historian Jeffrey
L. Ethell. Jeff had contributed
much to Wings of Fame, and will
be greatly missed by all in the
aviation publishing business. Our
sympathies go out to his family.

Wings of Fame™ is a registered
trademark in the United States of
America of AIRtime Publishing Inc.

Wings of Fame™ is published
quarterly and is available by
subscription and from many fine book
and hobby stores.

SUBSCRIPTION AND BACK
NUMBERS:

UK and World (except USA and
Canada) write to:
Aerospace Publishing Ltd
FREEPOST
PO Box 2822
London
W6 0BR
UK

(No stamp required if posted in the
UK)

USA and Canada, write to:
AIRtime Publishing Inc.
Subscription Dept
10 Bay Street
Westport
CT 06880, USA
(203) 838-7979
Toll-free order number in USA:
1 800 359-3003

Prevailing subscription rates are as
follows:
Softbound edition for 1 year:
   $59.95
Softbound edition for 2 years:
   $112.00
Softbound back numbers (subject to
availability) are $16.00 each, plus
shipping and handling. All rates are
for delivery within mainland USA,
Alaska and Hawaii. Canadian and
overseas prices available upon request.
American Express, Discover Card,
MasterCard and Visa accepted. When
ordering please include card number,
expiration date and signature.

U.S. Publisher:
   Mel Williams
Subscriptions Director:
   Linda DeAngelis
Charter Member Services
Manager:
   Janie Munro
Retail Sales Director: Jill Brooks
Shipping Manager: E. Rex Anku

WINGS
OF FAME™

CONTENTS

'Blue Angels'

For just over half a century, the United States Navy's Flight Demonstration Squadron has thrilled the public and provided inspiration to both serving and would-be naval aviators. In that time they have flown the best of the navy's combat aircraft at more than 3,500 displays and look set to do so for many more.

Of the eight main display aircraft used by the 'Blue Angels' in their half-century of thrilling the crowds and promoting naval aviation, perhaps the most fondly remembered is the diminutive A-4 Skyhawk. With a thrust-to-weight ratio rivalled only by the Bearcat, the A-4 had the shortest wingspan of all the 'Blues' aircraft, giving a superb roll-rate.

The US Navy Flight Demonstration Squadron (NFDS) – more popularly known as the 'Blue Angels' – celebrated its 50th anniversary in 1996, making it the oldest continuous aerobatic group in the world. This is not to say that it was the first aerial demonstration team, not even in the US Navy.

The first US Navy group to perform in public was organised by Lieutenant D. W. Tomlinson in late 1927. He had only recently been reassigned to US Navy Fighter Squadron VF-2B as the executive officer from non-flying duty as an instructor at the US Naval Academy, and he recognised the need to 'show the flag' in order to vie with the fledgling US Army Air Corps for funds and for authorisation to compete for missions. His peers agreed. Tomlinson selected two squadron pilots, Lieutenants (jg) W. V. Davis and A. P. Storrs, to train as the wingmen for the group, which would be known as the 'Seahawks'. They performed in their Boeing F2B-1 biplanes at various shows while based at North Island, near San Diego, California. That team disbanded in late 1929, when all three of the pilots received orders to report to new assignments.

Navy demonstration teams

Other units that performed under the banner of the US Navy were the 'High Hatters' of VF-1B, also flying F2B-1s; the 'Three Flying Fish' formed within the Tactical Section of the Naval Flight Test Group from NAS Anacostia; and the 'Three T'Gallants' from Training Squadron 5. The 'Flying Fish' flew Curtiss F6C-4 shipboard fighters and the 'T'Gallants' flew, at different times, F6C-4s, F4B-1s and F2B-1s, all carrier-capable biplane fighters.

After World War II, teams that performed included the 'Gray Angels', made up of rear admirals flying McDonnell FH-1 Phantom Is, as well as a Marine group from VMF-122 that also flew FH Phantoms. The A-4 Skyhawk, in addition to being the vehicle used by the 'Blue Angels', was used for a short time with the 'Albino Angels' formed within VA-113, and with the 'Air Barons', a USN reserve group from Glenview, Illinois.

Above: The biggest, heaviest, fastest and most powerful aircraft used by the 'Blue Angels' was the McDonnell Douglas F-4J Phantom. Impressive as it was, it was not ideal.

Left: The straight-wing Grumman F9F Panther was the first jet to serve with the 'Blue Angels', joining the team in 1949. It was replaced in 1955 by the swept-wing F9F-8 Cougar.

The unit that came to be known as the 'Blue Angels' was formed in 1946 at Jacksonville, Florida within the Naval Air Advanced Training Command after an initial suggestion floated down from the US Navy Public Affairs office of the Secretary of the Navy. The primary purpose of the proposed flying exhibition group was to bring a recruiting message to the public. After the cessation of the hostilities of World War II, the military services were top heavy in rank structure. To regain the proper mix to ensure a stable growth, new members were needed in both enlisted and commissioned ranks. It was felt that an exciting flying demonstration would help to draw in recruits from around the country. Also, an added incentive would be the help in projecting the Navy's message to the public of the advantages of a strong carrier-oriented force, to emphasise the foreign policy of the United States to the nations around the world.

When the directive reached the US Navy Air Advanced Training Command via the chain of command from topside, it was passed down until it reached the desk of Lieutenant Commander Roy 'Butch' Voris. He was the chief instructor for the Instructors Advanced Training Unit which was responsible for training Navy personnel to be instructors. Voris concurred in the "advisability of establishing such a team" and, after passing it back up the chain, the mechanism was established. Voris was selected as the first officer in charge (OIC) of the Navy Flight Exhibition Team. Fifty years later, 25 other US Navy leaders have also held the title of 'the boss' of this distinguished group of pilots.

In 1950, the team put aside its task of thrilling the viewers with its spectacular aerobatics and went to war. Lieutenant Commander John Magda, the skipper, led the transition of the team into US Navy Fighter Squadron VF-191 and prepared for action in Korea, where they flew two tours aboard the carrier USS *Princeton*. Sadly, Magda did not survive. He was killed during a strafing run on 8 March 1951 near Tanchon.

Squadron status

In October 1951, 'Butch' Voris was asked to reform the team and to be ready for the 1952 season. They continued as a team until 1974 when, during the switch to the McDonnell Douglas A-4F Skyhawk II, the organisation was upgraded to that of a squadron. That included the official assignment of such personnel as flight surgeon, supply, administration and other skilled personnel, who had formerly assisted on a part-time basis when needed.

Today, the US Naval Flight Demonstration Squadron, the 'Blue Angels', reports to the Chief of Naval Air Training Command (CNATRA) in the hierarchy of command, but represents the Department of Defense (as does the USAF 'Thunderbirds' team).

The Grumman F6F-5 Hellcat was initially selected as the vehicle to allow the team members to demonstrate their piloting skills. A North American SNJ-6 Texan trainer was also selected, to simulate a Japanese 'Zero' aircraft and to provide the solo manoeuvres during the routine.

Voris was given full authority to name the pilots, ground crew and other supporting personnel to accomplish the mission. The first pilots selected were Lieutenant Commander L. G. Barnard, Lieutenant (jg) M. W. Cassidy, and Lieutenant M. N. Wickendoll. Barnard was shortly reassigned to another command and Lieutenant Al Taddeo and Lieutenant (jg) Gale Stouse received orders to join the team, with Stouse flying the SNJ solo act.

The Hellcats received slight modifications, in that non-essential items were deleted to reduce weight. This consisted of the guns, ammunition boxes, armour and other small items. The aircraft were painted insignia blue, which was lighter than the standard blue used by the fleet aircraft, and the lettering was applied in yellow.

After six weeks of practice, Rear Admiral Ralph Davidson and Vice Admiral Frank Wagner approved the show. On 15 June 1946, the first public appearance was made at the Southeastern Air Show at Craig Field, Jacksonville, Florida. Although four Hellcats were assigned, the show were based on the three-man Vee formation, stressing low-altitude manoeuvres. The Vee formation was used to enable each aircraft to roll about its individual axis rather than about the formation axis. The SNJ would fly through the area and the Hellcats simulated gun runs with the ersatz 'Zero', which itself simulated being shot down. The

The first mount of the 'Blue Angels' was the F6F Hellcat. The team was an instant hit with the public and the top brass, and quickly re-equipped with the F8F Bearcat, seen below. The 'Blue Angels' name was that of a New York night club spotted by a team member in the listings section of the New Yorker magazine.

Above: The 'Blue Angels' performed their first public show at Craig Field, Jacksonville on 15 June 1946. The team chose the F6F Hellcat over the F4U Corsair and F7F Tigercat, beginning a 22-year association with Grumman products. One name considered for the new team before 'Blue Angels' was adopted was 'Blue Lancers'.

Below: The original display routine included a series of military formations and simulated air combat tactics rather than the 'show' formations of later years. The display altitude was as low as 10 ft (3 m). The team is seen here performing its last Hellcat show at Grumman's Bethpage factory.

The first commander of the 'Blues' was LCdr Roy Marlin 'Butch' Voris, seen here in his F6F-5. Voris flew combat in the F4F with VF-10 in 1942 (and was wounded at Guadalcanal) and the F6F with VF-2, scoring seven confirmed kills and one probable against 'Zeroes'. Voris returned to lead the team when they reformed with F9Fs in 1952.

Hellcats then continued with reverse echelon rolls, Cuban eights and inverted flying. The show routine was 17 minutes long and could be kept within the length of the 7,000-ft (2135-m) runway. Show altitude varied from 10 to 2,800 ft (3 to 855 m).

The F6Fs were used for three months before being replaced by the Grumman F8F-1 Bearcat. To further enhance its show appearance, the team switched to the Bearcat in 24 August 1946, at a show in Denver, Colorado. It continued to operate the Bearcat until 14 August 1949 when a transition to the Grumman F9F-2 Panther was made. The selection of the light, compact Bearcat proved to be a superb choice and, with some practice and two shows under its belt, the team performed at the 1946 Cleveland Air Races, at that time the premier air show in the world. The recognition received at that show resulted in world-wide attention. Appearance requests poured in to the team at a greatly increased rate.

New leader, new member

Initially, the team continued the three-aircraft Vee show. With the selection on 30 May 1947 of a new leader, Lieutenant Commander R. A. Clarke, the four-aircraft formation was introduced to more accurately portray the usual fighter formation of tactical naval aviation, comprising two sections of two aircraft. This permitted incorporating into the routine the Thach Weave, in which the two sections of aircraft would weave left and right to protect each other on offence and defence. With this manoeuvre, they also continued to 'attack' and shoot down the interloper SNJ/'Zero'. New manoeuvres added during the F8F era included the four-aircraft Cuban eight in a loose line-abreast position and the reverse echelon roll, in a 24-minute show. In 1949, the SNJ/'Zero' (which was also known as *Beetle Bomb)* was replaced with a Bearcat, continuing the pre-dominately yellow paint scheme used by the earlier simulated 'Zero'. During this period, the team consisted of five Bearcats (one a spare), the SNJ/'Zero' (replaced later with an additional Bearcat) and a transport borrowed from base operations, usually a Douglas R4D Skytrain. The operation was augmented with base personnel who assisted in narrating, operating the transport and other administrative details. The five demonstration pilots did not always fly the same spot, sometimes switching between positions. In addition to the demonstration pilots, a dedicated cadre of eight enlisted personnel was responsible for the unexpected – as well as the routine – maintenance necessary for the 'Blue Angels' to meet all their flying commitments.

In 1948 the team's parent organisation, the Naval Air Advanced Training Command, moved to Corpus Christi, Texas from Jacksonville, Florida. The 'Blue Angels' were led to their new location by Lieutenant Commander R. E 'Dusty' Rhodes, the team's third leader and a former Japanese POW.

A yellow-painted SNJ was used as the team's solo aircraft in the Hellcat and Bearcat eras. At first, the SNJ portrayed a 'Zero' in the show routine, complete with Japanese hinomaru insignia. The SNJ was 'shot down' in each show and a dummy backseat 'pilot' was thrown out by an airman to parachute down for prompt capture by a detachment of Marines.

While the prop-driven Bearcats piloted by the Navy's best pilots gave a spectacular and crowd-pleasing show, it was inevitable that they would be replaced as technology advanced the state of the art with turbine-powered aircraft. The Navy was anxious to show the public its new first line fighter, the Grumman F9F-2 Panther.

Jet-age 'Blues'

In June 1949, under skipper 'Dusty' Rhode's leadership, the team transitioned to turbine-powered aircraft. The initial training was accomplished in Lockheed TO-1 (P-80C) aircraft at North Island in a syllabus that gave each pilot about 10 solo hours. In July, they flew to Bethpage, Long Island, New York, the home of Grumman Aircraft Corporation, to pick up their new F9F-2 Panthers, and ferried them to Corpus Christi to prepare for the upcoming shows. For a while they continued to perform in the Bearcats until they could bring the Panther routine on line. Since the aircraft were new to the fleet also, not just to the team, some problems surfaced regarding to maintenance and the availability of some ground support equipment.

After an approval show at Pensacola for the admiral on 5 August 1949, the jet routine was taken to the public at Beaumont, Texas on 20 August 1949. The switch to jets also signalled a

When the 'Blue Angels' transitioned to the F8F-1 in late 1949, Grumman painted the aircraft at their factory. Seen here collecting their new mounts are (left to right) Lts William May and Maurice 'Wick' Wickendoll, LCdr Voris and Lt Chuck Knight. The first badge used by the team is also shown. Later, the aircraft on the crest changed to represent the particular type then in team use.

Right: The 'Blue Angels' Bearcats wore the team name on each side of the cowl, but no national insignia. The no. 5 aircraft was normally the team's show spare.

station change, with the team being reassigned to NAS Whiting Field near Pensacola, Florida. This move facilitated an auxiliary mission for the team, that of helping in the training and upgrading of pilots for jet aircraft. Whiting, with its longer runways, was more adaptable to the requirements of jet aircraft and was also the home of the Navy's jet training squadron, Jet Training Unit One (JTU-1).

The last F9F-2 show was flown 30 July 1950, at which time the team was disbanded and the members became the nucleus of VF-191. The squadron prepared for action in Korea under the leadership of Lieutenant Commander John Magda, who had relieved Lieutenant Commander Rhodes on 11 January 1950.

As was to be expected, flying the jets was radically different than flying the Pratt & Whitney R-2800 reciprocating engine-powered Bearcats. The jets could fly in much

In the early years a variety of transport aircraft were borrowed or assigned to support the team. Mostly they were Beech SNBs (C-45s) or R4Ds (C-47s). During 1953, when the team was based at NAS Corpus Christi, it used this R5C-1 (C-46).

Below: The Bearcats began to introduce tight formations into the routine as opposed to 'dogfight' manoeuvres. Nos 2 and 3 have always flown the right and left wing positions, respectively, with no. 4 in the slot.

Above: Despite moving into the jet era, the 'Blue Angels' retained one example of their previous mount to act as the 'enemy' and as the solo aircraft. This was an F8F-1 named Beetle Bomb, painted yellow with blue markings in a reversal of the team's normal scheme. It was lost in a crash in 1950. Another, 'blue' F8F replaced Beetle Bomb as the narrator's transport.

Left: The first jet used by the 'Blue Angels' was Grumman's successor to the Bearcat, the F9F Panther. In September 1949, the team re-equipped with the F9F-2 version, using four or five aircraft in the display routine. The Panther was faster and higher-climbing than the Bearcat but had a larger turning circle. This picture and the one above show the team's equipment at the National Air Races at Cleveland in 1949.

closer and flatter due to the absence of the propellers. This introduced a phenomenon known as the proximity effect, which affected the control forces and obligated the pilots to anticipate this effect. The turbine engines also produced less thrust at low speed, making it necessary to fly at higher speeds for all manoeuvres. The time required for the early jet engines to spool up also required the pilots to anticipate any additional power increases needed to manoeuvre the aircraft.

Trailing smoke was a feature introduced by the Panthers. Dyed fuel (red and blue) was released from the wingtip tanks to mark the flight path of the aircraft during the manoeuvres, as was a trail of white smoke emitted from the engine tailpipe. A low grade of oil, commonly used in construction and sometimes referred to as 'corvus' oil, was piped into the engine exhaust at the option of the pilot, producing a trail of dense, white smoke. This mirrored the practice of most private aerobatic aircraft.

Over 1,000 of the straight-wing Panthers were built in the F9F-2/3/4 and -5 series. The 'Blue Angels' used the F9F-2 and the F9F-5 variants.

After a 14-month standown brought about by the Korean conflict, the Chief of Naval

In June 1950, the 'Blue Angels' were ordered to form the nucleus of fighter squadron VF-191 'Satan's Kittens' for service in Korea. Here LCdr Johnny Magda leads F9F-2s of VF-191 over the Golden Gate Bridge prior to deployment on USS Princeton. Magda did not survive the tour.

Beetle Bomb served with the 'Blues' as a display aircraft in its own right and as transport for a narrator who described the team's manoeuvres to the show crowd. Between the main gear was a pod containing a dummy pilot and parachute.

Operations determined that there it would be advantageous to bring the 'Blue Angels' back for the 1952 season. The Vought F7U-1 Cutlass, then undergoing flight tests, appeared to be a prime choice for the demonstration vehicle. Its rate of roll and turning radius was, at that time, unsurpassed, and the aircraft would be able to perform new and spectacular manoeuvres. Lieutenant Commander 'Whitey' Feightner was selected to head the reformed team. Feightner was a World War II veteran fighter and test pilot, and was involved in the Cutlass flight test programme at Patuxent River. Upon hearing of the selection of the Cutlass as the prime aircraft, he convinced the authorities, based on his testing experience, that they should rethink their selection, since the F7U-1 had not been fully developed and lacked the reliability necessary to fulfil a year-long schedule of air shows. However, Feightner agreed that they could be used as solo demonstration vehicles, and he accepted the assignment to be one of the pilots. 'Mac' MacKnight, a former 'Blue Angel' from the 1948/49 team, returned to fly the second F7U-1 Cutlass.

Problematic Panther

A new version of the F9F Panther was then selected to be used, the F9F-5. Although similar in appearance to the -2, the new Panther had more power. It used the P&W J48-P-6, an adaptation of the Rolls-Royce Tay centrifugal flow turbine engine rated at 7,000 lb (31.5 kN)

static thrust. This 22 per cent power increase, coupled with only a 9 per cent increase in empty weight over the -2 Panther, did provide some added performance. The F9F-5's fuselage length was increased by 19 in (48.3 cm) and the tail height was increased over the F9F-2. The original leader from 1946/47, Lieutenant Commander 'Butch' Voris, was waiting for a new assignment and, being senior to Feightner, was then tasked with the job of standing up the organisation. Although Feightner was originally offered the leadership position, he never occupied it. The 'Blue Angels' used this straight-winged fighter until 1955.

After reforming, the team returned to NAS Corpus Christi, Texas as its base camp. Grumman delivered the six new F9F-5s to the 'Blues' in early 1952 but, for the most part, they were grounded until June because of fuel-control problems. The first F9F-5 show was flown for the public on 20 June 1952 at Memphis, Tennessee. Two F7U-1 Cutlasses, which had been brought aboard to act as additional soloists and to supplement the normal Diamond formation, became the primary show aircraft to cover for the grounded Panthers. When the F9F-5's fuel-control problems were fixed, the two Cutlass aircraft, which required

Grumman F6F-5 Hellcat

The 'Blue Angels' Hellcats were painted in insignia blue, a lighter shade than the midnight blue then current for USN fighters. The markings were actually applied in gold leaf during the brief F6F era.

Display aircraft of the 'Blue Angels'

Grumman F8F-1 Bearcat

Grumman painted the Bearcats assigned to the team in a shade of its own devising, which came to be known as 'Blue Angels Blue'. The actual hue has varied over the years.

Grumman F9F-5 Panther

The Panther was the first team aircraft to wear the 'Blue Angels' crest. The markings were basically identical on the earlier F9F-2s.

Chance-Vought F7U-1 Cutlass

The two Cutlasses were numbered '7' and '8' during their brief career with the team. The inscription 'Vought Cutlass' was carried on the inner vertical fin surfaces.

Grumman F9F-8 Cougar

The Cougars introduced the team name in script to the colour scheme and revised the position of the 'U.S. Navy' titles on the fuselage, compared to the Panther.

Grumman F11F-1 Tiger

The original 'short-nosed' F11Fs wore angular 'Blue Angels' titles at the beginning of their service with the team. Markings positions varied more during the Tiger period than with other team aircraft.

McDonnell Douglas F-4J Phantom II

The Phantoms wore enlarged versions of the yellow trim and underside arrowhead markings that had been introduced on the F11F. The forward Sparrow missiles were sometimes blue.

McDonnell Douglas A-4F Skyhawk II

The colours and markings on the Skyhawk were a slightly subdued version of those on the Phantom. As on the Phantom and Tiger, the underwing 'US Navy' titles were in a swept-back style.

McDonnell Douglas F/A-18 Hornet

Today's F/A-18s follow the pattern used since the later-model Tigers, with some revision to the 'Blue Angels' script and the addition of the manufacturer's 'Hornet' logo.

Below: The F9F-5s suffered from control problems which resulted in cancellation of some early shows with the Panther. Whether or not this scene was the result of such a problem, this 'Blues' Panther needed lots of muscle to unstick it from the mud, Detroit 1953.

Above: When VF-191 returned after its Korean sojourn, the 'Blue Angels' reformed with the F9F-5 version of the Panther. The 'dash-five' incorporated a new (J48 vs J46) engine, but the main external changes were a taller fin and a 2-ft (0.6-m) fuselage extension. 'Butch' Voris led the team again for the 1952 season and was followed by former VF-191 XO Ray Hawkins.

In January 1955, the 'Blues' transitioned to the faster and more powerful F9F-8 Cougar. An underside view of the 'Blue Angels' Cougars illustrates the main differences between the F9F-5 Panther and F9F-8 Cougar – swept wings and tailplanes and no tip-tanks. The team crest remained unchanged from Panther days.

F9F-5s. The F9F-6 aircraft were returned to the US Navy and were never used as a showplane.

Cougars were not assigned to the 'Blue Angels' until the 1955 season, when leader Commander R. L. 'Zeke' Cormier accepted the delivery of F9F-8B aircraft. The first Cougar show was flown at El Centro, the team's winter training practice site, on 22 January 1955. The final show for this aircraft occurred 12 July 1957 in Pensacola, where the 'Blue Angels' had again relocated in mid-season, 1955.

Most of the Cougars used by the team were F9F-8Bs (this version was readily available), the attack version that differed from the F9F-8 or fighter variant by having a low-level bombing system, cockpit instrumentation and the elimination of the engine air inlet ramp. Two F9F-8 fighters were assigned. The inflight-refuelling probe, normally installed in the nose, was removed on most of these 'Blue Angel' aircraft.

Supersonic Tiger

In 1956, newer aircraft were considered to replace the Cougars. Douglas A4D Skyhawks and North American FJ-3 Furies were evaluated, but were rejected because they were not equipped with a performance-enhancing afterburner. The rapid power and the noise produced by this device was thought to be a plus for the show. The Grumman F11F-1 met these requirements and, what is more important, the timing was right.

During the R & D phase of the Tiger's development, the aircraft was designated F9F-9 but changed to F11F-1 when production contracts were let. After first flying on 30 July 1954, the Tiger was delivered to VA-156 in March 1957. The Curtiss-Wright J65-W-18 Sapphire turbojet engine, built under licence for the British company Armstrong Siddeley Motors, normally developed 7,450 lb (33.14 kN) of static thrust and could be augmented to 10,500 lb (46.71 kN) of thrust. The initial 42 aircraft were built with 'short' noses, but they and the balance of the 199 built for the US Navy had the fuselage extended over 3 ft

high maintenance to keep them in the air, were retired and assigned to the Naval Air Technical Training Command at Memphis for practice by neophyte mechanics in training. Feightner by this time had been recalled to Patuxent River, the Navy's test facility, to perform the F7U-3 test programme.

In January 1953, Lieutenant Commander Ray Hawkins replaced Voris to become the team's sixth officer-in-charge (OIC).

In August of 1953, the team was assigned six

new Grumman F9F-6 Cougars, a swept-winged version of the Panther. The skipper, Lieutenant Commander Ray Hawkins, was forced to eject from his aircraft during the ferry flight from the Grumman factory to Corpus Christi, Texas. The supersonic ejection (a first for the Navy) was caused by a runaway horizontal stabiliser actuator that resulted in an uncontrollable dive. Fortunately, Hawkins was not seriously injured, but the ensuing grounding of the F9F-6s forced the team to revert to the straight-winged

The 'Blue Angels' flew their first display outside the US in September 1956 when they took their Cougars to Canada. Introduction of the Cougar had been scheduled for 1953, but a hydraulic failure during delivery of F9F-6s resulted in a supersonic ejection and the retention of Panthers for another two seasons.

(0.9 m). The fleet usage of the Tigers was brief due to the type's short range and minimal supersonic duration, and the aircraft were reassigned to Advanced Training Command. Their continued usage as the US Navy's standard advanced trainer helped to maintain spare parts in the supply system and was instrumental in allowing the team to continue using the F11F.

Six early production, short-nosed F11F-1 Tigers replaced the Cougars in April 1957. For the next three months, the team practiced with the F11Fs but used the F9F-8s for show. The initial Tiger show was flown on 12 July 1957. In 1959, the longer-nosed Tigers were delivered and the 'Blue Angels' continued to fly these supersonic-capable fighters until November 1968. This usage for 12 seasons was a record and was not exceeded until the run of the McDonnell Douglas A-4F Skyhawk IIs.

OICs who led the Tiger teams were Commanders Ed Holley, Zeb Knott, Ken Wallace, Bob Aumack and Bill Wheat. Commander Nick Glasgow was slated to relieve Ed Holley, but was killed during a practice session before he could assume command.

In order to preclude the possibility of the shortage of spare parts affecting the F11F-1 Tiger show, the team started to look for an aircraft replacement in 1967. The F11F-1s were beginning to be phased out of Training Command, which would reduce logistic sup-

Below and below right: The solo Bearcat was replaced by the Lockheed TO-2 in 1950. The role of this T-33 variant was not display, however, but transport for the team narrator and giving jet orientation flights to VIPs and media representatives. Three different TO-2s with many colour scheme variations were used between 1952 and 1957.

To complement the Panther show, and to show the public the new technology entering naval aviation, the 'Blue Angels' took on a pair of Chance-Vought F7U-1 Cutlasses in 1951. The Cutlass introduced twin engines, afterburners and complex hydraulic controls to the team. Maintenance problems and a number of spectacular near-accidents contributed to the abandonment of the Cutlasses, which were replaced in the show by an extra pair of F9Fs.

port. The LTV F-8 Crusader was considered but rejected for the same reason that necessitated the retiring of the Tiger: the F-8 was out of production. In addition, that aircraft was playing a vital part in the Vietnam conflict and there were no available aircraft in the inventory for the air show circuit.

The Northrop F-5 was given major consideration but was not acceptable because none existed in the US Navy's inventory at that time. The use of the McDonnell Douglas A-4 Skyhawk was also considered but, again, they were not available. All Skyhawk production was devoted to supporting the air war in Asia.

Phantoms for the 'Blues'

The F-4J Phantom II was assessed and seemed to meet the criteria. (Helping the selection was an indication that the USAF 'Thunderbirds' were also contemplating the switch to the Phantom from the North American F-100s.) With its two afterburning GEJ79 engines developing 17,500 lb (77.85 kN) thrust, a crowd attention-grabbing sound would bring the audience to their feet (and occasionally break windows with the sonic blast). There would be some modifications necessary, but the important fact was that the aircraft were available. The first 12 of the F-4J aircraft were completed early enough that the

Above and below: These views show the extreme nose-up ground angle of the Cutlass and the short nose and single nosewheel of the F7U-1. Compared to the F7U-3, the -1 was not nearly strong enough for carrier operations or high-g manoeuvres. The Cutlasses lasted for only half a season with the team, and wore the numbers '7' and '8' for their displays.

Left: The first markings worn by the Tigers differed significantly from those used on the team's other jets, in that the name was in an angular script and no squadron badge was displayed.

Below: The team is shown in 1958 performing a Diamond slow pass. At 170 mph (274 km/h), this was the slowest manoeuvre in the show.

Above: The 'Blue Angels' transitioned to the F11F Tiger in 1957. Their first Tigers were from the initial production batch which had short noses and a semi-retractable refuelling probe in the nose. Only 42 of these 'short nose' F11F-1s were delivered to the Navy. Taken at Miramar, this picture shows the aircraft without tail numbers.

would affect the control inputs. This arrangement forced the pilots to engage in a strong physical conditioning programme in order to withstand the tiring *g* forces.

The aircraft were also modified by the installation of VHF radios so the pilots could communicate with civilian airports. The four Sparrow missile positions were used to house Sparrow shapes: the front two carried smoke oil and the rear two were loaded with dye to colour the fuel that was occasionally dumped to trail what appeared to be red and blue smoke. This fuel-dumping arrangement was halted because of the problems of spotting objects that fell in the path of the descending fuel. The manoeuvre marking then became the white smoke produced by venting a low-grade oil into the engine tailpipe at the pilot's option.

New manoeuvres

The power-to-weight ratio of the Phantom II permitted some new manoeuvres to be worked into the routine, such as a dirty loop on take-off and a line-abreast loop. If the runway was wide enough (250-300 ft/76-91 m), six-aircraft delta landings were executed; if not, a four-aircraft echelon landing could be made if the crosswind was less than 5 kt (5.7 mph; 9.2 km/h) and the runway was a minimum of 200 ft (60 m) wide. In either case the trail aircraft landed first, followed by progressive touchings-down until the leader landed. The team could fly three different shows depending on the ceiling and visibility. The high show — which allowed the most spectacular manoeuvres — required a minimum of a 12,000-ft (3,660-m) ceiling and 5-mile (8-km) visibility. The low

AWG-10 pulse-Doppler radar fire control system could not be delivered in time for installation. The first production block was flown with ballast substituted for the weight of the radar and these aircraft were initially used for in-type training, eventually moving on to R & D flying positions. Six of these 'lead-nose' Phantoms were initially selected and transferred to the McDonnell Aircraft facility in St Louis for modifications to show requirements.

Phantom modifications

The Mach 2 flight envelope of which the Phantom was capable required a complex stability and control system whose feel system did not lend itself to the low-altitude, subsonic speeds and manoeuvres that were the team's forte. A simplified arrangement was developed that provided a 14-lb pull force throughout the manoeuvre range with full nose-down trim.

At the same time as the 'Blue Angels' swapped their Cougars for Tigers, they exchanged their TO-2 for another Cougar, this time an F9F-8T two-seat variant. This aircraft was initially numbered '0'. Seen behind the Cougar at Oakland in September 1957 is the team's R5D-2.

This system also had to be compatible with the cross-country flight requirements. Also installed was the team's custom pilot-restraining strap system that prevented the pilot from introducing inadvertent control inputs due to his movements under high-*g* loads. Peak forces were +7.5*g* and -3.5*g*. Since the pilots trimmed the aircraft such that the control stick usually rested against their leg, the use of *g* suits was rejected because the suit's pulsating bladder

Grumman F-11A Tiger

The 'Blue Angels' 1968

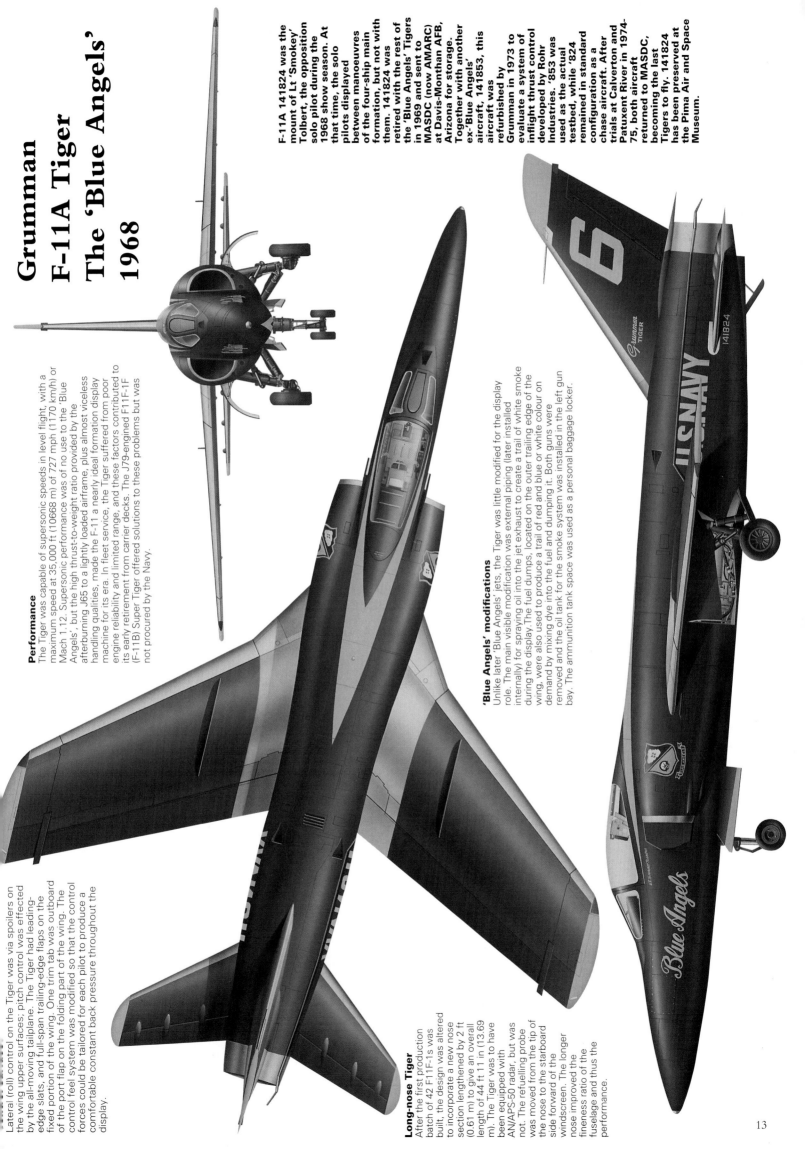

Lateral (roll) control on the Tiger was via spoilers on the wing upper surfaces; pitch control was effected by the all-moving tailplane. The Tiger had leading-edge slats, and full-span trailing-edge flaps on the fixed portion of the wing. One trim tab was outboard of the port flap on the folding part of the wing. The control feel system was modified so that the control forces could be tailored for each pilot to produce a comfortable constant back pressure throughout the display.

Long-nose Tiger

After the first production batch of 42 F11F-1s was built, the design was altered to incorporate a new nose section lengthened by 2 ft (0.61 m) to give an overall length of 44 ft 11 in (13.69 m). The Tiger was to have been equipped with AN/APS-50 radar, but was not. The refuelling probe was moved from the tip of the nose to the starboard side forward of the windscreen. The longer nose improved the fineness ratio of the fuselage and thus the performance.

Performance

The Tiger was capable of supersonic speeds in level flight, with a maximum speed at 35,000 ft (10668 m) of 727 mph (1170 km/h) or Mach 1.12. Supersonic performance was of no use to the 'Blue Angels', but the high thrust-to-weight ratio provided by the afterburning J65 to a lightly loaded airframe, plus almost viceless handling qualities, made the F-11 a nearly ideal formation display machine for its era. In fleet service, the Tiger suffered from poor engine reliability and limited range, and these factors contributed to its early retirement from carrier decks. The J79-engined F11F-1F (F-11B) Super Tiger offered solutions to these problems but was not procured by the Navy.

'Blue Angels' modifications

Unlike later 'Blue Angels' jets, the Tiger was little modified for the display role. The main visible modification was external piping (later installed internally) for spraying oil into the jet exhaust to create a trail of white smoke during the display. The fuel dumps, located on the outer trailing edge of the wing, were also used to produce a trail of red and blue or white colour on demand by mixing dye into the fuel and dumping it. Both guns were removed and the oil tank for the smoke system was installed in the left gun bay. The ammunition tank space was used as a personal baggage locker.

F-11A 141824 was the mount of Lt 'Smokey' Tolbert, the opposition solo pilot during the 1968 show season. At that time, the solo pilots displayed between manoeuvres of the four-ship main formation, but not with them. 141824 was retired with the rest of the 'Blue Angels' Tigers in 1969 and sent to MASDC (now AMARC) at Davis-Monthan AFB, Arizona for storage. Together with another ex-'Blue Angels' aircraft, 141853, this aircraft was refurbished by Grumman in 1973 to evaluate a system of inflight thrust control developed by Rohr Industries. '853 was used as the actual testbed, while '824 remained in standard configuration as a chase aircraft. After trials at Calverton and Patuxent River in 1974-75, both aircraft returned to MASDC, becoming the last Tigers to fly. 141824 has been preserved at the Pima Air and Space Museum.

Above: The 'Blue Angels' were one of the highlights of the 1967 Paris air show at Le Bourget. Although foreign tours are infrequent, the team has visited Iceland, the Netherlands, Denmark, Finland, the UK, Italy, Tunisia, Turkey, Central and South America, the Caribbean, Korea, Taiwan, Japan, the Philippines, Guam, Spain, Iran, Russia, Bulgaria and Sweden, in addition to many visits to Canada.

Left: The 'Blue Angels' demonstrate one of their set-pieces – the Diamond landing. A six-plane delta landing was also performed, which was even more difficult and spectacular. These new additions to the routine first appeared in 1962.

show required a ceiling of 3,500 ft (1070 m) and visibility of 5 miles (8 km). At ceiling conditions less than this, a rolling show could be flown if the visibility was 5 miles.

'Blue Angels' under threat

The Phantom II proved to be a milestone in 'Blue Angels' history, with its brute power and size. However, its use did present problems. The relatively extensive maintenance required and its high fuel consumption (especially during a fuel crisis) combined to force the US Navy to look elsewhere for a less expensive programme to present their message. In August 1973, after an unfortunate year of malfunctions and accidents, the remainder of the show season was cancelled and an overview was made of the entire operation, with the distinct possibility of ending the programme. The Secretary of the Navy, John Warner, leaned toward permanently suspending the programme, but he appointed a panel of six senior flag officers to review the situation. This board unanimously recommended the continuation of the 'Blue Angels', calling

the team a prime recruiting asset. They additionally reported that a survey showed that 40 per cent of about 2,500 aviation officer candidates surveyed considered the 'Blue Angels' to have had a significant influence on their decision to enter naval aviation. The Chief of Naval Operations, Admiral Zumwalt, concurred, and directed that the 'Blue Angels' were to continue, although changes were to be made both to aircraft used and organisational structure.

OICs of the teams flying the Phantoms were Commanders Bill Wheat, Harley Hall, Don Bently and Lieutenant Commander Skip Umstead.

After the decision was made that the cost of 'Blue Angels' operations was viable, and that the mission was justifiable, approval was given to reinstate the programme. At that time Captain Ken Wallace, who was the Tactical-Air-Plans Officer in the Chief of Naval Operations Office, was selected to make recommendations on the aircraft and the organisation that would operate those aircraft. He was named as the programme manager. Wallace was ably suited for this position as he had been a former team leader and had flown all positions during his seven years in three tours with the team. He would have liked to see the more complex Grumman F-14 Tomcat used because it represented the Navy's showcase aircraft. However, the cost of weapon systems that would have to be carried and not used for the team mission, as well the refinement of the control system, made the use of the Tomcat not practical. The next aircraft that Wallace surveyed was the LTV A-7 Corsair II, the Navy's front-line attack aircraft, but they were not available because of the more pressing needs of the Vietnam War. This combination of factors resulted in the selection of the Skyhawk, which later proved to be the most suitable of all the aircraft that the team had used since 1946.

Again, the timing was just right for the introduction of the agile Skyhawk. McDonnell had built 150 A-4F Skyhawks only because the Navy had experienced some production and operational difficulties getting the A-7 Corsair on-line. The increase in activity in Vietnam gave Douglas an opportunity to keep the production line of the A-4 open to fulfil the Navy's aerial commitments. When 100 A-4Fs were re-equipped with the Pratt & Whitney J52-P-408 engines developing 11,200 lb (49.82 kN) of unaugmented thrust (replacing the 9,300-lb/41.37-kN thrust P&W J52-P-8 engine), a superb show type was created. These

Above: This view shows why the Tiger was fitted with a tail bumper. The pilot of this aircraft, seen during one of the team's visits to the UK, has the canopy back in traditional naval fashion.

Below: From 1957, the 'Blue Angels' were permanently assigned their own transport aircraft. The first of these to wear the full team colours was R5D-3 BuNo. 56508, seen in 1967.

An important member of the team during the Tiger days was no. 9, the suitably-decorated portable air starter or 'huffer' that was essential in getting the team running.

'Blue Angels' Commanding Officers

LCdr* Roy M. 'Butch' Voris	1946-mid-1947	Grumman F6F-5/F8F-1	Formed Team. 7 kills WWII
	1952	Grumman F9F-5	Reformed team after Korea
LCdr Bob Clarke	Mid 1947-end 47	Grumman F8F-1	
LCdr R.E. 'Dusty' Rhodes	1948-1949	Grumman F8F-1	Joined team in 1947
	1949-	Grumman F9F-2	
LCdr Johnny Magda	1950	Grumman F9F-2	Joined team in 1949. When team disbanded in 1950 and reformed into VF-191, Magda assumed command but was killed in Korea
LCdr Ray Hawkins	1953	Grumman F9F-5/6	Also served on team 1948 to 1950. Credited 14 kills WWII
LCdr Robert "Zeke" Cormier	1954-1956	Grumman F9F-5/8	Also served in 1950. 8 kills WWII
LCdr Ed Holley	Mid-1957	Grumman F9F-8	
	Mid-1957-1958	Grumman F11F-1	
Cdr Nick Glasgow	1959		Named to be leader but was killed prior to assuming command
Cdr Zeb Knott	1959-1961	Grumman F11F-1	
LCdr Ken Wallace	1962-1963	Grumman F-11A	Also served in 1954, 1955, 1961 and 1974
LCdr Bob Aumack	1964-1966	Grumman F-11A	
LCdr Bill Wheat	1967-1968	Grumman F-11A	
	1969	McDonnell Douglas F-4J	
LCdr Harley Hall	1970-1971	McDonnell Douglas F-4J	
LCdr Don Bentley	1972-1973	McDonnell Douglas F-4J	Injured in winter training 1973, replaced by Umstead
LCdr 'Skip' Umstead	1973	McDonnell Douglas F-4J	Killed in collision, July 1973
Cdr Tony Less	1974-1975	McDonnell Douglas A-4F	First squadron commander
Cdr K.C. "Casey" Jones	1976-1977	McDonnell Douglas A-4F	
Cdr William Newman	1978-1979	McDonnell Douglas A-4F	
Cdr Denny Wisely	1980-1981	McDonnell Douglas A-4F	
Cdr Dave Carroll	1982-1983	McDonnell Douglas A-4F	
Cdr Larry Pearson	1984-1985	McDonnell Douglas A-4F	
Cdr Gil Rud	1986	McDonnell Douglas A-4F	
	1987-1988	McDonnell Douglas F/A-18A	
Cdr Pat Moneymaker	1989-1990	McDonnell Douglas F/A-18A	
Cdr Greg Wooldridge	1991-1992	McDonnell Douglas F/A-18A	
	Mid-1993	McDonnell Douglas F/A-18A	Temporarily relieved Cdr Stumpf
	1996	McDonnell Douglas F/A-18A	Relieved Cdr Cochran early 1996
Cdr Bob Stumpf**	1993-1994	McDonnell Douglas F/A-18A	
Cdr Donnie Cochran***	1995-1996	McDonnell Douglas F/A-18A	Also served in 1986 to 1989
Cdr George Dom	1997	McDonnell Douglas F/A-18A	

* Ranks are as upon assuming command

**Cdr Stumpf was temporarily relieved of command because of Tailhook accusations. He was cleared and returned to head the 'Blue Angels' for 1994.

***Resigned as leader in early 1996 and replaced with then-Capt Wooldridge

The 'Blue Angels' became famous for their tight formations, the aircraft separated by as little as 3 ft (0.91 m). This closeness generated a strong 'proximity effect' where the wingmen tended to force the leader upwards out of the formation, while the slot aircraft imparted a push on his tail. This effect varied with each type and was more pronounced with the Tiger than it had been with the Cougar.

In various guises, the Cougar was the longest-serving jet used by the 'Blue Angels', in use from 1955 until 1968. The TF-9J (F9F-8T) served throughout the Tiger era, wearing the number '7' from 1959.

aircraft were available because they were being withdrawn from front-line attack squadrons to be replaced by the A-7, which had begun to achieve its operational capabilities. Its superior bombing and range capabilities meant that the A-7 was a worthy replacement for the A-4 as a war machine.

In late 1973, Douglas submitted to the Navy a requested Engineering Change Proposal (ECP), outlining the A-4 modifications for eight single-place A-4Fs and one two-place TA-4J to convert them to demonstration aircraft. These alterations to the airframe resulted in an empty dry weight of 11,300 lb (5135 kg), and included:

1. Wing slats to be locked in the closed position to prevent inadvertent asymmetrical opening, which would be disastrous if it occurred in close formation;

2. Smoke oil tanks to be installed to contain the oil used in manoeuvre marking;

3. Internal fuel plumbing to be modified to provide for an additional 30 seconds of inverted flight time;

4. Horizontal stabiliser system to be altered to provide increased (3°) nose-down trim;

Above and left: As spectacular in its own way as the team itself, the 'Blue Angels' Constellation (BuNo. 131623) supported the team for two seasons. Delivered to the Navy as an R7V-1 in 1953, it later became a C-121J and then a VC-121J. Despite its graceful looks, the C-121 was not an ideal support aircraft as it required specialised loading equipment that was not always available at airfields visited by the team. Sent to storage at Davis-Monthan in 1972, the 'Connie' was sold for scrap in 1978.

Aircraft of the 'Blue Angels' 1946 – the present

Grumman F6F-5 Hellcat

1946

4 aircraft assigned, 3 used in routine
79049, 79393 , 79914, 80097

North American SNJ-5/6

1946-49

1 aircraft assigned and used
44008, 91047 (-5), 112193 (-6).

Grumman F8F-1 Bearcat

1946-49

5 aircraft assigned, 4 used in routine
94781, 94880, 94843, 94969, 94985, 94986, 94989, 94990, 94992, 94996, 95000, 95021, 95037, 95124, 95134, 95144,
Beetle Bomb (1949 -50) 95187

Grumman F9F-2 Panther

1949-50, 1951-52

5 aircraft assigned, 4 or 5 used in routine
122585, 122587, 122588, 123016, 123017

Chance-Vought F7U-1 Cutlass

1952

2 in team   124426, 124427

Grumman F9F-5 Panther

1952-55

7 aircraft assigned, 5 used in routine
125237, 125239, 125249.125258, 125278, 125283, 125286, 125294, 125305, 125943, 125989, 125993, 126070, 126071, 126101

Grumman F9F-6/-8/-8B Cougar

1955-57

7 aircraft assigned, 5 used in routine
128080, 128116, 128128, 128129, 128152, 128446 (-6)
131099, 131142, 131143, 131147, 131205, 131208, 131210, 131211, 131212, 131213, 138870 (-8B)
144279, 144368 (-8)

Grumman F11F-1 Tiger

1957-68

7 aircraft assigned, 6 used in routine
138633, 138639, 138640, 138641, 138642, 138643, 138644, 138645, 138647, 141738, 141764, 141765, 141775, 141777, 141790, 141797, 141802, 141811, 141812, 141816, 141823, 141824, 141829, 141831, 141837, 141847, 141849, 141850, 141851, 141853, 141859, 141863, 141867, 141868, 141869, 141870, 141871, 141872, 141873, 141874, 141876, 141882, 141883, 141884

McDonnell Douglas F-4J Phantom

1969-73

7 aircraft assigned, 6 used in routine
153072, 153073, 153074, 153075, 153076, 153077, 153078, 153079, 153080, 153081, 153082, 153083, 153084, 153085, 153086, 153839

McDonnell Douglas A-4F Skyhawk

1974-86

7 aircraft assigned, 6 used in routine
154176, 154177, 154179, 154975, 154983, 154984, 154986, 155029, 154202, 155056, 155033, 154180, 154172, 154217, 154992, 154211, 154973, 155000,
TA-4J 158722

McDonnell Douglas F/A-18A Hornet

1987-

7 aircraft assigned, 6 used in routine
161353, 161520, 161521, 161522, 161523, 161524, 161525, 161526, 161527, 161528, 161931, 161941, 161945, 161952, 161955, 161957, 161961, 161962, 161963, 161969, 161973, 161975, 161983, 161984
TF-18B 161932, 161943

Transport and support aircraft

Beech SNB

1949

Various

Douglas R4D-5/-7-8

1949-53

17123, 17281 (-5), 99838 (-7), 12437 (-8)

Curtiss R5C-1

1953

39507

Douglas R5D-2/-3/-4R

1955-68

50868 (-2), 56508, 91996 (-3), 90407 (-4R)

Lockheed C-121J

1968-70

131623

Lockheed C-130

1970-

150690, 149806, 148893, 149791 (KC-130F), 15191 (TC-130G)
163310 (KC-130T)

Lockheed TO-2

1952-57

128662, 128676, 137955

Grumman F9F-8T (TF-9J) Cougar

1957-69

142470, 144368

In 1969, the 'Blue Angels' switched manufacturer from Grumman to McDonnell Douglas and took delivery of the mighty F-4J Phantom. The dummy Sparrow missiles seen under the fuselages of these Phantoms in a Farvel formation contained smoke oil (forward) and coloured dye (rear), as well as helping to maintain the correct centre of gravity.

Right: A four-ship take-off was part of the Phantom routine. The two solo aircraft would make individual take-offs, one performing a dirty roll, the other entering an Immelmann climb.

5. Stick forces to be increased around the pitch axis for show manoeuvres but modulated for cross-country flight;

6. Extendible, stowable ladder to be installed in the area vacated by left-hand gun (this was dictated by the possibility that the airports from which the squadron would operate might not have the custom-designed boarding ladder that was normally used with the A-4);

7. Certain unused weapons system equipment and the upper avionics pod to be deleted;

8. Drag chute to be installed to facilitate landings at the smaller airports.

Eight of these uprated A-4Fs were selected and sent to the factory at Palmdale, California for the revisions that were felt would enhance their air show capabilities. In addition, a new TA-4J was selected for use by the squadron and was partially modified.

The organisational changes were incorporated and the team's ethos was altered to that of a full US Navy squadron. This gave the squadron commander much more control of his personnel, for they would be assigned to him and not be on loan. Added to the organisation were such personnel as flight surgeon, supply, administration, and public affairs. They joined the maintenance officer, the events co-ordinator and the transport pilots, who were already onboard. Also added were additional enlisted

The different aerodynamic characteristics of the F-4 required greater stepdown in formations to reduce proximity effects. The Phantom was regarded as more stable in turbulence than the Tiger and had larger reserves of power for manoeuvres such as a trail loop and the Immelmann on take-off.

personnel in the needed disciplines. The squadron stood up on 10 December 1973 with Commander Tony Less assuming command. This arrangement was considered a 'bonus' command as Less (and all succeeding skippers) had previously commanded a Navy squadron.

Spectacular Skyhawk

The Naval Flight Demonstration Squadron deployed to NAF El Centro in January 1974 to begin its winter training and to receive its aircraft from Douglas. They arrived without the normal 'Blue Angel' paint scheme applied, and practice commenced. The aircraft were gradually painted as time allowed. Although the Skyhawks did not have an afterburner, the nearly one-to-one thrust ratio provided an agility that made it an excellent vehicle for the intended purpose. The smaller turn-rate tightened up the show. With the high rate of roll, new manoeuvres were added such as the five-aircraft fleur-de-lis, a five-aircraft loop and double Farvel, plus the multi-aircraft landings introduced earlier were continued.

The A-4s served with the 'Blue Angels' until 1987, giving the type the distinction of being the longest-operated with that organisation. Following Less as the squadron commanders were Commanders Casey Jones, Bill Newman,

By 1974, neither the 'Blue Angels' nor the USAF 'Thunderbirds' flew Phantoms any more. The energy crisis and the expensive maintenance needs of the F-4, as well as several crashes, led to a 'downsizing' to the smaller and more nimble A-4F and T-38A, respectively.

Denny Wisely, Dave Carrol, Larry Pearson and Gil Rud.

In 1985 plans were being formulated to relieve the ageing A-4 as the US Navy's 'Blue Angel' show aircraft. A message from the Commander, Naval Air Systems Command to McDonnell Douglas Corporation stated: "A review of the NFDS A-4F fatigue life expenditure and projected loss rates indicated that the A-4F inventory could no longer support the 'Blue Angels' requirement without serious degradation to fleet advisory training." ('Topgun' and the various adversary squadrons were heavy users of the diminutive Skyhawk.) He went on to say that the F/A-18 was under consideration as a possible replacement for the A-4F and requested that the contractor "conduct and submit a preliminary cost estimate and feasibility analysis based on the conversion requirements listed." This projected programme would entail the modification of eight single-place and two two-place aircraft.

Some consideration was also given to the possible use of the T-45 Goshawk but this aircraft was undergoing some production and flight problems and was definitely not the choice of the aviators.

Subsequently, the F/A-18 was selected and was to be ready for the 1987 show season.

'Hotrod' to Hornet

The modifications necessary to bring the F/A-18A to demonstration standards were amazingly few. Lot IV aircraft (which were not carrier suitable and were available in the inventory) were chosen and modified thus:

Above: The 'Blue Angels' pioneered the mirror formation (which they called the Back-to-Back) for supersonic jets. The solo aircraft flew a mostly separate display to the main Diamond formation, with only two manoeuvres requiring five or six aircraft. The solo Phantoms would be 'on stage' a dozen times during a typical 45-minute show.

1. The flight control software was programmed for demonstration flying;
2. Provision were made to allow 30 seconds of negative g flight as well as 0g flight;
3. A 20-minute smoke capability was added. The 80-US gal (300-litre) tank, accumulators and boost pump were installed in the area normally used by the nose-mounted M61A 20-mm cannon, with plumbing running back to the left engine;
4. Communications were provided for both VHF and UHF frequencies;
5. A Collins VOR/ILS (VHF OmniRange/Instrument Landing System) was installed so the unit could operate safely from civil airports;
6. The standard 'Blue Angel' integrated harness and restraint arrangement for securing the pilot to the ejection seat was installed;
7. A spring cartridge was installed between the stick and the instrument panel to provide the download for pilots to fly the show with a pull force.

After extensive training at NAF El Centro,

The team worked up on its new Skyhawks in the winter of 1973/74 at NAS El Centro in California. While the team aircraft were being prepared, formations were completed with borrowed aircraft in normal colour schemes.

The Fortus is a variation on the Back-to-Back formation where the two solo 'Angels' pass down the flight line with no. 5 inverted. On a signal from the inverted jet, both lower their undercarriage and hook. As the crowd is passed, the aircraft are cleaned up, no. 5 rolls upright and the pair exits stage right.

the team began its first show season with Hornets in 1987. Added to the show was a high angle-of-attack/slow-flight routine to demonstrate the F/A-18's ability in that area. The multiple-aircraft landings previously used were discarded due to the Hornet's lack of sensitivity at low speeds with the control system.

Choice of three shows

In its display routine, the squadron continues to prepare three different shows, the choice of which is based on the available ceiling and visibility on the day. A normal or high show requires a minimum of 8,000-ft (2440-m) ceiling and 3 miles (5.4 km) of visibility, while the low show requires at least a 3,500-ft (1070-m) ceiling. If the altitude minimums are down to a 1,000-ft (305-m) base, a rolling show will be flown in which manoeuvres are limited to flat passes. The F/A-18 show operates

between a high of 7.5g to a low of -3g, in which the solo aircraft work the extremes.

The 'Blue Angels' are now in their 51st year of exhibition flying. To date they have flown over 3,500 shows for the general public and the future looks strong. In this time of military downsizing, there still is a vital need to show the public just what the military is all about. The 'Blue Angels' are adept at this.

Squadron bosses during the F/A-18 era have been Commanders Gil Rud, Pat Moneymaker, Greg Wooldridge, Bob Stumpf, Donnie

Cochran and George Dom.

To supplement the main show aircraft operation, the 'Blue Angels' have used other aircraft to either perform in the show or accomplish such services as providing VIP and media flights, and other logistic flights where necessary. These aircraft are in addition to the transports for ground equipment and maintenance personnel.

The first aircraft used in this manner was a two-place North American SNJ Texan, normally used for training. It was initially

The team's KC-130, in service since 1970, and its Marine Corps crew of nine are collectively known as 'Fat Albert Airlines'. The Hercules air refuels the team en route to the furthest shows and sometimes performs a JATO take-off as part of the show.

Bottom: When the 'Blue Angels' achieved squadron status, they were entitled to all the personnel of a normal Navy squadron. In 1983, there were 70 in the maintenance crew, in addition to support and administration personnel permanently based at Pensacola.

Despite its smaller size compared to the Tiger, and the lack of an afterburner, the Skyhawk was eminently suitable for the 'Blue Angels' needs, having the agility and turning radius to keep manoeuvres in front of the crowd. Here, the A-4s are on the upside of a six-ship Delta Loop.

Above: One of the most popular parts of the routine is the Knife Edge pass, or KE. Other opposing manoeuvres performed with the A-4s included four-point hesitation rolls and horizontal rolls.

Right: This is how close a separation of 3 ft (0.91 m) actually looks from the slot position, in this case from the team's TA-4J which occasionally filled in for displays.

Flying a tight six-ship formation at low level requires intense concentration from all concerned, and this shows in the face of the slot pilot during a training sortie. 'Blue Angels' pilots wear special USAF harnesses and helmets with a boom mike rather than an oxygen mask.

Below and below right: The 'Blue Angels' TA-4J was used for media and orientation flights, as was the Cougar in the Tiger era. From time to time, the 'T-bird' was down for maintenance and a normal Training Command TA-4 was used. These white aircraft were known as 'Caspar'. Likewise, USMC C-130s were sometimes borrowed and nicknamed 'Ernie' after the Sesame Street character.

painted yellow with a large red circle on the aft fuselage. During the flight demonstration, the Hellcats and later the Bearcats would pretend to shoot down this simulated Japanese 'Zero' fighter of World War II. As the hostile feelings for the war-time Japanese forces subsided, the words 'US NAVY' replaced the red circle. This aircraft was given the number '0' in the aircraft numbering system and referred to as *Beetle Bomb*. (Always coming in last.) Three different SNJ aircraft were used in this era, two SNJ-5s and one SNJ-6. In 1949 the SNJ was replaced with a Grumman F8F-1 Bearcat, also painted yellow, and was used until 1952 both as a show plane and for the narrator's transportation. The Bearcat (BuNo.98157) also carried the name *Beetle Bomb*.

Jet support

In 1952, the 'Blue Angels' replaced the Bearcat used for the narrator/public affairs officer with a two-place jet, the Lockheed TO-2 (T-33A). On the assignment of this aircraft, the 'Blue Angels' could provide media flights that were helpful to give a closer taste of the type of flying that was possible with turbine-powered aircraft and could demonstrate some of the manoeuvres that the team performed. The 'Blue Angels' used three different TO-2s from 1952 through 1956. In 1957 when the prime demonstration plane was changed to the Grumman F11F-1 Tiger, the support aircraft was also altered and a Grumman F9F-8T (TF-9J) Cougar was made available. For the first year, this aircraft was numbered '0' following the previous practice, but was changed in 1959 to the number '7'. The 'Blue

Angels' continued the use of the Cougar until the retirement of the Tigers in 1968. Two different Cougars were used over the years.

The year 1969 ended Grumman's record as the manufacturer of the show aircraft and McDonnell Douglas became the supplier, when the Phantom II became both the prime and the support aircraft. The F-4J could be used as the show aircraft spare. Two examples known to be used at one time as the support aircraft were BuNos 153079 and 153083

The A-4F Skyhawk II replaced the F-4J Phantom II in 1974 and a two-place TA-4J took the role of support aircraft. The new aircraft was partially modified at the Douglas factory by installing radios compatible with the civil activities; it was installed so it could be used in either the forward or rear seat. A drag chute was also added. The same aircraft was used for the entire 13 years of the Skyhawk service, except for three instances when the aircraft was in heavy maintenance and three other TA-4Js were temporarily assigned. Since these loaned aircraft were left in their normal white paint scheme, with some 'Blue Angels' identification applied, the crew referred to them as 'Caspar'. The permanently assigned aircraft was BuNo. 158722 and the 'Caspars' were 158107, 153477 and 153667.

With the change to the F/A-18A in 1987, two Lot VI TF-18Bs were allocated to perform the support function. The two-place Hornets were capable of performing the show manoeuvres, so were frequently used as a spare aircraft in the formation when required. They also were used during the early part of the season to train the new pilots. Both of these

Left: The top of a loop is seen from the TF-18 in the slot position. The two-seat Hornet is used for the narrator and for continuation rides as well as media flights. For the 1992 European tour, two TF-18s, coded '7' and '8', were part of the entourage.

Above: The solo Hornets flash by with little margin to spare at the mid-point of the solo opposing four-point hesitation roll. To bring about such precision requires dedicated crews in the air and on the ground. In 1997, the ground echelon numbers 109.

aircraft usually carried the number '7' on the tail, but during the 'Blue Angels' trip to Europe in 1992 both aircraft accompanied the group, and one was numbered '8' for that trip, reverting to '7' at its conclusion.

Various Navy transport aircraft were used to move the 'Blue Angels' maintenance and administration personnel between the home sites and the show locations around the country. At first these aircraft were station-assigned vehicles flown by base operation personnel who then filled in at the show with various duties. The aircraft were not marked with a unique colour, as were the show aircraft. Initially, the twin Beech SNB (C-45) was used. As the number of people involved and the distance to the shows increased, a larger Douglas R4D-5 Skytrain was used, from 1949. During the 1953 season, a station-assigned Curtiss R5C-1 Commando or a Douglas R4D-8 was used. When the team adopted a crest insignia in 1949, one was usually placed on the nose of the transport. The transports was marked as 'Corpus Christi' aircraft.

Permanent transport

After the team relocated to NAS Sherman Field at Pensacola, Florida, the Douglas R5D (C-54) was used as the transport. The first example used bore the station's name on the vertical tail. In 1958, skipper Ed Holley decided to consolidate his empire; he acquired control of the transport and assigned his maintenance officer as the pilot. This policy continued until a USMC KC-130F Hercules with a complete Marine Corps crew joined the team in 1970.

After 12 years of action, the Douglas Skymasters were retired and replaced with a Lockheed C-121J Constellation. Although graceful in appearance, the C-121J was difficult to use as a personnel/cargo transport. It sat so far off of the ground that loading of heavy and large equipment was difficult, requiring ground support equipment that was not usually available at the variety of airports from which the team operated. The Navy had no suitable assets available to relieve this condition, but the US Marine Corps came to the rescue when in 1970 it made available the last KC-130F Hercules delivered to it, plus a Marine crew.

Six different Hercules have been used since then, although some have been on temporary assignment while the prime aircraft underwent necessary maintenance and rework. These temporary aircraft have been referred to as 'Ernie', to differentiate them from 'Bert' or 'Fat Albert'. They and the Marines are still providing the logistics support. 'Fat Albert', as part of the air show, occasionally demonstrates a JATO-enhanced take-off.

Today, after 50 years of promoting naval aviation, the worth of the 'Blue Angels' is recognised by the high command and the future seems secure. What the team might be flying in another 50 years time may not yet have been invented, but it is certain it will be flown with the same flair that has made the 'Blues' one of the world's most famous display teams for the past half-century.

Harry S. Gann

The McDonnell Douglas F/A-18A has now served with the 'Blue Angels' for 11 seasons, and is sure to become the longest-serving aircraft with the team. Its most likely replacement is the F/A-18E Super Hornet, some time after 2000.

Above: The 'Blue Angels' show off their precise formation keeping in a Diamond 360° Pass. The fly-by-wire controls of the Hornet have made some manoeuvres easier, but others, such as formation landings, have been dropped.

The first five CANA Super Etendards are seen over the southern French coast prior to delivery to Argentina. Four of these would be deployed to Rio Grande for the conflict.

Super Etendard in the Falklands
2ª Escuadrilla Aeronaval de Caza y Ataque

Of all the weapon systems fielded by the Argentine forces, none was feared more by the British than the Super Etendard/Exocet combination. Here the pilots of 2ª Escuadrilla tell their story, and relate the three combat missions flown against the British Task Force during the 1982 Falklands/Malvinas conflict.

In late March 1982 this Comando de Aviación Naval Argentina strike–fighter squadron had a total of five Super Etendards, and towards the end of the year it received the remaining nine examples which had been temporarily embargoed by the French government. During the South Atlantic conflict it operated from Rio Grande naval air station,

in the remote Tierra del Fuego, where it had four aircraft. Its five available AM39 Exocet sea-skimming missiles destroyed two British ships, without any loss.

The following accounts of the combat are provided by the pilots themselves, providing a graphic insight into the operations and combat missions of the Super Etendard.

The CANA accepted the first five Super Etendards at BAN Comandante Espora, Bahia Blanca, on 17 November 1981. This aircraft remained at the base throughout the conflict, being used as a 'Christmas tree' to provide spares for the four operational aircraft.

Summary of Super Etendard combat missions

Date	Pilots/aircraft	Remarks
1 May	Lt Cdr Jorge Colombo (CO) Lt Carlos Machetanz	Returned to Rio Grande due to failure of the wingman's fuel to transfer during inflight refuelling
4 May	Lt Cdr Augusto Bedacarratz, 3-A-202 Lt Armando Mayora, 3-A-203	Attack on HMS *Sheffield*
23 May	Lt Cdr Roberto Agotegaray Lt José Rodríguez	Target not found, returned to Rio Grande
25 May	Lt Cdr Roberto Curilovic, 3-A-203 Lt Julio Barraza, 3-A-204	Attack on MV *Atlantic Conveyor*
30 May	Lt Cdr Alejandro Francisco, 3-A-202 Lt Luis Collavino, 3-A-205	Attack on British Task Force

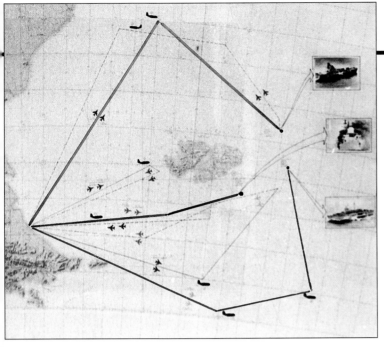

Left: This 2ª Eslla map shows the routes of the five SuE missions, including the two abortive sorties. The strike missions are shown as blue (Sheffield), green (Atlantic Conveyor) and purple (Invincible).

Above: Air and ground crew of 2a Escuadrilla gather in front of a Super Etendard on 31 May 1982. The commander, Capitán de Fregata J. Colombo, is fourth from left in the second row.

4 May 1982
Leader – *Sheffield* attack

Capitán de Corbeta (Lt Cdr) Cesar Augusto Bedacarratz

Augusto Bedacarratz undertook the naval aviator course in 1967 and the following year, after graduation, was posted to the 2ª Escuadrilla Aeronaval de Ataque, where he flew North American T-28P Fennec light strike aircraft. Bedacarratz obtained his carrier qualifications aboard the ARA Independencia. *During 1969 he was posted to Grupo 4 de Caza of the Argentine Air Force, where he did the fighter-bomber course. During the period 1970-1971 he was with the Escuadrilla de Busqueda y Salvamento (SAR squadron) where he flew the Grumman HU-16 Albatross. After two years in staff duties, from 1974 to 1978 he was posted to the 3ª Escuadrilla Aeronaval de Caza y Ataque with A-4Q Skyhawks, operating from the carrier* 25 de Mayo, *and during his last year there was the unit's executive officer. In 1980 he was sent to France for the Super Etendard course. He was the CO of 2ª Escuadrilla during 1983.*

"The deployment of 2ª Escuadrilla to Rio Grande took place on Monday 19 April 1982, with four of the five aircraft we had received from France by then. The fifth airplane remained at Base Aeronaval Comandante Espora as a source of critical spares, for the French government had suspended deliveries of any kind of logistic or technical support during the conflict. This deployment meant that the 'weapons system' for launching the AM39 missile was ready, and that all of us had trained in the tactics and techniques required for that missile, taking into account the British fleet defensive capabilities. It is worth noting that this intensive training took place in only 20 days, without any technical support from the expected Aérospatiale people who, according to the contract, had to come to Espora to ready the Super Etendard/Exocet system. On the other hand, the 10 pilots in the escuadrilla had received the minimum training required before

that date, amounting to 50 flying hours in France.

"The deployment to Rio Grande included the necessary personnel and material to operate continuously with the maximum number of aircraft in service (four), while the naval air station itself provided the needed infrastructure support for our operations, including providing meals for everybody. An idea of the effort made by this station during the conflict – the space limitations and the lack of comfort – can be got from the number of units deployed to this relatively small airfield.

Teniente de Navio Mayora prepares to launch on the 4 May mission which crippled the Sheffield. The aircraft, 3-A-203, was used on both successful missions, and was finally lost in a crash in 1997.

Besides 2ª Escuadrilla Aeronaval de Caza y Ataque, there were the Escuadrilla Aeronaval de Exploración (SP-2 Neptunes); 3ª Escuadrilla Aeronaval de Caza y Ataque (A-4Q Skyhawk); a division of Macchi MB.339As from 1ª Escuadrilla Aeronaval de Ataque; the Grupo de Busqueda y Rescate formed with our Beech King Air 200 and Prefectura Naval

Below: Only five AM39 Exocets were available to 2ª Escuadrilla during the war. An MM38 land-launched Exocet was also fired from Port Stanley, damaging HMS Glamorgan on 12 June.

Right: Capitán de Corbeta Cesar Augusto Bedacarratz sits in the cockpit of 3-A-204. This aircraft was used in the Atlantic Conveyor raid, although Bedacarratz was flying '202 during the Sheffield mission.

Ground crew swarm around the Super Etendard of Teniente de Navio Mayora at Rio Grande prior to the Sheffield *mission. The Exocet missile has just been fitted to the pylon, its transport canister being seen open in the foreground. Further deliveries of Exocets and Super Etendards were embargoed by the French until after the conflict.*

Skyvans; plus an air force squadron of Daggers, all with aircrews, ground crews and the necessary equipment to perform maintenance up to the second level.

"At 07.00 on 4 May, Neptune 2-P-112, which was performing a maritime surveillance sortie over the ocean area south of the Malvinas (Falklands), detected a medium-sized ship which it electronically identified as a destroyer. This initial detection prompted the work-up for launching the readiness section, to which I was assigned as leader, while my wingman was Teniente de Navio (Lt) Armando Mayora. The escuadrilla had been organised into five groups of two pilots each, leader and wingman, the former being senior officers and the latter junior officers. This organisation into groups allowed us to reach an excellent level of training with a very high level of mutual knowledge, understanding and confidence. Later, the maritime patrol aircraft located a force comprising one large ship and two medium-sized ones, sailing very close together, and 40 miles (65 km) from the first one we had detected. With this data we started to plan to mission, adapting to this particular mission the flight profile established by the escuadrilla. We took into account the capabilities of the early warning radars of the Type 42 destroyers and the need for an indirect course to the target in order to detect any picket ship,

and established the air refuelling control point with the air force KC-130 tanker.

"At 09.15 we were in the cockpits, performing the last post-start checks. We received the latest updates about the target location, provided by the Neptune which was performing the dangerous 'contact search' mode.

"At 09.45 we launched from Rio Grande, each with an AM39 missile. We were in total radio/sensor silence, as this was the only possible way to minimise the enemy's electronic countermeasures capabilities for decoying the missiles, whose capabilities were an unknown factor. We climbed on a heading to the refuelling point, intercepting the tanker at 10.04, and completed our refuelling at about 250 nm (287 miles; 462 km) from the target. We continued towards the target at the same flight level, although we started the descent some time before we had planned. We were flying over a cloud deck, so we had to 'hole' it, making visual contact with the ocean's surface at 500 ft (152 m). We encountered frequent rain/snow squalls which reduced visibility to about 3,280 ft (1000 m). At that time, we received a call from 2-P-112 updating the target's location. The clock on the dash panel marked 10.30, more than an hour since we had obtained the latest known position of the enemy, so this update was of the utmost

importance. The Super Etendard's Agave radar had been designed as an attack radar, and it sweeps a sector forward of the aircraft. We had been briefed to turn it on for only a few seconds, so as not to alert the enemy's electronic systems, but it was necessary to know the precise position of the target to guarantee its location and reduce the risk of being detected ourselves without knowing it.

"The Neptune told us that at 115 miles (185 km) there was one large and two medium-sized ships. I sent a signal to Lt Mayora informing him that we were heading towards the largest ship, which was our target. We were flying at less than 100 ft (30 m) over the sea.

"When we reached the distance we had established in the pre-briefed procedures, we climbed and turned on the radar to fix the targets, which should have appeared in our radar displays; nothing appeared in them. A few seconds later we turned off our sets and descended below 100 ft, continuing with our very low level navigation. We were at maximum speed then, for we had discovered it was necessary to reduce the time needed to reach the launch/attack area.

"I decided to continue for another 25 miles (40 km) in total radio/electronic silence; since the call from the maritime patrol aircraft at 10:30 I hadn't exchanged any words with my wingman. We

climbed again and repeated the procedure, and now, with both radars, we detected a medium-sized ship just at the 12 o'clock position and offset 30° to the right of the large ship, with two smaller ones very near. Quickly we turned right, while descending to make the last stage of the attack run. When we reached the distance established in our procedures, I used the radio to order Lt Mayora to launch his missile, while I did the same. He did not hear this order, so as he watched while my Exocet fell away and started its engine he asked if I had launched positively. I repeated the launch order, so he fired his missile five seconds later than mine. It was exactly 11:04.

"Now we made the escape leg, maintaining maximum speed and flying as low to the water as we dared, about 50 ft (15 m) . After having flown the distance we considered adequate to avoid a possible interception by Sea Harriers, we started to climb and established a direct heading to Rio Grande. We landed at 12.15. Both Super Etendards arrived at the dispersal area with all systems working, without any technical problems."

Seen on the carrier 25 de Mayo, *this is one of the SuEs delivered after the war. Each aircraft only carried one Exocet, the weight being balanced by a drop tank. In CANA service the aircraft also carries the Pescador short-range anti-ship missile, as well as bombs and rockets.*

4 May 1982
The wingman's view

Teniente de Navio (Lt) Armando Mayora

In 1975 as a midshipman Mayora took the naval pilot course, and during the next two years was posted to 1ª Escuadrilla Aeronaval de Ataque flying MB.326s. In 1978, already a lieutenant (jg), Mayora was chosen to make the transition course to the A-4 Skyhawk in the United States, but this was cancelled by the Kennedy amendment

on human rights. Until 1980 he was posted to 3ª Escuadrilla Aeronaval de Caza y Ataque, getting his carquals in the A-4Q aboard the carrier 25 de Mayo. *In 1979 he took the LSO course for the Skyhawk. In 1980 Lt Mayora took the Super Etendard course in France, and next year qualified as LSO for this type of aircraft. In 1982 he rose to the rank of teniente de navio (lieutenant).*

"The unit started a very intensive period of training during the first days of April, just after the Malvinas (Falklands) had been taken by our forces. The Operations Department (to which I belonged) had to devise the best attack profiles to be used, and before that could be done, several things had to be determined:
"– The capability of the Super Etendard to operate from a short runway like that of Puerto Argentino (Port Stanley). We performed tests of take-offs and

landings, and discovered that, with wet or icy runways, landings were at best marginal, and dangerous. Tests indicated that the airfield at Port Stanley should only be used in emergency. The decision was made to operate from Rio Grande naval air station in Tierra del Fuego.

"– Early on it was decided to settle on an attack unit of two aircraft. We took into account the kill probability provided from launching two AM39 Exocets; aircraft availability; the number of missiles available; and the number

Super Etendard in the Falklands

Badge of Base Aeronaval Rio Grande, from where the Super Etendard missions were launched.

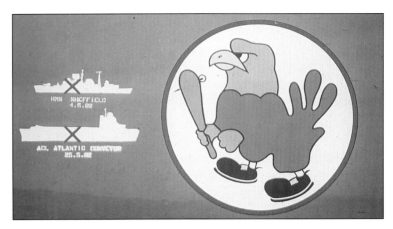

3-A-203 wore two kill markings, alongside the 2ª Escuadrilla badge.

of tanker aircraft for air refuelling. We also considered the mutual support and manoeuvring flexibility provided by a two-ship section, as well as the stealthiness needed to penetrate a fleet equipped with the most advanced early warning systems.

"- The flight parameters (height and speed) were determined for the penetration and escape phases.

"Once these steps were performed, the 10 pilots assigned to the escuadrilla were divided into five pairs, with the seniors as leaders and the juniors as wingmen. From then the sections were frozen, and underwent training together about the launching procedures and the tactics. This was so they could perform them as much like second nature as possible, and in total radio silence.

"After making several of these training missions, I went aboard the Argentine navy Type 42 destroyer ARA *Hércules* to observe from the receiving end how an attack developed. We learned that the possibilities of being detected before launching the missiles were quite low, and that during this stage we should keep out of range of the Sea Dart surface-to-air missiles. As the final element of our training days at Comandante Espora, each pair of aircrews undertook a complete mission, refuelling from an air force KC-130H and attacking a Type 42 destroyer that had been previously shadowed and detected by a Grumman S-2E Tracker.

"On 19 April the escuadrilla deployed to Rio Grande where the training missions continued, including testing the Agave radar performance in conditions of a higher return from the ocean's surface (due to higher waves). Early on the morning of 4 May, a Neptune maritime patrol aircraft was launched from Rio Grande for a surveillance mission south of the Malvinas. At approximately 07:00 the order was received to launch the readiness section (Lieutenant Commander Bedacarratz and myself) because the Neptune had a radar contact, which could be enemy surface shipping. New contacts later confirmed this, and they were assigned as our target. Carefully, but without losing any time, we planned the mission with an air refuelling 250 nm (287 miles; 462 km) from the known target position; after refuelling, we would start the penetration stage. With a new target update we went to the aircraft, and started the pre-flight checks on the aircraft and the AM39 missile.

"To understand our state of mind at that time it was necessary to remember that on 1 May the first engagements took place, and that the escuadrilla's first mission was frustrated when there was a fuel transfer failure in one of the Super Etendards taking fuel from a tanker. On the next day the cruiser ARA *General Belgrano* had been sunk by a British submarine, and on that day and the next one the readiness pair received scrambling orders but were later cancelled, in one instance when both fighters were on the runway's holding point ready for take-off.

"While taxiing to the runway, we checked the exactness of the points in the inertial navigation system, checking heading and distances obtained in our two aircraft, as well as making the last checks to the weapons system.

"We launched at 09.45 and headed in absolute radio/electronic silence to the air refuelling point with the tanker. We found it at the pre-established height and heading thanks to our navigation sets; there it was, the big fat Hercules with both hoses extended. We had already planned that the leader would take the left one, while the right one would be for me. We took all the needed fuel without any problems and continued with our mission. When we were about

120 nm (138 miles; 222 km) from the target, we received from the maritime patrol aircraft a new update about the target's position, and were informed that there was a small target and a larger one offset about 30 nm (35 miles; 56 km).

"After entering the positions into the navigation system we compared distances, and decided to go for the larger target. Weather conditions in the area were quite bad, the ceiling was about 500 ft (152 m) and occasional squalls substantially reduced visibility. Despite difficult navigation, I thought at the time that these were ideal weather conditions for the attack, since it would be difficult to discover us and to scramble Sea Harrier interceptors.

"The stress level was not the same as a training mission, and I was surprised that I was more worried about not forgetting things that could prevent the missile launching than I was about being intercepted. In spite of this, we paid close attention to our RHAW sets and continually checked our rear hemisphere.

"At the opportune distance we did our first pull-up and turned on the radar; nothing was found, so we turned it off and went back to low flying again. We ran 20 miles

(32 km) more and climbed again. This time I did see an echo in the radar display at a distance of 35 miles (56 km), 20° offset to the right. I immediately heard the leader's voice through the headset confirming the detection and ordering me to head directly towards it. I could discern what looked like a large echo, with two smaller ones to the sides. We accomplished the final procedures for launching the Exocet and at 11.02 we launched both missiles. I saw that both rocket motors ignited and the missiles descended to their sea-skimming flight height. After the launch, we executed a maximum-rate turn toward the escape route, along which we also flew at maximum speed. With no trouble we landed at Rio Grande, where our colleagues awaited us anxiously. At about 16.00, while we were in the long post-mission debriefing, we heard on the BBC International Service a British MoD communiqué announcing the attack on the destroyer HMS *Sheffield*."

HMS Arrow *(left) attempts to put out the fires aboard* Sheffield *after the Exocet attack, while rescuing the survivors of the crew. A memorial to the 21 men lost in the raid was erected on Sealion Island.*

Capitán de Corbeta Curilovic (flight leader, above) and Teniente de Navio Barraza (wingman, left) are seen climbing from their cockpits on the evening of 25 May, after having successfully hit the Atlantic Conveyor in the course of a 4-hour 7-minute mission. The vessel was only struck by one missile, the other almost certainly having been deflected by countermeasures. Indeed, it has been suggested that the missile which hit the ship had actually been deflected away from the carrier Hermes, which was only two miles from Atlantic Conveyor at the time.

25 May 1982
Attacking the *Atlantic Conveyor*

Capitán de Corbeta (Lt Cdr) Roberto Curilovic

In 1969 Curilovic took the naval pilot course, and was posted next year to the 2ª Escuadrilla Aeronaval de Ataque as a lieutenant (junior grade). In 1972 he was posted to the 1ª Escuadrilla Aeronaval de Ataque, where he flew MB.326s in the advanced training and light attack roles. From 1973 to 1980 he was posted to 3ª Escuadrilla Aeronaval de Caza y Ataque, flying the A-4Q. During that period, in 1974/45 he took LSO and flight instructor courses with US Navy squadron VT-21 at Kingsville, Texas, with the TA-4J. In November 1980, while acting as the escuadrilla's executive officer, Curilovic received orders to go to France to accept the Super Etendards and activate the new escuadrilla. In 1981 he obtained his qualifications as a Super Etendard pilot and LSO,

Seen heading this post-war line-up of SuEs armed with Exocets and Magics is 3-A-204, Barraza's mount during the 25 May mission. The CANA claimed both Exocets hit the Atlantic Conveyor, while the British admit to only one.

aboard the French navy carrier Clemenceau. Three years after the Falklands War, with the rank of commander, Curilovic took command of 2ª Escuadrilla.

"25 May, a very special day for the Argentines (the national holiday), started very early in Rio Grande for us. It was still night, and very cold, when my wingman Lieutenant Barraza and I walked to the readiness hangar to check the aircraft, missiles and ancillary systems, a job we concluded at about 07.30. About one and a half hours later, and with all the escuadrilla personnel in the operations room at Rio Grande, our CO briefed us about the position of the British Task Force, 110 nm (126 miles; 203 km) northeast of Puerto Argentino (Port Stanley), and the probable location of the aircraft-carriers.

"The position of these Sea Harrier floating bases was determined by the Falklands-based Combat Operations Centre and, after carefully studying the radar traces of incoming and outgoing British air raids, could be fixed with a certain degree of exactness. We planned our navigation, trying to choose a final approach route which the British could not predict. The last attack had been from the south, so this one would come from the north, although the distance was much longer. We would need an air refuelling on the way to the target, and we would land at Puerto Deseado airfield since lack of range prevented us from reaching Rio Grande. After an attempt to go to the aircraft at 10.00 we cancelled the take-off because the tanker was not available in the pre-established time slot (it is worthwhile to remember that there were only two KC-130Hs available for all the Argentine attack aircraft with air-to-air refuelling capability).

"We returned to pre-flight status and to our navigation procedures. We received information about British Sea Harrier CAPs between that position and the northern mouth of the Falklands Sound. We had to consider our route to the location of the destroyer HMS *Coventry*, which was on radar picket duties on that northern mouth.

"Finally we launched at 14.30 hours, heading to the co-ordinates 48° 00' south, 62° 00' west, where the Hercules tanker was waiting for us. Without any difficulties we started our refuelling at 15.00, and at an initial distance of 330 nm (379 miles; 610 km) from the Task Force we started our attack profile. Our RHAW sets did not indicate any radar pointing at us, so we assumed we had not been detected yet. At 16.28 at the opportune distance I made the first radar emission with the Agave, and I could see the expected echoes in the display. We continued with the attack run, at 500 kt (574 mph; 923 km/h) and 100 ft (30 m) over the sea, starting the missile launching procedure. We turned on the radar again and selected the largest target. I confirmed with my wingman (our first radio communication since take-off) the target to lock-on to, and the system started to work as advertised.

"With a full lock-on from the radar, in the optimum launch parameters at the co-ordinates 50° 38' south and 56° 08' west, we launched our missiles at 16.32. We still had no indication from our RHAW sets, so we were convinced that our attack was a complete surprise to the enemy. The first 70 miles (113 km) of the escape leg were at low level and maximum speed, and then we climbed for the cruise height. I contacted the tanker which, having heard about our request, had waited for us; I asked for directions to a new refuelling point, so there would be no need to land at Puerto Deseado. At 17.25, at the co-ordinates 48° 20' south and 63° 00' west, we engaged the fuel hoses, and once fully refuelled started the return leg to Rio Grande. At these southern latitudes night comes quickly, and in complete darkness and bad weather we made an ILS approach, and landed at Rio Grande at 18.37. We had logged four hours and seven minutes of flight, a tension-loaded day had passed, and we were extremely pleased by the welcome reception from our escuadrilla colleagues, who were waiting for us. The result of the mission was two hits on *Atlantic Conveyor*, and it later sank with 10 helicopters onboard and tons of vital equipment."

25 May 1982
Successful mission

Teniente de Navio Julio Hector Barraza

Barraza completed the naval pilot course in 1971 at the Naval Aviation School in Punta Indio. Next year he was posted to the 2ª Escuadrilla Aeronaval de Ataque, then equipped with T-28 Fennecs, and qualified aboard the carrier 25 de Mayo. *In 1974 he went to 1ª Escuadrilla Aeronaval de Ataque, equipped with Macchi MB.326s, where he stayed for three years. In 1977 he was posted to 3ª Escuadrilla Aeronaval de Caza y Ataque, although he took the Skyhawk course in the United States, flying the TA-4J. In 1981 he was selected to form part of the group of pilots who trained in France in the Super Etendard, and thus was a founding member of the reactivated 2ª Escuadrilla Aeronaval de Caza y Ataque.*

"After an unsuccessful mission flown on 23 May by Lieutenant Commander Roberto Agotegaray and Lieutenant José Rodríguez Mariani, it was our turn to cover the next pair of pilots on readiness. My leader was Lieutenant Commander Roberto Curilovic. There were no missions on 24 May, but next day, on 25 May, we received the order to attack a target which was located 110 nm (126 miles; 203 km) northeast of Puerto Argentino (Port Stanley).

"The first attempt to take-off, at about 11.00, was cancelled because the KC-130 tanker was not available, so the mission slipped into the afternoon. We went to the aircraft and cranked up, and lots of people wished us good luck and good hunting. At about 14.00 we launched and soon we were flying in the pre-established profile, heading towards the point where we had scheduled our refuelling

from the KC-130 tanker. During the mission's first stage I was concerned that we could not make contact with the Hercules at the planned altitude because a thick cloud deck jutted up at that height. Crossing the radial from Rio Gallegos, the clouds started to break, then disappeared. We were flying in complete radio silence. I saw a little dot on the horizon: the KC-130 was waiting for us with its hoses deployed, flying in a racetrack pattern at the proper height. With hand signals each of us went to a hose, I to the left, Lieutenant Commander Curilovic to the right. Then the turn stopped, and the Hercules established a west-northwest heading, towards the mainland. This could mean problems for us, as the distance to run after completing the tanking would be longer than pre-established. Lieutenant Commander Curilovic said over UHF, '070, 070', but there was no reply; he then tried over VHF, and the Hercules started to turn right. The rear observation windows of the tanker were full of the crewmen continuously waving at us. Refuelling took a long time, about 15 minutes.

"Just after disengaging, a message came from the KC-130: 'We have an important signal for you, please copy' and then transmitted in the clear updated co-ordinates of the target. I wrote them down, but doubted that I had copied them well. These co-ordinates were entered into the INS, and I found that the difference from the heading and distance that we had entered initially was quite small. We started our descent before we reached the pre-established distance from the Task Force, since our fuel

level allowed this. Now we were flying in combat spread, separated by 1.5 to 2 miles (2.4 to 3.2 km). At about 1,500 ft (460 m) there were broken clouds and we levelled at 100 ft (30 m) over the ocean, flying 500 kt (574 mph; 923 km/h).

"We detected the target on the radar, and at 39 miles (62 km) Lieutenant Commander Curilovic said, 'I've got a lock-on,' and I replied, 'Come on 39,' then he said, 'All right.' I had set all the switches I could on the armament panel, so the Exocet would fire by pushing the button on the stick. First to launch was Lieutenant Commander Curilovic, then one or two seconds later I did the same. The reason for that slight delay was that on the last stage of the attack run, I heard my leader say 'Launch,' and I concentrated my attention on his aircraft, how the missile fell ballistic for a few metres and then the rocket engine fired. We made a maximum rate turn to the left to get on our pre-established escape route, with throttles to the firewall and the needle almost touching the 600-kt (688-mph; 1108-km) mark, just above the water. I constantly swivelled my neck towards the rear hemisphere, to check if there was a Sea Harrier CAP behind us. Fortunately there wasn't any, and

we later learned that the destroyer *Coventry*, which was on radar picket duties near the northern entrance of the Falklands Sound, had been attacked by our air force aircraft and most of the CAPs were in that area. The return leg passed without any problems as we flew towards the co-ordinates where the KC-130 tanker was waiting for us. In the event of not finding it, or any other emergency, we had briefed to land at Puerto Deseado, where a support Beech King Air 200 had detached with ground crews. Our luck stayed with us and after refuelling we continued to Rio Grande, where we landed in total darkness after more than four hours of flight.

"Next day we learned that both Exocets had hit the *Atlantic Conveyor*, a container ship which had been requisitioned by the Royal Navy as an auxiliary carrier."

Julio Barraza refuels from a Grupo 1 de Transporte KC-130H 'Chancha' (mother sow), minutes before dropping down to wave-top height for the attack on **Atlantic Conveyor.**

MV Atlantic Conveyor *was hit at 1936Z, caught fire and later sank, carrying with it a Lynx, three Chinooks, six Wessexes and large supplies of tents and ammunition. Twelve crewmen lost their lives: Captain I. H. North was posthumously awarded the DSC.*

30 May 1982
The last attempt

Teniente de Navio Luis Antonio Collavino
In February 1971 Collavino received his naval aviator wing. His postings from then until 1982 were: 1972 – 2ª Escuadrilla Aeronaval de Ataque with T-28 Fennecs, including carrier carquals aboard 25 de Mayo. *1972-1973 – 1ª Escuadrilla Aeronaval de Ataque, flying Macchi MB-326 aircraft. 1974-1975 – 3ª Escuadrilla Aeronaval de Caza y Ataque, flying A-4Q Skyhawks including carrier deployments aboard* 25 de Mayo. *1976 – Flight Deck Officer,* 25 de Mayo. *1977 – Staff Course for Naval Aviators. 1978-1980 – Flight Instructor, Escuela de Aviación Naval. November 1980/July 1981 – Super Etendard course in France. 1980 – Primary Flight Control CO,* 25 de Mayo. *Just after Operation Rosario (the Argentine name for the landings in the Falklands) he was replaced in the carrier and sent to Rio Grande with 2ª Escuadrilla Aeronaval de Caza y Ataque.*

"The 30 May 1982 mission was the last attack performed by the escuadrilla and the last Exocet missile launch. The movements of the British fleet were studied carefully at Puerto Argentino. Using a Westinghouse AN/TPS-43E mobile early warning radar it was determined where the aerial bogies appeared or disappeared at the edges of the radar's horizon. It was known that the Sea Harrier's radius of action did not allow the British to go much further from the islands than about 100 nm (115 miles; 185 km). We were sure that in that area there was at least one aircraft-carrier. On 29 May the order was received that we should attack a target located 100 nm to the east of Puerto Argentino. The readiness section at the time was formed by Lieutenant Commander Alejandro Francisco and myself.

"After the sinking of *Atlantic Conveyor* on 25 May – which to our knowledge had been a nasty surprise for the British Task Force – most of the British ships had

sailed to the southeast from their previous position north-northeast of the Malvinas. We decided that, since most of Argentine air attacks were on an easterly heading, we would plan an attack with a northwesterly heading, to continue to exploit the surprise factor (which had been so successful in the *Atlantic Conveyor* attack that was done on a north/south heading). We also knew that the Task Force's staff had increased the number of advanced picket ships and they were positioned in the most dangerous approach areas, i.e. covering the western 180° of their fleet.

"The planned attack heading was actually the most compromised from a radius-of-action point of view, but it preserved the surprise element and avoided possible pickets. Most importantly, it necessitated two air refuellings and so increased the risk of cancelling the mission if any problem arose in the course of it. All through the morning of 29 May, we planned and verified all the minute details of navigation, attack and escape. All the escuadrilla pilots participated, each doing his best to accomplish the job: some contributed their hard-won experience, others good sense, and all boldness and aggression. At noon everything was ready and we were waiting for the take-off order in the ready room. Then Lieutenant Commander Jorge Luis Colombo, the escuadrilla CO, informed us that the Fuerza Aérea staff had signalled its desire that its fighter-bombers should participate in the operation. They requested the attack be a joint one with the A-4C Skyhawks deployed at San Julian airfield.

"This request was made because the Super Etendards had radar and a very accurate navigation system, which allowed them to attack targets in the open seas. This was not the case for the air force A-4Cs, unless they followed the Super Etendards on their attack. The good thing was that the number of weapons dropped over the target increased because each of

the four Skyhawks was armed with three 500-lb (226-kg) bombs; the bad thing was the risk of losing the surprise factor, since six aircraft flying together could not be discreet. Due to the brief time available in which to establish all the joint procedures we needed, and since the A-4Cs had not yet arrived at Rio Grande, and the target remained in the indicated area, it was decided to make the attack with only the two Super Etendards. We drove the aircrew van to the readiness hangar, cranked up the Atars and performed the avionics pre-flight check – and then over the radio we heard the bad news. The air force KC-130H tanker was returning to Rio Gallegos, its home base, due to a low fuel level, so the mission was postponed until the next day.

"On Sunday 30 May, while we waited for an update about the British fleet's new position, we met with the A-4C pilots in an extensive briefing. It included establishing the overall co-ordination of the flight, the importance of discretion and maintaining radio silence, and adapting the Skyhawk's flight profile to that already planned for the Super Etendards. Meanwhile, the two KC-130 Hercules tankers were flying towards the air refuelling point, pretending as much as possible to be innocent commercial traffic [they used a commercial airway]. It was 12.30 when at last we took off, followed by the four A-4Cs, with a five-minute lag between us and them. The Skyhawks were flown by First Lieutenant José Daniel Vázquez as flight leader, First Lieutenant Omar Jesús Castillo as number two (they were both shot down and killed during the attack), First Lieutenant Ernesto Ruben Ureta as number three and element leader, and Second Lieutenant Gerardo G. Isaac as number four. The join-up with the tankers was at the pre-established point at 20,000 ft (6097 m), southeast of Isla de Los Estados; the refuelling itself went smoothly, we went to one tanker and the Skyhawks to the other. The

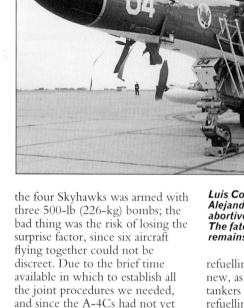

refuelling mode in this mission was new, as the attack aircraft and the tankers flew eastwards while refuelling, continuing together for about 150 miles (240 km), taking on fuel during almost the whole stage in order to complete this cruise leg with full fuel tanks, or at least with the maximum possible quantity. Everything worked very well.

"When we got to the most easterly point we disengaged from the Hercules and adopted the combat formation, with the Super Etendards leading, separated a mile in line abreast, and two Skyhawks flying wing on each one. At about 300 nm (345 miles; 555 km) from the target, we commenced the attack run, keeping a north/northwest heading. We descended to low altitude where we found bad weather, and each minute more clouds appeared. This made visibility among us difficult and caused a slight drift to the right of our course, but it did not worry us much thanks to the excellent nav/attack system of the Super Etendard, which allowed us to have control of the flight's parameters. It did mean that the attack would be carried out more from the east than originally planned, so the British fleet could be surprised to receive an air raid more than 100° offset from its air defence axis, which was turned towards the west. Soon we were flying at low level, less that 60 ft (18 m) over a stormy ocean, in radio silence. Flight discipline was being accomplished as briefed, as if we had flown together many times. When, according to our attack tactics, we climbed to turn on the radar, we found that the display showed several real and mock contacts. Once again we descended and continued with the low-level flying.

"A few minutes later we climbed again and the displays still showed the two kinds of echoes, but after

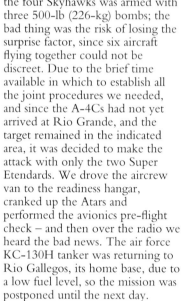

Francisco refuels from a KC-130H, carrying the last Exocet available to 2ª Eslla. Behind are three of the four Grupo 4 A-4Cs of ZONDA flight, which followed the missile in to attack Avenger (thinking it was Invincible). Although Francisco and his wingman returned without drama, two of the Skyhawks were hit by Sea Darts launched by Exeter and the others missed the target.

working on the radar we discerned which ones were true, and then pointed the antenna at (designated) the largest one. Lieutenant Commander Francisco launched the last missile (I did not carry a warload, only guns) from a distance and in conditions which should assure a hit on a target locked by his radar and also confirmed by my radar. Immediately we turned to the south, always at low level, maintaining maximum speed for almost 30 miles (48 km), then we started the climb to cruise height and returned home without making air-to-air refuelling.

"The four Skyhawks followed the Exocet's smoke trail, continuing with their attack run after accelerating to maximum speed, but soon the trail ended in a dark spot blurred by the fog. They had to drop their bombs into the ship hit by the missile. Two A-4Cs were shot down near the target. The other two fired their cannon and launched their bombs, overflying the ship quite close and almost colliding with its antennas, as it was enveloped in the smoke

The Super Etendard is still the main attack aircraft of the CANA, although operations are now mostly shore-based. The aircraft in the foreground carries an acquisition round of the Magic AAM.

cloud caused by the missile's hit a few seconds before.

"After the attack both Skyhawks refuelled from the tanker, which wasn't necessary but was done to increase the safety margin for the return flight. We landed at Rio Grande, and 15 minutes later the two surviving A-4Cs did the same, after three hours and 47 minutes of flight. The Skyhawk pilots were subjected to a very intensive debriefing, each in a different room. They related their recent experiences and both said the same thing: that the warship they attacked, according to what they had seen and the recognition silhouettes, was none other than HMS Invincible. They also said that the missile ran true and that its trail ended in the ship, proof that the missile had hit the ship.

"In my opinion, I think detailed analysis of what the 2ª Escuadrilla Aeronaval de Caza y Ataque accomplished during the war led to changes in more than one navy, regarding tactics and doctrine. Not only the results that were obtained, but above all the way the constant threat forced a powerful force like the Royal Navy to significantly change the course of its operations.

Attacking HMS *Invincible* – or not

The Royal Navy carrier HMS *Invincible* was not hit during the raid narrated by Luis Collavino, nor was it overflown by the Skyhawks, contrary to what the pilots claimed then and still claim. The fact is that they misidentified, both on radar and visually (due to very poor weather), the frigate HMS *Avenger* and the destroyer HMS *Exeter*, both on picket duties and sailing in close formation with the carrier. They were in a high stress situation: flying at extreme range, with little experience in this kind of operations, in bad weather, and seeing two of their colleagues shot down by Sea Darts. All these factors contributed to the two surviving Skyhawk pilots claiming with all honesty that they had bombed and overflown the carrier, but the truth is that they bombed (missing) and overflew both *Avenger* and *Exeter*.

As for the Super Etendards, it is likely that both targets appeared as one in their radar displays, due to the heavy sea state or perhaps jamming from the RN ships. Lieutenant Commander Francisco's Exocet was launched at 20 to 25 km (12 to 15 miles) from the target: possibly it was destroyed in flight by a lucky shot from one of the 4.5-in (11.43-cm) guns; perhaps it flew into the water and exploded relatively near the ships; more probably, it was decoyed by a cloud of chaff from one or more Curvus rockets launched by both warships. Skyhawk pilots claimed that the smoke trail ended in a blurred blot darker than the low clouds and fog, and they also stated that *Invincible* was enveloped in smoke.

Despite the denials and the hard facts, the 30 May 1982 attack against the British Task Force has become established within the Argentine navy and air force as the day that HMS *Invincible* was damaged, both by the Exocet and the bombs. This way, both services are satisfied.

"Once the supply of Exocets had been used up, the four available Super Etendards returned to Comandante Espora between 1 and 2 June. Using them in more conventional roles was considered, with slick and retarded dumb bombs, but since a new delivery of Exocet missiles was expected we started a very intensive training period in night operations, adapting the tactics and techniques we had used in daylight to the more demanding and dangerous night-time. Until the conflict ended on 14 June, the escuadrilla lived during the night. We planned, exchanged experiences and ideas during the afternoon, then we started flying in the evening almost until day, repeating the missile launch procedures and everything associated with this item."

Salvador Mafé Huertas

Lockheed's Blackbirds

A-12, YF-12 and SR-71

In the late 1950s the CIA had guessed that it would only be a matter of time before its high-flying yet flimsy U-2 would be shot down by the powerful Soviet SA-2 'Guideline' SAM. Accordingly, a programme was initiated to provide a follow-on which could produce overhead intelligence with vastly reduced vulnerability. The result was the Lockheed A-12, but due to the changing political climate following the forecasted U-2 loss in 1960, the aircraft never went into action over the Soviet Union. Instead, the A-12 saw only brief service over North Vietnam and North Korea. However, it was the highest-flying and fastest air-breathing aircraft ever built, breaking new technological ground in virtually every area. This experience was put to use in producing the YF-12, a Mach 3 interceptor which, although it was not chosen for production, was instrumental in developing the long-range radar and missile systems in service today. For strategic reconnaissance, the A-12 design evolved into the two-man SR-71, which for 25 years provided the United States with a unique window into the hot-spots of the world. Today, over 30 years after its first flight, the SR-71 is back in limited service, proving just how far ahead of its time it was when it was designed in the early 1960s.

The first operational flight undertaken by Central Intelligence Agency (CIA) pilot Harvey Stockman in Lockheed U-2 article number 347, on 4 July 1956, produced a photo-take of previously denied territory, the like of which had never been seen before. At a stroke the U-2 and its associated programme, Operation Overflight, established themselves as the pre-eminent means of gathering strategic intelligence concerning the USSR and its satellites.

Despite spectacular results, informed sources were concerned about the Soviets' ability to accurately track on radar the subsonic U-2. In November 1954, CIA director Allen Dulles recruited Richard Bissell, a brilliant economist and innovator who lectured at both Yale and Massachusetts Institute of Technology (MIT), and appointed him Special Assistant for Planning and Co-ordination. Bissell, 'Kelly' Johnson (the U-2 designer) and the Killian Committee (a Department of Defense-sponsored 'think-tank' to President Eisenhower, consisting of the chairman James R. Killian, president of MIT, and 14 other eminent professionals with science and technology backgrounds) believed that the U-2 would enjoy a period of no more than two years of invulnerability from the start of Operation Overflight. Accordingly, Bissell began organising research and development of follow-on systems. In the autumn of 1957, he contacted 'Kelly' Johnson and asked if the Lockheed Skunk Works team would conduct an operations analysis into the relationship of interceptability and an aircraft's speed,

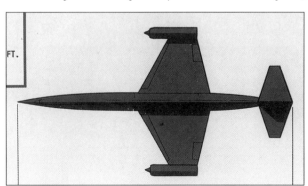

altitude and radar cross-section (RCS). Since Kelly was already immersed in related studies, he agreed to accept the project; the results concluded that supersonic speed coupled with the use of radar-attenuating materials (RAM) and radar-attenuating design greatly reduced, but not negated, chances of radar detection. Encouraged by the results, it was agreed that further exploratory work should be conducted. The CIA then focused on the possibility of operating a platform capable of flight at extremely high speeds and altitude, which also incorporated the best available radar-attenuating capabilities. During the closing months of 1957, the Agency invited Lockheed Aircraft Corporation and the Convair Division of General Dynamics to submit non-funded, non-contracted designs for a reconnaissance-gathering vehicle which adhered to the fore-mentioned performance criteria. Both companies accepted the challenge and were assured that funding would be forthcoming at the appropriate time. For the next 12 months, the Agency received designs that were developed and refined all at no expense!

High-risk programme

It was readily apparent to Bissell that developing such an advanced aircraft would be both high-risk and extremely expensive; government funding would be a prerequisite and in order to obtain this various high-ranking government officials would have to be brought into the programme and given clear, authoritative presentations on advances as they occurred. He therefore assembled a talented panel of six specialists under the chair of Dr Edwin Land. Between 1957 and 1959 the panel met on six occasions, usually in Land's Cambridge, Massachusetts office. Kelly and General Dynamics' Vincent Dolson were at times in attendance, as were the Assistant Secretaries of the Air Force and Navy, plus other select technical advisors.

Codenamed Project Gusto by the Agency, Lockheed's first submission, Archangel, proposed a Mach 3 cruise aircraft with a range of 4,000 nm (4,600 miles; 7400 km) at 90,000-95,000 ft (27430-29000 m). This, together with his Gusto Model G2A submission, were both well received by the Programme Office, as Kelly noted later. Convair, on the other hand, prepared the Mach 4-capable Super

Looking east across the Groom Dry Lake airfield, this line-up of Blackbirds is headed by the first A-12 built, behind which is the only A-12B two-seater. At the far end of the row are two YF-12As. Groom Lake, aka Area 51, 'the Ranch' or 'Dreamland', had been established as the flight test centre for the U-2; its proximity to the atomic weapon testing site deterred any unwanted guests, as did the security measures which were introduced. Beginning with a lakebed runway and a few shacks, the facility grew steadily in size throughout the U-2, A-12, F-117 and subsequent programmes, and now boasts a six-mile runway and a large complex of buildings.

Prior to the development which led to the A-12, the Lockheed Skunk Works was working on liquid hydrogen powered aircraft under Project Suntan. This design, designated CL-400-10, was over 160 ft (49 m) long and had two Pratt & Whitney 304 engines. The principal disadvantage of the liquid hydrogen powerplant was the lack of range, despite the fact that most of the aircraft's fuselage contained fuel.

Previous studies

Even before the U-2 of Francis Gary Powers was shot down, Lockheed (and others) was busy studying a follow-on aircraft which would be invulnerable to Soviet defences for the overflight mission. While most designs strove for greater speed and altitude, some tackled the then-novel idea of vastly reducing radar cross-section.

Above: During Project Gusto Lockheed produced designs from A-3 to A-12. Many, like the A-10 depicted here, featured the forward fuselage chine which was such a feature of the eventual A-12 aircraft. The A-11 was a very high-performance diamond-winged design but had a massive RCS. The A-12 attempted to combine the A-11's performance with a much lower radar cross-section.

Above: The Archangel I of autumn 1957 was the first of the high-speed studies. The name related to the U-2's 'Angel' nickname.

Left: Arrow I was another early study, with two engines mounted side-by-side in a large fairing. The design had two large vertical tail surfaces near the wingtips.

Above: Archangel II was the second of the high-speed designs (leading to the A-3/12 series). It featured a mixed powerplant of two turbojets for take-off and low-speed flight (inboard), and two large ramjets on the wingtips for high-speed flight.

Left: Dubbed Gusto 2, this large (wider span than a U-2) flying-wing design was slow but was designed to have a very low radar cross-section.

Hustler, which would be ramjet-powered when launched from a B-58 and turbojet-assisted for landing. As designs were refined and resubmitted, the Lockheed offerings' names were shortened to 'A' followed by an index number, running from A-3 to A-12. The design and designations from Convair also evolved, being known as the Kingfish. On 20 August 1959 final submissions from both companies were made to a joint DoD/Air Force/CIA selection panel. Though strikingly different, the proposed performance of both aircraft compared favourably.

	A-12	Kingfish
Speed	Mach 3.2	Mach 3.2
Range (total)	4,120 nm	4,000 nm
Range (at altitude)	3,800 nm	3,400 nm
Cruise altitudes		
Start	84,500 ft	85,000 ft
Mid-range	91,000 ft	88,000 ft
End	97,600 ft	94,000 ft
Dimensions		
Length	102 ft	79.5 ft
Span	57 ft	56 ft
Gross weight	110,000 lb	101,700 lb
Fuel weight	64,600 lb	62,000 lb
First flight	22 months	22 months

On 28 August Kelly was told by the director of the programme that Lockheed's Skunk Works had won the competition to build the U-2 follow-on. The next day Lockheed was given the official go-ahead, with initial fund-ing of $4.5 million approved to cover the period 1 September 1959 to 1 January 1960. Project Gusto was now at an end and a new codename, Oxcart, was assigned. On 3 September the Agency authorised Lockheed to proceed with anti-radar studies into aerodynamics, structural tests and engineering designs. The small engineering team, under the supervision of Ed Martin, consisted of Dan Zuck in charge of cockpit design, Dave Robertson on fuel system requirements, Henry Combs and Dick Bochme on structures, and Dick Fuller, Burt McMaster and Kelly's protégé, Ben Rich.

Tunnel testing

The final A-12 design was arrived at after many hours of tunnel testing, across the whole spectrum of the aircraft's speed envelope. Several features, such as canard foreplanes, were tested and discarded.

Below left: This tunnel model is recognisably the A-12 in a near-definition configuration, but has triangular foreplanes added in an attempt to improve the pitch stability.

Below: This tunnel model of the A-12, by then codenamed Oxcart, dates from 1960. It has the inboard elevons and all-moving tails of the final design, conventional rudders having been tested earlier. One feature subsequently altered was the elegantly curving wing/chine join.

Above: Photographed in January 1962, the first A-12 (Article 121, later 60-6929) is seen virtually complete in Building 82 (final check-out) of the Burbank assembly facility. Great secrecy surrounded the A-12 programme: the aircraft was by a wide margin the most advanced anywhere in the world. It was also to be the fastest, its top speed and altitude being higher than the SR-71 which followed.

Above right: This is the last A-12, Article 133, nearing completion at Burbank. Apparent is the size of the Q-bay, which housed large downward-looking cameras behind the pilot.

An A-12 model sits atop the Groom Lake RCS pole. It has been painted with ferrous 'Iron Ball' radar-attenuating paint to test its effect. The large fairings protruding from the jetpipes were used to emulate the radar signature of the afterburner plumes from the two J58s.

The ambitious scope of performance planned for the new aircraft cannot be overstated. The best front-line fighter aircraft of the day were the early 'Century Series' jets like the F-100 Super Sabre and the F-101 Voodoo; in a single bound, the A-12 would operate at sustained speeds and altitudes treble and double, respectively, those of such contemporary fighters. The technical challenge facing the Skunk Works team was enormous, and the contracted timescale in which to achieve it was incredibly tight. Kelly later remarked that virtually everything on the aircraft had to be invented from scratch. Operating above 80,000 ft (24390 m), the atmospheric pressure was 0.4 psi (2.7 kPa) and ambient air temperature was -56° C (-69° F) – but cruising at a speed of 1 mile (1.6 km) every two seconds meant that airframe temperatures varied from 245° to 565° C (473° to 1,050° F). At a Mach 3.2 cruise, the two engines required 100,000 cu ft (2830 m³) of air per second, the equivalent of 2 million people inhaling simultaneously.

A-12 construction

How and from what was such an aircraft built? The A-12 design is characterised by an aft-body delta wing with two large engines, each located at mid-semi-span. Two all-moving vertical fins were mounted on top of each engine nacelle and canted inwards 15° from the vertical to reduce the aircraft's radar signature and to aid the control of excess offset yaw-thrust during single-engine flight. A large aft-moving inlet spike or centre-body protruded forward from each engine nacelle, which helped to regulate mass airflow to the two powerful engines at speeds above Mach 1.4. Mission equipment was housed in a large bay behind the pilot in the A-12 (this bay was occupied by a fire control officer (FCO) in the YF-12 interceptor version and a reconnaissance systems officer (RSO) in the Air Force-operated SR-71.) Weapons, a fire control system and vari-

ous cameras and sensors were located in mission equipment bays, located in the underside of the chine (a boat-like hull-form which extended along both sides of the long fuselage forebody on the YF-12 and SR-71). In all three variants, flight crews wore a full pressure suit.

Sustained operation in extreme temperatures meant lavish use of the advanced titanium alloys that account for 85 per cent of the aircraft's structural weight, the remaining 15 per cent being comprised of composite materials. The decision to use such materials was based on considerations such as titanium's ability to withstand high operating temperatures; that it weighs half as much as stainless steel but has the same tensile strength; and that conventional construction was possible using fewer parts (high-strength composites were not available in the early 1960s). The particular titanium used was B-120VCA, which can be hardened to strengths up to 200,000 psi (1.38 million kPa). Initially the ageing process required 70 hours to achieve maximum strength but, with careful processing techniques, this was reduced to 40 hours. A rigorous (and expensive) quality control programme was established wherein for every batch of 10 or more parts processed, three samples were heat-treated to the same level as those in the batch. One was then strength-tested to destruction, another tested for formability and the third held in reserve should pre-processing be required. With more than 13 million titani-

Testing the A-12

The extreme performance and exacting mission requirements of the A-12 required extensive testing of the various systems. Those tests which could not be conducted behind closed doors were undertaken at the secret operating location at Groom Dry Lake, where radar cross-section pole tests and other visible trials could be performed in daylight and privacy. Once the first aircraft was reassembled at the base, high-speed taxi trials followed, during the course of which the aircraft took off inadvertently, on 25 April 1962.

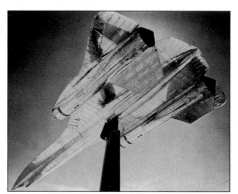

The second A-12, Article 122, was delivered to Groom Lake on 26 June 1962, and was used initially for RCS pole tests.

Tests of the Lockheed SR-1 ejection seat were made at Groom Lake, a hired 1961 Thunderbird being used to tow the test rig across the dry lakebed.

um parts manufactured, data is available on all but a few.

Using this advanced material, it was not long before problems arose. Titanium is not compatible with chlorine, fluorine or cadmium, so for example a line drawn on sheet titanium with a Pentel pen will eat a hole through it in about 12 hours. All Pentel pens were recalled from the shop floor. Early spot-welded panels produced during the summer had a habit of failing, while those built in the winter lasted indefinitely. Diligent detective work discovered that to prevent the formation of algae in the summer, the Burbank water supply is heavily chlorinated. Subsequently, the Skunk Works washed all titanium parts in distilled water. As thermodynamic tests got underway, bolt heads began dropping from installations; this, it was discovered, was caused by tiny cadmium deposits left after cadmium-plated spanners had been used to apply torque. As the bolts were heated over 320° C (610° F) their heads dropped off. All cadmium-plated tools were removed from tool boxes.

Corrugated skin

Another test studied thermal effects on large titanium wing panels. An element 4 ft x 6 ft (1.2 m x 1.8 m) was heated to the computed heat flux expected in flight and resulted in the sample warping into a totally unacceptable shape. This problem was resolved by manufacturing chord-wise corrugations into the outer skins. At the design heat rate, the corrugations merely deepened by a few thousandths of an inch and on cooling returned to the basic shape. Kelly recalled he was accused of "trying to make a

1932 Ford Trimotor go Mach 3," but added that "the concept worked fine." To prevent this titanium outer skin from tearing when secured to heavier sub-structures, the Skunk Works developed stand-off clips, which ensured structural continuity while creating a heat shield between adjacent components.

Chosen powerplant would be the Pratt & Whitney JT11D-20 engine (designated J58 by the US military). This high bypass ratio afterburning engine was the result of two earlier, ill-fated programmes: Project Suntan, a 1956 project which envisaged a 2.7-Mach hydrogen-fuelled aircraft built by Lockheed and designated CL-400, and which was axed three years after inception: and Pratt & Whitney's JT9 single-spool high-pressure ratio turbojet, rated at 26,000 lb (115 kN) in afterburner and developed for a US Navy attack aircraft, which was also axed. Nevertheless, the engine had already completed 700 hours of full-scale engine

Above: Following the inadvertent hop on 25 April, Lou Schalk flew the A-12 on its scheduled first flight the following day. He kept the undercarriage down throughout the 30-minute sortie, during which some wing and fuselage fillets were lost. Here Schalk is seen during that first landing.

Above left: On 30 April 1962 the A-12 made its first 'official' flight in front of a small gathering of government and company officials.

Lou Schalk was subsequently joined by Lockheed test pilots Bill Park, Jim Eastham and Bob Gilliland. Here Eastham pilots the first aircraft during refuelling trials in early 1963. The short-finned modified KC-135A was based at Groom Lake for the duration of the tests.

testing and results were very encouraging. As testing continued, however, it became apparent that due to the incredibly hostile thermal conditions of sustained Mach 3.2 flight, only the basic airflow size (400 lb/180 kg per second of airflow) and the compressor and turbine aerodynamics of the original Navy J58 P2 engine could be retained (even they were later modified). The stretched design criteria, associated with high Mach number and its related large airflow turn-down ratio, led to the development of a variable-cycle engine, later known as a bleed-bypass engine, a concept conceived by Pratt & Whitney's Robert Abernathy. This eliminated many airflow problems through the engine by bleeding air from the fourth stage of the nine-stage, single-spool axial-flow compressor. The excess air was passed through six low-compression-ratio bypass ducts and was reintroduced into the turbine exhaust, near the front of the afterburner, at the same static pressure as the main flow. This reduced exhaust gas temperature (EGT) and in addition produced almost as much thrust per pound of air as the main flow which had passed through the rear compressor, the burner section and the turbine. Scheduling

of the bypass bleed was achieved by the main fuel control as a function of compressor inlet temperature (CIT) and engine rpm. Bleed air injection occurred at a CIT of between 85° and 115° C (185° and 240° F) (approximately Mach 1.9).

To further minimise stalling the front stages of the rotor blades at low engine speeds, movable inlet guide vanes (IGVs) were incorporated to help guide airflow to the compressor. They changed from axial to a cambered position in response to the main fuel control, which regulated most engine functions. Set in the axial position to provide additional thrust for take-off and acceleration to intermediate supersonic speeds, the IGVs changed to the cambered position when the CIT again reached 85° to 115° C. If IGV 'lock-in' failed to occur upon reaching a CIT of 150° C (302° F), the mission would be aborted.

When operating at cruising speeds, the turbine inlet temperature (TIT) reached over 1100° C (2,012° F), which necessitated the development of a unique fuel, created jointly by Pratt & Whitney, Ashland Shell and Monsanto. It was known originally as PF-1 and latterly as JP-7. Having a

The 'Roadrunners'

Before the A-12 had flown, the CIA had begun the process of finding pilots for the programme. In all, 11 were chosen from Air Force units, all having undergone rigorous medical examinations and the CIA's own security 'sheep-dipping' process. Conversion flying carried on hand-in-hand with flight trials, the first Agency pilot flying the A-12 in the spring of 1963. The test programme reached a major milestone on 20 July, when Mach 3 was achieved for the first time. Serious intake problems were slowly overcome and by November 1965 the Oxcart team was declared operational. It was to be May 1967 before the A-12 actually went into action. In the intervening period the Oxcart pilots honed their skills, although not without the loss of four aircraft. The aircraft had been flown to Mach 3.56 and 96,200 ft (29322 m).

The CIA A-12 operation was designated the 1129th Special Activities Squadron. The roadrunner was adopted as its badge.

Early A-12 pilots christened the aircraft 'Cygnus'. Here one is seen emerging from its Groom Lake barn.

much higher ignition temperature than JP-4, standard electrical ignition systems were useless. Instead, a chemical ignition system (CIS) was developed, using a highly volatile pyrophoric fluid known as tri-ethyl borane (TEB). TEB is extremely flash-sensitive when oxidised, so the small TEB tank carried on the aircraft – to allow engine afterburner start-up both on the ground and aloft – was pressurised using gaseous nitrogen to ensure the system remained inert. Liquid nitrogen carried in three dewar flasks situated in the front nose gear well was used to provide a positive 'head' of gaseous nitrogen in the fuel tanks. This prevented the depleted tanks from crushing as the aircraft descended into the denser atmosphere to land or refuel. In addition, this inert gas reduced the risk of inadvertent vapour ignition.

Go-ahead from the CIA

Oxcart received a shot in the arm on 30 January 1960 when the Agency gave Lockheed ADP the go-ahead to manufacture and test a dozen A-12s, including one two-seat conversion trainer. With Lockheed's chief test pilot, Louis W. Schalk, onboard, work on refining the aircraft's design continued in parallel with construction work at the jet's secret test site in Nevada. Area 51, Groom Dry Lake (referred to variously as 'the Ranch' or 'the Area'), was initially built for the U-2 test programme in the mid-1950s. Located 100 miles (160 km) northwest of Las Vegas, the site offered an expansive dry lake bed, exceptional remoteness and good weather year round. Its 5,000-ft (1525-m) runway was too short, however, and all other facilities were inadequate for this new programme. A new water well was drilled and new recreation facilities were provided for the construction workers who were billeted in trailer houses. An 8,500-ft (2590-m) runway was constructed, and 18 miles (29 km) of off-base highway were resurfaced to allow 500,000 US gal (1.9 million litres) of PF-1 fuel to be trucked in every month. Three US Navy hangars together

with Navy housing units were transported to the site in readiness for the arrival of the A-12 prototype, expected in May 1961.

Difficulties in procuring and working with titanium, coupled with problems experienced by Pratt & Whitney, soon meant that the anticipated first flight date slipped. Even with completion date of the first aircraft put back to Christmas 1961 and initial test flight postponed to late February 1962, the J58 would still not be ready. Eventually, Kelly decided that J75 engines would be used in the interim to propel the A-12 to a 'halfway house' of only 50,000 ft (15245 m) and Mach 1.6.

The flight crew selection process evolved by the Pentagon's Special Activities Office representative (Colonel Houser Wilson) and the Agency's USAF liaison officer (Brigadier General Jack Ledford, succeeded by Brigadier Paul Bacalis) got under way in 1961. On completion of the final screening, the first pilots were William Skliar, Kenneth Collins, Walter Ray, Alonzo Walter, Mele Vojvodich, Jack Weeks, Jack Layton, Dennis Sullivan, David Young, Francis Murray and Russ Scott (only six of them were destined to fly operational missions). These elite pilots then began

60-6938 taxis at the 'Ranch' for an Oxcart training mission. Late in the programme the aircraft acquired an all-over 'Iron Ball' finish and national insignia. Those flying with 1129th SAS Det 1 at Kadena had no insignia and wore spurious five-digit serials (starting with '77') in red on the fin.

Bottom: The A-12B taxis for take-off at Area 51. It was never painted in the all-over black scheme, although it did receive the black edges.

Below: The 'Goose' approaches the tanker. The USAF established the 903rd ARS with KC-135Qs to support Oxcart flights.

The 'Titanium Goose'

Clarence L. 'Kelly' Johnson is seen in the rear cockpit of the A-12B, strapped in for a low-level flight. This was the only time Johnson ever flew in a member of the Blackbird family.

To aid pilot conversion the fourth aircraft (60-6927) was completed as the sole A-12B trainer, with a second, raised cockpit in the Q-bay. This aircraft retained its J75 engines throughout its career, restricting it to about Mach 1.6. It first flew in January 1963 and was based at Groom Lake until the end of the Oxcart programme in 1968. In addition to its regular use as a conversion tool, the 'Titanium Goose' was occasionally used for flight-test work where two pilots were required, although such work usually was accomplished in the simulator.

Black Shield

After many months of waiting, the 1129th SAS was finally given an operation on 17 May 1967. Three aircraft (127, 129 and 131) were dispatched to Kadena AB on Okinawa to fly missions over North Vietnam (and later Korea). The first mission was launched on 31 May, and the last on 8 May the following year. A total of 29 operational missions was flown.

The pilots of the 1129th SAS Det 1 were awarded the CIA's Star for Valor.

The 1129th SAS Det 1 Black Shield team used the large white hangars at top right. This complex was subsequently used by the SR-71s of the 9th SRW's OL-8 when they took over the Far East reconnaissance mission.

taking trips to the David Clark Company in Worcester, Massachusetts, to be outfitted with their own personal S-901 full pressure suits – just like those worn by the Mercury and Gemini astronauts.

In late 1961 Colonel Robert Holbury was appointed base commander of Groom Dry Lake; his director of Flight Operations would be Colonel Doug Nelson. In the spring of 1962 eight F-101 Voodoos to be used as companion trainers and pace/chase aircraft, two T-33s for pilot proficiency and a C-130 for cargo transportation arrived at the

remote base. A large 'restricted airspace zone' was enforced by the Federal Aviation Agency (FAA) to enhance security around 'the Area', and security measures were invoked upon North American Air Defense (NORAD) and FAA radar controllers, to ensure that fast-moving targets seen on their screens were not discussed. Planned air refuelling operations of Oxcart aircraft would be conducted by the 903rd Air Refueling Squadron at Beale AFB, California. The unit was equipped with KC-135Q tankers which possessed separate 'clean' tankage and plumbing to isolate the A-12's fuel from the tanker's JP4, plus special ARC-50 distance-ranging radios for use in precision, long-distance, high-speed join-ups with the A-12s.

With the first A-12 at last ready for final assembly, the entire fuselage, minus wings, was crated, covered with canvas and loaded on a special $100,000 trailer. At 02.30 on 26 February 1962, the slow-moving convoy left Burbank; it arrived safely at Area 51 at 13.00, two days later. By 24 April, engine test runs together with low- and medium-speed taxi tests had been successfully completed.

First flight

It was time for Lou Schalk to take to the aircraft on a high-speed taxi run that would culminate in a momentary lift-off and landing roll-out onto the dry salty lake bed. For this first 'hop' the stability augmentation system (SAS) was left uncoupled; it would be properly tested in flight. As A-12 article number 121 accelerated down the runway, Lou recalled: "I had a very light load of fuel so it sort of accelerated really fast. I was probably three or four per cent behind the aft limit centre of gravity when I lifted off the airplane, so it was unstable. Immediately after lift-off, I really didn't think I was going to be able to put the airplane back on the ground safely because of lateral, directional and longitudinal oscillations. The airplane was very difficult to handle but I finally caught up with everything that was happening, got back control enough to set it back down, and chop engine power. Touchdown was on the lake bed instead of the runway, creating a tremendous cloud of dust into which I disappeared entirely. The tower controllers were calling me to find out what was happening and I was answering, but the UHF antenna was located on the underside of the airplane (for best transmission in flight) and no one could hear me. Finally, when I slowed down and started my turn on the lake bed and re-emerged from the dust cloud, everyone breathed a sigh of relief."

Two days later Lou took the Oxcart on a full flight. A faultless 07.05 take-off was followed shortly thereafter by all the left wing fillets being shed. Constructed from RAM,

Left: This was the first picture released (in 1982) of the A-12, depicting 60-6932 which was the aircraft lost on an engine check flight just before it was due to return to the US at the end of Black Shield. The aircraft and its pilot, Jack Weeks, disappeared without trace.

Below: 60-6928 was also lost when a massive leak caused it to run out of fuel during a Groom Lake training flight. During the Black Shield deployment, training continued at Groom Lake. The final A-12 flight was conducted by Frank Murray in 60-6934 on 21 June 1968.

Tagboard

When the Powers shoot-down effectively ended US manned overflights, the idea of unmanned operations became highly attractive. Initially, the idea of a drone A-12 was discussed, before a smaller ramjet-powered vehicle was introduced. The first study authorisation was received from the CIA on 10 October 1962. The drone design drew heavily on the aerodynamics of the A-12, and used the Marquardt RJ43 engine from the Bomarc missile. Codenamed Tagboard, the drone was initially developed under the designation Q-12, later becoming the D (for Daughter) -21, while the launch vehicle, a converted A-12, became the M (for Mother) -21.

these elements were fortunately non-structural and Lou recovered the aircraft back at Groom Dry Lake without further incident.

On 30 April – nearly a year behind schedule – Lou took the A-12 on its 'official' first flight. With appropriate government representatives on hand, the 59-minute flight took the aircraft to a top speed and altitude of 340 kt (390 mph; 628 km/h) and 30,000 ft (9145 m). On 4 May the aircraft went supersonic for the first time and reached Mach 1.1. Kelly began to feel confident that the flight test programme would progress rapidly, and even recover some of the time lost during the protracted manufacturing process. Another Lockheed test pilot, Bill Park, joined the Skunk Works team to share the burden with Lou. On 26 June the second A-12 arrived at Area 51 and was immediately assigned to a three-month static RCS test programme. The third and fourth aircraft arrived during October and November. The latter was a two-seat A-12 trainer, nick-named 'the Goose' by its crews, and was powered through-out its life by two J75s. On 5 October another milestone

This series of photos shows the M-21/D-21 pair during captive carry tests from Groom Dry Lake. The M-21 arrived in August 1964 for flight trials, before being mated for the first flight with the drone on 22 December. During the trials in 1965 the D-21 was fitted with a frangible nosecone and exhaust fairing, later to be discarded. One of the problems faced was getting enough unrestricted airspace to reach the required launch speed.

Above and right: Without the D-21 drone, the M-21 had the same phenomenal performance as a standard A-12, but with the extra payload became very sluggish. Eventually, when the drone's intake and exhaust covers were discarded, the Marquardt ramjet was used to augment the thrust from the M-21's J58s. The drone engine was started at Mach 1.24, and fuel was transferred from the M-21 prior to launch to top up the D-21's tanks.

Below: In all-black scheme an M-21/D-21 combination taxis for a nosecone separation trial.

Below right: One of several methods tested for removing the nosecone was the use of pyrotechnics, with this result. It was virtually impossible for any system to be employed which did not damage the drone's airframe nor cause debris to be ingested.

was achieved when the A-12 flew for the first time with a J58 (a J75 was retained in the right nacelle until 15 January 1963, when the first fully J58-powered flight took place).

National priority

On 27 October 1962, Major Rudolph Anderson's U-2 was shot down by an SA-2 while monitoring Soviet SS-N-4 medium-range ballistic missile (MRBMs) and SS-N-5 intermediate-range ballistic missiles (IRBMs) build-ups during the Cuban missile crisis. Just like the Gary Powers shoot-down two and a half years earlier, the U-2's vulnerability had been demonstrated in a spectacular fashion; regrettably, Major Anderson lost his life in the incident. The significance of this event was certainly not lost on intelligence communities involved in Oxcart, and the successful prosecution of that programme now became a matter of highest national priority.

With test pilot Jim Eastham also recruited into Oxcart, the programme was still beset with problems, which were focused around the engines and air inlet control system

(AICS). The AICS regulated massive internal airflow throughout the aircraft's vast flight envelope, controlling and supplying air to the engines at the correct velocity and pressure. This was achieved using a combination of bypass door and translating centre-body spike position. At ground idle, taxiing and take-off, the spikes were positioned in the full-forward position allowing air to flow unimpeded to the engine's compressor face. In addition, supplementary inflow air was provided through the spike exit-louvres and from six forward bypass exit-louvres.

Early tests revealed that the engine required an even greater supply of ground air when operating at low power settings, a deficiency that was overcome by installing additional bypass doors just forward of the compressor face. The size of these variable-area 'inlet ports' was regulated by an external slotted-band and could draw air through two sets of doors. The task of opening or closing the doors was manually controlled by the pilot initially, but much later was accomplished automatically when a digital automatic flight control system computer was developed. Together, the forward bypass doors and the centre-body spikes were used to control the position of the normal shockwave just aft of the inlet throat. To avoid the loss of inlet efficiency caused by an improperly positioned shockwave, the shockwave was captured and held inside the converging-

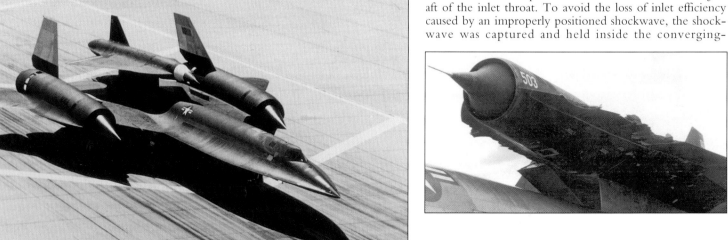

Lockheed M-21/D-21
Groom Dry Lake, Nevada
1965/66

The D-21 Tagboard programme resulted in two M-21s and 30 D-21s. There were four launches, all using the second M-21, 60-6941. The first launch was undertaken on 5 March 1966. Although the D-21 only flew for 120 miles (195 km), the launch process had been demonstrated successfully. On 27 April the second flight reached over 1,200 nm (2220 km; 1,380 miles) while the third, on 16 June, reached about 1,600 nm (2960 km; 1,840 miles) and completed eight pre-programmed turns. The only problem was that the drone failed to eject the sensor systems package. The M-21/D-21 programme was cancelled following the disastrous fourth launch.

D-21 system package

The D-21 had a package mounted on a hatch in the lower nose which accommodated the high-value systems, including the Hycon camera and its film, inertial navigation system, automatic flight control system, and command and telemetry electronics. At 60,000 ft and Mach 1.67 the package was ejected, deploying a parachute and broadcasting a beacon signal. A specially-equipped Hercules then attempted to catch it in mid-air.

Paint scheme

In the early part of the programme both M-21 and D-21 retained a natural metal finish edged in black to cover the sections of RAM. Both later received an all-black scheme.

M-21 mother-ship

The M-21 differed little from the standard A-12, but incorporated a second cockpit for the launch systems operator in the Q-bay. A single dorsal pylon was provided to mount the drone, aerodynamically clean but strong enough to carry the 11,000-lb (4990-kg) D-21. The pylon included a fuel line for topping off the drone's tanks and emergency jettison equipment.

The loss of '941

On 30 June 1966 Bill Park (pilot) and Ray Torick (launch system operator) attempted the fourth D-21 launch, using a level 1 g launch instead of the slightly pitching forward 0.9 g method used in the three previous attempts. At the moment of launch, the D-21 experienced an asymmetrical unstart, with only one side of its burner operating. The drone rolled to the right, causing the M-21 to pitch up. Despite Park's rapid reactions in pushing the stick forward, the drone hit the mother-ship. At Mach 3.25, the aircraft did not stand a chance, and the nose broke off. Both crew ejected safely, but Torick was tragically drowned.

D-21 anatomy

From front to rear the D-21's body contained a narrow conical inlet section which fed a duct which arced over the sensor/system hatch. The duct ran back to the Marquardt RJ43 ramjet. Fuel was held in most of the remaining structure, with control runs to the simple rudder and elevon control surfaces.

D-21 camera

Made by Hycon, the HR-335 camera peered through a window in the lower part of the hatch. It was mounted longitudinally with a 45° prism. Resolution was in the order of 6 in (15 cm).

D-21 launch

The D-21 was not forcibly ejected from the M-21 pylon, being allowed to float free after engine ignition at Mach 3.25. Initially it was decided that a gentle pushover manoeuvre would be required to provide sufficient separation at launch, but after the first three successful launches it was felt that the demanding rigours of maintaining a precise 0.9g contour were too exacting for all but highly experienced test pilots. Consequently, the straight and level launch was adopted, with disastrous results.

Mike Badrocke

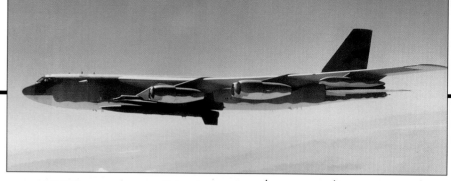

Senior Bowl

Even before the loss of the M-21, Lockheed was proposing that the B-52H would make a much safer launch platform for the D-21 drones. In order to achieve the necessary speed and altitude for launch, a booster rocket was required. The 4200th Test Wing was established at Beale to operate the Senior Bowl programme, although initial tests were flown from Groom Lake.

Above: A boomer's eye view of a D-21B and its booster while the B-52H carrier refuels. The test programme got off to a bad start when a drone accidentally fell from a B-52 and the booster ignited. The first scheduled launch was on 6 November 1967, the flight ending in failure. It was not until 16 June 1968 that a D-21B flew its 3,000-nm (5555-km; 3,452-mile) design range, achieving over 90,000 ft (27432 m) and ejecting its film package successfully.

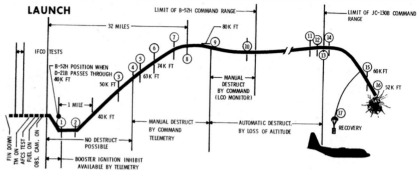

D-21B Sequence of Events

BOOSTER IGNITION-		5	DESTRUCT ALTITUDE SWITCH OPEN	9	AUTOMATIC DESTRUCT CIRCUITRY ARM	14 FUEL "OFF"
5° PITCH-UP, FOLLOWED BY 1°/SEC PULL-UP		6	ENGINE IGNITION; AUTO DESTRUCT CIRCUIT COMPLETE	10	COMMAND AND T/M "OFF"	15 EJECT HATCH
TRANSITION TO FINAL CLIMB TRAJECTORY		7	APU LOAD TAKE-OVER	11	COMMAND "ON"	16 AUTOMATIC DESTRUCT
MANUAL DESTRUCT CIRCUIT COMPLETE		8	BOOSTER JETTISON, AFCS TO MACH HOLD	12	BEACONS "ON" AND T/M "ON"	17 HATCH RECOVERY
				13	DESTRUCT DISABLE	

Above left: This view shows a D-21B (as the B-52 version was known) under the specially designed carrier on a B-52H. The pylon used the Hound Dog missile attachments under the inner wings of the bomber.

diverging nozzle slightly behind the narrowest part of the 'throat', allowing the maximum pressure rise across the normal shock.

Once airborne and with landing gear retracted, the forward bypass doors would close automatically. At Mach 1.4 the doors began to modulate automatically to obtain a programmed pressure ratio between 'dynamic' pressure at the inlet cowl on one side of the 'throat' and 'static' duct pressure on the other side. At 30,000 ft (9145 m) the inlet spike unlocked and began its rearward translation at Mach 1.6, achieving its full aft translation of 26 in (66 cm) at the design speed of Mach 3.2 (the inlets' most efficient speed). Spike scheduling was determined as a function of Mach number, with a bias for abnormal angle of attack, angle of sideslip, or rate of vertical acceleration. The rearward translation of the spike gradually repositioned the oblique

Left: Only four operational D-21B launches were made, on 9 November 1969, 16 December 1970, 4 March 1971 and 20 March 1971. Two drones were lost, including one in the target area, and neither of the others managed to return the sensor packs.

Below: The solid fuel booster took the D-21 to 80,000 ft and Mach 3.2.

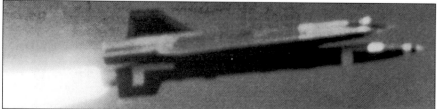

shockwave which extended back from the spike tip and the normal shockwave which stood at right angles to the airflow, and increased the inlet contraction ratio (the ratio between the inlet area and the 'throat' area). At Mach 3.2, with the spike fully aft, the 'capture-airstream-tube-area' had increased 112 per cent (from 8.7 to 18.5 sq ft/0.8 to 1.7 m²), while the 'throat' restriction had decreased by 46 per cent of its former size (from 7.7 to 4.16 sq ft/0.7 to 0.4 m²).

A peripheral 'shock trap' bleed slot (positioned around the inside surface of the duct, just forward of the 'throat' and set at precisely two boundary layer displacement thickness) 'shaved off' seven per cent of the stagnant inlet airflow and stabilised the terminal (normal) shock. It was then rammed across the bypass plenum through 32 shock trap tubes spaced at regular intervals around the circumference of the shock trap. As the compressed air travelled through the secondary passage, it firmly closed the suck-in doors while cooling the exterior of the engine casing before it was exhausted through the ejector nozzle. Boundary layer air was removed from the surface of the centrebody spike at the point of its maximum diameter. This potentially turbulent air was then ducted through the spike's hollow supporting struts and dumped overboard through nacelle exit louvres. The bypass system was thus able to match widely varying volumes of air entering the inlet system with an equal volume of air leaving the ejector nozzle, throughout the entire speed range of the aircraft.

Increasing the pressure differential

The aft bypass doors were opened at mid-Mach to minimise the aerodynamic drag which resulted from dumping air overboard through the forward bypass doors. The inlet system created internal pressures which reached 18 psi (124 kPa) when operating at Mach 3.2 and 80,000 ft (24390 m), where the ambient air pressure is only 0.4 psi (2.7 kPa). This extremely large pressure differential led to a forward thrust vector which resulted in the forward inlet producing 54 per cent of the total thrust. A further 29 per cent was produced by the ejector, while the J58 engine contributed only 17 per cent of the total thrust at high Mach.

Inlet airflow disturbances resulted if the delicate balance of airflow conditions that maintained the shockwave in its normal position was upset. Such disturbances were called 'unstarts'. These disruptions occurred when the normally placed supersonic shockwave was 'belched' forward from a

Above: Jim Eastham (left) made the first flight of the YF-12A on 7 August 1963. Standing with him is one of the test fire control officers, Ray Scalise.

Below: This single photograph of the prototype YF-12A was released in February 1964, the first tangible evidence of the Mach 3 aircraft programme.

'Kelly' Johnson stands proudly in front of the third and final YF-12 at Groom Lake. During the early test period the aircraft had only the RAM edges painted, and carried 'FX' buzzcodes.

AF-12 interceptor

Initially known as the AF-12, what became the YF-12A was a development of the A-12 optimised for long-range interception, utilising the Hughes AN/ASG-18 fire control system developed for the cancelled F-108 Rapier. The seventh, eighth and ninth A-12s were redirected to AF-12 development.

balanced position in the inlet throat, causing an instant drop in inlet pressure and thrust. With the engines mounted at mid-semi-span, the shockwave departure manifested itself in a vicious yaw toward the 'unstarted' inlet; sometimes they were so violent that crew members' helmets would be knocked hard against the canopy framing. To break a sustained unstart and recapture the disturbed inlet shockwave, the pilot would have to open the bypass doors on the unstarted inlet and return them to the smooth-flowing but less efficient position that they were in just prior to the disturbance. Early A-12 test flights involved increasing the aircraft's speed by increments of one-tenth of a Mach number and manually selecting the next spike position. If the inlet dynamics worked well the aircraft was decelerated and recovered back to 'the Area', where the dynamics would be further analysed and incorporated into the sched-

ule. More often, however, there would be a mismatch between spike position and inlet duct requirements and a vicious unstart would result. It took 66 flights to push the speed envelope from Mach 2.0 to Mach 3.2, and the incidence of unstarts was greatly reduced only when pneu-

Article 1001, the first YF-12A, is seen at Groom Lake. The streamlined pods under each engine nacelle contained cameras to record the launch and separation of the Hughes AIM-47 missiles. Note the folded ventral fin under the rear fuselage and the 'porthole' aft of the FCO position – painted on to confuse.

The first YF-12A touches down at the 'Ranch' after a successful maiden flight. The existence of the YF-12 was made public at an early date (although President Johnson referred to the aircraft as the 'A-11') to deflect the rumours circulating regarding the far more sensitive A-12 Oxcart programme.

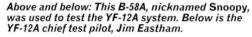

System tests

The ASG-18/AIM-47 was developed as the first pulse-Doppler long-range look-up/look-down weapon system, and after the YF-12 programme terminated was evolved into the AWG-9/AIM-54 used by the F-14. The system was thoroughly tested prior to fitment on the YF-12, including a series of tests mounted in a converted B-58. The entire system proved to be generally successful, despite its complexities.

The bulky radome covered a massive 40-in (1.02-m) diameter radome for the ASG-18. Note that both the port missile bays are open.

Above and below: This B-58A, nicknamed Snoopy, was used to test the YF-12A system. Below is the YF-12A chief test pilot, Jim Eastham.

Another aircraft used in the YF-12A test programme was this Boeing JQB-47E, which survived two AIM-47 missile shots.

Below right: Jim Eastham prepares to fly the second YF-12A on a test mission from Area 51. Note that a fairing has been fitted to hide the infra-red search and track sensors. Eastham took a YF-12A to Mach 3.23 in January 1965.

Below: Marked for the three YF-12A records, 60-0936 poses with an AIM-47 (earlier GAR-9) missile. The weapon, of which three were carried, had a 250-kT nuclear warhead.

matic pressure gauges that had been installed on the inlet systems to sense pressure variations of as little as 0.25 psi (1.72 kPa) were replaced by an electrically controlled system from aircraft number nine (60-6932).

During December 1960, a separate project group under Russ Daniell was organised in the Skunk Works, working

independently of the A-12 team. From joint 715 (a point perpendicular to where the inboard wing leading edge meets the fuselage chine), the entire forward fuselage forebody of an A-12 was modified to create a Mach 3.2 interceptor. Originally designated AF-12, the aircraft would be equipped with the 1,380-lb (625-kg) Hughes AN/ASG-18 pulse-Doppler radar that had been intended for the North American F-108 Rapier, which was cancelled on 23 September 1959. DoD officials decided that development of this outstanding radar and the integrated 818-lb (371-kg) GAR-9 (later redesignated AIM-47) missile system should continue on a 'stand alone' basis. Hughes continued R&D work with both systems on a specially modified Convair B-58A Hustler (serial 55-665, nicknamed *Snoopy 1*).

AF-12 review

On 31 May 1960 the Air Force conducted a mock-up review of the AF-12, and was impressed. By June, AF-12 wind-tunnel tests revealed directional stability problems resulting from the heavily revised nose and cockpit configuration. As a result, a large folding fin was mounted under the aft fuselage, as were two shorter fixed fins beneath each nacelle. A bomber version of the A-12, designated RB-12, also reached the mock-up stage, but was still-born because

An AIM-47 is seen on its lowered rack in a YF-12A. The first powered launch was undertaken on 18 March 1965, after an earlier separation-only test. Six out of seven AIM-47 tests resulted in hits, including one launched from 75,000 ft at Mach 3.2, fired at a target approaching head-on at 1,500 ft.

A-12 cockpit

One glance inside the cockpit of the A-12 gives an impression of the kind of piloting ability required by the few candidates selected to fly the type. Not only did the pilot have to control a hugely complex machine, he also had to navigate accurately while travelling at unprecedented speeds. Furthermore, the pilot was responsible for monitoring and operating the reconnaissance systems.

The cockpit itself was dominated by the circular display for the driftsight, which allowed him to look downwards for visual checks on his progress, and to check for cloud cover in the target area. With so many instruments to cram in to a restricted dashboard area, there was little pattern to the layout, and many instruments had smaller read-outs than would otherwise be normal. The principal flight/navigation instruments were grouped to the left of centre, including radio compass, airspeed indicator, altimeter, attitude indicator and turn-and-bank indicator. Beneath these were four dials for manual control of the forward bypass doors and inlet spikes. To the right of centre was the vertical speed indicator and a strip of duplicated engine instruments.

The pilot sat on a Lockheed **SR-1** ejection seat, which was fired by pulling the prominent **D-ring** pull.

This is the rear cockpit of the A-12B trainer. Although the instrumentation is the same as that in the front seat, the major difference is the lack of the circular driftsight.

YF-12 cockpit

Shown below is the front cockpit of the YF-12A, which is ergonomically friendly compared to the A-12. The upper circular display was a radar screen, while below that was the large attitude indicator and radio compass. To the left of these were strip displays for airspeed (in Mach and knots), while to the right were strip indicators for vertical speed and altitude. The engine instruments were again in a double column to the right, and further to the right were the fuel controls.

Below is the rear cockpit of the YF-12A, a good deal less complicated than the front. The fire control officer had large display screens for the radar and **IR**. On either side of these are elegant strip displays for speed (left) and altitude (right). Note that the **Fire Control Officer** has an early form of track-ball control on the right-hand console. The cockpit layout was subsequently altered during **NASA** test programmes.

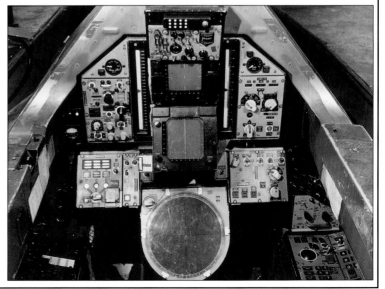

Above: After the first two AIM-47 launches had been accomplished using the second YF-12, the first and third (illustrated) flew to Eglin to fire the next five. This aircraft notched up three launches, two against Q-2C drones and one against the JQB-47.

Right: A great indication of the aerodynamic effectiveness of the forward fuselage chines is provided by the amount of extra keel area needed by the YF-12A to counter the lack of nose chines. In addition to the two undernacelle fins, a large folding ventral fin was added.

Right: Immediately prior to the official announcement of the existence of the 'A-11', two YF-12As were flown into Edwards AFB and operated from there. They were finally introduced to the media on 30 September 1964 although it was to be some time further before public cameras were allowed near the type.

Below: This underview of a YF-12A shows graphically the series of auxiliary doors located along the engine nacelles.

it represented too much of a threat to the highly political North American XB-70A Valkyrie. On 7 August 1963, several weeks after being moved to Groom Dry Lake, Jim Eastham climbed aboard the interceptor prototype and took aircraft 60-6934 (the seventh A-12) for its first flight; he later modestly described it as a 'typical production test flight'.

On 24 May 1963, the programme received a temporary set-back when Agency pilot Ken Collins was forced to eject from A-12 60-6926 during a subsonic test flight. The crash occurred 14 miles (22.5 km) south of Wendover, Utah. To preserve secrecy, a media cover story referred to the aircraft as a Republic F-105 Thunderchief. An accident investigation established the cause of the incident as a pitot-static system failure due to icing.

Preparing to go public

As 1963 drew to a close, nine A-12s at Groom Dry Lake had notched up a total of 573 flights totalling 765 hours. A year later, 11 A-12s had logged over 1,214 flights amounting to 1,669 hours – only six hours 23 minutes were at Mach 3 and only 33 minutes at the design speed of Mach 3.2. As Oxcart grew in both size and cost, concern was expressed within both the Agency and Air Force about how much longer the programme could be kept a secret. It was also noted that technological data accumulated during the project would be of immense value in conjunction with 'white world' feasibility studies into supersonic transport. In November 1963, President Johnson was briefed on the programme, after which he directed that a formal announcement be prepared for release early in the new year. Kelly Johnson noted in his diary: "Plans going forward for surfacing of the AF-12 programme. I worked on the draft to be used by President Johnson and proposed the terminology 'A-11' as it was the non-anti-radar-version."

On Saturday 29 February 1964, a few hours prior to the President announcing the existence of the programme, two AF-12s – 60-6934 and 60-6935 – were flown from Groom Dry Lake to Edwards AFB by Lou Schalk and Bill Park, thereby diverting attention from Area 51 and the 'black world' A-12 programme. At Edwards, a 'buzz' had gone out to some senior staff that something special might be happening on the first morning of their weekend off. In consequence, a few dozen people witnessed the arrival of the extremely sleek aircraft, the like of which no-one outside the programme had seen before – except for desert

dwellers and the occasional incredulous sighting by airline crews. Lou Schalk remembers taxiing to their assigned hangar as eyes bulged and heads nodded in utter disbelief. Unfortunately, the arrival lost a touch of elegance when, to aid push-back into the hangar, they turned the aircraft 180° at the entrance. Lou recalls, "This turnaround sent hot engine exhaust gases flooding into the hangar, which caused the overhead fire extinguishers valves to open. These valves were big – like the flood valves on hangar decks of aircraft-carriers – and the desert had not seen so much water since Noah's embarkation!"

Air Force fighter

Now an Air Force programme, the aircraft's designation was changed to YF-12A to suit USAF nomenclature. The third YF-12A, 60-6936, soon joined the other two examples at Edwards, and Jim Eastham continued the envelope

extension programme. On 16 April 1964, the first airborne AIM-47 missile separation test was conducted. Unfortunately, as onboard cameras showed, the weapon's nose-down pitch was inadequate; had rocket motor ignition also been conducted, the missile would probably have ended up in the front of the cockpit! Back at 'the Ranch', on 9 July 1964, Bill Park experienced a complete lock-up of his flight controls in aircraft 60-6939 as he descended for landing following a high-Mach flight. Despite trying to save the brand-new aircraft from rolling under while turning on to final approach, he could not stop the bank angle from increasing and was forced to eject. Punching out at 200 kt (370 mph; 600 km/h) in a 34° bank, no more than 200 ft (60 m) above the ground, Park was extremely lucky to survive unscathed.

A milestone in the programme was reached on 27 January 1965, when an A-12 flew a 2,580-mile (1170-km)

The F-12 interceptor programme officially ended on 5 January 1968, although the chances of the programme going ahead had slowly evaporated during 1967, despite the excellent results shown by the missile tests. The first aircraft was used to create the SR-71C trainer, and the remaining aircraft were loaned to NASA, albeit continuing some Air Force work. In 1970/71 the USAF used this, the third aircraft, to mimic MiG-25 'Foxbats' for air defence studies. During the course of these it was lost on landing at Edwards.

Left: The first YF-12A is seen at Edwards in full interceptor configuration, with missile bay doors open and infra-red turrets. The aircraft was grounded on 14 August 1966.

F-12B fighter

The F-12B would have been the production interceptor, based on the YF-12A design which had largely been seen as a technology demonstrator. The key change was the shoe-horning of the ASG-18 radar antenna into a slimmer, chined nose. On 14 May 1965 a development contract was received but no production decision was ever taken.

Right: This is the full-size mock-up of the proposed F-12B fighter which was displayed to USAF officials in July 1964. The return to the chined forward fuselage eliminated the need for the extra fin area employed by the YF-12A.

The YF-12A programme was very successful, thanks in part to the 'pick and shovel' work already done by Lockheed (on the A-12) and Hughes (on the ASG-18). The cancellation was resented by many in Lockheed, especially as it was accompanied by an order to cut up the jigs for the entire Blackbird programme.

$500,000 for the production version of the interceptor, designated F-12B. No production go-ahead was given with the engineering contract but considerable optimism was generated. An equivalent sum was granted on 10 November to keep alive basic F-12B design work. Similarly, Hughes received $4.5 million to continue development of the AN/ASG-18 radar and fire control system.

On 28 December Mele Vojvodich took aircraft 60-6929 for a functional check flight (FCF) following a period of deep maintenance. On applying back pressure to the stick for rotation to lift-off, the aircraft's nose yawed viciously to one side. Mele attempted to correct the yaw with rudder, but this caused the nose to pitch up. The rush of instinctive responses which followed resulted in a series of counter-movements, completely opposite to what a pilot would expect to occur. Despite all the odds, Mele managed to get the aircraft to about 100 ft (30 m), where he ejected after just six seconds of flight. Incredibly, he survived and escaped serious injury. An accident investigation discovered that the pitch stability augmentation system (SAS) had been connected to the yaw SAS actuators, and *vice versa*, when the unit was reinstalled following maintenance. Thereafter, the SAS connectors were changed to ensure incorrect wiring was impossible.

The end of the F-12

On 29 March 1966, Kelly had a long meeting with Colonel Ben Bellis, System Project Officer (SPO), Hughes Aircraft Company and various members of the F-12 test force, during which he was asked to take on the task of integrating the weapons systems. He agreed to do so, and fire control tests were continued. However, Secretary of Defense McNamara opposed production of the aircraft and, as a result, on three occasions over the next two years he denied the Air Force access to $90 million worth of funds which had been appropriated by Congress to begin F-12B production. Following a Senate Armed Services Committee hearing into the future of continental air defence, it was decided, in the light of intelligence available at the time, to downgrade Aerospace Defense Command, which in turn

sortie in one hour 40 minutes, with three-quarters of the flight time spent at Mach 3.1. On 18 March, YF-12A '935 successfully engaged a Q-2C target drone at 40,000 ft (12195 m), while the interceptor flew at Mach 2.2 and 65,000 ft (19815 m). Aware of the number of world speed and altitude records held by the USSR, the DoD informed Kelly of its desire to use the YF-12A to wrestle several of those records from the Soviets. Accordingly, on 1 May 1965 (five years to the day that Gary Powers was shot down in his U-2 by a Soviet SA-2), six records were smashed by 60-6936 (see table below for details). Fourteen days later, the Skunk Works received a contract for

YF-12 records

The USAF was eager to reclaim important world records from the Soviets and so Lockheed was instructed in August 1964 to use the YF-12A. Although Lockheed managed the attempts, which took place at Edwards, naturally it was Air Force crews flying the aircraft. The record runs did not take place for some time, but easily shattered the existing marks.

Absolute Altitude, 80,257.86 ft (24468.86 m)
1 May 1965   Pilot, Col Robert L. 'Fox' Stephens. FCO, Lt Col Daniel Andre   YF-12A 60-6936
Absolute Speed over a straight course, 2,070.101 mph (3331.41 km/h)
1 May 1965   Pilot, Col Robert L. 'Fox' Stephens. FCO, Lt Col Daniel Andre   YF-12A 60-6936
Absolute Speed over a 1000-km closed course 1,643.041 mph (2644.146 km/h)
1 May 1965   Pilot, Lt Col Walter F. Daniel. FCO, Maj. Noel T. Warner   YF-12A 60-6936

For the record attempts the YF-12s were painted with a large white cross on the undersides for tracking purposes. Six records were set, including three absolutes. The five crew involved were Colonel Robert Stephens (centre), Lt Col Daniel Andre, Major Walter Daniel, Major Noel Warner, and Captain James Cooney.

NASA and the YF-12

In 1967 a deal was struck between NASA and the USAF, whereby NASA was given access to early A-12 wind tunnel data and in exchange agreed to provide a small team of highly skilled engineers to work on the SR-71 flight test programme. Under the leadership of Gene Matranga, the team from the Flight Research Center (FRC) at Ames was engaged on various stability and control aspects of the SR-71 at Edwards. This work helped hasten the SR-71 into the inventory and led to the establishment of a close working relationship between the Air Force and NASA.

On 5 June 1969, a memorandum of understanding was signed between the Air Force and NASA, which permitted the latter access to the two remaining YF-12s in storage. NASA paid for operational expenses and ADC supplied maintenance and logistic support. After both aircraft were fully instrumented, phase one of the programme got under way when, on 11 December 1969, the first YF-12 to fly in three years climbed away from Edwards. Phase one of the programme was controlled by the Air Force, and consisted of developing procedures establishing limitations for command and control and for working out possible bomber penetration tactics against an interceptor with YF-12 capabilities. This phase of the programme was terminated on 24 June 1971, during the closing stages of the 63rd flight of 60-6936, which had been used throughout the tests by the Air Force. Lieutenant Colonel Jack Layton and systems operator Major Bill Curtis were approaching the traffic pattern before recovery back at Edwards when a fire broke out as a result of a fuel line fatigue failure. The flames quickly enveloped the entire aircraft, and while on base leg both crew members safely ejected; '963 crashed into the middle of the dry lake bed and was totally destroyed.

While the YF-12s were being readied for flight, Donald L. Mallick and Fitzhugh L. Fulton Jr, the two NASA pilots who flew most of phase two of the programme, were checked out in the SR-71B. Later, Victor Horton and Ray Young, the two NASA backseaters, were checked out by Lieutenant Colonel Bill Campbell in a YF-12, and the civilian programme began. Utilisation of the high-speed platform was extensive, since NASA engineers at Langley were interested in aerodynamic experiments and testing advanced structures. Lewis Research Establishment wanted to study

propulsion, while Ames concentrated on inlet aerodynamics and the correlation of wind tunnel and flight data. In addition, the aircraft was used to support various specialised experimentation packages. Taken together it was hoped that problems 'worked around' during the early test programme could be designed out of any future commercial SST venture, thereby avoiding expensive mistakes.

After the 22nd flight of '6935 on 16 June 1970, the aircraft was grounded for nine months for instrumentation changes. Following an FCF on 22 March 1971, four flights were flown without the folding ventral fin, to asses directional stability up to Mach 2.8.

NASA needed more aircraft, and as a result the Air Force supplied an SR-71A (article 2002, serial 64-17951) on 16 July 1971. This aircraft had been involved in the contractor flight test programme from the beginning, but the Air Force stipulated that it should only be used for propulsion testing. The first NASA flight of this aircraft – which at the behest of the Air Force was serial 60-6937 and referred to throughout the NASA test programme as a YF-12C – occurred on 24 May 1972.

During the course of various studies, it was discovered that inlet spike movement and bypass door operations were almost as effective as elevons and rudders in influencing the aircraft's flight path at high speed. In addition, propulsion system and flight control integration was an aspect of controlled testing by NASA in an effort to improve future mixed-compression inlet design.

Honeywell and Lockheed funded the Central Airborne Performance Analyser (CAPA). It was installed and tested by NASA and proved so successful that it was later fitted to operational SR-71s. The integrated automatic support system isolated faults and recorded the performance of 170 sub-systems (relating primarily to the inlet controls), on 0.5-in (1.27-cm) magnetic tape. Pre- and post-analysis of this onboard monitoring and diagnostic system proved highly cost effective and reduced maintenance manhours.

YF-12C 60-6937 (SR-71A 64-17951) was retired from the programme and placed in storage at Palmdale after its 88th flight with NASA on 28 September 1978. YF-12A 60-6935 continued operating until the programme ceased after its 145th NASA flight, flown by Fitz Fulton and Vic Horton on 31 October 1979. A week later, Colonel Jim Sullivan and Colonel R. Uppstrom ferried the aircraft to the Air Force museum at Dayton, Ohio, where it is displayed as the sole example of the YF-12.

Above: 60-6935 bore the brunt of the NASA operations, flying from December 1969 until its 145th and last NASA flight on 31 October 1979. It then made one more journey, to the USAF Museum at Wright-Patterson AFB for display. The YF-12A offered NASA a unique research vehicle, being able to cruise at over 2,000 mph and altitudes over 80,000 ft for extended periods of time. As much of the Administration's research efforts were aimed at supersonic transport aircraft, the YF-12's abilities were particularly welcome, allowing the investigation of many areas of flight control, structure and aerodynamics. Experiments could be carried externally, although most were carried in the converted fighter's missile bays. Some sorties were lengthy affairs, requiring inflight refuelling from the 100th ARW's KC-135Q force flying from nearby Beale.

Above: NASA's Ames Research Center proposed using the YF-12As as high-speed testbeds for various propulsion tests, using externally mounted experimental installations. This wind-tunnel model is seen with a dorsal installation of an experimental high-speed ramjet. The main load-bearing pylon would have been augmented by four bracing struts.

Right: Flying with a T-38A chase aircraft, the second YF-12A is seen carrying the Coldwall experiment. This was used to acquire heat transfer data for application to a future high-speed transport. It consisted of a stainless steel tube covered by a frangible ceramic coating.

SR-71A

Development of the A-12 had led to studies for various reconnaissance and bomber derivatives, including the RB-12, RS-12 and R-12. The latter was a pure reconnaissance aircraft, with a stretched fuselage housing more fuel and a second crew member. It was ordered into production for the Air Force, initially under the RS-71 designation. This was neatly transposed to become the SR (Strategic Reconnaissance)-71.

The SR-71 wing is built on a network of ribs and spars. The area inboard of the engine nacelles forms a large fuel tank. The skin sections do not form a perfect seal at low temperatures, and the tanks are often seen leaking.

Most of the Blackbird's shape is edged in a structure incorporating radar-absorbent material in the shape of re-entrant triangles. This is an early SR-71, still labelled as an R-12. Note the upper skin corrugations.

Five SR-71s are seen on the Burbank production line in 1965. The Senior Crown aircraft followed on the line directly from the A-12/F-12.

Right: The prototype SR-71A is seen at Palmdale prior to its first flight. It has only been partially painted at this point.

Below: Article 2001, the prototype SR-71A, turns lazily over the Mojave desert. The aircraft wore unique white markings during its career. It was lost on 10 January 1967 during braking trials on a wet runway.

rendered the F-12B unnecessary. On 5 January 1968, official notification was received from the Air Force to 'close down the F-12B'; the YF-12A programme was formally ended on 1 February.

So it fell to the 'black' A-12 Oxcart programme to validate the concept of high-altitude, sustained Mach 3 plus flight in an operational environment. By late 1965, all of the Agency pilots were Mach 3 qualified and the A-12 was ready for operational testing. Despite this, political sensitivities surrounding the Gary Powers shoot-down five years earlier conspired to ensure that the aircraft would never carry out missions over the USSR – the very country it was originally built to overfly. The initial site to which to deploy this multi-million dollar national security asset was decided as Cuba. By early 1964, Project Headquarters had already begun planning contingency overflights under the programme codename Skylark. On 5 August 1965, the director of the National Security Agency, General Marshall S. Carter, directed that Skylark achieve emergency operational readiness by 5 November; this capability was achieved (albeit on a limited basis), but never deployed.

Combat debut

Instead, 'Cygnus', as Agency pilots referred to the A-12, received its baptism of fire in the skies over Southeast Asia. Moves had begun on 22 March 1965 when, following a meeting with Brigadier General Jack Ledford (the CIA/USAF liaison officer), Secretary of Defense Cyrus Vance granted $3.7 million to provide support facilities at

Kadena AB, Okinawa for a planned deployment of 'Cygnus' aircraft under a project codenamed Black Shield. On 3 June, Secretary McNamara consulted the Secretary of the Air Force about the build-up of SA-2s around Hanoi and the possibility of substituting the more vulnerable U-2s with A-12s to conduct reconnaissance flights over the North Vietnamese capital. He was informed that once adequate aircraft performance was validated, Black Shield could be cleared to go.

Four A-12s were selected for Black Shield operations, Kelly Johnson taking personal responsibility for ensuring the aircraft were completely 'sqwark-free'. On 20 November 1965 a 'Cygnus' aircraft completed a maximum endurance flight of six hours 20 minutes, during which the A-12 reached speeds above Mach 3.2 and altitudes approaching 90,000 ft (27440 m). On 2 December the highly secretive 303 Committee received the first of many proposals to deploy Oxcart to the Far East. However, the proposal was rejected, as were several other submissions made throughout 1966. On 5 January 1967 another tragedy hit the programme when A-12 60-6928 crashed 70 miles (112 km) short of Groom Dry Lake. Its pilot Walt Ray ejected but was killed when he was unable to gain seat separation.

Oxcart deployment

In May 1967, the National Security Council was briefed that North Vietnam was about to receive surface-to-surface ballistic missiles. Such a serious escalation of the conflict would certainly require hard evidence to substantiate it, and consequently President Johnson was briefed on the threat. Richard Helms of the CIA proposed that the 303 Commit-

tee authorise deployment of Oxcart, since it was ideally equipped to carry out the task, having a superior camera to that used by U-2s or pilotless drones and being 'invulnerable to shoot-downs'. President Johnson approved the plan and in mid-May an airlift was begun to establish Black Shield at Kadena AB, on Okinawa.

At 08.00 on 22 May 1967 Mele Vojvodich deployed A-12 60-6937 from Area 51 to Okinawa during a flight which lasted six hours six minutes and included three inflight refuellings. Two days later Jack Layton joined Mele in 60-6930. 60-6932 flown by Jack Weeks arrived on Okinawa on 27 May, having been forced to divert to Wake Island for a day following INS and radio problems. The detachment was declared ready for operations on 29 May.

Above: The prototype SR-71A, 64-17950, first flew from Palmdale on 22 December 1964, piloted by Bob Gilliland with the rear cockpit left vacant. The one-hour plus flight topped 1,000 mph and ended up in this low flypast for the gathered officials at the request of 'Kelly' Johnson. Flying chase in the F-104 was Jim Eastham.

Left: Robert J. Gilliland poses in the cockpit of an SR-71A. Gilliland had been the fourth pilot in the Blackbird programme, following Lou Schalk, Bill Park and Jim Eastham.

An early photograph shows the first SR-71B trainer. This aircraft is the longest serving of all the Blackbirds. Having been the first aircraft delivered to the USAF, it was still active in the late 1990s with NASA.

SR-71B

Experience with the A-12 had shown the value of the 'Goose' two-seat trainer, so two SR-71B trainers were incorporated into the Senior Crown production programme at an early stage. These were the seventh and eighth aircraft built. 64-17956 was the first SR-71 delivered to the USAF, accepted at Beale AFB by the 4200th SRW on 7 January 1966 following a first flight on 18 November 1965. The second trainer first flew exactly a month later.

Left: The raised second cockpit of the SR-71B eroded performance slightly, although not to any drastic effect. The cockpit did reduce directional stability, requiring the addition of YF-12-style ventral fins under the engine nacelles.

YF-12C

Following the loss of one of its YF-12As, NASA requested the loan of an SR-71A to make up its test fleet. With an accepted surfeit of aircraft, the Air Force promptly loaned the second aircraft (64-17951), which received a new identity of YF-12C 06937 when it arrived at Edwards. Fitz Fulton and Victor Horton made the first NASA flight on 24 May 1972. The aircraft was used on many high-speed programmes, including Shuttle work.

Perhaps the only time different members of the Blackbird family flew together was during NASA programmes. Here the YF-12C partners the second YF-12A, the latter carrying high-speed cameras under the engine nacelles and the Coldwall high-speed heat exchange experiment.

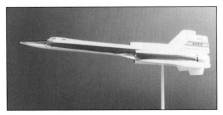

NASA proposed painting its Blackbird fleet in the house scheme of white with a blue band. This was dropped for a number of reasons: the scheme would have been difficult to keep clean, and the black paint did much to radiate heat.

Redolent of the M-21/D-21 combination, NASA proposed using the YF-12C as a launch platform for a hypersonic research drone.

SR-71A 2003 first flew on 24 March 1965, and was used heavily on the flight trial programme until it was lost on 25 January 1966. The pilot, Bill Weaver, survived, despite not using the ejection seat, but sadly the RSO, Jim Zwayer, perished.

Following weather reconnaissance flights on 30 May, it was determined that conditions were ideal for an A-12 camera run over North Vietnam, so project headquarters in Washington placed Black Shield on alert for its first operational mission. Avionics specialists checked various systems and sensors, and at 16.00 Mele Vojvodich and back-up pilot Jack Layton attended a mission alert briefing. At 22.00 (12 hours before planned take-off time) a review of the weather confirmed the mission was still on. The pilots went to bed, to ensure they received a full eight hours of 'crew rest'.

They awoke on the morning of 31 May to torrential rain – a new phenomenon to the desert-dwelling A-12s. However, meteorological conditions over 'the collection area' were good and at 08.00 Kadena received a final 'go'

from Washington. On cue, Mele engaged both afterburners and made the first instrument-guided take-off of an A-12. A few minutes later Mele burst through cloud and flew 60-6937 up to 25,000 ft (7620 m), where he topped off the tanks from a KC-135. Disengaged from the tanker's boom, he accelerated and climbed to operational speed and altitude, after informing Kadena that aircraft systems were running as per the book and the back-up services of Jack Layton would not be required. Mele penetrated hostile airspace at Mach 3.2 and 80,000 ft (24390 m); the so-called 'front door' entry was made over Haiphong, then Hanoi, exiting North Vietnam near Dien Bien Phu. A second air refuelling took place over Thailand, followed by another climb to altitude and a second penetration of North Vietnamese airspace made near the Demilitarized Zone. Mele landed back at Kadena after three instrument approaches in driving rain.

In all, the flight had lasted three hours 40 minutes. Several SA-2s were fired at the aircraft but all detonated above and well behind their target. The photo-take was downloaded and sent by a special courier aircraft to the Eastman Kodak plant in Rochester, New York for processing. 60-6937's large camera successfully photographed 10 priority target categories, including 70 of the 190 known SAM sites. By mid-July A-12 overflights had determined with a high degree of confidence that there were no surface-to-surface missiles in North Vietnam.

SAM activity

During a sortie flown by Denny Sullivan on 28 October 1967, he had indications on his radar homing warning receiver (RHWR) of almost continuous radar activity focused on his A-12 while both inbound and outbound over North Vietnam, which also included the launch of a single SA-2. Two days later he was again flying high over North Vietnam when two SAM sites tracked him on his first pass. On his second pass, approaching Hanoi from the east, he again noted he was being tracked on radar. Over the next few minutes he counted no fewer than eight SA-2

Right: Refuelling became an important and regular part of SR-71 flying, and was tested at an early stage. The tankers were specially-modified KC-135Qs provided by the 9th SRW. Here the recipient is the ill-fated '952, complete with optical tracking mark just visible under the engine nacelle.

detonations in "the general area though none were particularly close." After recovering the aircraft back at Kadena without further incident, a post-flight inspection revealed that a tiny piece of shrapnel had penetrated the lower wing fillet of his aircraft and become lodged against the support structure of the wing tank.

Pueblo missions

During 1967, a total of 41 A-12 missions was alerted, of which 22 were actually granted approval for flight. Between 1 January and 31 March 1968, 15 missions were alerted, of which six were flown, four over North Vietnam and two over North Korea. The latter two came about following seizure on the night of 23 January of the USS *Pueblo* – a US Navy signal intelligence (Sigint) vessel – by North Korea. The first sortie was attempted by Jack Weeks on 25 January, but a malfunction on the A-12 resulted in an abort shortly after take-off.

The next day, Frank Murray completed the task. "I left Kadena, topped off, then entered northern airspace over the Sea of Japan via the Korean Straits. My first pass started off near Vladivostok, then with the camera on I flew down the east coast of North Korea where we thought the boat was. As I approached Wonsan I could see the *Pueblo* through my view sight. The harbour was all iced up, except at the very entrance, and there she was, sitting off to the right of the main entrance. I continued to the border with South Korea, completed a 180° turn and flew back over North

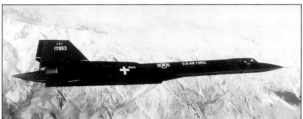

Korea. I made four passes, photographing the whole of North Korea from the DMZ to the Yahu border. As far as I know, I was undetected throughout the flight, but when I got back to Kadena some folks told me that the Chinese had detected me and told the North Koreans, but they never reacted."

Back at Kadena, the 'take' was immediately flown to Yakota AB, Japan where the 67th Reconnaissance Technical Squadron had been activated to enable the more timely exploitation of such data by theatre commanders.

On 8 May 1968 Jack Layton successfully completed a mission over North Korea, which proved to be the final operational flight of an A-12. After three years, a long-standing debate had been resolved concerning whether the A-12 or a programme known as Senior Crown should carry forward the strategic reconnaissance baton: Oxcart was vanquished. In early March 1968, SR-71s began arriving at Kadena to assume the Black Shield commitment.

Above: The first six SR-71As were used for the flight trials programme. These were followed by the two SR-71B trainers, and then the operational aircraft, which began with 2009/64-17958, which was delivered to Beale on 4 June 1966. Despite a temporary halt in deliveries, due mainly to plumbing problems, aircraft arrived quickly afterwards. This machine, the fourth operational aircraft, became something of a 'hangar queen'.

Above left: '953 was the fourth SR-71 built, and is seen here during initial flight tests, marked with a photo-calibration cross. It was lost on a test flight in December 1969.

This Lockheed drawing shows the B-71 proposal, which carried AGM-69 SRAM missiles in the chine bays and an attack radar in the recontoured nose. The aircraft was intended as an attacker of high-value targets.

B-71 bomber proposal

Despite the rejection of the RB-12 and RS-12, Lockheed continued to pursue a bomber Blackbird with the B-71. This was submitted to the Air Force following the cancellation of the XB-70 Valkyrie.

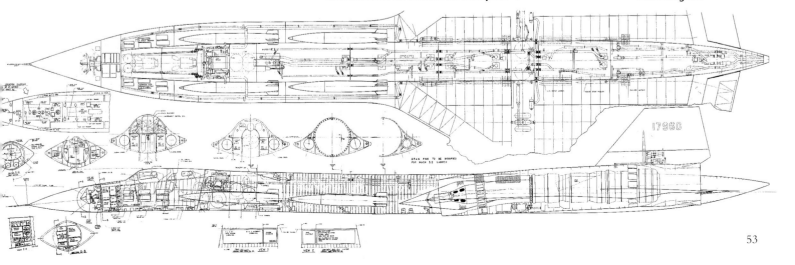

Giant Scale

Above: SR-71s operating from Kadena were adorned with 'Habu' mission marks. This is 64-17974, which was named Ichi Ban.

Top right: '972 taxis in at Kadena at the end of a Giant Scale mission over North Vietnam. In the revetments are the special C-135s (including an RC-135M Combat Apple) of the 4252nd (later 376th) Strategic Wing.

Far right: An SR-71A slides away from the KC-135Q during a refuelling over the South China Sea. Giant Scale missions occasionally involved a 'double-header' flight with two loops through North Vietnamese airspace.

Those A-12s back at 'the Area' were flown to Palmdale and placed in storage by 7 June. At Kadena, the three aircraft that had performed all the Black Shield missions were readied for a return transpacific ferry flight. On 2 June 1968 tragedy once again hit the Oxcart programme, when Jack Weeks was killed during an FCF in 60-6932. The aircraft and its pilot were lost without a trace in the Pacific Ocean. The two remaining A-12s on Okinawa – 60-6930 and 60-6937 – were ferried back to Area 51 before being flown to Palmdale, the last flight being made by Frank Murray on 21 June 1968 in aircraft '937.

Tagboard and Senior Bowl

On 10 October 1962 Kelly Johnson received authorisation from the CIA to carry out study work on a drone that would be mated with an A-12. At the root of the request was the US government's decision to discontinue manned overflights, following the Gary Powers shoot-down. Fourteen days later, Kelly, Ben Rich and Russ Daniell met representatives from Marquardt to discuss ramjet propulsion system options. Progress was rapid, and on 7 December a full-scale mock-up was completed on the craft, which within the Skunk Works was referred to as the Q-12. Still to receive mission specifications from the Agency, Kelly

worked on producing a vehicle with a range of 3,000 nm (3,450 miles; 5550 km) hauling a Hycon camera system of 425 lb (193 kg) that would be capable of a photographic resolution of 6 in (15 cm) from operating altitude. The engine to be used was the Marquardt RJ43-MA-3 Bomarc, and by October 1963 the overall configuration for the Q-12 and its launch platform – two purpose-built, modified A-12s – was nearing completion. It was codenamed Tagboard. The designation of both elements was also changed, the carrier vehicle becoming the 'M' – standing for 'Mother' – 21 and the Q-12 becoming the 'D' – for 'Daughter' – 21.

The 11,000-lb (5000-kg) D-21 was supported on the M-21 by a single, dorsally mounted pylon. Reaching launch point, the mother ship's pilot maintained Mach 3.12 and initiated a 0.9-g push-over. Once released by the launch control officer (LCO) who sat in what on other A-12s would be the Q-bay, the D-21 flew its sortie independently. Equipped with a Minneapolis-Honeywell inertial navigation system, the D-21 would fly a pre-programmed flight profile, executing turns and camera on/off points to produce the perfect photo-reconnaissance sortie. Having completed its camera run, the drone's INS system then sent signals to the auto-pilot system to descend to a predetermined 'feet wet' film collection point. The entire palletised unit containing INS, camera and film was then ejected at 60,000 ft (18290 m) and Mach 1.67, and parachuted towards the ocean. As the drone continued its

Above: Although SR-71s occasionally were diverted into Udorn, the missions attempted to end at Kadena if possible. Unfortunately, this 'Habu', 64-17978, suffered irreparable damage during a landing at Kadena in a severe crosswind.

Right: Complete with large 'Habu' tail artwork and mission symbols behind the RSO's cockpit, Ichi Ban is seen shortly after its return to Beale. This aircraft was the last SR-71 to be lost.

descent it was blown apart by a barometrically activated explosive charge. Meanwhile, the air retrieval was executed by a JC-130B Hercules. On 12 August 1964 the first M-21 was dispatched to Groom Dry Lake and on 22 December the first D-21/M-21 combination flight took place with Bill Park at the controls. Troubles dogged Tagboard and it was not until 5 March that the first successful D-21 launch was accomplished. The second launch on 27 April saw the drone reach Mach 3.3 and 90,000 ft (27440 m), and fly for 1,200 nm (1380 miles; 2220 km), holding course within 0.5 mile (0.8 km) throughout. The flight came to an end after a hydraulic pump burned out and the D-21 fell out of the sky.

Drone disaster

The Air Force remained interested in the drone and on 29 April 1966 a second batch of D-21s was ordered. On 16 June a third successful launch was made and the D-21 flew 1,600 miles (2575 km), completing all tasks on the flight card except ejecting the all-important camera pallet. The fourth and final D-21 sortie from the M-21 occurred on 30 July 1966 and ended in disaster when the drone collided with '941 moments after achieving launch separation. The impact caused the mother ship to pitch up so violently that

the fuselage forebody broke off. Both Bill Park and his LCO, Ray Torrick, successfully ejected and made a 'feet wet' landing, but unfortunately Torrick's pressure suit filled with water and he drowned before he could be rescued. Bill Park spent an hour in the ocean before he was brought aboard a US Navy vessel.

The D-21 was grounded for a year while a new launch system was developed. This new operation, codenamed Senior Bowl, involved the drone being launched from the underwing pylons of two modified B-52Hs of the 4200th Test Wing based at Beale AFB, California. Upon launch, the D-21B was accelerated to Mach 3.3 and 80,000 ft (24390 m) by a solid propellant rocket developed by Lockheed Propulsion Company of Redlands, California. When cruise speed and altitude had been achieved, the booster was jettisoned and the drone's flight continued as described earlier. The first launch attempt from a B-52 was made on 6 November 1967; it proved unsuccessful, as did three other attempts. Success was finally achieved on 16 June 1968. Between 9 November 1969 and 20 March 1971, a total of four operational flights over China was attempted. To maintain tight security, the B-52 with its unique payload departed Beale at night and lumbered westwards to the Pacific island of Guam. Just before dawn the

During the early years of the SR-71 programme the detachment at Kadena was the most important operating location, although the aircraft also began to take an interest in Cuba. Twenty-nine SR-71A aircraft were built, of which six were earmarked for test purposes. The remaining operational fleet was obviously too large for the tasks with which it was set, and many aircraft were put into storage. They were rotated with the active aircraft periodically to spread utilisation across the fleet. This practice continued throughout the career of the aircraft. At the end the USAF had 10 aircraft, of which six were active: two at Beale for training and two at each of the dets.

Three crews participated in the record flights. Shown below are Major George Morgan (left) and Captain Eldon Joersz, who captured the speed record. Above is the aircraft they used: 64-17958.

SR-71 records

During early 1976 the US Air Force approved a series of record flights which would eclipse those marks set by the YF-12A. The absolute speed record still stands, although the sustained altitude record was beaten on 26 April 1995 by Roman Taskaev in a MiG-29 with a height of 90,092 ft (27460 m).

Two SR-71As, '958 and '962 (illustrated), were earmarked for the record flights, each painted with a large white cross for ground tracking. The record attempts were staged out of Edwards AFB.

Date	Crew	Aircraft
Altitude in Horizontal Flight, 85,068.997 ft (25935.669 m)		
27/28 July 1976	Pilot, Capt. Robert C. Helt. RSO, Maj. Larry A. Elliott	SR-71A ?
Speed over a Straight Course (15/25 km), 2,193.167 mph (3529.464 km/h)		
27/28 July 1976	Pilot, Capt. Eldon W. Joersz. RSO, Maj. George T. Morgan	SR-71A 64-17958
Speed over a Closed Course (1000 km), 2,092.294 mph (3367.128 km/h)		
27/28 July 1976	Pilot, Maj. Adolphus H. Bledsoe Jr. RSO, Maj. John T. Fuller	SR-71A ?

next day the flight resumed, the bomber departing Guam and heading for the launch point. Upon vehicle separation, the 'BUFF' made its way back to Guam, while the D-21 embarked upon its pre-programmed day-time reconnaissance run. Achieving only limited success, Senior Bowl was cancelled on 15 July 1971.

Senior Crown

While working on Oxcart in the early spring of 1962, Kelly had mentioned the possibility of producing a reconnaissance/strike variant for the Air Force. Lockheed was issued with a 90-day study contract wherein the various Air Force mission options were identified and defined in terms of the A-12 platform. By the end of April 1962, two different mock-ups were under construction, referred to as the R-12 and RS-12. On 18 February 1963 Lockheed received pre-contractual authority to build six aircraft with the understanding that 25 aircraft would be ordered by 1 July. Colonel Leo Geary had been the RS-12 System Program Officer (SPO), but after protracted debate it was decided that the A-12 project group under Colonel Templeton would inherit the R-12, which became designated SR-71 by the Air Force. The RS-12 and later the B-12/B-71 proposals for a strike version of the aircraft failed to win production contracts, despite Kelly having demonstrated to the Air Force the unique capabilities of such a platform. This was largely due to the far greater lobbying powers of the XB-70 and later FB-111 fraternity.

In a speech made on 24 July 1964 President Johnson revealed to the world the existence of the SR-71. Externally, the aircraft differed in shape from the A-12 by having a more elliptical nose plan. A second crew member, known as a reconnaissance systems officer (RSO), sat behind the pilot in what was the A-12's Q-bay. Sensors carried by the SR-71 also differed from its predecessors. To enhance mission flexibility, the nose section was interchangeable, variously housing a sideways-looking airborne radar (SLAR), or an optical bar camera (OBC) for horizon-to-horizon coverage, or an empty unit for routine, Stateside-training sorties. Cameras onboard the SR-71 were located on palletised units which were housed in slim bays in the underside of the chine. The physical length of the 'close-look', technical objective camera (TEOCS) was reduced by using cassegrain or 'folding optics' technology. It is ironic

that initially the resolution of these units was inferior to that produced by the large Hycon camera carried in the A-12's Q-bay. However, as technology progressed the resolution of the SR-71's camera system also improved. (Following a recent 10 per cent improvement, it is believed that today's resolution is between 1.75 and 1.5 in (4.4 to 3.8 cm) from cruising altitude. That is to say, if a series of lines 1.75 in wide were painted on the ground 1.75 in apart, a photo interpreter could count the number of lines applied.)

In August Kelly phoned Bob Murphy and asked him if he wanted to work on the SR-71 programme. At the time, Murphy was a superintendent in charge of D-21 drone production. The first drone was undergoing final check-out while nine others were at various stages of assembly. Bob accepted the offer and was immediately briefed by Kelly, who said, "I want you to go to Palmdale and get Site 2 away from Rockwell. Hire the people you need. The pieces of the SR-71 will be up to you on November 1st and I want her flying before Christmas. Oh, I also want you to move up there because I don't want you to commute." Rockwell controlled all three sites at Palmdale, using Sites 1 and 3 for B-70 production; Site 2 housed a paint shop, telephone exchange and other facilities.

New assembly location

Following a meeting with the base commander and various Rockwell representatives, 'Murph' successfully managed to gain control of Site 2 for Lockheed. The prototype SR-71A, serial 64-17950 (article number 2001), was delivered from Burbank to Site 2, Air Force Plant 42, Building 210, at Palmdale for final assembly on 29 October, by two large trailers specifically designed for the task. At that point Bob Murphy's team 'went into overdrive' in an attempt to meet the extremely tight deadline set by Kelly. Earlier that year Kelly had promoted the charismatic Robert J. Gilliland to the position of chief project pilot for the SR-71, a post for which Bob was admirably qualified, having gained a great deal of experience as a member of the F-104 and A-12 test teams. Bob worked closely with Dick Miller who led the flight test engineering effort for the entire contractor test programme, as it was Dick's responsibility to implement specific tests to be completed on individual flights.

With two J58s installed, '950 conducted its first engine

SR-71 cockpit

The front cockpit of the SR-71A (seen here with the F-1 ejection seat removed) was less complex than that of the A-12 as many of the sensor and navigation systems had been moved to the backseat.

The display was dominated by two attitude indicators at top centre (primary below and secondary right at the top), with a horizontal situation indicator below. Below that was a screen which projected a moving map image. To the left of the large primary attitude indicator was an airspeed indicator, while to the right was the altimeter. Below this was the vertical speed indicator. To the left of the HSI was the triple display indicator (**TDI**), which presented the key figures of Mach number, KEAS (knots, equivalent airspeed) and altitude at one glance. Below the moving map was the annunciator panel for warning.

To the right of the central instrument display were the engine instruments and at the extreme right was the fuel control panel. On the left-hand side were controls for aircraft systems, such as temperature and pressurisation for the cockpits and sensor bays, undercarriage, ejection seats and inlet/bypass system.

The left-hand console had the throttle quadrant, aft bypass door control, engine restart controls, standby oxygen and the UHF radio. The right-hand console mounted panels for the ILS, flight control system, VHF radio and intercom system. At the rear of both side consoles were banks of circuit breakers. Visible emergency handles included gear release to the right of the annunciator panel and canopy release next to the throttles.

Left: The **RSO**'s console was dominated by a large radar display in the centre, above which was a viewsight display. Included in the other instruments is a **TEOC** camera look-angle indicator. The **DEF** (defensive electronics) were operated from the left-hand console.

Right: This is the rear (instructor's) cockpit of the SR-71B, which differs in only minor detail from the front cockpit. Note the trim thumbswitch on the top of the stick.

Lockheed's Blackbirds

Palmdale test

During the SR-71 programme the Skunk Works and AFSC/AFLC maintained one aircraft as a test vehicle for evaluating new systems and operating procedures. For much of the SR-71's career the task was handled by 64-17955.

The test aircraft usually wore the Lockheed Skunk Works badge on the fin.

Two famous products of the Lockheed Skunk Works fly together from Palmdale. The U-2R was the ASARS-2 development aircraft. SR-71A '955 had performed the test work on ASARS-1 for the 'Habu' fleet.

64-17978 was a well-known 'Habu' thanks to its Playboy bunny tail art, which led to it being called the Rapid Rabbit. Here it is seen here over the snow-capped Sierra Nevada mountains close to the Palmdale base.

The Palmdale test fleet was initially assigned the first six aircraft for testing. Four were lost in accidents and '951 was transferred to NASA, leaving just '955 (above). This flew until grounded in January 1985. 64-17972 (below) then took over the test role.

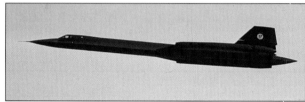

test run on 18 December 1964. Three days later, a 'non-flight' was conducted during which Gilliland accelerated the aircraft to 120 kt (138 mph; 220 km/h) before snapping the throttles back to idle and deploying the large 40-ft (12-m) drag 'chute.

SR-71 first flight

On 22 December 1964, Gilliland (using his personal call-sign DUTCH 51) got airborne from runway 25 at Palmdale in SR-71A, 64-17950. The backseat, or RSO's position, remained empty on this historic flight for safety reasons. After take-off Bob immediately retracted the landing gear, reduced afterburners to 'min', turned right and continued his climb northbound over Edwards' test range until he levelled off at 20,000 ft (6097 m) and Mach 0.9. Jim Eastham was flying chase in one of three F-104s, the other two being flown by USAF test pilots Colonel Robert 'Fox' Stephens and Lieutenant Colonel Walt Daniels. Eastham tucked his F-104 into close formation on '950's right wing, while both pilots calibrated and verified accurate pitot static derived flight data. A series of handling checks was then flown during which the aircraft's static and dynamic stability was assessed. These checks were carried out with the stability augmentation system (SAS) axes switched 'on' and 'off', both 'individually' and 'collectively'. Performance

comparisons of predicted values of speed versus thrust and fuel consumption were also recorded, followed by a climb to 30,000 ft (9145 m) where cabin pressure, oxygen flow and temperature control were checked. Having passed Mojave, he headed west before completing a 180° turn to the left and rolling out on a southerly track over the snow-covered Sierra Nevadas.

As all systems were performing well, it was time to complete a supersonic dash. So, with Jim sticking to the 'SR' like glue, Bob eased the two throttles into 'min burner', scanned the engine parameters and slid the throttles up to the 'max'. The light test-jet accelerated very rapidly to 400 kt (459 mph; 739 km/h) in level flight and then on up to supersonic speed. At Mach 1.4 Bob's attention was drawn to the flashing of the 'master caution' warning lights. A glance at the annunciator panel identified the problem as 'canopy unsafe'. Visually checking the two canopy locking hooks, Bob verified that the canopy was really 'fully locked'. The pressure-sensitive micro-switches which transmitted the electrical 'unsafe' signal had triggered due to an aerodynamic low-pressure area above the aircraft which had sucked the canopy up, against the locking hooks. In reality, the canopy remained locked, and having analysed the situation as safe Bob advanced the throttles once again, continuing his acceleration and climb while closely scanning the instruments. On reaching 50,000 ft (15245 m) and Mach 1.5, Bob eased the throttles out of 'burner into 'mil' and began a deceleration to 350 kt (402 mph; 647 km/h) indicated airspeed, whereafter he descended to 20,000 ft (6097 m) to allow the engines to cool down.

Approaching Palmdale, Bob was advised by Test Ops that Kelly had requested a subsonic flyby down the runway. Happy to comply, Bob and the accompanying '104s streaked by to highlight the successful completion of the first flight. Downwind, with the gear down and locked, he turned '950 onto a wide base leg and set up a long final approach at 185 kt (212 mph; 342 km/h). Touching down smoothly on Palmdale's runway 25, he gently lowered the nose and deployed the drag 'chute. At 50 kt (57 mph; 92 km/h) the 'chute was jettisoned. The aircraft was turned off the active runway and taxied back towards the crowd of USAF dignitaries and Lockheed engineers and technicians, who awaited Bob's debriefing.

After congratulations from Kelly and the others, Bob narrated details of his first flight chronologically from start-up to shut-down. Clarifying questions were then fielded by some of the technicians, after which a typescript of the recorded briefing was circulated to all concerned. Further details were gathered for later dissemination from cockpit-mounted camera recordings and other 'automatic observer' panels. Aircraft '951 and '952 were added to the test fleet for contractor development of payload systems and techniques. Shortly after the Phase II, Developmental Test Program was started, four other Lockheed test pilots were brought into the project: Jim Eastham, Bill Weaver, Art Peterson and Darrell Greenamyer.

Developmental efforts within Lockheed were matched by Air Force Systems Command (AFSC) where Colonel Ben Bellis had been appointed the SR-71 SPO. His task was to structure a Development and Evaluation Program that would evaluate the new aircraft for the Air Force. This programme was undertaken by the SR-71/YF-12 Test Force at the Air Force Flight Test Center, Edwards AFB. Both Phase I Experimental and Phase II Development test flying had moved to Edwards where SR-71As '953, '954 and 955 were to be evaluated by the 'blue suiters'. On 18 November and 18 December 1965, the two SR-71B pilot trainers, '956 and '957 respectively, successfully completed their first flights, but the SR-71s were plagued by problems associated with the electrical system, tank sealing and obtaining design range.

Air Force base

While these problems were being worked on, Beale AFB, chosen home for the newcomer, had been undergoing an $8.4 million construction programme which included the installation of an army of specialised technical support facilities. The 4200th Strategic Reconnaissance Wing was activated at Beale on 1 January 1965, and three months later four support squadrons were formed. In January 1966, Colonel Doug Nelson was appointed commander of the new wing – a job for which he was eminently qualified, having been the Director of Operations for the Oxcart project. Doug began by selecting a small group of competent sub-commanders and Strategic Air Command (SAC) fliers to form the initial cadre of the SR-71 unit. Colonel Bill Hayes became the deputy commander for maintenance; Lieutenant Colonel Ray Haupt, chief instructor pilot; Colonel Walt Wright commanded the medical group; Colonel Clyde Deaniston supervised all Category III flight test planning; and the flight crews were recruited from the best SAC bomber pilots and navigators in the service. The first two of eight Northrop T-38 Talons arrived at Beale on 7 July 1965.

They were used as 'companion trainers' to maintain overall flying proficiency for the SR-71 crew at a fraction of the cost of flying the main aircraft. On 7 January 1966 Colonel Doug Nelson and his chief instructor, Lieutenant Colonel Ray Haupt, delivered the first SR-71B to Beale AFB. Five months later, on 14 April, Nelson and Major Al Pennington took delivery of Beale's first SR-71A, serial 64-17958. On 25 June 1966, the 4200th was redesignated the 9th Strategic Reconnaissance Wing (SRW), its component flying squadrons being the 1st and 99th Strategic Reconnaissance Squadrons (SRS).

Crew training and Category III operational testing

Tanker support

Fifty-six KC-135Qs were procured to support the Blackbird operations, most assigned to the 9th SRW (after 1982) but with a few allocated to the Plattsburgh-based 380th BW. The Q had a separate fuel system for the SR-71's JP-7 fuel, although it could burn the special fuel itself in an emergency. Similarly, the JP-7 tanks could also be used to house standard fuel, although they required a thorough purging afterwards. Additional communications and navaids were provided for SR-71 operations.

proceeded in earnest. Unfortunately, progress came at some cost. The first SR-71 loss occurred on 25 January 1966 when Bill Weaver and his test engineer, Jim Zwayer, took off from Edwards in SR-71A '952. The main objectives of the flight were to evaluate navigation and reconnaissance systems and to investigate procedures for improving high Mach cruise performance by reducing trim drag, thereby lowering fuel burn and increasing range. This research required that the centre of gravity (CG) be moved further aft than normal to compensate for the rearward shift of the centre of pressure at high Mach. After inflight refuelling, DUTCH 64 climbed back to cruising altitude. While in a

Seen prior to refuelling, an SR-71A glides under the KC-135Q with its refuelling receptacle open. The Q had special air-to-air TACAN equipment for radio-silent rendezvous.

Left: Most SR-71 missions, including training flights, involved at least one refuelling. Standard procedure was to launch the tanker(s) ahead of the SR-71, which followed them and topped off its tanks after take-off and a climb to around 26,000 ft. Occasionally two tankers were needed for the top-off. Here an SR-71 waits at the end of the Beale runway with its two assigned top-off tankers.

Middle East missions

During and immediately after the Yom Kippur War of 1973, two SR-71s flew nine missions to the war zone from East Coast bases. Four sorties were launched from Griffiss AFB and five from Seymour Johnson AFB, the last on 6 April 1974. At nearly 11 hours, and with six refuellings, the flights were gruelling affairs.

Above: Seen wheeling high over Beale, '964 was one of the two aircraft involved in the marathon flights into the Middle East war zone in late 1973. The flights not only covered the Suez theatre, but also the Israeli front with Syria.

Above right: '979 and '964 are seen in the hangar at Griffiss AFB during late 1973. '979 flew six of the nine long round-trips to the Middle East. The T-38 Talon, callsign TOXON 01, was at Griffiss to act as chase-plane to test SR-71 '955, which was conveniently at the New York base for a series of trials, thereby providing a ready-made cover for the operational missions.

64-17964 floats across the western end of the Beale runway. The SR-71A handled much like any other delta at low speed, its large wing area providing a measure of air cushioning at the high landing speeds, making touchdowns benign.

35° right back turn, manually controlling the right forward bypass doors at Mach 3.17 and between 77,000 and 78,000 ft (23470 and 23775 m), Weaver experienced a right inlet unstart. Bank angle immediately increased from 35° to 60° and the aircraft entered a pitch-up that exceeded the restorative authority of the flight controls and SAS. The aircraft disintegrated, but miraculously Weaver survived; unfortunately, Jim Zwayer was killed in the incident. The problem of excessive trim drag was solved by Kelly, who designed a 'wedge' which was inserted between the aircraft's forward fuselage and its detachable nose section. This moved the centre of lift forward, thus reducing static margin and trim drag. The visual result was a distinctive 2° nose-up tilt.

Early losses

The SR-71 prototype was written off on 10 January 1967 during an anti-skid brake system evaluation at Edwards AFB. Lockheed's test pilot Art Peterson escaped with a cracked disc in his back. Three months later, on 13 April, Beale lost SR-71A '966 following a night air refuelling. It was Captain Earle Boones's ninth training sortie and he was flying with Captain 'Butch' Sheffield because it had been discovered during the pre-flight medical that his regular RSO had a cold which prevented him from equalising his middle ear pressure. Leaving the tanker, Earle turned to avoid thunderstorms which straddled his planned acceleration-to-climb track. As he climbed prior to performing a 'dipsy doodle' manoeuvre to hasten fuel-consuming transonic breakthrough, he suffered a series of engine stalls and his airspeed drifted down to 170 kt (195 mph; 314 km/h) at 37,000 ft (11280 m). The heavy jet shuddered in the stall and Earle fought hard to regain control, but '966 suddenly entered a pitch-up rotation from which there was no recovery. Both men safely ejected as '966 made its grave not far from that of Bill Weavers's aircraft, in northern New Mexico.

On the night of 25 October 1967, a black-tie dinner was being held at the Beale Officers' club with Kelly Johnson as guest of honour. At the same time, Major Roy St Martin and Captain John Carnochan were flying a night sortie in aircraft '965. As Roy eased the aircraft into the decent profile over central Nevada, the gyro-stabilised reference platform for the ANS drifted without a failure warning. This was the source of attitude reference signals to the primary flight instruments and guidance information to the autopilot, so the aircraft entered an increasing right bank; however, the flight director and the attitude director indicator instruments displayed no deviation from wing-level flight. In the autumn, at 20.25 at high altitude over Nevada, there is no visual horizon for external reference. The aircraft rolled over, the nose fell far below a safe descent angle and it plunged through 60,000 ft (18290 m). The crew sensed something was wrong when Roy glanced at the standby artificial horizon (a small instrument awkwardly positioned low in the cockpit) and was alarmed to see it indicate a "screaming dive and roll-over toward inverted flight." He attempted a "recovery from unusual positions manoeuvre," and managed to roll the wings level but, roaring through 40,000 ft (12195 m) well above the speed from which level flight could be achieved, both men had to eject. The RSO went first, full into a Mach 1.4 slipstream, and just as Roy ejected he heard the warning horn that the aircraft was now below 10,000 ft (3050 m). Aircraft '965

SR-71C – The 'Bastard'

The loss of the second SR-71B trainer, 64-17957, on 11 January 1968 caused a shortfall in pilot conversion capacity. Accordingly, Lockheed created the SR-71C, a hybrid aircraft using the rear fuselage of the first YF-12A and a static test forward fuselage. The aircraft, inevitably called the 'Bastard', was disliked and little-flown, spending much of its life in a barn at Beale. The aircraft was easily distinguishable by its short tail, inherited from its YF-12 origins.

Overseas appearances

Throughout its operational career the SR-71 remained a sensitive programme, and overseas public appearances were rare. The first major public trip was to the 1974 SBAC show at Farnborough. The 9th SRW took the opportunity to set an unmatchable time between New York and London on the way to the show, shattering the previous record which had been held by a British Phantom. After a week as the undisputed star of the static display, sitting next to a C-5 Galaxy, the aircraft used the return flight to set a new London-Los Angeles record. Further European appearances included the Paris air show, and the aircraft became a regular at selected UK air shows when Det 4 was established at Mildenhall.

Date	Crew	Distance	Time	Aircraft
Speed over a Recognised Course – New York to London				
1 September 1974	Pilot, Maj. James V. Sullivan. RSO, Maj. Noel F. Widdifield	3,490 miles (5616 km)	1 hr 54 min 56.4 sec	SR-71A 64-17972
Speed over a Recognised Course – London to Los Angeles				
13 September 1974	Pilot, Capt. Harold B Adams. RSO Capt. William C Machorek	5,645 miles (9084 km)	3 hr 47 min 35.8 sec	SR-71A 64-17972

Above: This SR-71 appeared at the Paris Salon in 1989 after having flown in from Det 4 at Mildenhall.

Above left: Major Noel Widdifield (RSO, left) and Major James Sullivan (pilot, right) pose at Beale immediately prior to the record-breaking run to Farnborough.

Left: Sullivan streams the brake 'chute as '972 arrives at a wet Farnborough at the end of its record-breaking transatlantic run. The 3,490-mile (5616-km) distance from new York to London was accomplished at an average ground speed of 1,817 mph (2924 km/h).

plunged into the ground near Lovelock, Nevada like a hypervelocity meteorite. Luckily, both men survived without permanent injuries. Following an accident board of investigation, several instrument changes were implemented on the fleet together with an amended training programme containing less night flying until crews had accumulated more daytime experience in the SR-71.

Retiring Oxcart

With Lockheed having completed its 30th SR-71 on 25 September 1967, and with the Agency operating its small fleet of Oxcart aircraft, it was inevitable that accountants would begin to ask their age old question: "is it really necessary?" Questions were mooted by the Bureau of the Budget (BoB) as far back as November 1965, and a memo from that office questioned the requirement not only for the number of such high-performance aircraft, but also the necessity for separate 'covert' CIA and 'overt' USAF operations. Since the SR-71 was not scheduled to become operational until September 1968, the SECDEF rightly declined to consider the proposal. In July 1966, BoB officials proposed that a tri-agency study be set up to again establish ways of reducing the cost of both programmes. After the study was completed, a meeting was convened on 12

December 1966 and a vote taken on available options. Three out of four votes cast were in favour of the motion to "terminate the Oxcart fleet in January 1968 (assuming an operational readiness date of September 1967 for the SR-71) and assign all missions to the SR-71 fleet." The memorandum was transmitted to President Johnson on 16 December despite protestations from the CIA's Richard Helms, who was the sole dissenting voice in the vote. Twelve days later, Johnson accepted the BoB's recommendations and directed that the Oxcart programme be terminated by 1 January 1968. In the event, the Oxcart run-down lagged, but the original decision to terminate the programme was reaffirmed on 16 May 1968 and, as seen earlier, the first Kadena-based A-12 began its flight back to

Below left: In March 1982 the SR-71B became the first aircraft to notch up 1,000 missions. It was flown on this landmark flight by Lieutenant Colonel Dave Peters and Major Jerry Glasser.

Below: The early SR-71s exhibited an almost perfect chine planview. Later the lines were distorted by the addition of radar warning receiver pimples near the nose.

Beale operations

Situated in the Sacramento Valley, California, Beale AFB was the headquarters for the SR-71 operation. The base played host to all of the training effort, employing the SR-71B and C dual-control aircraft, T-38As and some standard SR-71As for this task, in addition to ground simulators. Many operational missions were also flown from Beale aimed at Cuba (originally codenamed Giant Plate, and subsequently Clipper); they initially involved overflights but later were amended to constitute a pass along the southern and northern coasts of the island. In 1984 Beale-based SR-71s also overflew Nicaragua.

Top: The crew of '958 lowers the gear during the downwind leg at Beale. The right-hand end of the apron accommodated B-52s and KC-135s; the left-hand end housed recce aircraft. The line of small barns on the far side of the apron was the accommodation for the SR-71s, and U-2Rs inhabited the wide hangars (two at a time) on the near side.

Above right: Most SR-71 pilots took their first ride in trusty '956, seen here over the Sierra Nevada mountains.

Below: The one-off SR-71A(BT) first flew in this guise on 11 December 1974, crewed by Darryl Greenamyer and Steve Belgeau.

the US on 7 June.

As the 9th SRW approached the time for overseas deployment, much talk in the crew lounge was devoted to anti-SAM tactics. The plan was to penetrate enemy airspace at Mach 3. If fired upon, the pilot would accelerate to Mach 3.2 and climb, thereby forcing the missile's guidance system to recalculate the intercept equation. One idea was to also dump fuel so that the aircraft would become lighter, enabling a more rapid climb, but a crew ended the debate during a sortie over Montana by dumping fuel for 10 seconds to see if the afterburner would ignite the fuel trail. Instead, it turned instantly into an ice cloud in the -55°F (-48°C) stratosphere and left a 5-mile (8-km) contrail-finger pointing directly to the aircraft. The pilot reported that he could see the trail for hundreds of miles after having turned back towards the west!

Halving the trainer fleet

During this work-up period, another incident befell the 9th SRW on 11 January 1968. Lieutenant Colonel 'Gray' Sowers and 'student' Captain Dave Fruehauf, on his third training sortie, experienced a double generator failure in SR-71B '957, near Spokane, Washington. They immedi-

ately switched off all non-essential electrically powered equipment to conserve battery power and made repeated attempts to reset both generators, which would come on briefly only to fail again. With most of the bases in Washington state unsuitable for diversion, the crew hoped to make Portland, Oregon, only to discover that they were weathered out. They had little option therefore but to press on for Beale. Their long straight-in approach looked good until the 175-kt (200-mph; 323-km/h) 'final' placed the aircraft in its natural 10° nose-up angle of attack. This allowed some dry-tank fuel inlet ports to 'suck air', which in turn interrupted the gravity flow of fuel to the engine combustion chambers, because the fuel boost pumps were inoperative. This caused cavitation, both J58s flamed out, and at 3,000 ft (915 m) Gray ordered bail-out. Both crew members survived as '957 'pancaked' inverted only 7 miles (11 km) north of Beale's long runway.

OL-8

As the 1st SRS neared operational readiness, decisions were made by Colonel Bill Hayes (9th SRW commander) and Colonel Hal Confer (Director of Operations) about which crews would be first to be deployed to Kadena AB, on the island of Okinawa. The eight crew members selected began training for the deployment, flying simulator sorties depicting the oceanic route they would fly. It was also decided that the same sequence of crew deployment to Kadena would be repeated when it became time to fly operationally over Vietnam. Three aircraft and four crews would be deployed and the crews themselves pulled straws to decide the 'batting order'; the fourth crew would be standby for the three deploying aircraft and, if their services were not needed, would arrive on Kadena by KC-135Q tanker. Command of the operating location (OL-8) would alternate between the 9th SRW's wing commander and vice commander (and later deputy chief of operations). The OL's numbered designation was arrived at sequentially after the 9th SRW's U-2 detachments. Two days before

Glowing Heat (the codename for the deployment), six KC-135Q tankers were positioned at Hickam AFB, Hawaii. Emergency radio coverage was set up on Wake Island.

On 8 March 1968, Majors Buddy Brown and his RSO Dave Jenson left Beale in '978 and became the first Senior Crown crew to deploy to Kadena. The flight involved three air refuellings. Buddy recalls, "We had taken off from Beale at 11.00 and arrived at Kadena at 09.05 – nearly two hours earlier than take-off time, but in the next day because we had crossed the international date line. We beat the sun by a good margin." Two days later Major Jerry O'Malley and Captain Ed Payne delivered '976 to the OL. They were followed on 13 March by Bob Spencer and Keith Branham in '974. Finally, three days later in late evening rain, Jim Watkins and Dave Dempster, the back-up crew, were wearily disgorged from the KC-135. The crews and their aircraft were ready for business.

Due to maintenance problems, Buddy Brown and Dave Jenson missed their chance of being the first crew to fly the

SR-71 operationally; instead, that accolade went to Major Jerry O'Malley and Captain Ed Payne in '976. The mission was flown on Thursday 21 March 1968 and their route was similar to that flown by Mele Vojvodich in his A-12, 10 months earlier. However, with its large high-definition camera in the Q-bay, the A-12 was a photographic platform only. For its first operational mission, the SR-71 carried a downward-looking vertically-mounted terrain objective camera in the centre of the fuselage, ahead of the nose gear. Behind the cockpits in the P and Q chine bays were the left and right long focal-length 'close-look' technical objective ('TEOC' or 'Tech') cameras. Behind them, in bays S and T, were two operational objective cameras ('OOCs'), but of greater significance was the Goodyear side-looking airborne radar (SLAR) located in the detachable nose section, and its associated AR-1700 radar recorder unit in the N-bay, within the right chine.

Having refuelled after their first run, Jerry climbed and accelerated on track for their final 'take' for the mission, which was to be flown over the DMZ. For this run, the

Above: 'Big Tail' refuels from a KC-135Q during its two-year test programme. This came to an end on 29 October 1976 after the USAF lost interest in the concept, following the end of the war in Southeast Asia. The programme had been successful, offering a greater level of versatility with little performance penalty, and allowing the SR-71 to carry bigger mixed Sigint/optical loads.

Left: The SR-71A(BT)'s tail is seen here in the full 8½° up position, used to provide sufficient clearance at take-off and initial touchdown. Controls in the cockpit allowed the pilot to employ the tail as a trimming device in normal flight.

Below: 64-17959 lands at Palmdale during an early test flight, the 'Big Tail' modification sporting photo-calibration marks. Immediately after touchdown the tail was deflected from the full up position to 8½° down, after the wheels had touched the runway, to avoid fouling the brake 'chute.

'Big Tail'

The 'Big Tail' conversion was initially proposed as a way of housing more defensive electronic equipment, but rapidly evolved into a means of increasing sensor-carrying space. In one configuration the SR-71A(BT) carried OBC cameras in both nose and tail so that simultaneous frames could produce stereoscopic images. The tail section provided an additional 49 cu ft (1.39 m³) of capacity.

adopted a tanker callsign for security reasons; the three-ship formation made its slow, lumbering way to Ching Chuan Kang. On arrival, the SR-71 was quickly hangared. The next day, the 'take' was downloaded and despatched for processing – the film to the 67th RTS at Yokota AB, Japan and the SLAR imagery to the 9th RTS at Beale AFB. After two nights at CCK, Jerry and Ed ferried '976 back to Kadena and a superb reception by their friends.

Post-mission intelligence results were stunning. The SLAR imagery had revealed the location of many artillery emplacements around Khe Sanh, and a huge truck park which was used to support the guns. These sites previously had eluded US sensors on other reconnaissance aircraft. Over the next few days, airstrikes were mounted against both targets, reducing their effectiveness dramatically. After a 77-day siege, Khe Sanh was at last relieved on 7 April 1968 (two weeks after '976's discovery sortie). As a result of their highly successful mission, Major Jerome F. O'Malley and Captain Edward D. Payne were each awarded the Distinguished Flying Cross. On its very first operational mission, the SR-71 had proved its value.

Early OL-8 operational sorties were typified by problems involving the SR-71's generators, which often led to the aircraft having to divert into one of the USAF bases in Thailand. Of the 168 SR-71 sorties flown by OL-8 throughout 1968, 67 were operational missions over North Vietnam, the remaining being FCFs or for crew training. In addition, the first of many aircraft change-arounds took place when, over a period of seven days in September, '980, '970 and '962 took over from '978, '976 and '974. Crew rotation also took place, with no fewer than 21 crews having taken the SR-71 into battle over the same period (Bob Spencer and his RSO Keith Branham returned for a second temporary duty (TDY) stint).

'Habu'

While operating out of Kadena, the SR-71 received its nickname of 'Habu'. The habu is a poisonous pit viper found on the Ryuku islands; though non-aggressive, it can inflict a painful bite if provoked. Although resisted by officialdom, the name 'Habu' has proved to be permanent among all associated with Senior Crown.

OL-8 lost its first 'Habu' after more than two years of Kadena operations. On 10 May 1970 Majors Willie Lawson and Gil Martinez had completed one pass over North Vietnam and had air refuelled '969 near Korat RTAFB. Initiating an afterburner climb to prepare for a transonic 'dipsy doodle', they discovered that they were surrounded by heavy thunderclouds extending up to 50,000 ft (15245 m). The aircraft needed climb distance to get above the clouds before the dip-manoeuvre which established the

Above: An SR-71A fitted with chine-mounted RWR antennas closes on the boom of a KC-135Q during a Stateside training sortie.

The SR-71's unique shape was optimised not just for speed, but also for RCS reduction.

primary sensor was the SLAR. On arrival back at Kadena Jerry and Ed were confronted with a base completely fogged in. Despite a good ground-controlled approach (GCA), Jerry never saw the runway, and climbed back to contemplate further options. The SR-71 was low on fuel, so another tanker was launched and 25,000 lb (11340 kg) of fuel was taken onboard. The crew then received a two-figure encoded number which told them to divert to Taiwan. The SR-71 flew in company with two tankers and

Mach 1 airspeed needed for a higher rate of climb. The Mach 0.9 preliminary climb was sluggish with a full fuel load, and Willie eased '969 into a slightly steeper climb, trying to clear a 30,000 ft (9145 m) saddle-back of cloud. At that moment the aircraft entered turbulent cloud and both engines flamed out. The aircraft's angle of attack increased, then suddenly the nose pitched up and recovery was impossible. Both crew members ejected safely and landed resplendent in their silver moon suits, near U-Tapao. To date, four SR-71s have been lost in pitch-up incidents.

OL-8 against the Soviets

Although the vast majority of early 'Habu' flights from Kadena were in support operations in Vietnam, this was not exclusively the case. On the night of 27 September 1971, Majors Bob Spencer and 'Butch' Sheffield completed post take-off tanking and established '980 on a northerly track. US Intelligence had obtained details of the largest-ever Soviet naval exercise to be held near Vladivostok, in the Sea of Japan. Such an event could prove a rich fishing ground for an intelligence data trawl, and the 'Habu' was an ideal vehicle for stirring up the Soviet fleet's defence systems.

National security officials were especially interested in obtaining signal details relating to the Soviets' new SA-5 SAM system. Accordingly, Major Jack Clemance, an inventive electronic warfare officer who worked in the 9th SRW's Electronic Data Processing Centre, jury-rigged one of the aircraft's Elint sensors which allowed it to receive continuous-wave signal data.

As '980 bore down on the target area, dozens of Soviet radars were switched on; just short of entering Soviet airspace, the 'Habu' rolled into a full 35° banked turn, remaining throughout in international airspace. However, on approach to the target area, Bob noted that the right engine's oil pressure was dipping. Clearing the area, Bob once again scanned the engine instruments to discover the reading had fallen to zero. He shut down the engine and was forced to descend and decelerate to subsonic speeds. Having stirred up a hornets' nest, they were now sitting ducks for any Soviet fast jets sent up to intercept the oil-starved Habu. Worse still, at lower altitude they were subjected to strong headwinds which rapidly depleted their fuel supply. 'Butch' calculated that recovery back to Kadena was impossible – instead, they would have to divert into

South Korea.

The OL commander had been monitoring '980's slow progress and as the 'Habu' neared Korea, US listening posts reported the launch of several MiGs from Pyongyang, North Korea. In response, USAF F-102s were scrambled from a base near Hon Chew, South Korea and vectored into a position between the 'Habu' and the MiGs. It was later established that the MiG launch was unconnected with the SR-71's descent. Bob recovered '980 into Taegu, South Korea, without further incident. In all, their EMR 'take' had recorded emissions from 290 different radars, but the greatest prize was 'capture' of the much sought-after SA-5 signals – a first.

On 20 July 1972, while returning to Kadena from an operational mission, Majors Denny Bush and Jimmy Fagg were caught by excessive cross winds shortly after touch-down in '978. They jettisoned the 'chute as per the book, to prevent the aircraft from 'weather-cocking' sharply into wind, but the extended roll-out caused the aircraft to roll off the end of the runway and, in a twist of fate, the aircraft hit the concrete housing the emergency crash barriers. One of the main landing gear struts was badly damaged, which in turn caused substantial additional damage. Both crew members were unhurt, but '978 was written off. It was not

Det 1 – Kadena

Kadena was the site for the first overseas operational deployment, SR-71s taking over from the CIA A-12s. Known successively as OL-8, OL-RK and OL-KA, the Kadena operation finally settled as Det 1 of the 9th SRW in August 1974, and operated as such until retirement of the aircraft in 1990. Missions from this base were flown against Vietnam, Korea, China and the Soviet Far East. Four marathon missions were also launched against Iran.

Det 4 – Mildenhall

The 9th SRW began operations from RAF Mildenhall in 1976 with sporadic single-aircraft detachments of both the U-2R and SR-71A. Det 4 was established as such in April 1979 with a single U-2R, while SR-71 deployments increased. The U-2s primarily provided Sigint coverage and the SR-71s were used for photography (later radar imagery). In 1981 the detachment was heavily committed to covering the situation in Poland, which was under threat of Soviet intervention. By late 1982, Det 4 was assigned two SR-71s on a near-permanent basis, operations being regularly conducted along the East-West German border, in the Baltic and around the North Cape. The SR-71 operation was fully formalised in 1984.

Top: With KC-135Qs trailing in the background, 64-17964 is seen wearing the name **The Bodonian Express** *on its tail, a reference to a diversion into the Norwegian airfield at Bodø during a 1981 mission to the North Cape from Beale.*

Below: David Clark S-1030 pressure suits provided full protection in the event of a cabin depressurisation at altitude. Special ports in the helmet allowed the crew to eat and drink during the flight.

until 21 April 1989 that Kadena lost another 'Habu'. On that occasion one of the engine compressor discs disintegrated during Mach 3 flight, the debris severing one hydraulic system and damaging the other. Lieutenant Colonel Dan House and Major Blair Bozek decelerated and descended '974 down to 400 kt (459 mph; 739 km/h) and 10,000 ft (3,048 m) when the remaining hydraulic system ran dry. Both men safely ejected just a few hundred yards off the coast of Luzon and were rescued by Filipino fishermen. They were later picked up by an HH-53 'Super Jolly Green Giant' and flown to Clark AFB.

OL-8 was redesignated OL-RK on 30 October 1970, became OL-KA on 26 October 1971 and finally Detachment 1 or Det 1 of the 9th SRW in August 1974, a title it retained until deactivated in 1990. During 22 years of service, the unit flew missions to Vietnam, Laos, Cambodia, Thailand, North Korea, airspace off the USSR and China,

and four 11-hour return flights to the Persian Gulf during the Iran-Iraq War.

Operations from the USA

Despite four 9th SRW aircraft losses between 13 April 1967 and 10 October 1968, Category III 'Operational' Testing ended in December 1968. The wing was awarded the Presidential Unit Citation for meeting the challenges of bringing the 'most advanced' reconnaissance system of its day to operational readiness.

Rolling down Beale's runway 14 in '977, in October 1968, were new pilot/RSO team Majors Abe Kardong and Jim Kogler. Approaching V1, a wheel failed, throwing shrapnel into the fuel cells and causing a fuel fire. Abe aborted take-off at high speed, which caused the remaining tyres on that leg to burst. The brake 'chute blossomed, only to be consumed by the fire. With one wing low and the aircraft off centre to the runway, '977's sharp inlet spike knifed through the barrier cable at the end of the runway, rendering it useless. Now on the overrun, Jim ejected while Abe rode out the high-speed sleigh ride. When the dust settled, he was helped from the cockpit by the mobile control crew for that day, Willie Lawson and Gil Martinez.

On 11 April 1969 Lieutenant Colonel Bill Skliar and Major Noel Warner lined up SR-71A 64-17954 on runway 04 at Edwards and began a maximum gross weight take-off. DUTCH 69 had just rotated when one of the left main gear tyres blew. Unable to support the additional weight, the other two on that leg also went. Bill immediately aborted the take-off, but red hot shrapnel from the disintegrating wheel hubs punctured the fuel tanks and triggered a fire which engulfed the entire aircraft. Once at a standstill, Bill exited the aircraft to the right and assisted Noel from his rear cockpit. '954 never flew again. After this accident the Goodrich tyres were 'beefed up'.

The third pitch-up accident happened on 18 December 1969, when Director of the Test Force Lieutenant Colonel Joe Rogers and RSO Lieutenant Colonel Gary Heidelbaugh were accelerating and climbing '953. They heard a

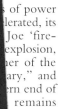

Left: A scene repeated many times throughout the 1980s: an SR-71 trails its 'tiger tails' past Mildenhall church as it launches into the East Anglian dawn at the start of a European mission. Most sorties were in and around northern Europe, but the Det 4 'Habus' occasionally ventured into the Mediterranean.

defence system from the East Coast base; this would also provide a convenient security cover for the operation. Accordingly, at 22.00 on 11 October 1973, Lieutenant Colonel Jim Shelton and Major Gary Coleman left Beale in '979 and headed for Griffiss. On arrival they were met by an angry base commander and three Lockheed tech reps after they had laid "a heavy late night sonic boom track" down into New York state as they descended from altitude. Jim phoned Al Joersz and John Fuller (who would fly a second SR-71 into Griffiss) and advised them to move their descent profile over the Great Lakes to minimise the effects of the boom on urban eastern states. With the amendment incorporated into their flight plan, no boom complaints accompanied the arrival of '964. Unfortunately, this second aircraft developed a hydraulic problem that forced an engine change, leaving the new detachment with one mission-ready aircraft until specialised equipment could be flown in from Beale. An hour after the arrival of '964, the first tanker from Beale touched down carrying Tom Estes (the operation officer), three mission planners and a number of the 9th's best intelligence and maintenance personnel. At 06.00 a secure teleprinter clattered out the final details of the first sortie which was to be flown just 22 hours later.

When the crews met the mission planners the former voiced concerns about diversionary fields, but no-one could offer a satisfactory answer. Later that morning, the tanker from Mildenhall arrived and technicians began preparing '979 for the longest operational sortie to date. By mid-afternoon it was suggested that the crew should get some sleep since they had been up nearly 36 hours and would soon be readying themselves for a 16-hour day. They were directed to old quarters where they discovered their rooms

An SR-71 returns to Mildenhall after an early morning mission. Two purpose-built barns were erected at the base to house the pair of operational aircraft, which were usually supported by around six KC-135Qs. A large hangar provided housing for the reconnaissance interpretation equipment.

Below left: During their time in Europe the Det 4 SR-71s occasionally posed with other NATO aircraft for photographs. This is a Jaguar from No. 41 Sqn, one of the RAF's tactical reconnaissance units.

Below: A spirited display by '960 at the 1986 Mildenhall air show resulted in this dramatic spectacle. As vortices streamed from the aircraft in the moist air, unburned fuel ignited in two fireballs. The following year an even more aggressive flying routine resulted in '973 being overstressed irrevocably.

A-12/SR-71 details

Above: The nosewheel strut mounted a pair of landing/taxiing lamps. The housing alongside the lamps contained the steering actuator.

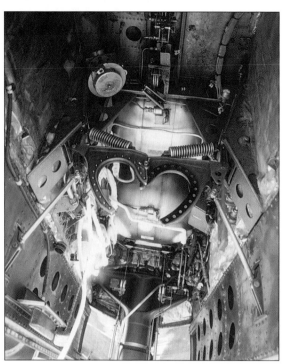

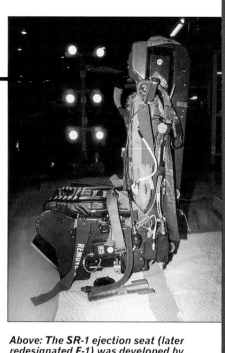

Above: The SR-1 ejection seat (later redesignated F-1) was developed by Lockheed from the C-2 seat used in early F-104 Starfighters.

Above: This view shows the nosewheel bay, looking aft toward the strut mounting. When retracted, the strut assembly was locked in place by large callipers.

Left: This is the mainwheel bay, showing the shroud which housed the wheel when retracted. All three wheel units had these heat protection measures.

Left: The mainwheel unit was retracted by a single hydraulic jack. The wheel hub was a single titanium forging.

Right: Detail of the mainwheel shows the dual brake runs and door attachments. The strut was painted black, while the wheel hubs were usually either red or green.

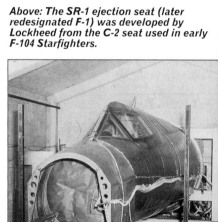

Above: To test the A-12 cockpit's ability to withstand the heat experienced at operational speed and altitude, this section was tested in an oven.

Above: The tilting panel for the buried refuelling receptacle also functioned as a slipway for the boom.

Above and right: For start-up, the J58 engine was turned by a ground power cart which fed air to the compressor. The attachment for the ducts was on the underside of the nacelle.

68

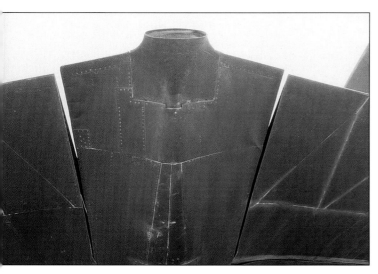

bove: This is the underside of an A-12's tail, showing the simple grilled perture. The SR-71 had a longer fuselage, and a distinct tailcone. Note the rge RAM wedges in the elevon structure.

Above: The sophisticated inlet system had a repositionable spike to correctly position the shock wave in the throat of the inlet and to increase capture area. The spike had a band of slits around it to remove boundary layer air.

Left: The SR-71 had interchangeable nose sections with four main attachment points. Note the circular fuselage structure with added chine sections.

Below: A partially disassembled aircraft displays the rib construction of the engine nacelle. The large row of attachment points along the top allowed the outer part of the nacelle, complete with outer wing panel, to be hinged up for easy access to the engine.

bove: The SR-71 mounted most of its sensors nd navigation equipment in underfuselage bays. his is the E-bay, which housed electronics. On e other side of the nosewheel bay was the R-ay, which housed radios. Outboard of these bays ere the chine-mounted K- and L-bays, usually sed for DEF (defensive electronics) equipment.

ight: This view looking forward into the engine acelle shows the intake spike assembly, fixed to e nacelle with four struts. The centrebody was ollow to allow the dumping of boundary layer air.

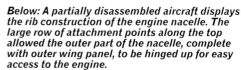

elow and right: The Nortronics astro-tracker as housed in a bay behind the cockpit, peering owards through a small circular window in a movable spine panel.

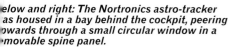

Below: Lifted upper wing panels show the internal multi-spar construction of the wing. The internal void formed an integral fuel tank. Note the chord-wise corrugations of the upper surface.

Fuel

Early problems in the Blackbird programme prompted Pratt & Whitney, Ashland Shell and Monsanto to develop a new high-flashpoint fuel. Originally known as PF-1 and later designated JP7, this fuel would only ignite at high temperatures, reducing the risk of inadvertent fires caused by the high operating temperatures encountered at high Mach numbers. For operational flights a chemical known as A-50 was added to the fuel, this reducing the frequency response of the afterburner plume, which had been shown to produce a large radar return when untreated. Other additives included fluorocarbons to improve lubricity, and toluene and mentyl isobutylketone which further reduced the fire risk. This was especially important as the fuel was used as a hydraulic fluid to operate the afterburner nozzle, which caused it to be heated to 600°F (316°C). The high-flashpoint fuel required chemical ignition by triethyl borane (TEB), which ignited on contact with the fuel.

Compared to the A/F-12, the SR-71 had a lengthened fuselage for more fuel. Whereas the internal capacity of the YF-12 was 9,785 US gal (37040 litres), that of the SR-71A was 12,219 US gal (46254 litres). There were six tanks which occupied most of the main circular fuselage structure aft of the refuelling receptacle, and the wings between the fuselage and the engine nacelles. The wing tanks were punctuated by the wheel wells. Sixteen pumps moved fuel between tanks, engines and heat-exchangers, the engines being fed by a Chandler Evans-built main fuel pump specially housed in steel to protect it from the high temperatures. The fuel itself was used as an efficient heat sink for a number of systems, including the ECS, oil systems and TEB tank. It was also used to trim the aircraft by fore/aft movements to maintain the centre of gravity within limits. Three liquid nitrogen tanks were carried which were used to pressurise the fuel tanks, preventing crushing of the tanks by aerodynamic loads. The nitrogen also served to 'inert' the tanks as a further fire precaution.

DAFICS

Between 1980 and 1985 the SR-71 fleet underwent a major modification programme which replaced the old analog flight control and inlet system with DAFICS (digital automatic flight and inlet control system). This consisted of three Honeywell HDP-5301 digital computers housed in a Faraday cage to protect them from electromagnetic pulse. Two of the computers were used as primary systems for controlling the aircraft's stability augmentation systems, autopilot and the programmed inlet control system. The third comput was a monitoring system containing BIT (built-in test) software for continuous checking for faults. Air data from the pitot system was digitised and fed into the two main computers, which then calculated and commanded appropriate actions. The monitoring computer store the BIT data which could be downloaded by maintenance technicians upon landing for fault rectification and rescheduling of the inlet contro programme if required.

Automatic inlet control was considered vital to the SR-71's missior so critical were the parameters at high Mach and high altitude. The inlet spikes and auxiliary doors were programmed to maintain the shock wave in the correct position in the throat of the inlet, from where it could easily be expelled (an 'unstart'). The DAFICS (and earli analog system) maintained the shock in the correct position as far as possible, and automatically recaptured the shock wave if an 'unstart' should occur. Manual control of the inlet and bypass door system wa possible from the cockpit should the system fail, although this was less precise than the automatic system.

y controlled and hydraulically actuated, primary power
ssory drive system (with back-up from the right). Gear
tely 14 seconds. A cable-controlled emergency release
avity in the event of a hydraulic failure. The mainwheel
on a hollow axle so that any wheel could be changed
side of the tyres were impregnated with aluminium to
to the wheel well, the outer walls being close to the hot
ion was by nitrogen. Braking was also powered by the left-
ng forward the upper portion of the rudder pedals.
low speeds. To aid braking a large parachute was fitted in
e was pulled from its housing by a smaller drogue chute.

Lockheed SR-71A 'Blackbird'
1st Strategic Reconnaissance Squadron
9th Strategic Reconnaissance Wing
Strategic Air Command, US Air Force

What became known as the SR-71A was the outcome of a series of proposals made by Lockheed to the US Air Force based on the technology of the A-12 single-seater. At the time the USAF's major programme was the North American XB-70 Valkyrie Mach 3 bomber, and any proposal that was seen to challenge it was to be avoided. However, Lockheed schemed the B-12 as a nuclear bomber which could penetrate deep into hostile airspace and clean up any targets which had not been hit in the first opening round of strikes. The proposal met with great interest, and a contract for six pre-production aircraft and 25 others was awarded on 4 June 1962. This aircraft was given the Air Force designation RS-71 (for reconnaissance-strike), and followed on in the bomber sequence from the B-70, which had been redesignated RS-70. Lockheed's refined design became known in-house as the RS-12. In the early 1960s the advent of the ICBM caused the Pentagon to radically review its thoughts, with the result that the special weapons which needed to be developed for the RS-71 were never ordered. Based on this lack of commitment, Kelly Johnson feared a cancellation of the project, and rapidly produced a pure reconnaissance version, the R-12. In May 1964 Secretary of Defense McNamara cancelled the RS-70 Valkyrie, and soon after announced that the SR-71 (neatly transposing Reconnaissance-Strike with Strategic Reconnaissance) would be built for the USAF, a modification to the existing RS-71 contract. But for the foresight and rapid reaction of Kelly Johnson, the aircraft may never have been built.

Navigation system

One of the many key technological problems which had to be surmounted in the Blackbird programme was that of navigation. Accurate navigation was essential when flying in sensitive areas and over large distances, while the aircraft would often be far away from reliable ground stations. Consequently, the NAS-14V2 Astro-inertial Navigation System (ANS) was developed by Nortronics. The ANS combined three main reference components: a highly accurate (to five milliseconds) chronometer, an inertial platform and a star-tracker. The latter had 52 permanently visible stars logged in its memory, of which at least three were sequentially tracked at any given time by a gimbal-mounted tracker located in the top of the navigation bay aft of the RSO's cockpit. By cross-correlating the positions of the stars, an accurate position could be gained, and compared with the inertial platform.

In addition to the ANS, the SR-71 also carried a standard inertial system. This was originally the Flight Reference System (FRS), which only provided heading and attitude information, but in June 1982 was replaced by the Singer-Kearfott SKN-2417 (as used in early F-16s). This standard INS provided a useful and accurate back-up should the primary ANS fail. It was housed in the R-bay, along with other nav/comms equipment. This included an ARA-48 automatic direction finder (ADF), TACAN receiver with distance-measuring equipment, instrument landing system (ILS), and HF/VHF/UHF radios. An IFF transponder was located in the D-bay.

Drawing data from the primary ANS, the system produced a moving map strip projection in each cockpit as the main navigation display. The RSO also had a video viewsight for looking beneath the aircraft to cross-check known ground positions against ANS/INS predictions. The viewsight (with either 44° or 114° selectable fields of view) was also useful for spotting SAM launches or checking cloud cover over the target during photographic missions.

Autopilot

Most of the mission was flown using the autopilot, which, in AUTONAV mode, was slaved to the ANS. Prior to the sortie a pre-planned route was prepared using a series of destination points (DPs). These were loaded by tape into the ANS computer prior to take-off. Once airborne, the ANS commanded the autopilot to follow these DPs around the route of the mission. None of these DPs was ever actually flown over, as the system automatically commanded the turn before arriving at the DP so that the aircraft would cut the corner in order to roll out on the next leg precisely on track. The turn position was calculated based on the aircraft's speed and preset desired bank angle. At Mach 3.2 the maximum preset bank angle was 42°, which allowed a margin of 3° over the permissible airframe limit of 45°.

Undercarriage

The tricycle undercarriage was electrica coming from the left-hand engine's acc retraction and extension took approxima system allowed the gear to extend by g struts each mounted three wheels, eac without removing the other two. The ou reflect heat when they were retracted i upper and lower skins of the wing. Infla hand hydraulic system, operated by flex Nosewheel steering became operativ a compartment in the spine. The mai

Lockheed SR-71A OL-8, 9th SRW, Kadena

The first operational deployment for the SR-71A was to Kadena, from where missions were flown over North Vietnam and, later, Korea, China and the Soviet Far East. This aircraft, 64-17978, was the first of three to be deployed in the initial phase, leaving Beale for Okinawa on 8 March 1968. After flying nearly 300 hours from the detachment, '978 returned to Beale in September, having gained the reputation of being a very reliable aircraft. When it returned to the detachment in 1972, it ruined its reputation by having a double generator failure over North Vietnam, causing the crew to overfly Hanoi at a perilous 41,000 ft and at only marginally supersonic speed, well within SAM range. Soon after this mission, its SAS failed while travelling at Mach 3.17 in a 30° bank, causing the crew some anxious moments and leaving them with a long subsonic slog back to Kadena. '978's luck finally ran out on 20 July 1972, when the crew attempted to land it in a fierce crosswind. Having used the brake chute on a first attempt at landing, Major Denny Bush had no such luxury on the second attempt. The cross-wind was too strong, and Bush could not keep the SR-71 straight. It ran off the runway and was damaged beyond repair, although thankfully the crew emerged unscathed. While at the Kadena detachment the aircraft acquired the then-popular 'Playboy' bunny logo on its vertical fins, and became known as the 'Rapid Rabbit'.

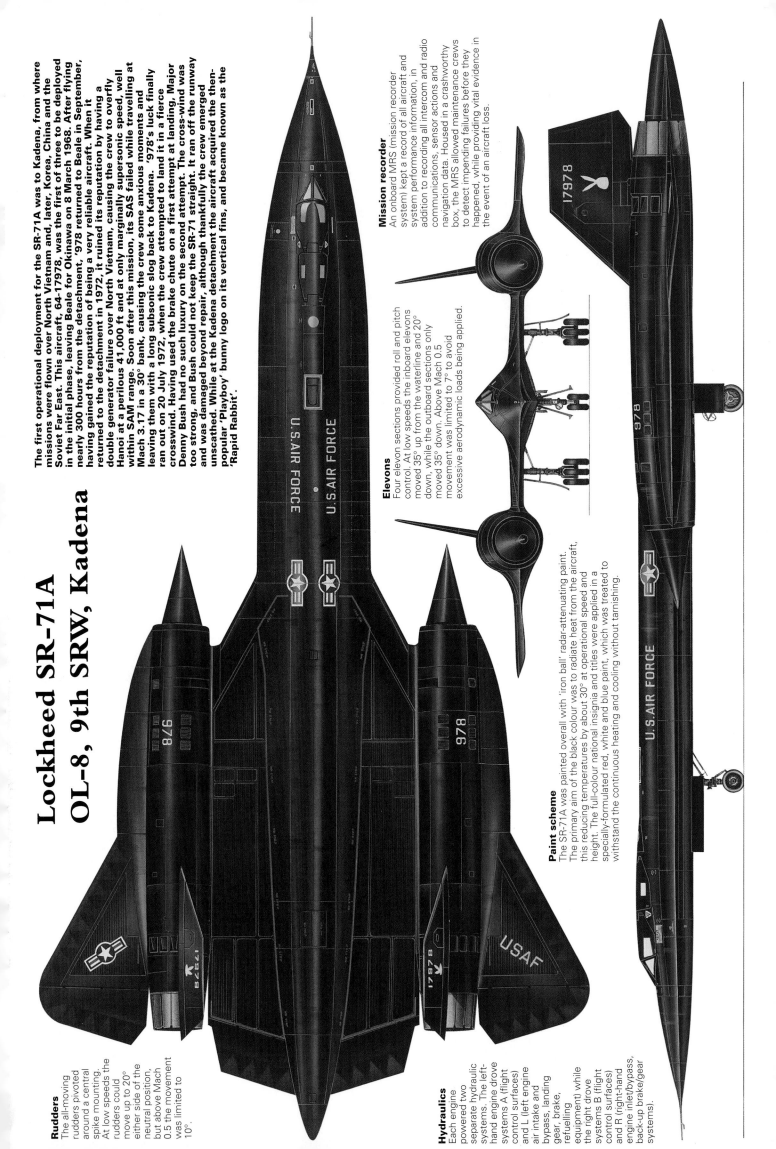

Rudders

The all-moving rudders pivoted around a central spike mounting. At low speeds the rudders could move up to 20° either side of the neutral position, but above Mach 0.5 the movement was limited to 10°.

Hydraulics

Each engine powered two separate hydraulic systems. The left-hand engine drove systems A (flight control surfaces) and L (left engine air intake and bypass, landing gear, brake, refuelling equipment) while the right drove systems B (flight control surfaces) and R (right-hand engine inlet/bypass, back-up brake/gear systems).

Mission recorder

An onboard MRS (mission recorder system) kept a record of all aircraft and system performance information, in addition to recording all intercom and radio communications, sensor actions and navigation data. Housed in a crashworthy box, the MRS allowed maintenance crews to detect impending failures before they happened, while providing vital evidence in the event of an aircraft loss.

Elevons

Four elevon sections provided roll and pitch control. At low speeds the inboard elevons moved 35° up from the waterline and 20° down, while the outboard sections only moved 35° down. Above Mach 0.5 movement was limited to 7° to avoid excessive aerodynamic loads being applied.

Paint scheme

The SR-71A was painted overall with 'iron ball' radar-attenuating paint. The primary aim of the black colour was to radiate heat from the aircraft, this reducing temperatures by about 30° at operational speed and height. The full-colour national insignia and titles were applied in a specially-formulated red, white and blue paint, which was treated to withstand the continuous heating and cooling without tarnishing.

SR-71 details

These views show the inlet spike in the full out (above) and fully retracted (below) positions, the centre-body travelling 26 in (0.66 m) between the two. The forward position is used at speeds up to Mach 1.6, above which the spike starts retracting to its full aft position achieved at Mach 3.2.

Access to the Pratt & Whitney J58 engine is by a novel folding wing/nacelle method. Most of the outer nacelle, apart from the forward section, hinges upwards along the centreline, taking the outer wing panel with it. This allows the J58 to be accessed easily for in situ *maintenance or removed completely. Note the special jacked cradle which is used to lower down and then transport the removed engine.*

Lockheed SR-71A cutaway

1 Pitot tube
2 Air data probe
3 Radar warning antennas
4 Nose mission equipment bay
5 Panoramic camera aperture
6 Detachable nosecone joint frame
7 Cockpit front pressure bulkhead
8 Rudder pedals
9 Control column
10 Instrument panel
11 Instrument panel shroud
12 Knife-edged windscreen panels
13 Upward-hinged cockpit canopy covers
14 Ejection seat headrest
15 Canopy actuator
16 Pilot's Lockheed F-1 'zero-zero' ejection seat
17 Engine throttle levers
18 Side console panel
19 Fuselage chine close-pitched frame construction
20 Liquid oxygen converters (2)
21 Side console panel
22 Reconnaissance Systems Officer's (RSO) instrument display
23 Cockpit rear pressure bulkhead

24 RSO's Lockheed F-1 'zero-zero' ejection seat
25 Canopy hinge point
26 SR-71B dual-control trainer variant, nose profile
27 Raised instructor's rear cockpit
28 Astro-inertial navigation star tracker
29 Navigation and communications systems electronic equipment
30 Nosewheel bay
31 Nose undercarriage pivot fixing
32 Landing and taxiing lamps
33 Twin nosewheels, forward retracting
34 Hydraulic retraction jack
35 Cockpit environmental system equipment bay
36 Air refuelling receptacle, open

37 Fuselage upper longeron
38 Forward fuselage frame construction
39 Forward fuselage integral fuel tanks
40 Palletised, interchangeable reconnaissance equipment packs
41 Fuselage chine member
42 Forward/centre fuselage joint ring frame
43 Centre fuselage integral fuel tanks; total system capacity 12,219 US gal (46254 litres)
44 Beta B.120 titanium alloy skin panelling
45 Corrugated wing skin panelling
46 Starboard main undercarriage, stowed position
47 Intake centre-body bleed air louvres
48 Bypass duct suction relief louvres

49 Starboard engine air intake
50 Moveable intake conical centre-body
51 Centre-body retracted (high-speed position)
52 Boundary layer bleed air holes
53 Automatic intake control system air data probe
54 Diffuser chamber
55 Variable inlet guide vanes
56 Hinged engine cowling/outer wing panel
57 Pratt & Whitney JT11D-20B (J58) single-spool bleed-bypass engine

61 Afterburner fuel manifold
62 Tailfin fixed root section
63 Starboard outer wing panel
64 Under-cambered leading edge
65 Outboard roll control elevon
66 All-moving starboard fin
67 Continuously operating afterburner duct

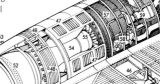

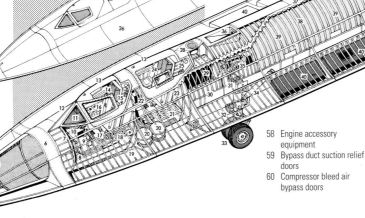

58 Engine accessory equipment
59 Bypass duct suction relief doors
60 Compressor bleed air bypass doors

68 Afterburner nozzle
69 Engine bay tertiary air flaps
70 Exhaust nozzle ejector flaps
71 Variable-area exhaust nozzle
72 Starboard wing integral fuel tank bays
73 Brake parachute doors, open

74 Ribbon parachute stowage
75 Aft fuselage integral fuel tanks
76 Skin doubler
77 Aft fuselage frame construction
78 Elevon mixer unit

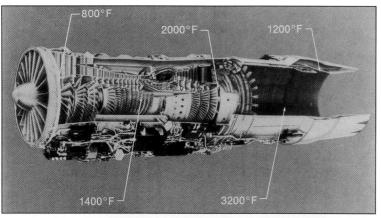

Above: This drawing shows a cutaway of the J58 engine, together with selected temperatures under normal operating conditions. In the afterburner section temperatures reached a fierce 3,200°F (1760°C).

This engine is one of the YJ58 powerplants built for test purposes, and differed from production engines by having some gold-plated parts. Around 150 J58s were built for the entire Blackbird programme.

Stills from a Lockheed film show the modified Convair F-106B (left) used to test the SR-1 ejection seat, and an aerial test with an instrumented dummy (above).

Right: Three nose sections were regularly carried: empty (for ferry or training), OBC and ASARS-1. This is the latter, easily identified by its bulged contours forward of the joint with the fuselage. Also of note is the knife-edge section mounted ahead of the windscreen.

Left: Little has been released about the SR-71's DEF (defensive electronics) system, although the aircraft has several small antennas around the airframe. This forward-facing receiver is located under the forward fuselage.

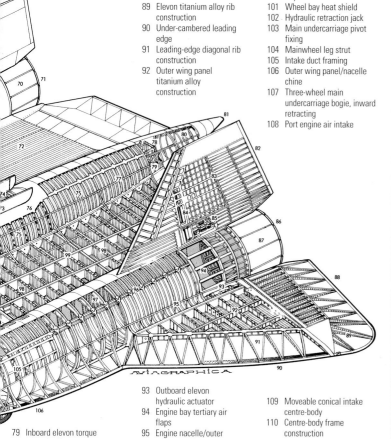

87	Ejector flaps
88	Port outboard elevon
89	Elevon titanium alloy rib construction
90	Under-cambered leading edge
91	Leading-edge diagonal rib construction
92	Outer wing panel titanium alloy construction

100	Main undercarriage wheel bay
101	Wheel bay heat shield
102	Hydraulic retraction jack
103	Main undercarriage pivot fixing
104	Mainwheel leg strut
105	Intake duct framing
106	Outer wing panel/nacelle chine
107	Three-wheel main undercarriage bogie, inward retracting
108	Port engine air intake

79	Inboard elevon torque control unit
80	Tailcone
81	Fuel vent
82	Port all-moving fin
83	Fin rib construction
84	Torque shaft hinge mounting
85	Fin hydraulic actuator
86	Port engine exhaust nozzle

93	Outboard elevon hydraulic actuator
94	Engine bay tertiary air flaps
95	Engine nacelle/outer wing panel integral construction
96	Engine cowling/wing panel hinge axis
97	Port nacelle ring frame construction
98	Inboard wing panel integral fuel tank bays
99	Multi-spar titanium alloy wing construction

109	Moveable conical intake centre-body
110	Centre-body frame construction
111	Inboard leading-edge diagonal rib construction
112	Inner wing panel integral fuel tank
113	Wingroot/fuselage attachment root rib
114	Close-pitched fuselage titanium alloy frames
115	Wing/fuselage chine blended fairing panels

Above: A technician runs a bench check on an OBC camera prior to installation in the nose section of an SR-71A. The camera is housed within its own environmentally controlled casing. The OBC is a horizon-to-horizon panoramic camera.

Left: Seen through the viewscope of a U-2, technicians work on a TEOC camera. This camera was mounted lengthways in the chine bays (P or Q) with the 45° prism peering downwards through a window in the rear of the bay.

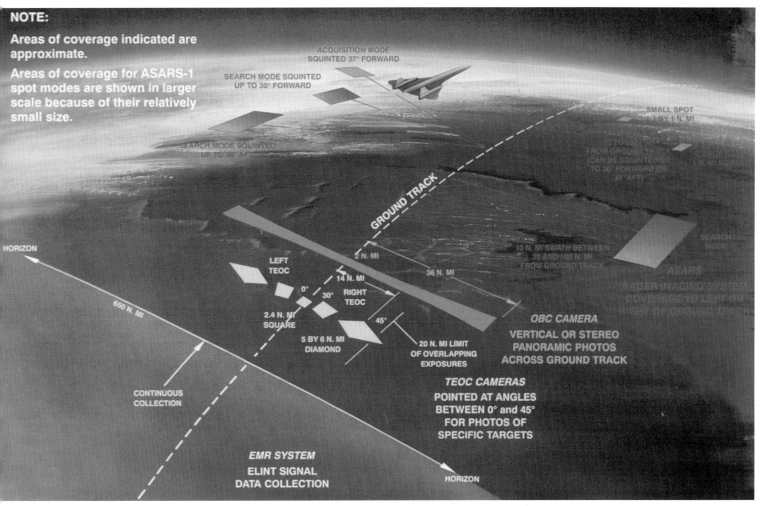

ACQUISITION MODE SQUINTED 37° FORWARD

SEARCH MODE SQUINTED UP TO 30° FORWARD

SEARCH MODE SQUINTED UP TO 30° AFT

SMALL SPOT 1.1 BY 1 N. MI

HORIZON

GROUND TRACK

650 N. MI

LEFT TEOC

2 N. MI

14 N. MI

36 N. MI

10 N. MI SWATH BETWEEN 20 AND 100 N. MI FROM GROUND TRACK

0°   30°

RIGHT TEOC

2.4 N. MI SQUARE

45°

5 BY 6 N. MI DIAMOND

20 N. MI LIMIT OF OVERLAPPING EXPOSURES

SEARCH MODE

ASARS RADAR IMAGING SYSTEM COVERAGE TO LEFT OR RIGHT OF GROUND TRACK

OBC CAMERA
VERTICAL OR STEREO PANORAMIC PHOTOS ACROSS GROUND TRACK

CONTINUOUS COLLECTION

TEOC CAMERAS
POINTED AT ANGLES BETWEEN 0° and 45° FOR PHOTOS OF SPECIFIC TARGETS

EMR SYSTEM
ELINT SIGNAL DATA COLLECTION

HORIZON

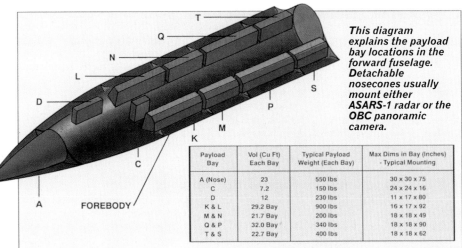

This diagram explains the payload bay locations in the forward fuselage. Detachable nosecones usually mount either ASARS-1 radar or the OBC panoramic camera.

FOREBODY

Payload Bay	Vol (Cu Ft) Each Bay	Typical Payload Weight (Each Bay)	Max Dims in Bay (Inches) - Typical Mounting
A (Nose)	23	550 lbs	30 x 30 x 75
C	7.2	150 lbs	24 x 24 x 16
D	12	230 lbs	11 x 17 x 80
K & L	29.2 Bay	900 lbs	16 x 17 x 92
M & N	21.7 Bay	200 lbs	18 x 18 x 49
Q & P	32.0 Bay	340 lbs	18 x 18 x 90
T & S	22.7 Bay	400 lbs	18 x 18 x 62

SR-71 sensors

The SR-71's sensors fall into three groups: optical, radar and Elint. The diagram above depicts examples of the kind of coverage options available with the aircraft flying at 80,000 ft. The brown area is the continuous horizon-to-horizon Elint coverage, yellow is for the TEOC cameras, blue for the OBC panoramic and orange for the ASARS-1 radar. Electronic steering in the radar allows for a degree of forward or rearward squint, while the radar can operate in both a wide-area search mode or detailed spot mode.

Right: This diagram illustrates two typical mission profiles, the red ribbon being for a short-range mission with a top-off refuelling after launch, while the blue depicts a longer mission with three refuellings.

Below: An illustration of the clarity achievable by the SR-71's cameras is provided by this view of the Seattle dome.

Above: '967 is seen with the Q-bay open. This usually housed the palletised TEOC (Technical Objective Camera).

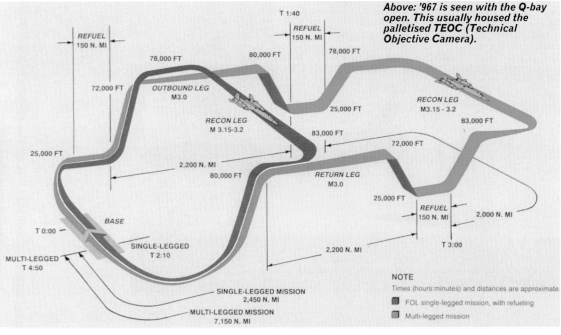

T 1:40

REFUEL 150 N. MI

REFUEL 150 N. MI

78,000 FT

78,000 FT

80,000 FT

72,000 FT

OUTBOUND LEG M3.0

RECON LEG M3.15 - 3.2

25,000 FT

RECON LEG M 3.15-3.2

83,000 FT

83,000 FT

72,000 FT

25,000 FT

2,200 N. MI

80,000 FT

RETURN LEG M3.0

25,000 FT

REFUEL 150 N. MI

2,000 N. MI

BASE

T 0:00

SINGLE-LEGGED T 2:10

2,200 N. MI

T 3:00

MULTI-LEGGED T 4:50

SINGLE-LEGGED MISSION 2,450 N. MI

MULTI-LEGGED MISSION 7,150 N. MI

NOTE
Times (hours:minutes) and distances are approximate.

▪ FOL single-legged mission, with refueling
▪ Multi-legged mission

Libya

Operation El Dorado Canyon, the reprisal raid on Libya, was flown on the night of 14/15 April 1986. Three post-strike photo-reconnaissance missions were flown by Det 4 SR-71s, the first departing even before the USAF's F-111 bombers had returned to their bases. So important were the missions that both aircraft were launched, one acting as an air-spare.

Below: '980 had three camel markings applied to the left nose gear door following its 15/16/17 April missions.

Above and above right: Some of the post-strike imagery was released to the press, the first time that SR-71 photographs had been made public, although the quality was reduced to hide capability. The aircraft were fitted with two TEOC cameras each, with an OBC panoramic camera for horizon-to-horizon coverage.

Although most tanker support was provided by the KC-135Q, the SR-71 could also refuel from a KC-10A. This capability was first used operationally during the 1986 Libya missions. The SR-71s returned to Libya in 1987 during another period of tension.

were hot and their beds uncomfortable. Gary Coleman recalled, "No-one could snore like Jim Shelton and I got no sleep at all, but I consoled myself with the thought that at least my pilot was getting some solid rest!"

The belligerent attitude of usually helpful allies necessitated that JP7 fuel and tanker crews be repositioned from Mildenhall and Turkey to Zaragoza in Spain, and emergency landing sites were still proving all but impossible to find. Nevertheless, Jim Shelton cranked '979's engines on cue, and lifted off from Griffiss and headed east at 02.00. Just off the East Coast he made good the first of many ARCPs (air refuelling contact points), topped off and continued east to the next cell of tankers awaiting the thirsty 'Habu', just beyond the Azores. Returning again to speed and altitude, they made a high-Mach dash through the Straits of Gibraltar and let down for a third air refuelling just east of the heel of Italy. Due to the proximity to the war zone and Libya, the US Navy provided a CAP (combat air patrol) from carrier-based aircraft on station in the Mediterranean.

The SR-71 then resumed its climb and acceleration to

coast-in over Port Said. Gary Coleman said, "There was no indication of anything launched against us, but everyone was painting us on their radars as we made our turn inbound. The DEF panel lit up like a pin-ball machine and I said to Jim, 'this should be interesting.'"

In all, '979 spent 25 minutes over 'denied territory'. Entering Egyptian airspace at 11:03 GMT, they covered the Israeli battle fronts with both Egypt and Syria before coasting out and letting down towards their fourth ARCP, which was still being CAPped by the US Navy. Their next hot leg was punctuated by a fifth refuelling, again near the Azores, before a final high-speed run across the western Atlantic towards New York. Mindful of his own fatigue, Gary was in awe of his pilot who completed a textbook sixth air refuelling, before greasing '979 back down at Griffiss after a combat sortie lasting 10 hours 18 minutes (more than five hours of which was at Mach 3 or above) and involving 11 tanking operations from the ever-dependable KC-135Qs. Their reconnaissance 'take' was of high quality and provided intelligence and defence analysts with much needed information concerning the deposition of Arab forces in the region, which was then made available to the Israelis.

Back to the war zone

Aircraft '979 paid a second successful visit to the Yom Kippur War zone on 25 October, this time crewed by Majors Al Joersz and John Fuller. A third mission was chalked up by the same aircraft eight days later. Majors Jim Wilson and Bruce Douglas took '964 on its first sortie to the Mediterranean on 11 November. The 10-hour 49-minute flight departed Griffiss and terminated as planned at Seymour Johnson AFB, North Carolina, the reason behind this detachment move being to avoid the New York winter weather.

Despite hostilities between the factions officially ending with a Soviet-backed motion in the United Nations on 24 October, fierce fighting continued to break out at regular intervals. It was to cover disengagement that the SR-71's monitoring system continued to be called upon, with five more marathon flights being flown from Seymour Johnson AFB.

In total, these nine flights represent a pinnacle of operational professionalism and serve as a tribute, not only to the dedication of the aircrews, but also to that of the staff planners, tanker crews and of course the unsung heroes, that small group of top ground technicians who maintained the SR-71s away from home. The sorties also stand as a testament of the long-reach capability of the aircraft and its ability to operate, on short notice, with impunity in a high-threat environment.

As part of the United States bicentennial celebrations,

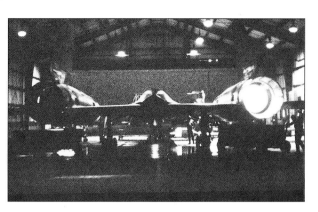

SAC and HQ USAF agreed to reveal some of the SR-71's performance capabilities, by securing more records for the nation. Initially, the plan was to set an 'around the world at the equator' speed record. Pat Bledsoe and John Fuller were the senior crew at the time and were chosen to make the flight. Initial planning showed it could be done in 16 hours 20 minutes with fuel taken onboard from seven air refuelling tracks. The only modification for the SR-71 would have been an additional liquid dewar. Alas, the planning came to an abrupt halt when HQ USAF generals saw the cost of deploying fuel and tankers to forward bases around the world – it would involve nearly 100 KC-135 flights! Instead, a new set of world speed and altitude records were set by the 9th on 27 and 28 July 1976 (see table, page 55).

Cuba

Early in the Senior Crown programme, Cuban reconnaissance sorties became a task for the 9th SRW. They were flown from Beale and initially codenamed Giant Plate, but the designation was later changed to Clipper. Most sorties were 'stand-off' runs, flown abeam the island in international airspace. Such a mission would typically take three and a half hours to complete and was considered very routine.

Occasionally, however, the track was modified to take the aircraft directly over Cuba. When the Carter administration entered office, they suspended all overflight actively in an act of 'goodwill'. In 1978, though, a reconnaissance satellite photographed a Soviet freighter in Havana harbour surrounded by large crates that were being moved to a nearby air base where aircraft were being reassembled. It appeared that 15 MiG-23s had been supplied to Castro's air force. The MiG-23BN 'Flogger-H' was known to be capable of carrying nuclear weapons, and if it was this variant

Above: Simple barns were used to house the SR-71, with doors at either end to allow start-up inside the barn.

Above left: Due to the high flashpoint of JP7 fuel, a unique starting method was required. A ground cart or compressed air spun up the engine spool, while a TEB (tri-ethyl borane) shot provided chemical ignition, resulting in this greenish glow.

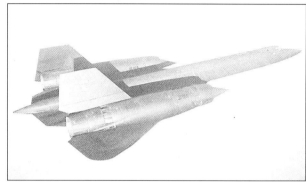

that had been exported, then the shipment violated the 1962 Soviet pledge of not deploying 'offensive' weapons to Cuba.

Two sorties were flown by SR-71s over Cuba in November 1978. They verified that the MiGs were MiG-23Ms 'Flogger-Es' optimised for air defence, evidence which substantiated Soviet claims.

UK operations

Early in the Senior Crown programme, the total number of operating SR-71s was scaled down. The two flying squadrons became one in April 1971. As the US disengaged itself from Vietnam, and with the Yom Kippur War over, the number of unit-authorised aircraft also declined. By 1977, the SR-71A primary authorised aircraft (PAA) stood at six aircraft, and funding reduced proportionately. Since the SR-71 was primarily an imagery platform, it had lost support from the National Intelligence Committee, which had become enamoured with satellite products. Having lost much of the high-level support of that powerful constituency, the SR-71 had to be funded by the Air

64-17968 sports one of the tail-art designs which appeared sporadically throughout the SR-71's career. Such artwork was applied in chalk, as this did not damage the 'iron-ball' paint, and could easily be washed off. Artworks usually appeared at the detachments, being removed when the aircraft rotated back to Beale.

Physiological Support

A key part of the SR-71 operation was the work of the PSD (Physiological Support Division), which was responsible for all aspects of the crew's well-being, including maintenance of the pressure suits and helmets, provision of food and drink, transportation to and from the aircraft, and medical support. The work was vital to ensure the safety of the crew in the event of an emergency at high altitude, where any depressurisation would result in blood 'boiling' in the veins.

Right: A front restraint strap was fitted to stop the aircrew's head being thrown back when the pressure suit inflated. The crew rode to the aircraft in a van fitted with reclining armchairs.

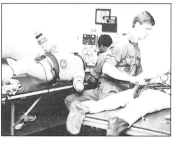

PSD technicians regularly checked the suits for leaks by inflating them. The main suit was protected by an outer orange cover.

A thorough medical preceded suiting up. The crew pre-breathed pure oxygen to purge any nitrogen from the bloodstream.

A vital check during suit-up was to ensure that the glove and helmet seals were secure. Note the helmet port for food and drink tubes.

An SR-71 lopes along over the California countryside after a refuelling. When the airframe is cold the wing tanks do not seal properly, so fuel leaks from various joints on the upper surface. When the aircraft is at maximum operational altitude and speed, the airframe heats up and expands, sealing the cracks.

Companion trainer

A large fleet of Northrop T-38A Talons was assigned to the 9th Strategic Reconnaissance Wing to act as companion trainers for the SR-71 force. The Talon provided low-cost flight hours for the crews, and its landing and subsonic handling characteristics proved to be a fair mimic of the SR-71. The Talons were also used on various chase duties, and later provided co-pilot flight hours for the KC-135 fleet.

Force, although it was tasked by national agencies to support a variety of theatre intelligence requirements. HQ SAC was hostile to Senior Crown because it diverted funds from its bomber and tanker mission. Although part of SAC's Single Integrated Operational Plan (SIOP), the SR-71 was not capable of gathering 'long on-station' samples of Sigint like the RC-135s and U-2Rs. The loss of its SAC patronage left Senior Crown increasingly isolated and vulnerable. To survive continued budgetary raids, it was apparent that the SR-71's utility had to be improved in order to become competitive with overhead systems.

In order to compete on a level playing field with satellites and other sensor platforms, the SR-71 needed updated sensors and, most importantly, it had to be equipped with an air-to-ground datalink system which would give it a 'near real-time capability'.

A new 'marketing package' was assembled which included details of the SR-71's performance and imagery capabilities. In the mid-1970s, Senior Crown advocates embarked on a public relations campaign within the Washington intelligence community to gather support for what

appeared to be a mortally wounded programme. Following an SR-71 briefing to intelligence officers of the Navy's Atlantic fleet, Bill Flexanher (an analyst at the Naval Intelligence Support Center at Suitland, Maryland) expressed an interest in the SR-71's sea-scanning radar capabilities to detect submarines in their home ports in the Baltic and Arctic areas. Flexenhar requested those areas to be 'SLAR-imaged' for his analysis.

A strong possibility existed that a new requirement could arise which would give Senior Crown a new lease of life. A call was made to the SAC reconnaissance centre for SR-71 missions over those areas, but at the time it was not possible. Instead, two missions were flown over the Soviet Pacific fleet near Vladivostok to test the concept. The results were impressive and another presentation was made to high-level naval and national intelligence officials.

Farnborough visit

As noted earlier, the first planned visit of an SR-71 to England was to have been 11 October 1973, during the Yom Kippur War. Instead, it was not until 9 September 1974 when Majors Jim Sullivan and Noel Widdifield in '972 established a new New York to London transatlantic speed record of less than two hours. Eighteen months later '972 returned as BURNS 31, and two aborted missions were flown in a bid to obtain SLAR imagery of the Soviet Northern Fleet. Due to abnormally warm weather conditions, fuel calculations made by the two RSOs during the missions showed that their fuel burn was so high that they would be unable to make their next ARCP. The 10-day deployment was an intelligence-gathering failure, but important lessons were learned about operating procedures in Arctic air masses.

Aircraft '962 arrived during Exercise Teamwork on 6 September 1976, and flew the very next day on a Barents Sea mission codenamed Coldfire 001. Majors Rich Graham and Don Emmons flew that and another round-robin sortie out of RAF Mildenhall, Suffolk, before returning '962 to Beale on 18 September. On 7 January 1977 SR-71A '958 arrived at Mildenhall as RING 21. It left at the end of a 10-day deployment as POWER 86. The same aircraft returned to 'the Hall' on 16 May as INDY 69, going back to Beale 15 days later as RESAY 35. The concept of using the SR-71's SLAR and camera systems 'to gather simultaneous, synoptic coverage' of the Soviet submarine fleet based on the Kolskiy Polustrov, in Murmansk and bases on the Baltic had been validated.

To fulfil the requirement it would be necessary to permanently base two SR-71s at Mildenhall. Such a move would reduce mission response times and be much more cost effective. A permanent operating location in Europe would require permission from Britain's Prime Minister and the Ministry of Defence, and would need close co-ordination with the US State Department and Congressional Intelligence Oversight Committee. More funding would be needed for new support facilities at Mildenhall (a maintenance complex, two single-aircraft hangars, added fuel storage and an engine run-up 'hush house'). Estimated cost was $14 million, which it was believed would be far too much for the necessary approval. Cost-cutting elements were therefore incorporated into the proposal, including recycled Beale hangers, a renovated mobile processing centre (MPC) and civilian contract maintenance. Such measures brought costs down to about $10 million. Missions were planned at a rate of 10 per month – the actual requirement was greater, but this was kept from SAC HQ, which would then have insisted upon a three-aircraft complement, which in turn would have escalated costs to a point that would have jeopardised the entire proposal. After some imaginative manoeuvring, the SR-71 programme element manager (PEM) at the Pentagon finally managed to steer the programme objective memorandum (POM) through the political minefield, and the POM leapt from 450th position in the order of priorities to seventh. Concurrence came in from all parties, and Senior Crown was alive and well to fulfil its new role from Mildenhall.

On 24 October, SR-71A '976 arrived at Mildenhall for a 23-day stint of TDY, returning to Beale on 16 November. During 1978, the same SR-71 was deployed on two occasions, first on 24 April for an 18-day stay and again on 16 October for 17 days. After nearly two years of these short TDY deployments, on 31 March 1979 Detachment 4 (Det 4) of the 9th SRW was activated at RAF Mildenhall to support U-2R and SR-71 operations.

Yemen

During the early spring of 1979, tensions between Saudi Arabia and the People's Republic of Yemen were strained to the point where the US intelligence community believed that the republic was on the brink of invading its northern neighbour. As a result, on the morning of Monday 12 March, Majors Rich Graham and Don Emmons deployed '972 from Beale to Det 4 in order to furnish decision makers with the necessary intelligence information. After two early morning ground aborts due to cloud cover over the 'collection area', a mission finally got underway. 'Buzz' Carpenter and his RSO John Murphy got airborne and headed for their ARCP off Land's End. Unfortunately, 'Buzz' suffered a violent attack of diarrhoea while on the tanker boom, but despite his discomfort he

At subsonic and low-sonic speeds the inlets of the J58 engines remained in the fully forward position, and the bypass doors were open. As the aircraft accelerated past Mach 1.6 the spikes began translating to the aft position, while the bypass doors were closed.

The last SR-71 loss was that of '974, seen here being pulled from the sea off the Philippine island of Luzon in 1989. The crew had ejected successfully.

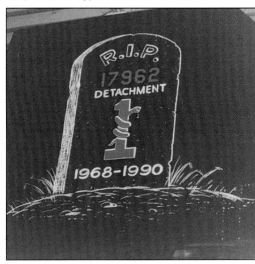

SR-71 operations came to an abrupt end in October 1989, although training continued for another month. '962 returned for the last time from Kadena wearing this tail art.

elected to continue the mission. Having convinced John that he now felt much better, they completed the full fuel off-load and accelerated due south.

Since they were unable to overfly France, it became necessary to skirt the Iberian peninsula. They therefore entered the Mediterranean Sea through the Straits of Gibraltar and completed a second refuelling before returning to high Mach flight. After overflying the Suez Canal, they descended for their third tanker rendezvous over the Red Sea. The planned double-loop coverage of the collection area was interrupted by the ANS, which tried to initiate a pre-programmed turn prior to reaching the correct

In February 1990, soon after the termination of SR-71 operations, Lockheed gathered together 11 surviving aircraft at Beale for a family photograph. At the rear of the group was the short-tailed SR-71C, which had been in storage for many years.

Above: The three SR-71s loaned to NASA pose on the Dryden facility ramp, with Rogers Dry Lake in the background. Steve Ishmael was the first NASA pilot to fly the aircraft in its second career with the Administration, and was checked out in the SR-71B on 1 July 1991 by USAF instructor pilot Rod Dyckman.

Right: Refuelling support for the NASA SR-71 operations is provided by the 412th Test Wing's fleet, in this case an NKC-135E. Beneath is the Edwards facility, the NASA complex being visible behind the ruddervators of the tanker's boom.

The SR-71B arrived at NASA Dryden on 25 July 1991 after a flight from Palmdale which completed Steve Ishmael's check-out. The next three flights allowed Ishmael to qualify Rogers Smith as the second NASA pilot. The first 19 NASA flights were accomplished using 831.

destination point (DP). Upon recognising the error, the crew flew the aeroplane manually while trying to work out what had caused the autonav 'glitch'. As a result of this miscue, they overshot the turn point but completed the rest of the route and made their way back to the tankers for another Red Sea top-up. A fifth air refuelling was completed east of Gibraltar, and an hour-and-a-half later they recovered '972 back to Mildenhall after a full 10-hour mission.

The mission had generated considerable interest within the 9th SRW as well as at SAC headquarters and in Washington. As a result, 'Buzz' and John were greeted by a large number of their colleagues as they stepped off the gantry, including Colonel Dave Young, the 9th SRW vice commander, who presented 'Buzz' with a brown SR-71 tie tack to commemorate the inflight incident when, to misquote a well known phrase, 'the world fell out of Buzz's bottom'.

When the 'take' was processed, it was of exceptional quality and the incident which had delayed their turn had yielded the most important information. That unexpected

success made additional flights to the area unnecessary. Consequently, Rich Graham and Don Emmons returned '972 to Beale on 28 March. Deployments continued to the Suffolk base throughout the early 1980s, the main 'collection areas' being the Barents and Baltic Seas in support of US Navy intelligence requirements.

On 9 July 1983, British aviation enthusiasts 'manning' the many off-base vantage points of Mildenhall noted the arrival of aircraft '962, an aircraft that had pulled TDY at the base on previous occasions. Majors Maury Rosenberg and Ed McKim had just completed a seven-hour operational flight from Beale to Mildenhall via the Barents/Baltic areas in the Palmdale flight test aircraft '955. The false serial number had been applied to ensure unwelcome attention was not drawn to the unique operational test deployment underway. In its detachable nose section, '955 was equipped with Loral's Advanced Synthetic Radar System (ASARS-1), a system that provided a quantum leap in radar resolution. With maritime data collected during the inbound flight, Majors B. C. Thomas and John Morgan conducted a 2.6-hour ASARS operational test sortie of land-based targets in East Germany nine days later. On 21 July, Maury and Ed took their turn on a four-hour mission. The final ASARS operational proving flight was conducted by B. C. and John on 30 July, when they flew '962 ('955) on a 7.3-hour flight back to Beale, again via the Baltic and Barents Seas. The series of tests was extremely successful, and following further tests back at Palmdale two production radar sets for the operational fleet were funded and deployed.

Watching the Gulf

The early 1980s also brought a resurgence of Islamic fundamentalism which was sparked off when Ayatollah Khomeini and his supporters declared Iran to be an Islamic

NASA operations

The SR-71 was retired in November 1989 amid much controversy. Six aircraft were earmarked for contingency purposes, of which three were loaned to NASA for continuing high-speed, high-altitude trials programmes, but they were theoretically available for USAF use if the need arose. The remaining three were placed in flyable storage. In the event NASA only flew two of its aircraft, using the type for a variety of experiments aimed chiefly at future supersonic airliner design and in aid of the X-30 NASP (National Aerospace Plane) programme before it was cancelled. Further trials will primarily be in support of the X-33 programme.

republic, a move that most Western intelligence sources agreed was very destabilising for the Middle East. During this period, SR-71s from Mildenhall occasionally ventured into the eastern Mediterranean to monitor the movements of various contraband supplied by sympathetic states to Islamic jihad soldiers and key terrorist leaders as their small executive support aircraft slipped from one tiny desert airstrip to another.

One such Middle Eastern SR-71 sortie took place on 27 July 1984 when, at 07.30, Majors 'Stormy' Boudreaux and Ted Ross departed Mildenhall in '979 using the callsign BOYCE 64. Due to French politicking with various Arab nations, France refused overflight transit access into the Mediterranean, which necessitated entry to the area via the Straits of Gibraltar. In addition, the flight was further complicated by inlet door and spike control problems which meant that 'Stormy' was forced to control the inlets and spikes manually. After two refuellings, and recycling all inlet switches, the 'glitch' refused to clear, but since by this time the crew had come so far, they reasoned they may as well press on. Flown in this configuration, the aircraft's emergency operating procedures dictated that performance should be limited to Mach 3 and 70,000 ft (21340 m). The mission called for a single high-speed, high-altitude pass over the target area, which the crew completed operating in the less fuel-efficient 'manual' inlet configuration.

Fuel problems

The run ended in a notably depleted fuel state. Ted urgently contacted the tankers which were orbiting near the island of Crete and asked that they head east to meet the thirsty 'Habu'. As BOYCE 64 descended, 'Stormy' caught sight of the tankers 30,000 ft (9145 m) below and

executed what he described loosely as "an extremely large variation of a barrel roll" and slid in behind the tankers "in no time flat." They stayed on the boom 12 to 15 minutes longer than normal in order to regain the pre-planned fuel disconnect point, and then cleared the tanker, accelerated and cruise-climbed back to Mildenhall. The flight, of nearly seven hours duration, produced a 'take' of exceptional quality as a result of a cold front which covered the eastern Mediterranean, the very clear air delivering 'razor sharp' photographic imagery. Det 4's commander, Colonel Jay Murphy, was especially proud of his crew's notable mission accomplishments, even though 'the book' dictated that words had to be spoken about flying a 'degraded' aircraft over a known Soviet SA-5 SAM site. However, like Jay, the National Photographic Interpretation Center (NPIC) in Washington was extremely pleased with this valuable 'take'.

Tension between the United States and much of the Arab world continued, and after a series of incidents President Reagan's patience came to an end. On 15 April 1986, Operation El Dorado Canyon was mounted, a co-ordinated strike on targets in Libya by air elements of the US Navy and 18 USAF F-111s from RAF Lakenheath. Lieutenant Colonels Jerry Glasser and Ron Tabor took off from

Above: 64-17980 is seen on the Dryden ramp shortly after its arrival. It shares the flight line with two Hornets.

Left: Four D-21 drones were recovered from Davis-Monthan AFB and delivered to NASA Dryden for possible use in a future high-speed research programme.

Below left: 844 is seen in 1996 being prepared with the LASRE (Linear Aerospike SR-71 Experiment), a dorsally mounted engine intended for the X-33 next-generation Space Shuttle.

Below: NASA's SR-71B was used to requalify Air Force pilots for the reborn 'Habu' programme.

The last records

The last round of SR-71 records was set on 6 March 1990 by Lt Col Ed Yeilding (pilot) and Lt Col Joseph T. Vida (RSO) while delivering 64-17972 to the National Air and Space Museum's Dulles facility. The records were all established for recognised city pairs and the all-important transcontinental flight. The times and speeds were as follows:

Coast to Coast (2,086 miles/3357 km). Time 1 hr 07 min 53.69 sec, average speed 2,124.5 mph (3418.9 km/h)
Los Angeles to Washington, DC (1,998 miles/3215 km). Time 1 hr 04 min 19.89 sec, average speed 2,144.83 mph (3451.67 km/h)
St Louis to Cincinnati (311.44 miles/501.20 km). Time 8 min 31.97 sec, average speed 2,189.94 mph (3524.27 km/h)
Kansas City to Washington, DC (942.08 miles/1516.08 km). Time 25 min 58.53 sec, average speed 2,176.08 mph (3501.96 km/h)

Right and top right: '972 arrives at Washington's Dulles airport after its coast-to-coast dash in March 1990. The St Louis to Cincinnati speed was only a few miles per hour short of the overall speed record set many years before. With the rebirth of the SR-71 programme, there is some unofficial desire to recapture the sustained altitude record lost to the MiG-29.

Right: Some idea of the size of the 'Habu' can be gained from this view of NASA's SR-71B refuelling from an NKC-135E during a test hop from Edwards. A key part of the requalification process for Air Force pilots was the practising of aerial refuelling, for which the KC-135T (re-engined KC-135Q) is now used.

Below: Resplendent in the dartboard badge of Det 4, 64-17980 arrives at Edwards. It was reserialled as 844 and used by NASA as Dryden's only flying SR-71A.

Mildenhall as scheduled at 05.00 in SR-71 '980 (callsign TROMP 30). Their mission was to secure photographic imagery for post-strike bomb damage assessment. To achieve this it would be necessary to overfly those targets hit earlier, but this time in broad daylight and with the sophisticated Libyan defence network on full alert. Such was the importance of the mission that SR-71A '960 (TROMP 31), flown by Majors Brian Shul and Walt Watson, launched at 06.15 as an airborne spare in case TROMP 30 aborted with platform or sensor problems. In the event, all aircraft systems, the two chine-mounted technical objective cameras (TEOCs) for spot coverage and the nose-mounted optical bar cameras (OBC) for horizon-to-horizon coverage worked as advertised aboard the primary aircraft, and '960 was not called upon to penetrate hostile airspace. Despite launches against '980, the SR-71 again proved that it could operate with impunity against such SAM threats, and at 09.35 TROMP 30 landed safely back at 'the Hall'. The mission's 'take' was processed in the MPC located in one of Mildenhall's disused hangers. It was then transported by a KC-135 (TROUT 99) to Andrews AFB, Maryland, where national-level officials were eagerly awaiting post-strike briefings.

Two more missions over Libya were conducted on 16 and 17 April, with minor route changes and different callsigns. This intense period of reconnaissance activity scored many new 'firsts' for Det 4: the first occasion that both aircraft were airborne simultaneously; the first time KC-10s had been used to refuel SR-71s in the European theatre; the first time that photos taken by the SR-71s were released to the media (although the source was never officially admitted and the image quality was purposely severely degraded to hide the true capability). All in all, the missions were a great accomplishment and reflected well on the detachment's support personnel under the command of former SR-71 RSO, Lieutenant Colonel Barry MacKean.

Shutdown

The Senior Crown programme was 'living on borrowed time' without an electro-optical backplate for the camera system and a datalink system which would permit camera imagery and radar data from ASARS-1 to be downlinked in near real time. Eventually, funds were appropriated for the development of Senior King, a secure datalink via satellite, but its development was too late to save the SR-71.

By the late 1980s the people articulating an anti-SR-71 posture were as wide and varied as they were powerful.

Dewain Andrews and Bob Fitch, serving on the Senate's House Permanent Select Committee on Intelligence (HPSCI), made the Senior Crown programme shutdown a personal crusade. Within the Air Force at that time, the main detractors were Chief of Staff General Larry Welch, AF/XO General Dougan, CinCSAC General John Chain, AF/Programme Requirements General Ron Fogleman, Chief of SAC Intelligence (SAC/IN) General Doyle, Colonel Tanner also of SAC/IN, and General Leo Smith of the Budget Review Board. As their assault got underway the main thrust of their argument orientated around cost and the marginal benefits of operating the SR-71 instead of satellites. In addition, the Pentagon contended that an air-breathing replacement was under development, and during a meeting on Capital Hill Welch testified (incorrectly) that the SR-71 had become vulnerable to SA-5s and SA-10s.

Stay of execution

By 1988 it looked as though the efforts of these people would be successful. But all was not quite lost: Admiral Lee Baggott, Commander in Chief, Atlantic (CinCLANT) required SR-71 coverage of the Kola peninsula because there were no other means of obtaining the quality of coverage required. He took the battle to retain the SR-71 in Europe right to the Joint Chiefs of Staff (JCS) and obtained funding for Det 4 for a another year. Meanwhile, the SR-71 PEM and his action officer were able to secure a commitment from a staffer on the Senate Appropriations Committee for $46 million to keep Kadena and Palmdale open for another year.

After that, however, the antagonists got their way. What was considered to be the final flight of an SR-71 took place on 6 March 1990, when Ed Yeilding and J. T. Vida flew '972 on a West to East Coast record-breaking flight of the United States, before landing at the Smithsonian National Aerospace Museum, Washington, DC, where the aircraft was handed over for permanent display. Thereafter, three SR-71As ('962, '967 and '968) were placed in storage at Site 2, Palmdale. Two SR-71As ('971 and '980), together with the sole surviving SR-71B ('956), were loaned to NASA. The remaining 13 aircraft (including the hybrid trainer designated SR-71C which consisted of the forward fuselage from a static specimen mated to the wing and rear section of YF-12A 60-6934) were donated to museums throughout the US, despite more than 40 members of Congress, and many other well-placed officials and senior officers, voicing their concern over the decision.

During the course of the Gulf War, two requests were made to reactivate the Senior Crown programme; both were turned down by the same SECDEF who had presided over the aircraft's shutdown – Dick Cheney. That Desert Storm was an overwhelming success for coalition forces is

Preserved aircraft

At the end of the Blackbird programme in 1989/90, the surviving aircraft (including the A-12s) not assigned to NASA or Air Force storage were put up for preservation, and there were many takers. By 1997 aircraft were on display at Palmdale (A-12, SR-71A and D-21), USS *Intrepid* in New York, Huntsville, Minneapolis, San Diego, USS *Alabama* at Mobile (A-12s), Los Angeles (A-12B), Seattle (M-21/D-21), Wright-Patterson AFB (SR-71A and YF-12A), Tucson, Edwards AFB, Robins AFB, Eglin AFB, Castle AFB, Chicago, Beale AFB, Offutt AFB, Dulles Airport, March AFB, Lackland AFB (SR-71As) and Hill AFB (SR-71C).

Above: One of the best preserved aircraft is A-12 '931, which resides at Minneapolis. Thanks to the efforts of the Minnesota ANG, and Crew Chief James C. Goodall, the aircraft is in immaculate condition. It wears the all-black scheme and spurious serials it would have carried when it was part of the 1129th SAS Det 1 Black Shield operation at Kadena.

A-12 '933 is now on display outside the San Diego Aerospace Museum.

For many years the surviving A-12s were shoehorned into a hangar at Palmdale.

YF-12A '935 was delivered to the USAF Museum on 7 November 1979.

The Blackbird Air Park at Palmdale has an A-12, SR-71A and D-21 drone on display.

64-17975 is now at March AFB, where it has joined a U-2C in the museum.

Beale's SR-71A, 64-17963, is on special display below the tower.

Above: Devoid of markings, one of the two SR-71As reactivated for the Air Force is seen undertaking an engine run at Palmdale during its final checks before taking to the air again.

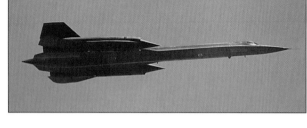

Right: The reborn SR-71 made its first major public appearance at the celebrations of the USAF's 50th anniversary, held at Nellis AFB in April 1997. One of the aircraft was on static display while the other flew in from Edwards for a couple of passes. Note the small radome housing the data downlink antenna on the underside of the fuselage.

The two SR-71As back in USAF service wear tactical-style tailcodes and serial presentations. The badge is that of Air Combat Command, while the tailstripe belongs to the 9th Reconnaissance Wing.

beyond dispute. However, there were lessons to be learned from the 41-day campaign, not least of which was the lack of timely reconnaissance material available to General Schwarzkopf's field commanders.

Renaissance

It was not until March/April 1994 that events in the international arena once more took a turn. Relations between North Korea and the United States, at best always strained, reached a new low over the north's refusal to allow inspection of their nuclear sites. At this point Senator Robert Byrd took centre stage. Together with several members of the Armed Services, and various members of Congress, he contended that in 1990 the Pentagon had consistently lied about the supposed readiness of a replacement for the SR-71. The motivation behind such commitments was not the usual politicking, but one of genuine concern for the maintenance of a platform capable of broad area synoptic coverage.

The campaigning and lobbying paid off, as noted in the Department of Defense Appropriations Bill 1995, report 103-321 dated 20 July, wherein provision was made for a modest, "three-plane SR-71 aircraft contingency reconnaissance capability," at a cost of $100 million, for FY95. Of the three SR-71As placed in deep storage at Site 2, Palmdale, only '967 was called to arms. The other A model to be recommissioned was '971, which had been loaned to NASA, renumbered 832 and regularly ground tested but never flown by its civilian caretakers. Pilot trainer SR-71B, together with the brand new flight simulator, would be shared between the Air Force and NASA, and in a further

Det 2 – Edwards

The reborn SR-71 programme is now based at Edwards AFB, residing in buildings at the north end of the main AFFTC complex. This location is close to the NASA Dryden facility. Two aircraft ('967 and '971) are on charge.

move to keep operating costs to a minimum the new detachment, designated Det 2, would, like NASA, operate its aircraft from Edwards AFB, California. Det 2's commander is a former 'Habu' RSO, Colonel Stan Gudmundson; overall command and control is still via the 9th RW at Beale AFB.

Aircraft reactivation began on 5 January 1995 with a fuel leak evaluation of '967. Seven days later, at 11.26, NASA crew Steve Ishmael and Marta Bohn-Meyer got airborne from Edwards in '971 on a 26-minute ferry flight which terminated at Lockheed Martin's Skunk Works, Plant 10 Building 602, Palmdale. Over the next three months ASARS and other sensors previously in storage at Luke AFB, Arizona were installed. At 10.18 on 26 April, NASA crew Ed Schneider and Marta Bohn-Meyer completed a 34-minute FCF in '971. A month later Ed, and Marta's husband Bob Meyer, conducted '971's second and final FCF which lasted 2.5 hours. It took seven more FCFs to wring out all the 'glitches' in '967, the final one of which was successfully completed on 12 January 1996.

Three Air Force crews were selected to fly the aircraft: pilots Gil Luloff, Tom McCleary and Don Watkins, together with RSOs Blair Bozek, Mike Finan and Jim Greenwood. The plan was that two crews would always be mission ready qualified and the third crew would be mission capable. While crew proficiency training got underway in the simulator and the B model, R&D funds were used to develop and install the long overdue datalink, the antenna for which is housed in a small radome just forward of the front undercarriage wheel well. A digital cassette recorder system (DCRsi) provides recording and playback of both Elint and ASARS data. Near real time data can be provided if the aircraft is within 300 nm (345 miles; 555 km) line-of-sight range of a receiving station; if not, the entire recorded collection can be downloaded in 10 minutes once within station range.

Budgetary battles

As qualified Air Force crews began to acquaint themselves with their operational aircraft, a long-running battle between the various factions supporting or not supporting the resurrected programme came to a head. Exploiting a complex technical loophole in the legislation concerning the deployment of funds which had been appropriated by the Senate Appropriations Committee in the FY 1996 Defense Appropriations Bill, but not authorised in two other pieces of supporting legislation, it was decided that technically it was illegal to operate the SR-71. Consequently, at 23:00 (Z) on 16 April 1996 a signal was despatched from the Pentagon suspending SR-71 operations with immediate effect. The war between various Senate committees then went into overdrive, when protagonists of the SR-71 programme serving on the Senate Appropriations Committee threatened to eliminate section 8080 of the Appropriations Act and defeat the Intelligence

Authorization Act for FY97. This would effectively ensure that all intelligence activities for FY97 would grind to a halt – one can imagine the sheer panic this action would produce in USAF, DIA, CIA and NSA circles!

Perhaps not surprisingly, the tactic worked. Of the $253 billion defence budget for 1997, $30 million has been allocated for SR-71 operations and maintenance and another $9 million for procurement. This outlay has been ratified and signed off by the President. The three flight crews are once again up to full proficiency and the ASARS-1 datalink is now working extremely well. The next major sensor enhancement will take place with the deployment of an electro-optical backplane for the TEOCs. These units, being developed by Recon Optical, located in Barrington, Illinois, will replace film and instead facilitate the focused high-quality, close-lock image, to be transmitted via the datalink in real time, directly to theatre commanders.

Replacement questions

It is now known that the widely speculated 'platform', supposedly named Aurora, was nothing more than uninformed hype and fiction that had its origins in a classified budget line item, used to hide funds for the maniacally expensive B-2 programme. The proposed replacement for the SR-71 was not a 'warp speed'-capable stealth platform (many aviation journalists fail to appreciate the ramifications of supersonic or hypersonic speed when applied to a 'stealth' platform), but a subsonic, highly stealthy unmanned aerial vehicle (UAV). Built by Lockheed Martin/Boeing, the highly classified (and highly expensive) Tier 3 became a victim of budget constraints born from the peace dividend that followed the end of the Cold War. In its place the cheaper, Tier 3 Minus (Darkstar) and the Tier 2 Plus (Global Hawk) UAVs are in competition to be selected as a possible/probable replacement for the SR-71.

The world in which the SR-71 was conceived has thankfully changed dramatically, but the need for reconnaissance and intelligence gathering remains. We have seen how satellite doctrine upheld in certain influential circles of the intelligence community evolved into entrenched satellite dogma; we have also seen the short-sightedness of such policies. Could UAVs be going the same way? Surely what is needed is a mutually inclusive approach to the development of the airborne reconnaissance-gathering triad – satellites, UAVs and aircraft – as each brings its own unique capabilities. **Paul F. Crickmore**

A-12/SR-71 operators

Central Intelligence Agency
1129th Special Activities Squadron

This unit was established at Groom Dry Lake, Nevada, to operate the A-12 Cygnus aircraft. The base had an Air Force commander and director of flight operations, although the CIA was technically in charge of the Oxcart programme. Personnel from both government organisations, together with Skunk Works staff, worked side-by-side to

bring the A-12 into operational service. In addition to the A-12 and A-12B, the Groom Lake operation also flew the McDonnell F-101 Voodoo as a trainer, T-33s, U-3s and helicopters for utility work, a C-130 as a transport and an F-104 for high-speed chase. Refuelling support was provided by the 903rd ARS of the 456th Bomb Wing, detached from Beale AFB. The Oxcart

squadron was declared operational on 20 November 1965, with four aircraft ready for deployment to Kadena.

After a considerable wait, the orders to deploy came on 17 May 1967. The first aircraft flew to Kadena on 22 May, followed by two more, and all three were declared operational on 29 May. The first of 29 operational sorties was flown on 31 May 1967, and the last on 8 May 1968. The decision to end the det's Black Shield operation was reaffirmed on 16 May, and the aircraft began returning on 9 June, for storage at Palmdale. The final flight, and the end of the 1129th SAS, occurred on 21 June 1968 when aircraft 131 was ferried from Groom Lake to Palmdale.

4200th Strategic Reconnaissance Wing

The 4200th SRW was established at Beale AFB on 1 January 1965 to prepare for SR-71 operations, the first T-38A companion trainer arriving at the California base in July 1965. On 6 January 1966 the 4200th SRW

received its first Blackbird in the form of the trainer '956. The first operational aircraft arrived on 4 April 1966. Soon after, on 25 June 1966, the 4200th inherited the heritage and numberplate of the 9th Bomb

Wing, becoming the 9th Strategic Reconnaissance Wing.
The number was then assigned to the 4200th Test Wing, still at Beale, which became the unit responsible for testing and

employing the D-21B drone, using two B-52Hs as mother ships. This programme began in late 1966. The first launch was not undertaken until 6 November 1968, at which time the 4200th TW was flying from Groom Lake. Later launches took place from Beale, and the programme was terminated on 23 July 1971.

9th Strategic Reconnaissance Wing
1st and 99th Strategic Reconnaissance Squadrons

One of the premier bomber wings in the USAF, the 9th BW had been based at Mountain Home AFB, Idaho, operating B-47s, KC-97s and controlling a Titan missile complex. Bomber/missile operations were run down during the first half of 1966 pending the numberplate being assigned to the 4200th SRW, the SR-71 unit at Beale. The formal activation of the 9th SRW occurred on 25 June 1966.
Training and tactical development occupied the wing for the first months, and it was declared fully operational in December 1968. The wing was arranged into two flying squadrons, the 1st and 99th

Strategic Reconnaissance Squadrons. Both numberplates had been long associated with the 9th BW. Initially it was decreed that each squadron would have eight SR-71As and one SR-71B. The SR-71 reconnaissance effort was never as great as had originally been envisaged, and could easily be accomplished by one flying squadron. Accordingly, the 99th SRS 'Red Buffaloes' was deactivated on 1 April 1971.
Throughout the early period tanker support for the SR-71 was provided by the KC-135Qs of the 9th and 903rd ARS, 456th BW. The 456th BW was inactivated on 30 September 1975, the two tanker squadrons being then directly assigned to the 9th SRW. On 1 July 1976 Strategic Air Command formalised the consolidation of its high-altitude strategic reconnaissance assets when the U-2Rs of the 100th SRW became part of the 9th. The old U-2 wing number and two of its squadron numbers were reassigned to the KC-135Qs, which became the 349th and 350th ARS of the 100th ARW. The U-2Rs had already been using the 99th SRS number since 1972, and continued to do so after the amalgamation with the SR-71 force. Later the 9th SRW established the 4029th SRTS (renumbered 5th SRTS) as the U-2 training unit.
In addition to the ongoing training tasks, which utilised the standard SR-71As, SR-71B/C trainers and T-38s, the wing headquarters was also tasked with important reconnaissance missions as well as supporting the overseas deployments.

An SR-71A launches from Beale for a night mission. Most Beale sorties were for training, but the base was also used for operational sorties, notably those over Central America and the Caribbean.

The first major Beale-led missions were to the Middle East (using Griffiss AFB and Seymour Johnson AFB) in 1973/74. Other operational sorties launched from Beale went to Cuba, Nicaragua and occasionally to Europe.
Operational flying was ended on 1 October 1989, although training flights continued until 22 November 1989. The retirement ceremony for the SR-71 was held at Beale on 26 January 1990.

Kadena detachment (OL-8, OL-RK, OL-KA, Det 1)

Glowing Heat deployments to Kadena, Okinawa (known as the 'Rock') were first undertaken in March 1968, and for a while the SR-71 crews were co-based with their 'grey-suit' colleagues from 'the Agency'. The SR-71 detachment was known as OL (Operating Location) -8, and was declared

operationally ready with three aircraft on 15 March 1968. It flew its first combat mission on 21 March 1968. In early 1970, as the need for reconnaissance grew, the detachment was enlarged to four aircraft. On 30 October 1970 it was redesignated OL-RK (for Ryukyus, the island chain in

which Okinawa was situated) and on 26 October 1971 became OL-KA (for Kadena).
A high level of activity was maintained through the last months of the war in Southeast Asia, although with the end of the war the detachment was reduced in size to two aircraft. On 1 August 1974 OL-KA was redesignated as Detachment 1 of the 9th SRW. Reconnaissance missions in

the post-war years were naturally aimed at the Soviet Far East, China, North Korea and Vietnam, although Det 1 was tasked with marathon flights over the Persian Gulf during the Iran/Iraq war. All operations ceased on 22 November 1989 and the two aircraft were returned to Beale.

SR-71 patches changed with rapidity at the Kadena detachment in the early 1970s. The Habu pit viper remained a constant motif.

64-17968 taxis for a mission at Kadena in the early 1970s. In the background are civil airliners used on trooping flights.

Mildenhall detachment (Det 4)

An SR-71 was first deployed to Mildenhall for operations in Europe in early 1976. The UK government stipulated that these early deployments should be no longer than 20 days and required UK permission for each sortie. However, the deployments gradually became more frequent and the aircraft stayed longer. In March 1979 Mildenhall was the operating location for a Yemen reconnaissance flight. Detachment 4 of the 9th SRW was established in April 1979 with a single U-2R employed in Europe on Senior

Ruby Elint missions, and continued to support the periodic SR-71 visits. In 1981 Mildenhall was used for monitoring the situation in Poland.

By late 1982 the demands in Europe resulted in a second aircraft arriving at Mildenhall, while in July 1983 the base played host to the first operational test of an

ASARS-equipped aircraft. By this time Det 4 had ceased U-2R operations, which had been transferred to the newly-established 17th Reconnaissance Wing (with TR-1As) at Alconbury. Finally, on 5 April 1984, Prime Minister Margaret Thatcher announced that Det 4 would be a permanent SR-71 detachment with two aircraft, with some UK control remaining for the more sensitive sorties.

The two-aircraft detachment ceased operations on 22 November 1989, and the last aircraft left for Beale on 18 January 1990.

Det 4 usually mounted three sorties each week, covering the German border, Baltic coastline and the Kola Peninsula. The latter was home to the Soviet Northern Fleet.

9th Reconnaissance Wing

Detachment 2

Following the retirement of the SR-71, the 9th SRW continued its U-2R operations, and in June 1991 took over the UK operations at Alconbury from the 17th RW, shortly before the wing dropped the 'Strategic' from its designation. At Beale the 5th SRTS adopted the old SR-71 squadron number (in July 1990) to become the 1st Reconnaissance

Squadron (Training).

In October 1994 Congress directed the US Air Force to reactivate three SR-71s, utilising two aircraft which had been put into flyable storage at Palmdale, and one which had been loaned to NASA. The first

rework was completed by Lockheed in mid-1995. Further political debates have resulted in considerable delays to the SR-71 reactivation, and a drop to two aircraft. The USAF SR-71 operation is now conducted from a location at Edwards AFB, next door to the NASA SR-71s and conveniently close to the Skunk Works facility at Palmdale. The unit is administered

from Beale and is known as Detachment 2 of the 9th Reconnaissance Wing. The previous Det 2, a U-2 detachment at Osan, South Korea, was raised to squadron status (5th RS) in 1994.

Seen at Edwards in late 1996 is one of Det 2's SR-71s, alongside a black-painted T-38 used for training.

Test units

Various units have operated Blackbirds for test purposes. Test work from Edwards AFB was accomplished by the 4786th Test Squadron, which was formed on 1 June 1965. At Palmdale an Advanced Systems Project Office was established to function as an acceptance test centre. After initial manufacturer test flights, the ASPO took the aircraft and performed an exhaustive series of FCFs (functional test flights) before delivering the aircraft to Beale. Following the final delivery, the ASPO became heavily involved in all forms of testing for the SR-71 fleet. Initially the first six aircraft from the line were assigned to test purposes, but following transfers and

losses only one ('955) remained. This became the dedicated test aircraft until retired in 1985, being flown on joint Skunk Works/US Air Force test programmes.

On 31 December 1970 the Palmdale trials task was handed over from Air Force Systems Command to Air Force Logistics Command, which established Det 51 to perform the task. In September 1977 this unit became Det 6, 2762nd Logistics Squadron. A detachment at Norton AFB looked after the spares and logistics supply for the fleet. Det 6 operated right to the end of the SR-71 programme, using '972 as its dedicated test airframe in the late 1980s. The unit's last flying task was to fly the aircraft to Dulles on 6 March 1990, the last flight by an SR-71 before reactivation.

NASA

Operating from the Dryden Flight Research facility at Edwards AFB, NASA has enjoyed two spells operating the Blackbird. From 1969 to 1979 a single YF-12A was flown on a wide variety of high-speed trials, augmented by another YF-12A from 1969-71 and an SR-71A (rechristened YF-12C) from 1971 to 1978.

At the end of the USAF SR-71 programme, NASA elected to restart high-speed research programmes using an

SR-71A and an SR-71B. A third aircraft was assigned, although it never flew with NASA and was later reactivated by the US Air Force. The NASA SR-71B proved of great

value for requalifying USAF pilots, while the SR-71A is assigned to test programmes in support of the X-33 next-generation Space Shuttle.

As part of its future supersonic airliner trials programme, NASA used an F-16XL to measure sonic booms from the SR-71A 844.

Individual aircraft details

Lockheed A-12

60-6924/121
First flight 26 April 1962. Prototype A-12. Towed from Plant 42, Palmdale storage area to Blackbird Air Park display area, Palmdale

60-6925/122
Used for ground tests prior to first flight. Transported from Plant 42, Palmdale to USS *Intrepid*, New York for display. Due to vandalism the aircraft is to be repaired by Lockheed and moved for display at CIA HQ, Langley, Virginia

60-6926/123
First flight 24 May 1963. Second A-12 to fly. Lost during training/test flight after aircraft stalled due to inaccurate data being displayed to pilot. Pilot Ken Collins ejected safely

60-6927/124
Only two-seat pilot trainer. To be trucked to California Museum of Science, Los Angeles for display

60-6928/125
Last flight 5 January 1967. Lost during training/test flight. Pilot Walter L. Ray successfully ejected but was killed after he failed to separate from his ejection seat

60-6929/126
Lost seconds after take-off from Groom Dry Lake following incorrect installation of SAS. Pilot Mele Vojvodich ejected safely

60-6930/127
Deployed to Kadena from 24 May 1967 to June 1968 in support of Operation Black Shield. Was stored at Plant 42, Palmdale. Trucked to Space and Rocket Center Museum, Huntsville, Alabama for display

60-6931/128
Was stored at Plant 42, Palmdale. Transported by C-5 on 27 October 1991 to Minnesota Air National Guard, Minneapolis, for display

60-6932/129
Last flight 5 June 1968. Deployed to Kadena from 26 May 1967 in support of Operation Black Shield. Lost off the Philippines during an FCF prior to its scheduled return to the USA. Pilot Jack Weeks was killed

60-6933/130
First flight 27 November 1963. Last flight August 1965. Was stored at Plant 42, Palmdale. Trucked to San Diego Aerospace Museum, California for display

60-6937/131
Deployed to Kadena from 22 May 1967 to June 1968 in support of Operation Black Shield. Was stored at Plant 42, Palmdale. Disposition to be determined

60-6938/132
Was stored at Plant 42, Palmdale. Trucked to USS *Alabama*, located at Mobile, Alabama for display

60-6939/133
Last flight 9 July 1964. Lost while on approach to Groom Dry Lake during test flight due to complete hydraulic failure. Lockheed test pilot Bill Park ejected safely

60-6940/134
One of two A-12s converted for Project Tagboard as carrier for D-21 drones. Trucked to the Museum of Flight, Seattle, Washington for display

During the Oxcart programme all of the A-12s flew from Groom Dry Lake, the secret test location in Nevada. Twelve aircraft were completed as standard A-12s, one was diverted to be the only two-seat trainer, while the final two were completed with a second cockpit for a launch systems officer for the D-21 drone. This group is joined by two of the YF-12As at the far end.

60-6941/135
Last flight 30 July 1966. One of two A-12s converted for Project Tagboard as D-21 drone carrier. Lost during tests off the coast of California. Pilot Bill Park and launch control officer Ray Torick, both Lockheed employees, ejected safely. However, Ray Torick was tragically drowned in the subsequent feet-wet landing

Lockheed YF-12A

Above: YF-12A 60-6934 at Edwards AFB

Right: YF-12A 60-6936, flying from Edwards

60-6934/1001
First flight 8 August 1963. Last flight (as YF-12) 14 August 1966. Prototype YF-12A was used by Colonel Robert L. Stephens and his fire control officer Lieutenant Colonel Daniel Andre to establish new speed and altitude records. Due to technical problems the actual records were set by '936. Aircraft was subsequently transformed into SR-71C 64-17981

Below: YF-12A 60-6935 in NASA service

60-6935/1002
First flight 26 November 1963. Last flight 7 November 1979. After initial YF-12 test programme the aircraft was placed in storage at Edwards AFB, California. It was later made available to NASA and flew again on 11 December 1969. On completion of NASA test programme it was delivered by air to the USAF Museum at Wright-Patterson AFB, Ohio for display

60-6936/1003
First flight 13 March 1964. Last flight 24 July 1971. This aircraft was used to obtain all absolute world speed and altitude records on 1 May 1965. After a brief period of retirement the aircraft was made available to a joint Air Force/NASA/ADP test programme but was lost on 24 June 1971. Lieutenant Colonel Jack Layton and Major Billy Curtis ejected safely

Lockheed SR-71

64-17950/2001
First flight 23 December 1964. Last flight 10 January 1967. First prototype SR-71A. Lost during anti-skid brake system evaluation at Edwards AFB, California. Pilot Art Peterson survived.

64-17951/2002
First flight 5 March 1965. Last flight 22 December 1978. Operated by NASA from 16 July 1971 and known as YF-12C, serialled 60-6937. Removed from Palmdale storage and trucked to Pima Air and Space Museum, Tucson, Arizona for display

64-17952/2003
First flight 24 March 1965. Last flight 25 January 1966. Lost during test flight from Edwards AFB, California. Pilot Bill Weaver survived but RSO Jim Zwayer was killed. Incident occurred near Tucumcari, New Mexico

64-17953/2004
First flight 4 June 1965. Last flight 18 December 1969. Lost during test flight from Edwards AFB, California. Pilot Lieutenant Colonel Joe Rogers and RSO Lieutenant Colonel Gary Heidelbaugh ejected safely. Incident occurred near Shoshone, California

64-17954/2005
First flight 20 July 1965. Last flight 11 April 1969. Lost on runway at Edwards AFB, California during take-off. Pilot Lieutenant Colonel Bill Skliar and RSO Major Noel Warner escaped without injury

64-17955/2006
First flight 17 August 1965. Last flight 24 January 1985. Operated extensively by Air Force Logistics Command from Plant 42, Palmdale as the dedicated SR-71 test aircraft. This aircraft is on display at Edwards AFB, California

64-17956/2007
First flight 18 November 1965. Still flying 1997. One of two SR-71B dual-control pilot trainers. In 1997 was still on loan to NASA at the Ames Research Center, Hugh L. Dryden Research facility, Edwards AFB and used to train both NASA and USAF crews. Reserialled NASA 831

64-17957/2008
First flight 18 December 1965. Last flight 11 January 1968. One of two SR-71B dual-control pilot trainers. It was lost following fuel cavitation while on approach to Beale AFB, California. Instructor pilot Lieutenant Colonel Robert G. Sowers and student Captain David E. Fruehauf ejected safely

64-17958/2009
First flight 15 December 1965. Last flight 23 February 1990. Used on 27/28 July 1979 by Captain Eldon W. Joersz and RSO Major George T. Morgan Jr to establish speed run over 12/25-km course of 2,193.167 mph. Flown to Robins AFB, Georgia for display

64-17959/2010
First flight 19 January 1966. Last flight 29 October 1976. Underwent 'Big Tail' modification to increase and enhance sensor capacity/capability. Trucked to Air Force Armament Museum, Eglin AFB, Florida for display

64-17950, SR-71A prototype

SR-71A 64-17951 in NASA service, serialled '06937' and designated YF-12C

64-17952, wearing calibration markings

64-17953, lost on 10 January 1967

64-17954, lost on 11 April 1969

64-17955, Palmdale test aircraft

SR-71B 64-17956, later NASA 831

Wreckage of SR-71B 64-17957, 11 January 1968

64-17958 during speed/altitude record attempts

SR-71A(BT) 64-17959 'Big Tail' at Palmdale

Lockheed's Blackbirds

64-17960/2011
First flight 9 February 1966. Last flight 27 February 1990. This aircraft flew 342 operational missions, more than any other SR-71. Flown to Castle AFB Museum, California for display

64-17961/2012
First flight 13 April 1966. Last flight 2 February 1977. This aircraft was delivered to Chicago, Illinois for display

64-17962/2013
First flight 29 April 1966. Last flight 14 February 1990. Although no funds available for upkeep, this is one of two aircraft in storage at Site 2, Palmdale and still owned by the USAF

64-17963/2014
First flight 9 June 1966. Last flight 28 October 1976. Towed to current display area at Beale AFB, California

64-17964/2015
First flight 11 May 1966. Last flight 20 March 1990. Flown to Offutt AFB, Nebraska for display

64-17965/2016
First flight 10 June 1966. Last flight 25 October 1976. Lost during night training sortie following INS platform failure. Pilot St Martin and RSO Carnochan ejected safely. Incident occurred near Lovelock, Nevada

64-17966/2017
First flight 1 July 1966. Last flight 13 April 1967. Lost after night refuelling in a subsonic high-speed stall. Pilot Boone and RSO Sheffield both ejected safely. Incident occurred near Las Vegas, New Mexico

64-17967/2018
First flight 3 August 1966. Last flight 14 February 1990. Reactivated and overhauled for use by 9th RW Det 2 at Edwards AFB

64-17968/2019
First flight 3 August 1966. Still flying. Held in storage at Site 2, Palmdale after last flight 12 February 1990. Although no funds available for upkeep, this is one of two aircraft held in storage at Site 2, Palmdale, and is still owned by the USAF

64-17969/2020
First flight 18 October 1966. Last flight 10 May 1970. Lost after refuelling in subsonic high-speed stall. Pilot Lawson and RSO Martinez ejected safely. Incident occurred near Korat RTAFB, Thailand

64-17970/2021
First flight 21 October 1966. Last flight 17 June 1970. Lost following mid-air collision with KC-135Q tanker. Tanker able to limp back to Beale AFB, Pilot Buddy Brown and RSO Mort Jarvis both ejected safely. Incident occurred 20 miles east of El Paso, New Mexico

64-17960 at 1986 Mildenhall air show

64-17961, now on display in Chicago

64-17962 during speed/altitude record attempt

64-17963, now on display at Beale AFB

Below: 64-17964 marked as The Bodonian Express

64-17968, currently stored at Palmdale

64-17965 with T-33A before its loss in October 1976

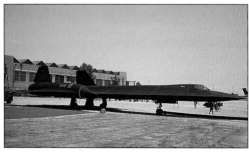

64-17967, Det 4 Mildenhall. Aircraft later resurrected for use by Det 2, 9th Reconnaissance Wing at Edwards AFB

Right: 64-17969, lost on 10 May 1970 over Thailand

64-17970, on display with other Beale aircraft

64-17971/2022
First flight 17 November 1966. Still flying. One of two SR-71As loaned to NASA at Edwards AFB although the aircraft was not used. Reclaimed by USAF for service with 9th RW Det 2 at Edwards AFB

64-17972/2023
First flight 12 December 1966. Last flight 6 March 1990. Flown on 1 September 1974 by Major James Sullivan and RSO Major Noel Widdifield from New York to London in record time of 1 hour 54 minutes 56.4 seconds. Flown on 6 March 1990 by Lieutenant Colonel Ed Yielding and RSO Lieutenant Colonel Joseph T. Vida from Los Angeles to Washington, DC in 1 hour 4 minutes 20 seconds. West to East Coast record set at 1 hour 7 minutes 54 seconds. On display at Smithsonian Institute, Dulles Airport

64-17973/2024
First flight 8 February 1967. Last flight 21 July 1987. Damaged while being demonstrated at RAF Mildenhall by Major Jim Jiggens. Aircraft was placed on display at Blackbird Air Park, Palmdale

64-17974/2025
First flight 16 February 1967. Last flight 21 April 1989. One of three aircraft used on first operational deployment to Kadena AB, Okinawa. Lost in 1989 while outbound from Kadena on an operational sortie following engine explosion and complete hydraulic failure. Pilot Major Dan E. House and RSO Captain Blair L. Bozek both ejected safely

64-17975/2026
First flight 13 April 1967. Last flight 28 February 1990. Flown from Beale AFB to March AFB, California for display

64-17976/2027
First flight May 1967. Last flight 27 March 1990. One of three aircraft used on the first operational deployment to Kadena AB, Okinawa. Flown by Major Jerome F. O'Malley and RSO Captain Edwards D. Payne on 9 March 1968 on the first operational SR-71 sortie. Flown to the US Air Force Museum, Wright-Patterson AFB, Ohio for display

64-17977/2028
First flight 6 January 1967. Last flight 10 October 1968. Lost at the end of Beale runway following a wheel explosion and runway abort. Pilot Major Gabriel A. Kardong rode the aircraft to a standstill, RSO Captain James A. Kogler ejected - both survived

64-17978/2029
First flight 5 July 1967. Last flight 20 July 1972. One of three aircraft used on first operational deployment to Kadena AB, Okinawa. Lost after a landing accident at Kadena. Pilot Captain Dennis K. Bush and RSO Jimmy Fagg both escaped unhurt

64-17979/2030
First flight 10 August 1967. Last flight 6 March 1990. This aircraft flew the first three of nine sorties from the eastern seaboard of the USA to the Middle East during the 1973 Yom Kippur War. Flown to Lackland AFB, Texas for display

64-17980/2031
First flight 25 September 1967. Still flying. Following last USAF flight on 5 February 1990 was one of two SR-71As loaned to NASA and flown from the Ames Research Center, Hugh L. Dryden Research Facility at Edwards AFB. Reserialled NASA 844

64-17981/2000
First flight 14 March 1969. Last flight 11 April 1976. Designated SR-71C, this hybrid dual-control aircraft combined the wing and rear section of YF-12A 60-6934 with a static test forward fuselage. After long period in storage at Beale was trucked to Hill AFB, Utah for display

64-17979, about to launch from Mildenhall

Below: 64-17980 landing at Det 4, Mildenhall

64-17971 at Det 4, Mildenhall

64-17972, Palmdale test aircraft

64-17973, now on display at Palmdale

64-17974, previously named Ichi Ban

64-17975 at the Alconbury air show, 1984

64-17976 with 9th SRW badge

64-17977 after a wheel explosion at Beale

64-17978, Rapid Rabbit

Below: 64-17981, the sole SR-71C

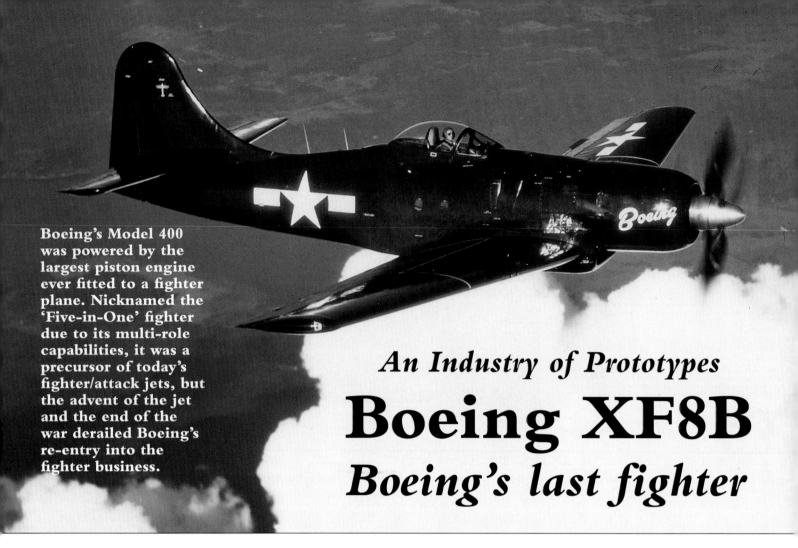

Boeing's Model 400 was powered by the largest piston engine ever fitted to a fighter plane. Nicknamed the 'Five-in-One' fighter due to its multi-role capabilities, it was a precursor of today's fighter/attack jets, but the advent of the jet and the end of the war derailed Boeing's re-entry into the fighter business.

An Industry of Prototypes

Boeing XF8B
Boeing's last fighter

In December 1945, the Boeing Airplane Company in Seattle, Washington was finally allowed to show off an aircraft it had been flying for a year. The aircraft was the Boeing Model 400, designated XF8B-1 by the US Navy and belatedly dressed in the Navy's gloss sea blue paint scheme.

While newsreel photographers aimed their cameras – one shooting from the roof of a car – test pilot Bob Lamson posed in front of the XF8B-1, strapped in, and demonstrated the aircraft at low altitude over Boeing Field, flying at less than 50 ft (15 m) above the runway. Boeing's company newspaper celebrated the removal of "shrouds of secrecy" from the XF8B-1 and noted that it was "as fast or faster than any other ship in the armed forces."

The paper also reported that Lamson put the "little ship" through its paces for the press. The XF8B-1 was 'little' only by the standards of a company that was turning out enormous four-engined bombers. The XF8B-1 was conceived as a powerful, multi-purpose, carrier-based warplane; for a single-seater, it was colossal. With a wing span of 54 ft (16.44 m) and a gross weight of 20,508 lb (9302 kg), it was less a fighter than a bomber (replete with an internal weapons bay) and was built to a requirement similar to the Martin BTM-1 (AM-1 Mauler), Curtiss XBTC-2 and Douglas BT2D-1 (AD Skyraider): for long-range strikes against Japan. The XF8B-1 also had much in common with the Army's XP-72 fighter being developed by Republic Aviation in Farmingdale, Long Island.

Unfortunately, by the time of its debut in

Pictured at Boeing Field in December 1944 is the first XF8B-1, BuNo. 57984. Markings were minimal, restricted to national insignia, some warning stencils and tiny model designator BuNo., and 'Navy' on the fin and rudder. This aircraft is parked in front of the old UAL hangar, camouflaged as an office building.

front of newsreel cameras, the Boeing XF8B-1 fighter was past any prospect for production or squadron service. The surrender of Japan removed its original purpose, which had been to fly long-range missions in the invasion of the Japanese homeland. There were other good reasons to build the XF8B-1 – in many respects, it was what the United States needed, and did not have, in Korea five years later – but there existed a stronger reason not to. Boeing was the principal builder of the big jet bombers. With the post-war era turning into the Cold War, no-one wanted to interfere with the B-47 or B-52 in order to make factory floor space available for a fighter, regardless of its merits.

'Five-in-One' fighter

In 1943 – while Americans were pondering their needs for the expected invasion of Japan – a Boeing negotiating team headed by R. H. Jewett got the nod for a big, long-range fighter. Boeing was eventually to refer to the XF8B-1 as the 'Five in One' since it could serve as a fighter, interceptor, dive bomber, torpedo

The first of three XF8B-1s flies over Washington state circa 1946. Boeing, once the main supplier of fighters to the US Navy, stuck to making bombers and transports after the F8B programme ended. Merger with McDonnell Douglas may once again see 'Boeing' fighters flying from US carriers.

bomber, or level bomber. The company won permission to develop it under a hands-off contract that would reduce Navy intervention with design changes while it was being built. Boeing had not produced a fighter since its promising but unsuccessful XF7B-1 monoplane of 1933.

On 10 April 1943, Boeing received the go-ahead to build three XF8B-1s, BuNos 57984-57986, identified within the company by their constructor's numbers of 8484-8486.

The XF8B-1 would be built to meet Navy Bureau of Aeronautics (BuAer) specification SD-349: for a maximum speed of 342 mph (550 km/h), a ceiling of at least 30,000 ft (9144 m), take-off in a 25-kt (29-mph; 46-km/h) wind within 262 ft (80 m), and a rate of climb at sea level of 3,760 ft (1146 m) per minute.

On 6 September 1943, Boeing's R. (Dick) Stith melded the existing XF8B-1 effort into a project team of 55 men, including Ed Wells who had played a critical role in the design of the B-17. Stith had been the manufacturer's representative with the US Seventh Fleet in the South Pacific, and was familiar with the Navy's experience with current fighters. From the beginning, Stith's team rejected a small aircraft in favour of adequate fuel for warm-up, mission, combat reserves, loitering near the carrier – and, of course, long range. After Wells left the project at an early stage, Lyle A. Wood became chief engineer. There was a lot of talent behind the XF8B-1: the engineering component had 14 men with 203 years experience under their belts, causing this programme to be nicknamed the 'Boeing Engineers' Pension Project'.

XF8B-1 described

The XF8B-1 was a tail-dragger broadly resembling the Hawker Sea Fury. It was substantially larger, however, with 50 per cent greater wingspan. The XF8B-1 weighed more than even the twin-engined Boeing 247 transport of the previous decade.

The XF8B-1 was powered by the biggest reciprocating engine then available, the Pratt & Whitney R-4360-10. The installed armament of six 0.50-in (12.7-mm) Browning M2 machine-guns with 400 rounds per gun was interchangeable with the same number of 20-mm cannons with 200 rounds each. The XF8B-1 used the Navy's standard Mk 23 computing gunsight.

The internal bomb bay in the fuselage was to accommodate a torpedo or up to 3,200 lb (1450 kg) of bombs. Another 3,200 lb (1450 kg) of bombs could be hung externally on one Navy Mk 51 Model 9 bomb shackle under each wing. The XF8B-1 reflected Boeing's hard work (later successful in the B-47 Stratojet bomber) at perfecting 'snap-open' bomb bay

doors which would remain closed until release, enabling a run-in on the target at high speed while hiding until the last instant the intention to drop bombs. The company had considerable difficulty with the bomb bay door configuration on the B-29 Superfortress and had devoted considerable attention to this feature. The bay contained four racks each with three stations, of which two could be employed simultaneously, using B-11 shackles. A variety of bomb loads could be carried, including four 100-lb (45-kg) M30A1, four 250-lb (114-kg) M57A1, four 500-lb (227-kg) M64A1, or two 1,000-lb (907-kg) M65A1 bombs. The bay employed an AN-A-2A bomb release mechanism. The bay could also accommodate 270 US gal (1022 litres) of fuel, enabling a carrier air group commander to choose between range and weapons-carrying capacity, depending on the mission.

The broad wing was equipped with conventional, sealed-balance ailerons and Fowler flaps. The backward-folding feature of the XF8B-1 undercarriage had been used on the Boeing Monomail, B-9 bomber and XF7B-1 fighter, but the company had never fully exploited a system it designed in the 1930s which also pivoted the gear 90° to lie flat in the wing. In

The sleek lines of the XF8B-1 were broken by the huge oil cooler scoop and the giant (13.5-ft/ 4.1-m) propellers. The contraprops absorbed the torque of the massive R-4360, allowing safe low-speed handling.

1934, Curtiss-Wright licensed the design and used it extensively in fighters. The XF8B-1 became the only Boeing aircraft ever to use this system.

The XF8B-1 was described in Boeing literature as having a "quick-change power egg" (the engine and all engine accessories) for ease of maintenance, plus a completely retractable (although non-steering) tailwheel and an arrester hook for carrier landing. Radio equipment was described as fitting in a 'parcel' which could be readily installed or removed.

The size and shape of the XF8B-1 was essentially finalised with the first preliminary design. Details were not, however. As initially sketched out, the aircraft had low wings, a Grumman-style wing-fold mechanism, cooling intakes in the wingroots, and outward-retracting landing gear. With its huge bomb bay, the aircraft would be exceedingly versatile. Based on wind tunnel tests, the cooling air intakes were relocated to a large, chin-mounted

'Corn cob' Fighters

In an effort to squeeze the last ounces of performance out of existing airframe designs, American manufacturers bolted larger and larger engines onto fighter aircraft. The ultimate expression of this was the Pratt & Whitney R-4360 Wasp Major which had the same frontal area of the R-2800, but four, rather than two, rows of cylinders, giving 28 in all. The shape of this lengthy powerplant led to the 'corn cob' nickname. The -4360 was tested in a variety of airframes with a range of propellers. The XF8B-1 was the first all-new design to fly with this giant engine.

Above and left: The R-4360 was trialled in an early-model Corsair, designated the F4U-1WM, which is seen here with a standard aircraft. This installation led to the post-war F2G with a four-bladed propeller, although the F4U-1WM and an XF4U-4 (left) were fitted with the AeroProducts six-bladed contraprop as fitted to the XF8B-1.

Below: The Republic XP-72 'Ultrabolt' was designed around the R-4360, and the second of two aircraft built was fitted with the AeroProducts contraprop. This aircraft was lost at an early stage of testing, although it did achieve 479 mph (772 km/h) at sea level in February 1944.

intake that extended below the wingroots. As design work progressed, a new, overhead wing-folding mechanism was adopted. This neatened the shape of the wing and decreased its weight.

Boeing finalised the design of the XF8B-1 on 7 October 1943. In addition to air intakes, wing-fold and gear retraction, engineers added a vertical stabiliser similar to the B-17 and B-29 unit. Later that year, it was decided to add a second seat behind the pilot for a flight engineer. This 'piggyback' would enable flight tests to progress more quickly. In operational service, the F8B would remain a single-seater. The second seat installed for the test programme was cramped, requiring the engineer to sit high behind the pilot in a hunched-over position, and afforded virtually no chance of escape from the aircraft in an emergency if the pilot were incapacitated.

Reporting to company vice president Welwood Beall, the XF8B-1 team began assembly at the Seattle plant. Wings and undercarriage were manufactured at the nearby Renton facility. From the start, minor but annoying engineering problems arose because the experimental fighter was being assembled in a environment where the company was producing big bombers as fast as it could. One expected problem that did not materialise, however, was with the new fighter's power-plant. Adoption by this single-seater of the largest piston engine ever to enter production proved relatively painless.

Four-row radial

The Pratt & Whitney R-4360-10 Wasp Major four-row, 28-cylinder radial engine was rated at 2,500 hp (1,865 kW) at 2,500 rpm. It was an audacious powerplant for a fighter (though it eventually served well on the Martin AM-1 Mauler, among others) and maintenance people found it a challenge, but there were never any serious flaws. Pratt & Whitney passed to Boeing the data from its tests of the XR-4360 on a Vought F4U-1WM Corsair (BuNo. 02460) in Hartford, Connecticut from May to August 1944, in which test pilot A. Lewis MacClain wrung the monster engine through all power settings. MacClain's work

Below and below right: Crammed behind the pilot in these views of the first aircraft is a test engineer. A one-stop trans-continental flight was made with such a passenger in March 1945.

resolved air flow problems, engine surging, and ignition difficulties above 20,000 ft (6096 m), which otherwise might have plagued the engine early in flight testing of the Boeing aircraft. Test work with the F4U-1WM later led to limited production of the Goodyear F2G Corsair series powered by the R-4360 engine.

The Republic XP-72 with R-4360 engine had made its first flight on 2 February 1944 and, since July, had been flying with an Aeroproducts contra-rotating propeller which was under consideration for the XF8B-1. The propeller unit was also being tested on an F4U-4 Corsair (the F4U-1WM had a conventional propeller). In addition, Boeing was considering a Curtiss-Wright contra-rotating unit for its aircraft. Eventually, it was the contra-rotating propeller that bestowed one of the most remarkable flight characteristics of the XF8B-1 – its lack of torque.

Propeller problems

Engineers expected that either propeller installation would bring vibration problems. There was some prejudice in favour of the Curtiss propeller, but that unit was delayed and Boeing went with the six-bladed, 13-ft 6-in (4.11-m), co-axial Aeroproducts unit. It was decided that at a later date Aeroproducts would supply a feathering unit which, among other things, would prevent the front and rear blades from locking together during a gear-up landing.

Finding a chief test pilot for the XF8B-1 was a challenge to a company that manufactured big bombers and had not turned out a single-seat aircraft for a decade. Fortunately, Robert 'Bob' Lamson was available. Lamson, 29, had logged 1,875 hours including 142 hours in pursuit types like the P-12 and P-26. To prepare for the new aircraft, Lamson made flights in the F4F, TBF, F6F and other single-seaters. He also visited the P & W facility in Hartford and consulted with XP-72 pilot MacClain.

In October 1944, the first XF8B-1, BuNo. 57984, known to the builder as 8484, was completed at Plant 1 in Seattle and towed to Plant 2 on Boeing Field for its pre-flight trials. The aircraft was in natural metal and remained so until its public debut a year later. On 2 November 1944, test pilot Lamson began engine run-ups. The Wasp Major engine was initially found difficult to start, a problem eventually resolved with alterations to the

carburettor. Eight days later, engineers mounted the XF8B-1 on its main gear and a tail jack for 10 hours of propeller vibration tests in a level attitude. Thereafter, Lamson took the aircraft on taxi tests which resulted in a case of overheated brake drums and brake drag.

On 27 November 1944, following high-speed taxis and two quick 'hops' off the ground, Lamson made the first flight. He was aloft for almost an hour with the undercarriage extended. Flight tests proceeded through the holidays and into the new year, revealing that aileron force was high, and the aircraft performed well in a stall. On 3 January 1945 engineer Bud Zerega became the first 'piggy-back' rider in the extra seat.

Navy pilot Commander Jock Sutherland flew the XF8B-1 on 9 January 1945. Sutherland was impressed with landing and stall characteristics, ground handling, visibility, cruise speed and the relative quiet inside the enclosed cockpit. He found the ailerons heavy above 105 mph (169 km/h) and noted a few other problems, principally the sluggishness of the prop control, which had to be moved more than an inch before it would affect the propeller.

On 31 January 1945, the second ship, BuNo. 57985 (c/n 8485), was rolled out. The aircraft was unpainted at first; more importantly, it was without an engine. Nearly 11 months passed before this XF8B-1 got into the air.

Meanwhile, Boeing installed new exhaust gills on ship no. 1. On 13 February, Lamson and Zerega performed high-speed taxi tests to check the temperature on the newly-installed exhaust gills. While they accelerated down the runway at Boeing Field, the aircraft swerved. Lamson lifted into the air momentarily, attempting to realign the aircraft on the runway – and possibly contemplating getting high enough to do a go-around. For a split-second, Lamson was between heaven and earth, not

On a damp day in December 1945, the XF8B-1, by now painted overall gloss sea blue, was unveiled to the media for the first time. Up until this point absolutely nothing had emerged about Boeing's fighter, and the onlookers were impressed by Bob Lamson's display. With the war over, Boeing then had to publicise its product in a world without seemingly unlimited defence budgets.

high enough to fly but not quite on the ground.

Abruptly, the gear retracted, the nose dipped and the contra-rotating propeller bit into the concrete with a shrieking sound. The propeller blades intermeshed, split at the seams, and wrapped around each other like spaghetti. The XF8B-1 slid to a stop. Lamson actuated the CO_2 fire extinguisher and he and Zerega scrambled out, unhurt.

Lamson speculated that a brake had locked or propeller wash from a B-29 running up on the apron had caused the XF8B-1 to swerve. He said he did not know what had caused the gear to retract. Others believed that Lamson had retracted the gear hoping to become fully airborne, then lowered it again when the propeller scraped the runway. The undercarriage had begun its extension cycle and the gear lever was in the down position.

Cleaning up after the mishap was no easy task. Attempts to raise the aircraft with three cranes proved unsuccessful. Eventually, the damaged fighter was lifted high enough to lock the gear into the down position, and a vehicle towed the XF8B-1 to its hangar.

In the aftermath of Lamson's unintended belly landing, studies showed that the landing gear could be retracted or extended by applying pressure on the gear handle even without moving it. Under certain circumstances, the gear could be down when the handle was in the up position, and *vice versa*. A faulty microswitch was remedied while a new R-4360 was installed on ship no. 1, which was repaired with new

bomb bay doors, air intake scoop, gear doors and propeller.

Ship no. 1 returned to the air on 4 March 1945. On 10 March, Lamson and engineer George Edmonstone were tasked to fly the aircraft to the Naval Air Test Center at NAS Patuxent River, Maryland. This marathon flight, with one stop in Wichita, Kansas, passed with only one hitch: the 'relief tube' discharged its contents violently into the cockpit, soaking both men.

Trials at Patuxent

Navy and Marine pilots flew the XF8B-1 under a variety of circumstances at Patuxent, including comparison trials with the Grumman F7F Tigercat and Bell P-59 Airacomet. At first, handling problems were noted because pilots were trimming the aircraft for torque, when it had none. While airborne, the contra-rotating propellers created a stroboscopic effect that could disorient, or at least irritate, the pilot when bright sunlight poked through blades rotating 7,500 times per minute. This had not been deemed a problem when only one pilot was flying the aircraft, but if the XF8B-1 was to become operational, the strobic effect would require further evaluation.

Marine Corps Major Marion Carl went aloft in ship no. 1 at Patuxent to study the strobic effect at various power settings. As Carl was easing back on the power, he inadvertently feathered the propellers, and was forced to put the aircraft into a dive to retain control of the propellers at high speed and low altitude.

The flight test effort at Patuxent was exhaustive, and the pilots' evaluations were merciless. The XF8B-1 got high marks for sturdiness and survivability, even after one pilot put it into a ground loop. Navy and Marine

pilots disliked the ground handling because of the poor brakes and found the control surfaces too heavy. The XF8B-1 achieved mixed results against the F7F and P-59. At Patuxent, 31 pilots flew the aircraft for 44.5 hours in 21 days. Lamson then took the aircraft to nearby NAS Anacostia in Washington, DC where 10 pilots flew it in two days. On 9 April 1945, Lamson and Edmonstone flew ship no. 1 back to Seattle.

Control response improved

On 14 July 1945, after extensive trial and error testing aimed at resolving the control heaviness, ship no. 1 was pulled into the hangar for a complete rebuilding of its aileron controls. The factory installed newly-designed trim tabs and a mechanical link to the ailerons. When the XF8B-1 flew again on 22 October – by which time the war for which the aircraft had been built was over – control response was improved significantly at low speed and somewhat at higher speed.

On his second flight on 22 October 1945, Lamson experienced an electrical fire caused by a malfunctioning circuit breaker. He landed among construction equipment, becoming the first pilot to touch down at the soon-to-be-completed Bow Lake airfield, the site of today's Seattle-Tacoma International Airport. The XF8B-1 was undamaged.

XF8B-1 no. 2 belatedly made its first flight on 27 November 1945, a year to the day after the first ship. By then, BuNo. 57985 (c/n 8485) was painted in Navy gloss sea blue.

The second aircraft had been modified while on the production line when the Engineering Division of the Army's Air Technical Service

The new, lower-profile canopy fitted during testing of the first XF8B-1 can be seen here. The new unit improved the appearance of the aircraft but leaked, rattled, and opened and closed too slowly. The aircraft suffered from no faults that could not have been corrected in service.

Specification

Powerplant: one Pratt & Whitney R-4360 Wasp Major four-row, 28-cylinder radial engine rated at 2,500 hp (1,865 kW) at 2,500 rpm
Performance: max speed 432 mph (695 km/h) at 26,500 ft (8077 m); cruising speed 190 mph (305 km/h); rate of climb 3,660 ft/min (1115 m/min); service ceiling 37,500 ft (11430 m)
Weights: empty weight 14,190 lb (6436 kg); gross weight 20,508 lb (9302 kg)
Armament: six 0.50-in (12.7-mm) Browning M3 machine-guns or six 20-mm or six 30-mm cannon; four 500-lb (227-kg) bombs or two 1,600-lb (725-kg) bombs in bomb bay; two 500-lb (227-kg) bombs, two 1,000-lb (907-kg) bombs or two 1,600-lb (725-kg) bombs in external racks
Dimensions: span 54 ft (16.44 m); length 43 ft 3 in (13.17 m); height 16 ft 3in (4.94 m); wing area 489 sq ft (45.43 m²)

Command (ATSC) showed interest in the potential of a production F8B and put forth a scenario for Army flight tests. Ship no. 2 introduced new dive flaps (at Army request), a reshaped fairing on the chin intake, and a revised canopy. The new canopy had a more rakish windscreen and a lower-set, more streamlined 'bubble', although it drew criticism for visibility and leaking problems. It appears that the 'piggyback' engineer's seat fitted to the first ship was not fitted in either of the subsequent XF8B-1s.

Once ship no. 2 was flying, Boeing relegated ship no. 1 to hangar storage and removed its engine for installation aboard the third XF8B-1. There was never an occasion when two XF8B-1s flew together, let alone three.

On 26 December 1945, Lamson's aircraft suffered a power loss while being hounded over Washington state by a quartet of Navy F4U Corsairs. He landed the XF8B-1 on a soggy strip at Marysville, Washington where the blue fighter upended itself, balancing on main gear and propeller with tail pointing skyward. The propellers were stopped by ground contact before they could intermesh, repairs were made, and the XF8B-1 resumed flying.

On 14 February 1946, ATSC pilot First Lieutenant Walter J. McAuley (a veteran of P-39, P-40 and P-47 combat in Italy and China) ferried the XF8B-1 and took ship no. 2 to Wright Field, Ohio via an overnight stopover at Hill Field, Utah. N. D. Showalter, chief of flight test for the Boeing Engineering Division, and project engineer Stith packed their bags to go to Wright Field to support the Army's evaluation. It was planned that ship no.

The F8B would have made an effective strike aircraft, with its internal weapons bay, 20-mm cannon and long range. One of the few doubts about its design was the question of pilot fatigue (or hypnosis) on a long mission caused by the flickering propeller blades.

2 would subsequently proceed to Eglin Field, Florida for armament and ordnance tests – but like so much relating to the XF8B-1, things did not work out according to plan.

Army evaluation

The end of the war and the arrival of jet aircraft meant that the original purpose of the XF8B-1 was long ago overtaken by events. The Army's interest was serious, nevertheless, and the Army evaluated ship no. 2 at Wright Field. Unfortunately, at a critical juncture, the aircraft suffered an engine failure at Wright Field – attributed to fatigue in the blower drive, brought on by the hard landing at Marysville. The Wright Field effort had to be cut short and the aircraft was unable to proceed to Eglin.

A report was compiled covering 35 hours of flying time by 18 pilots at Wright Field between 15 February 1946 and 15 March 1946. Pilots found the general features of the cockpit, including most of the controls, switches and instruments, to be conveniently located. The seat, adjustable for height only, was deemed uncomfortable, and the absence of a parking brake was noted. Criticism of the canopy – the new one, introduced with ship no. 2 – was considerable: "The canopy on the test airplane is poorly designed as to size and reduces the critical Mach number of the airplane. Fit of the canopy to the fuselage also is poor, and even with it closed as completely as possible cracks and gaps are present between the bubble and windshield and around the lower edge of the canopy. Side vision is somewhat distorted by imperfections in the plastic bubble. The canopy is operated by a hand crank on the right side of the cockpit. Crank gear ratio is too high, causing slow canopy operation. The canopy latch…is not very satisfactory."

The Wright Field report on ship no. 2 also noted that brakes were only adequate for the weight of the XF8B-1. The aircraft

demonstrated a take-off roll of 800 to 1,000 ft (240 to 300 m), with take-off performance satisfactory. Most aspects of flight performance were deemed satisfactory, although stall warning was rated 'marginal' – consisting of a slight buffeting and a sinking sensation 2 to 3 mph before the actual stall.

The report indicated that tests to obtain maximum range and endurance were not completed due to the malfunction of the engine, and concluded: "…an airplane as large as the XF8B, and designed to carry the load, also [should] have the added safety of two engines. The advantages as a long-range fighter are greatly reduced by excessive fatigue of the pilot. High-speed performance, manoeuvrability, and stability have been sacrificed for low-speed stability and control."

It appears that ship no. 2 languished at Wright Field, unflyable, from March through August 1946.

Enter ship no. 3

The first flight of XF8B-1 no. 3, BuNo. 57986, was made in early 1946. It was hastily pressed into duty as a substitute for no. 2 for the Army. The third ship arrived at Eglin on 23 July 1946. Unfortunately, ship no. 3 lacked the dive flaps that had been installed on the second craft at the Army's request. Still, tests went ahead to see how the XF8B-1 with its six-gun armament would perform as a fighter-bomber and, thereafter, to rate the aircraft as a bomber.

Some 33,530 rounds of 0.50-in (12.7-mm) ammunition were put through the XF8B-1 in ground firings and aerial strafing runs. In one of these tests a bullet ricocheted, broke the canopy (which had to be replaced), and dented the vertical fin and horizontal stabiliser leading edges, which were repaired. In this mishap, one of the guns suffered damage that could not be repaired on the scene – as with the engine, there were simply no spare parts for the armament – so tests were completed firing five of the six guns.

It was time to use the XF8B-1's internal bomb bay for the first time. The Army did not want the AN-MK7 mod 1 internal bomb hoist that Boeing had installed on the aircraft for the Navy, and loaded bombs from the ground with

Boeing XF8B

The second XF8B-1 was at Wright Field from February to August 1946, although for much of that time it was in semi-storage following an engine failure. This may be 57985, although there appear to be no other surviving images of the Wright Field tests or the number two XF8B-1.

Below: Despite the long period spent by two XF8B-1s at Eglin, there are few photographs of their time there. This view is also unusual in that it shows an external load of two drop tanks. The XF8Bs were tested with a variety of internal and external loads.

relative ease using a T65 bomb lift trailer.

It is not clear why the Army kept testing the XF8B-1 long after any prospect of a production order must have faded. The tests continued until 24 January 1947. "Everybody at Eglin flew it," remembered Colonel Don Lopez, who was a young test pilot in 1945. "It was big. Impressive. The sportiest part was taxiing. It seemed awkward – I was flying P-80s a lot and this was a much heavier-handling airplane." Lopez noted that the kaleidoscopic effect from the contra-rotating propellers "could be hypnotic on a long mission."

Weapons tests

Army pilots flew the XF8B-1 in simulated dive-bombing and horizontal bombing missions with 384 US gal (1454 litres) of fuel in the wings and four 1,000-lb (454-kg) bombs, two internal and two external. The XF8B-1 was to fly out to a combat radius of 270 miles (434 km). Each sortie began at a gross weight of 22,960 lb (10414 kg), which was about 10 per cent heavier than the Douglas BT2D-1(AD-1) Skyraider bomber then being developed for the Navy (although the latter gained weight before entering service). In all, bomb tests consumed 46 air and 23 ground tests.

The bomb tests were far from a complete success. Under some circumstances, the bomb bay doors would start closing before the bombs released. On early missions the doors would not open until speed was decreased to 130 mph (209 km/h) due to negative pressure inside the bay, a problem that was solved by cutting a 4-in (10-cm) hole into each bomb bay door at the aft end and one hole in the aft bulkhead.

Army pilots generally liked the XF8B-1 but found plenty of fault with the aircraft in the bombing role. They found the XF8B-1 unsuitable as a dive-bomber because it accelerated too rapidly and was longitudinally unstable. ("This unstable condition can detract much of the pilot's attention from full concentration on the target because he must constantly fight the airplane to keep it in the proper angle of dive...and to keep it from building up high speeds which result in inaccurate dive

bombing.") The absence of the dive flaps (built only on ship no. 2, still languishing at Wright Field) contributed to this conclusion. Pilots had better reports on the XF8B-1 as a level bomber and skip-bomber: the aircraft was stable and its 5° nose-down attitude in level flight, coupled with the 9° downslope of the nose ahead of the windshield, gave superb visibility. For anything requiring flexibility or manoeuvring, however, the XF8B-1 was regarded as an inferior fighter-bomber to the P-47 or P-51.

Build 600 aircraft? No thanks

Boeing's Dick Stith travelled to Washington, DC in late 1945 looking for favourable news of a possible production contract. Over the years the myth has grown that by the time Stith arrived in the capital, another Boeing official – a man concerned with bomber production – had turned down a Navy proposal to build 600 aircraft. As the legend goes, by the time Stith and Beall explained that the proposed contract had been rejected by the wrong official at Boeing, it was too late. The story is a good one but there is no proof today that the Navy ever placed an order for 600 airplanes.

Ship no. 1 was rebuilt with the new canopy and painted in the same fashion as ship no. 3, in gloss sea blue with the word 'Boeing' in script on its nose. On 8 October 1946, with ship no. 1 returned to test status in Seattle, the XF8B-1

scored its only 'kill': Lamson blew over a Piper J-3 Cub while running up for take-off. A week later, Lieutenant Frank J. Shaw ferried ship no. 1 from Seattle to Patuxent River with a stop in San Diego, California. Soon afterward, the Navy formally accepted ship no. 2. The first two ships were eventually transferred to the Navy in Philadelphia where they were struck on 31 January 1948 and scrapped. Bob Lamson wanted to acquire an XF8B-1 in the late 1940s, hoping to use it in the National Air Races, but it was not to be.

Testing of ship no. 3 was concluded at Eglin on 11 December 1946. Officially accepted by the Navy on 1 August 1947, ship no. 3 appeared in Philadelphia, Seattle and San Diego before being struck on 16 March 1950 and scrapped. Three months after this, the US Air Force (an independent service since September 1947) and the Navy were in need of an effective air-to-ground combat plane in Korea. Not enough F-47 Thunderbolts could be found and the Air Force had to settle for the F-51D Mustang, which was never ideal for air-to-ground work. The Navy, of course, had the AD Skyraider, which was in many respects similar to the Boeing aircraft.

Right place, wrong time

None of the problems encountered by the Boeing XF8B-1 during its development and testing was anything but routine, and it was clear from performance results that the XF8B-1 could have been an operational success. Unfortunately, the XF8B-1 arrived at the wrong time – with a war ending and jet aircraft emerging on the scene. Any other time, the XF8B-1 would have been a winner.

Robert F. Dorr

At the end of a brief career, the third aircraft, BuNo. 57986, was shunted from place to place before finally being scrapped. Here it sits out to grass, probably at San Diego, California, wearing the post-1947 national insignia. This picture gives a rare view of the wings in the folded position.

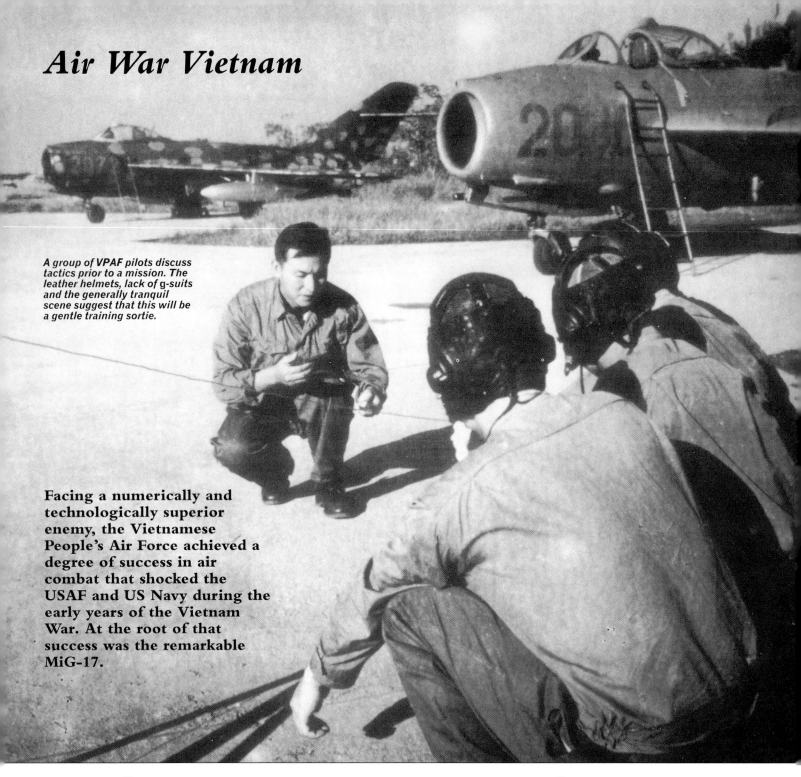

Air War Vietnam

A group of VPAF pilots discuss tactics prior to a mission. The leather helmets, lack of g-suits and the generally tranquil scene suggest that this will be a gentle training sortie.

Facing a numerically and technologically superior enemy, the Vietnamese People's Air Force achieved a degree of success in air combat that shocked the USAF and US Navy during the early years of the Vietnam War. At the root of that success was the remarkable MiG-17.

MiG-17 over Vietnam

In March 1956 the first group of 110 Vietnamese military pilot candidates who would form the backbone of the developing air force departed for China and the Soviet Union for training. The Chinese dealt with the would-be bomber and fighter pilots, while the Soviets instructed the transport aircrews. The 50 fighter students in China were led by Pham Dung, who was later succeeded by Dao Dinh Luyen.

In an attempt to establish basic training at home, the Vietnamese intended to form the air club of the Vietnamese Airlines (Hang khong Viet Nam) at Cat Bi airfield in Haiphong Province. To provide instructors for the air club, a delegation of 12 Vietnamese was sent to Czechoslovakia in mid-1956 to gain proficiency on Zlin Trener aircraft. At the end of 1956, the Ministry of Defence organised the 1st Flying School (truong hang khong so 1) at Cat Bi.

With the help of Chinese instructors, the first courses were launched to provide support personnel for future air units. The 2nd Flying School was established at Gia Lam airfield in Hanoi Province.

In 1957, few members of the first group on transport pilot training in the Soviet Union that had been shifted to fighter training units started general handling sorties on MiG-15. This year also saw fresh groups of Vietnamese being sent abroad to begin their studies in flying schools. Coming from a desperately poor country, most of the Vietnamese students were handicapped by scanty mechanical background – and by malnutrition. On at least one occasion, a Soviet flight surgeon held back a fresh group from flight training until their physical conditions improved with proper nourishment.

By the beginning of 1959, reconstruction of the French-built airfields in the North was close

to completion. For structuring and organising the air force, on 24 January 1959 the MoD set up the Directorate of Aviation (Cuc Khong quan) headed by Dang Thinh.

In April 1959, 25 pilots who had been trained on Zlin Treners in Czechoslovakia and Yak-18s in China returned, to become the instructors of the 1st Flying School. The first flying course with 30 students was launched on 31 May.

On 30 September 1959 the MoD issued order 429/ND regarding the formation of the 910th Air Wing (trung doan khong quan 910) and the Vietnamese Air Forces' School (truong khong quan Viet Nam) at Cat Bi.

In 1960 52 pilots who had already completed their Yak-18 basic training programme at Cat Bi advanced to MiG-17 training in China. By this time, 31 of the Vietnamese fighter pilot candidates who had arrived with the first group

Left: A pair of Vietnamese MiG-17s launches on a mission. The aircraft were only employed under tight GCI control, and only when they stood a good chance of successfully engaging American aircraft.

An aircraft diving ablaze over the characteristic North Vietnamese landscape became a familiar sight from 1965 onwards. Many of them crashed into the jungle or off the coast, so the recovery of the remains and the examination as to why they were lost will never be possible.

in 1956 were flying MiG-15s. Still lacking an airfield suitable for jet operations, Vietnam was not yet prepared to welcome its fledgling fighter pilots. Under the agreement between the MoDs of the two nations, they moved to the Chinese Son Dong air base to begin their transition to the MiG-17. There they joined 200 Vietnamese from various trade groups who were learning the support tasks necessary for fighter operations. It was the first stage of a process that evolved into the formation of the first Vietnamese fighter unit.

Two years later, still in China, they were flying in four-ship formations under visual flight rule conditions. By this time the ground personnel had completed their training. The Soviet Union gave 36 MiG-17s to Vietnam to equip its first fighter wing.

In 1963 the Vietnamese contingent was transferred from Son Dong to Mong Tu air base in Van Nam Province, near the Vietnamese border. They were ready to deploy back to Vietnam in case of need.

On 3 February 1964 Lieutenant General Hoang Van Thai, Deputy Minister of Defence, signed order 18/QD regarding the establishment of the 921st 'Red Star' Fighter Wing (trung doan khong quan tiem kich 921, Sao Do) under the command of Lieutenant Colonel Dao Dinh Luyen. Brigadier General Tran Quy Hai, Deputy Chief of Staff, presented the unit flag known as the 'Invincible Flag'.

Building the nest

In parallel with training its first generation of jet pilots abroad, Vietnam was feverish to build an air base where the fighters would take up residence. Pham Van Dong, the Prime Minister of North Vietnam, charged the Ministry of Transportation and the MoD with the construction of the airfield, the Ministry of Heavy Industry with supplying electrics and lighting, the Ministry of Construction with raising office blocks and apartments, the Ministry of Control of Materials with building kerosene and weapon storage facilities, the Post with the development of the telecommunication system, and the Ministry of the Interior with security measures. Two authorities from Vinh Phu Province paid close attention to and arranged for matters of great importance like manpower recruitment and food supply. In building the so-called Object No. 130, services of Chinese experts were also engaged.

On 1 May 1960 Phan Trong Tue, then Minister of Transportation, laid the foundation stone of Noi Bai airfield in Kim Anh District, Vinh Phu Province. By the middle of 1964, the most important facilities of the air base were finished and Noi Bai became suitable for jet fighter operations.

Back home

On 2 August 1964, the destroyer USS *Maddox* came under attack by North Vietnamese torpedo boats while sailing in territorial waters and apparently assisting a covert South Vietnamese commando raid. This, and a fictitious second torpedo attack two days later, resulted in Operation Pierce Arrow, a reprisal air raid on 5 August. Carrierborne aircraft launching from USS *Constellation* and USS *Ticonderoga* flew 64 sorties against North Vietnamese torpedo boat bases and support facilities. It was high time for the North Vietnamese to call home their fighters.

Chief of the General Staff Van Tieng Dung commanded the secret X-1 project. Lieutenant Colonel Nguyen Van Tien, Deputy Commander of the Vietnamese People's Air Forces (VPAF), revealed the project to the pilots in China.

On the morning of 6 August 1964, a valedictory ceremony was held at Mong Tu air base with a Vietnamese flag hoisted on the control tower. Ground crew conducted final checks on the flight line while the fully kitted pilots were awaited take-off. Noi Bai reported sunshine, but the sky over southern China was overcast until noon. When the weather cleared, flares were shot up and flights of four MiG-17s began to roar into the sky heading southeast. Wing Commander Dao Dinh Luyen led the first flight. His wingman was Pham Ngoc Lan, and number three was Tao Minh with Lam Van Lich on his wing.

The Noi Bai control tower, filled with expectations and high-ranking officers, zeroed in on the approaching MiGs. Pham Ngoc Lan touched down first, and his squadron mates followed him successfully. Van Tien Dung shook hands with each pilot after they rolled to a stop.

The four pilots selected to begin alert duty in the afternoon of arrival were Pham Ngoc Lan, Lam Van Lich, Tranh Hanh and Nguyen Nhat Chieu. The neophyte pilots of the 921st Fighter Wing were eager to fight, but long months of maturation and practice were to come before the first duel would take place.

Preparations for combat

Following the arrival of the 'silver swallows' – as the jet fighters were affectionately referred to by the Vietnamese – the military Party Committee and Vietnamese People's Air Forces – Anti-Aircraft Forces (VPAF-AAF) Command held conferences to discuss ideas and draw up the details of preparations to succeed in the first engagement. A handful of young, inexperienced pilots flying obsolete aircraft would fight against a numerically and technically superior

Lam Van Lich is seen prior to a mission. The improved MiG-17F introduced a new ejection seat with face curtain and stabilising panels.

enemy. However, the Vietnamese had the advantages of flying over friendly territory and of collaboration with radar and anti-aircraft units.

An intense training period began. MiG-17s were rumbling through the airspace of Hanoi and the northern provinces seven days a week. After four months at home, the Vietnamese airmen had logged more flying time than during one year in China. Rude mock-up cockpits made of bamboo were used for after-hours training.

Pilots regularly talked over their ideas about air combat tactics. One enthusiast recommended suicide attacks by ramming the enemy aircraft on a one-to-one basis, if necessary. Although this evidence of dedication and self-sacrifice was greatly appreciated, the idea of kamikaze-style *tai-atari* did not find adherents in the upper echelons; they preferred tactics that

ensured victory at the expense of the smallest possible own loss. Le Trong Long, who had served in a commando unit before joining the air force, suggested surprise attacks similar to commando assaults. Tranh Hanh explained how he would evade cannon fire, and Lam Van Lich held forth on how to avoid being caught from behind. Le Minh Huan reviewed the capabilities of the American air-to-air missiles.

Dao Dinh Luyen was the first fighter wing commander of the VPAF. In March 1956 he led the first group of 30 Vietnamese which started bomber pilot training on Tu-2 aircraft in China, but soon was assigned to the group on fighter pilot training. On 3 February 1964 he was selected to be the commander of the 921st Fighter Wing, and on 6 August led the first flight of Vietnamese MiG-17s home from Mong Tu air base, China. Upon the separation of the VPAF and the AAF in May 1977, Colonel Luyen became the Commander in Chief of the air forces.

Vietnamese pilots met captured American airmen to get to know the enemy, and studied photographs of US aircraft to aid recognition. Anti-aircraft gunners from the Militia and Anti-Aircraft Forces reported their observations during struggles against air raids.

As the months passed, the pilots gained more experience. To achieve a kill on the first pass, they practised opening fire from 300 m (985 ft) or even 150 m (492 ft). Besides the three cannon, agility was the MiG-17's other advantage over American aircraft, so close-in engagements were emphasised while learning air combat tactics.

Pilots were carefully selected for each flight. A few were destined to be aces, but team players were equally important. Skill, experience, character and a lack of personality conflict were all taken into account. Captain Tran Hanh, who it seemed could make a MiG-17 talk, became a flight leader; his wingman, Pham Giay, was quiet, studious and helpful. Numbers three and four of that flight, Le Minh Huan and Tran Nguyen Nam, had been born in neighbouring provinces and were close friends. Lieutenant Pham Ngoc Lan, an outstanding pilot, led another flight with the less skilled but disciplined Phan Van Tuc on his wing. Ho Van Quy, the number three, was good at navigation, while Tran Minh Phuong, flying the fourth aircraft, had a flair for air-to-air gunnery.

On 11 November 1964 President Ho Chi Minh paid a visit to the fighter unit. High-ranking party and government leaders like Le Duan, First Secretary of Central Committee and Truong Ching, President of the National Assembly accompanied him. These visits were not just to inspect the fighting units, but to fire the pilots with enthusiasm. The speeches of Bac Ho (Uncle Ho) were quite effective in motivating the audience.

Ho Chi Minh told them, "The Vietnamese way of warfare is distinctive. Even a rudimentary weapon becomes effective in the hands of the Vietnamese. We should exploit it and should not fear that the enemy has much more modern weaponry."

VPAF Command decided to send the fight-

ers into combat as soon as North Vietnamese territories above the 20th Parallel were attacked. Following the retaliatory strikes Flaming Dart I and II on 7 and 11 February 1965 against targets just north of the DMZ, a sustained bombing campaign, Operation Rolling Thunder, was initiated, on 2 March. In a month, it was extended against the North Vietnamese heartland. American aircraft would soon face not only the fiercest anti-aircraft fire in the history of air warfare, but audacious hit-and-run attacks by nimble little MiG-17s.

Display of presence

The misty morning of 3 April 1965 offered a horizontal visibility of only 4-5 km (2.5-3.1 miles) at Noi Bai. Cloud was 6/10 with its base at 300 m (985 ft). Weather at Thanh Hoa, the supposed location of this day's raid, differed little with a visibility of about 10 km (6 miles), 5-6/10 cloud and 700 m (2,296 ft) base.

At 07.00, radars detected enemy aircraft entering North Vietnamese airspace, apparently on a reconnaissance mission. It was likely that a massive air strike would follow against the Ham Rong highway and railroad bridge crossing the Song Ma River.

Colonel Phung The Tai, Commander in Chief of the VPAF, briefed the coming mission: six aircraft in two elements were to be launched to ambush the American strike force. Pre-flight briefing continued with time and callsign check.

At 09.40 the enemy was about to attack the Tao, Do Len and Ham Rong Bridges. From 09.45, the 921st Fighter Wing was held at a high state of readiness. At 09.47, flight two with Tran Hanh and Pham Giay departed for a deception manoeuvre. Flight one with Pham Ngoc Lan, Phan Van Tuc, Ho Van Quy and Tran Minh Phuong took off one minute later and turned on 210° heading to Thanh Hoa Province. Tran Quang Kinh was tasked with GCI and vectored the flights in two different directions, but abruptly lost radar contact both with the enemy and the Vietnamese aircraft. Two minutes later, specks appeared on the radar display, which turned out to be the MiGs of Pham Ngoc Lan's flight.

At 10.08 flight one approached within 45 miles (27.95 km) of Thanh Hoa, while flight two was still flying over Ninh Binh Province. A moment later the American formation was

picked up again on the radar. Flight one was ordered to jettison its external fuel tanks.

The US strike force, unaware of the MiGs sneaking up on them, separated and began bombing runs in pairs against the Ham Rong Bridge. Tran Hanh's flight was also about to join the battle. Pham Ngoc Lan, with Phan Van Tuc on his wing, closed on an F-8 and opened fire. The Crusader exploded. Ho Van Quy and Tran Minh Phuong bounced another element of enemy fighters, just to squeeze the trigger before closing to firing range.

At 10.15 Phan Van Tuc spotted an F-8 on his right. He radioed to Pham Ngoc Lan, who ordered his wingman to attack the Crusader while he gave cover. The MiGs set up a closing course, and shot down the American fighter.

Low on fuel, the Vietnamese flight was directed home at 10.17. All but one made it back successfully; Pham Ngoc Lan ran out of fuel short of the air base. Ignoring the order to eject, he lined up with a long strip of sand stretching along the bank of Duong River and force landed with only minor damage to the aircraft. Curious people living nearby rushed to the MiG, formed a guard and informed the air force.

Commemorating the victory, 3 April became Air Forces' Day. Although success had come in their first engagement, there were flaws in departure, tactics, gunnery and arrival. Every aspect of the mission was thoroughly discussed during the debriefing held that evening. The fliers had expended 160 37-mm and 526 23-mm cannon shells to shoot down two aircraft. It was understood that if all pilots had refrained from shooting until they were within firing range, this ratio might have been better. Vietnamese sources refer to MiG-17 gun camera films that recorded the blazing F-8 Crusaders; US sources claim only one F-8E of VF-211 'Checkmates' damaged by MiGs, with two other aircraft lost to air defence units.

Failing to destroy the Ham Rong Bridge, the enemy was expected to try again on the very next day. VPAF decided to let the anti-aircraft units to take their toll first and then to send three flights into combat, one of them with an

auxiliary task. The deception element would take off first and head west at 7000-8000 m (22,965-26,246 ft), then the attack flight would follow, heading southeast on the deck. Dao Ngoc Ngu was tasked with GCI.

Three that did not come back

Following pre-strike reconnaissance flights, an air raid was undertaken early on 4 April 1965 against the Ham Rong Bridge and the Thanh Hoa thermal power plant. The mixed strike force was dominated by bomb-hauling F-105 Thunderchiefs and Sidewinder-armed F-100s flying combat air patrol.

The VPAF reacted at 10.20 by launching a flight of four MiG-17s. Le Trong Long, Phan Van Tuc, Ho Van Quy and Tran Minh Phuong climbed to 8000 m (26,246 ft) and, cruising over Vu Ban, Phu Ly in Nam Ha Province, tried to attract the attention of the enemy. The second flight with Tran Hanh, Pham Giay, Le Minh Huan and Tran Nguyen Nam departed at 10.22. Three of them met their deaths during this day's encounter.

Flying in leaden skies with haze underneath, the attack flight was ordered to descend and head east, then southeast on the deck. Ingressing the combat area, they zoomed to altitude and spotted a flight of four F-105s about to release its bombs.

Tran Hanh ordered his wingman Pham Giay to follow and check his six, then set up a 'Thud' and finished it from 400 m (1,312 ft) with a burst from his triple cannon. When the American fighters realised that they were under attack, they immediately ploughed into the middle of the Vietnamese formation, splitting it

This wartime photograph illustrates the strategic Ham Rong Bridge in Thanh Hoa Province, carrying a railway track and the two roadways of the Highway 1 across the Song Ma River. It witnessed some of the fiercest air battles of the war.

Numerous aircraft of both sides were lost to unknown causes over North Vietnam. In cases like this the crew perished almost instantly, sometimes even without noticing that they were under attack. Crediting lost American aircraft speculatively to Vietnamese air defence forces rather than MiGs was always preferable.

into two elements. Tran Hanh and Pham Giay remained north of the Song Ma River, while numbers three and four found themselves south of the Ham Rong Bridge. Le Minh Huan with Tran Nguyen Nam providing cover downed another F-105D. Finally, however, all but one Vietnamese pilot of the attack flight lost his life during the mission. (The Vietnamese believe that all three MiGs were downed by USAF aircraft, but only one 416th TFS F-100D Super Sabre pilot was listed as having a 'probable' kill on that day.)

Only Tran Hanh could avoid being shot down. Breaking off, he discovered that he had lost radio contact with the GCI station and that his fuel tanks were just about dry. He decided not to eject but to execute a forced landing in Ke Tam Valley, Nghe An Province. He succeeded, just to be arrested by local people as soon as he brought the aircraft to a halt. When his VPAF badge was noticed, they led him to the district headquarters where the commander turned out to be Tran Hanh's friend, with whom he had fought against the French in the

The flight of Pham Ngoc Lan, Phan Van Tuc, Ho Van Quy and Tran Minh Phuong from the 921st Fighter Wing was credited with the first air-to-air victories gained by VPAF MiG-17s. Pham Ngoc Lan and Phan Van Tuc (first and second from left) shot down one F-8 Crusader each during the mission on 3 April 1965.

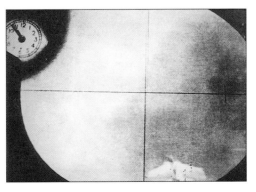

This frame from a MiG-17 gun camera film illustrates an F-105D Thunderchief moments before it was shot down by Captain Tran Hanh on 4 April 1965.

Air War Vietnam

This is one of the two F-105 Thunderchiefs shot down on the afternoon of 19 May 1966 by a pair of MiG-17s from the 923rd Fighter Wing. The Vietnamese pilots were Vo Van Man and Nguyen Bien.

Although the significance of observer posts did not diminish throughout the war, fighter operations, especially when under strict ground control, demanded sophisticated surveillance systems. This P-15 early warning and target acquisition radar was mounted on a Zil-157 6x6 truck, which provided the necessary cross-country mobility for the system.

320th Army Division. After bidding his host farewell, the pilot returned to his unit.

Reduction in numbers

The summer of 1965 brought decimation to the still-maturing fighter force. Combat losses were due to lack of combat experience, inferior hardware, and – last but not least – the 'over-efficient' air defence units. Heavy casualties were also a consequence of the high accident rate. Subsequent to the first encounters with MiGs, Lockheed EC-121D Warning Star radar surveillance aircraft were deployed to South Vietnam to fly airborne early warning missions off the coast of North Vietnam, monitoring VPAF air activity in an attempt to prevent surprise attacks.

On 17 June a flight of four MiG-17s scrambled to engage a fleet of US Navy aircraft, and downed two F-4B Phantoms over Nho Quan, Ninh Binh Province. Three of the Vietnamese aircraft failed to return. Two were shot down by the American fighters (two F-4Bs of VF-21 'Freelancers' from USS *Midway*), while the third

A MiG-17 is towed away from the flight line by a Chinese copy of the Soviet Zil-131 6x6 truck. The Chinese Shenyang Aircraft Factory began the production of MiG-17F fighters under the designation J-5 (or F-5) in 1955 with Soviet assistance. Early examples were assembled mainly from Soviet-made parts, while from 1956 all the components, including the engines, were manufactured by the Chinese. The Vietnamese generally did not differentiate the MiG-17Fs of Soviet and Chinese origin. Thus, aircraft described as MiG-17Fs could be either the original Soviet product or a Chinese-manufactured Shenyang J-5.

pilot misjudged his altitude and manoeuvred into a mountainside.

Lack of practice resulted in a similar accident on 20 June, when two MiG-17s caught six A-1Hs over Mai Chau, Hoa Binh Province. The Vietnamese flight leader fired seven times before he observed hits. His wingman reported a score, but a low-altitude manoeuvre dropped him into the ground. (Two VA-25 'Fist of the Fleet' pilots shared credit for downing this MiG-17, which – according to Vietnamese sources – actually was lost due to pilot error.)

Exactly a month later, a pair of MiG-17s brought down an F-4 Phantom over Tam Dao, Vinh Phu Province. Neither of the Vietnamese pilots returned from this mission. There were no confirmed American victories on that day, so the MiGs might have been the victims of friendly anti-aircraft artillery, or mishap.

This thinning-out went far beyond an acceptable level, and the VPAF found itself in simply no condition to oppose the enemy. Air Force Command analysed the situation and found many deficiencies in air combat tactics. For example, instead of attacking the heavily laden strike aircraft, Vietnamese pilots regularly tangled with escort fighters. Some flight leaders had acted in confusion or, because of the first successes, had contempt for the Americans.

In the third quarter of 1965 the 921st Fighter Wing was ordered to cut back its combat activity. For two months MiGs were cleared to

attack only if they could be sure of a favourable outcome. During these brisk encounters they attempted, first of all, to gain more combat experience.

A pause for build-up

In May 1965, the government ordered the building of new air bases and the development and repair of some of the existing ones. Kep in Ha Bac Province was scheduled for completion by September, to receive a new Vietnamese fighter unit. Roughly 4,000 people recruited from the Bac Giang chemical fertiliser factory and the 305th Army Division worked hard to remove 500000 m³ (17.6 million cu ft) of soil. By the end of June it became obvious that they were not meeting the deadline, so the MoD ordered the blowing-up of hills all over the construction area. Advisers from the University of Technical Sciences assisted the 2nd Engineering Division to place 250 tons of explosive. A river that crossed the site and was used to irrigate nearby fields was diverted into a canal outside the airfield. Some 700 m³ (24,720 cu ft) of concrete was used daily for the construction of taxiways, service roads and the runway.

On 7 September 1965 the airfield was opened for business. The 923rd 'Yen The' Fighter Wing (trung doan khong quan tiem kich 923, Yen The), commanded by Major Nguyen Phuc Trac, was formed on the same day. The wing was named after Yen The, a village in North Vietnam whose fame dates to the Franco-Viet Minh war. Kep became a key factor in the defence of the strategically important road and rail network in the northeast region.

Development of the fighter force was made possible by the return of 30 freshly trained pilots from the Soviet Union and China, and by the arrival of MiG-17F/PF and MiG-21 aircraft. The number of aircrew doubled while that of aircraft tripled in the second half of 1965.

The 921st Fighter Wing received the MiG-21 supersonic fighters, and the 923rd Fighter Wing was equipped with MiG-17s. In addition to the new aircraft, the capability of the VPAF was enhanced by the introduction P-35 and PRV-11 radars.

By this time, Anti-Aircraft Forces were fully engaged with the installation of SA-2 surface-to-air missile batteries. The Militia continued to be a major threat to low-flying enemy aircraft, and its strength was increased from 1.4 to 2 million.

Right: Lam Van Lich, after finishing his fighter pilot training in China, flew home on 6 June 1964 as number four of the first flight of the 921st Fighter Wing. Shooting down two Skyraiders on 3 February 1966, he gained the first night victories of the VPAF with MiG-17 aircraft.

Skirmishes resume

From the summer of 1965 air operations against North Vietnam were focused on the significant supply routes in the vicinity of Lang Son, Lao Cai, Haiphong, Hanoi and in the 4th Military Zone. Dogfights flared up again in September. Using the knowledge they accumulated during training in the previous months, Vietnamese pilots stressed close-in engagements with bomber elements of strike packages and tried to lure them low, into the reach of anti-aircraft artillery.

On 20 September, Highway 1 between Lang Son and Hanoi became the target of a US Navy air strike. A flight of four MiG-17Fs of the 921st Fighter Wing departed from Noi Bai. Pham Ngoc Lan, Nguyen Nhat Chieu, Tran Van Tri and Nguyen Ngoc Do climbed away and spotted the enemy aircraft flying over Yen Tu at 3000 m (9,842 ft). The Vietnamese pilots were ordered to drop their wing tanks, accelerate and attack. They immediately turned right and bounced an element of four F-4s.

The Phantom pilots apparently had not noticed the MiGs coming at them until it was too late. Two F-4s pulled hard up while the other pair broke starboard. Not intending to get into a vertical fight, the MiGs stayed with the turning Phantoms. One of them was attempting to disappear into a cloud, while his wingman plunged earthward. Nguyen Nhat Chieu was in ideal position to follow the former, which started to turn left into the cloud. The Phantom's predictable flight path allowed the Vietnamese pilot to take a short cut and close in.

Popping out of the cloud, the F-4 headed for the sea with the MiG on his tail. From 400 m (1,312 ft), Nguyen Nat Chieu opened fire. Trailing black smoke, the Phantom began a descent and tried to escape just to receive another – now lethal – burst from the MiG's

Pilots and curious technicians group in the shadow created by the tail of a MiG-17 to hold an outdoor briefing. Although they were flying over friendly territory, Vietnamese airmen regularly carried sidearms.

triple cannon and to crash into a mountain near Nha Nam, Ha Bac Province. The Vietnamese flight returned home safely.

Once the MiGs cleared the area, air defence units began firing at the enemy aircraft. Protecting the bridge over the Hoa River, the 83rd Anti-aircraft Battalion of the 238th Missile Regiment shot down one of them, which crashed at Huu Long village. The 40th Anti-aircraft Company defending the Luong Bridge in Ha Bac Province hit an A-4E Skyhawk, which augered in near Hoanh Bo, Quang Ninh Province.

The 15th and last aerial victory of 1965 went to the flight of Tran Hanh, Ngo Doan Nhung, Pham Ngoc Lan and Tran Van Phuong. The helicopter they shot down on 6 November was endeavouring to rescue imprisoned American aircrew in Hoa Binh.

MiGs patrol these skies

On 24 December 1965 Rolling Thunder was halted for 37 days, to be restarted on 31 January 1966. Three days later Lam Van Lich from the

Left: The entire aft section of the MiG-17's fuselage could be pulled off, thus providing easy access to the engine and its accessories. The VK-1 was a single-spool turbojet with centrifugal compressor. With the introduction of the afterburner on the MiG-17F, the thrust increased by about 25 per cent.

Below: Alerted pilots rush to their hastily camouflaged MiG-17Fs. The cockpit area and, in some cases, the external fuel tanks were left in natural metal.

Although the MiGs enjoyed far more success than a paper comparison of the opposing forces would have suggested, the traffic was far from one way. Here a MiG-17 receives a lethal burst from the 20-mm cannon of Major Kuster's F-105D in June 1967.

921st Fighter Wing was credited with the first VPAF night kill with jet aircraft. Flying a MiG-17 on the night of 3 February 1966, he shot down two A-1H Skyraiders over Cho Ben, Hoa Binh Province.

4 March was noted for an other 'first', this time the combat debut of the 923rd Fighter Wing. At 15.42 an enemy formation was detected entering Yen Bai-Phu Tho airspace. Phan Thanh Chung, Ngo Duc Mai, Tran Minh Phuong and Nguyen The Hon were ordered to scramble from Kep.

At 16.00 they caught sight of an element of F-4s and ran a perfect intercept. Flight lead and his wingman went after one Phantom. Phan Thanh Chung squeezed the trigger, but missed. After changing position, Ngo Duc Mai tried from 500 m(1,640 ft); he missed, too. Closing in to 200 m (656 ft), he fired two bursts, the second of which slapped into the American fighter and blew it up. By this time numbers three and four were also tangling with enemy aircraft, but without success.

Upon dashing home, the Vietnamese flight noticed F-4s trying to get at them. Number two reversed just to see the Phantoms turn tail and leave the area. Low on fuel, Ngo Duc Mai succeeded in making an emergency landing at 16.20.

On 26 April a flight of MiG-17s led by Ho Van Quy shot down two F-4C Phantoms and damaged a third one over Bac Son-Binh Gia, Lang Son Province.

The huge Mi-6 helicopters could easily lift the fully armed and refuelled MiG-17s, and transport them from their dispersals in the mountains to the airfields. After completing their missions, the fighters would soon be delivered back and hidden from the enemy bombers.

Growing battles

By the summer of 1966 a growing proportion of American bombing raids reached military and industrial targets in the Hanoi-Haiphong area. Air battles began in earnest on 4 June. During the summer months a dozen enemy aircraft fell to the cannons of VPAF MiG-17s in 10 engagements.

On 5 June two pairs of MiG-17s shot down two Crusaders. The Vietnamese pilots returned home safely.

Two more F-8s (one a VF-211 F-8E) were shot down in a ferocious dogfight on 21 June over Kep-Chu, Ha Bac Province. The four MiG-17s were flown by Phan Thanh Trung, Duong Trung Tan, Nguyen Van Bay and Phan Van Tuc from the 923rd Fighter Wing.

On 29 June bombing efforts were made against petrol facilities in Duc Giang, Hanoi Province; Thuong Ly, Haiphong Province; and the capital. Attempting to oppose the raids, the 923rd Fighter Wing sent four MiG-17s into combat. Tran Huyen, Vo Van Man, Nguyen Van Bay and Phan Van Tuc struck an element of 12 F-105 Thunderchiefs and downed two of them over Tam Dao, Thai Nguyen Province. (Major Fred L. Tracy was the first 'Thud' pilot credited with a MiG-17 kill. Reportedly, he was hit by the Vietnamese lead (probably Tran Huyen), who overshot only to be hit by Tracy's cannon fire; the Vietnamese pilot did a split-S (standard evasive manoeuvre) into a cloud at about 600 m (1,968 ft), leading the American pilot to believe his victim had fallen. This credit seems to be speculative. Vietnamese records do not mention losses on this day but, on the other hand, Tran Huyen's name does not appear in later missions. To add to the discrepancy, US sources do not mention own losses to enemy aircraft either, only damage to both Tracy's and his lead's aircraft.)

Phan Thanh Trung from the 923rd Fighter Wing destroyed an enemy aircraft on 13 July over An Thi, Hai Hung Province. Next day, fighting over the same place, Ngo Duc Mai shot down an F-8E of VF-162.

On 19 July radars detected an approaching formation of 12 enemy aircraft in flights of four, separated by 3 km (1.8 miles). Flying over Tam Dao, Vinh Phu Province between 600 and 1500 m (1,968 and 4,921 m), they were heading for Hanoi. Nguyen Bien and Vo Van Man was ordered to attack, and were instructed not

North Vietnamese air bases, especially the ones which could operate MiGs, were high-priority targets of the US bombing campaign. Thanks to the assistance of the civil population living nearby, the airfields usually became operational by the next day of the attack. Defusing and removing of unexploded bombs, like this high-drag Snakeye, however, was done by specialists.

to open fire unless closing to at least 400-600 m (1,312-1,968 ft). At 14.50 two MiG-17s of the 923rd Fighter Wing took off and soon ran into two pairs of F-105s separated by 1500 m (4,921 ft). The lack of bombs and the missile armament implied that the enemy aircraft were on a MiG-hunting mission. The F-105s were probably carrying either Shrike anti-radiation or Bullpup air-to-surface missiles, because they were equipped with Sidewinders only from 1967.

The Vietnamese pilots increased speed and a steep climb brought them behind a Thunderchief. Nguyen Bien opened fire from 600 m (1,968 ft) but the 'Thud' had noticed him and evaded. Getting behind the MiG, the American pilot tried to shoot it down with numerous bursts, but missed. A furious dogfight developed upon the arrival of the remaining eight 'Thuds'. Attempting to bait their chasers into the fire of the anti-aircraft artillery, the MiGs rushed for Noi Bai. East of the base Vo Van Man abruptly reversed and got behind the 'Thuds'. After two bursts one of the enemy aircraft crashed, and its pilot was killed. Despite the determination of the American pilots to shoot down the MiGs, their efforts were defeated by fierce anti-aircraft fire. Two minutes later another Thunderchief fell victim to Nguyen Bien, while the third was hit by flak and exploded over Tuyen Quang. The two MiGs landed at Gia Lam.

By the end of 1966, six more enemy aircraft had been downed by MiG-17s, two of them – a pair of F-8 Crusaders – on 5 September. At the conference held by the VPAF in December, the 1st squadron of the 921st Fighter Wing and the 2nd squadron of the 923rd Fighter Wing were awarded, as were individual pilots such as Tran Hanh, Nguyen Van Bay and Lam Van Lich.

Airfields in danger

With the air raid against Dong Hoi airfield on 30 March 1966, an uneasy period for Vietnamese air bases began. On 8 May Vinh airfield was struck by American aircraft. Two days later VPAF Command and the Political Bureau assembled to analyse the situation and to form a strategy of countering this new threat.

At the request of the MoD and commanders

Above: Following devastating strikes against the MiG bases, aircraft were evacuated to villages and forests in the vicinity of the airfields. People living nearby assisted the military to hide the fighters by means of camouflaged nets and branches.

Right: Later the MiG bases received urgent defences in the form of earthworks and shelters. Here a pair of MiG-17s is seen in their revetment at Phuc Yen, photographed by a passing tac recon aircraft in September 1966.

Hangars like this hiding a battered MiG-17F were dispersed in villages or agricultural co-operatives, and could easily be taken for bamboo huts from the air.

of the VPAF, Prime Minister Pham Van Dong ordered the provinces to mobilise their populations and materials and to work by the side of technical units and services of the armed forces to repair the damaged airfields. Committees were set up at province, district and village levels to co-ordinate the combined effort. With the support of local people, Noi Bai, Kep, Kien An, Gia Lam and Hoa Lac airfields were hastily restored to proper condition.

Designed by the Scientific Research Institute and built by numerous state factories, more than 70,000 steel-reinforced concrete plates that could be used to quickly repair damaged runways and taxiways were assembled near the air bases. Thousands of bamboo stems were carried to the airfields to provide protection against splinters, fragmentation and steel-pellet anti-personnel bombs. Aircraft revetments were made of earth and, later, hut-shaped shelters were constructed of rails and covered with earth and grass. Underground command posts were also built.

Similarly to Operation So Tan – the evacuation and dispersal of factories, schools, laboratories and hospitals of towns and industrial centres into the countryside and jungle – aircraft were dispersed into the mountains. Mi-6 helicopters carried the fighters to the dispersals tunnelled into the mountainsides 10-30 km (6.2-18.6 miles) from the air bases. Later, aircraft, armament and fuel were also hidden in villages and agricultural co-operatives. In Soc Son District, Vinh Phu Province, hundreds of thousands of trees were planted to conceal the MiGs evacuated from Noi Bai. These efforts were so successful that it is still believed that the aircraft – at least the MiG-21s – were temporarily withdrawn to Chinese airfields.

Thanks to the preparations and co-ordination mentioned above, damage suffered by Noi Bai on 22 November and by Kep on 2 December was quickly repaired.

MiG-17s go it alone

In the dry seasons of 1966-67, aerial offensives against North Vietnam continued with increased intensity. Key targets were power plants, industrial centres, military bases and air defence units in Hanoi, Haiphong, Viet Tri, Thai Nguyen and Quang Ninh Provinces. The Americans were attempting to isolate the capital from Haiphong and the two cities from other regions. Bombing campaigns against water-

MiG-17 cockpit

The MiG-17 was designed in the early 1950s, and its cockpit reflected its vintage. A cumbersome gunsight dominated the cockpit, which differed little between variants apart from the radar screen of the MiG-17PF.

Above: The instruments on the left-hand side of the panel included airspeed indicator (top left, reading 480 km/h), altimeter (bottom left, reading 2550 m) and attitude indicator (top right, showing a left 45° bank).

The gyro gunsight of the MiG-17 was crude but effective at close range. Below it was the display for the ARK-5 radio compass. The pilot was protected by a 64-mm armoured windscreen.

Above: The right-hand side of the MiG-17PF cockpit was dominated by the screen and associated hood for the RP-1 Izumrud radar.

On display in the VPAF Museum in Hanoi is a control column from a MiG-17. Shown alongside are rounds from the 37-mm N-37 cannon. The MiG-17 carried one of these guns, which was armed with 40 rounds. Although only effective over short range, the destructive power was devastating.

works, weirs and the banks of the Red River were also expected.

Trying to make good use of the small fighter force, activity was concentrated on the defence of Hanoi. Although MiG-21s had already been initiated into the war, the major share of battling was still falling to the proven MiG-17s. Combined use of the two types, utilising their capabilities to the full, was regarded to have paramount importance. Unfortunate circumstances surrounding MiG-21 operations in January, however, led to the type's temporary withdrawal from combat. MiG-17s had to tackle alone the tough job of intercepting enemy aircraft until April 1967. Co-ordination of the fighter and anti-aircraft units was still to be improved.

On 5 February 1967 a MiG-17 shot down a Phantom over Luong Son, Hoa Binh Province. Another F-4C fell to the cannon of a MiG-17 on 26 March over Hoa Lac, Ha Tay Province.

Realising that MiGs had become a considerable threat to its aircraft, the US was driven to refine air combat tactics. The Vietnamese observed that the proportion of fighters protecting the bomber force was increased to 1:1 or even 2:1 in strike packages. The bomber formations approached the target area under the umbrella of escort fighters at 4000-5000 m

Lead and wingman stand in front of their MiG-17s in February 1967. By this time VPAF MiG-21s were still maturing and could not be counted on in the air defence of North Vietnam.

Above: This photograph is claimed to illustrate the final moments of Colonel Norman Gaddis's F-4C. It was one of the three Phantoms downed on 12 May 1967 over Hoa Lac, Ha Tay Province with the co-operation of the 923rd Fighter Wing and the anti-aircraft units.

Below: Photograph of Colonel Norman Gaddis's identification card. After spending six years in North Vietnam as POW, he was released in 1973 under Operation Homecoming.

(13,123-16,404 ft), and returned immediately after bomb release. Electronic warfare operations, including employment of RB-66C, EB-66B/C ECM aircraft to counter North Vietnamese air defence radars, were intensified.

On 24 March General Vo Nguyen Giap, Minister of Defence, issued order 04./QD-DP regarding the organisation of radar and missile units of the VPAF-AAF. The new designation of VPAF became 371st Air Division, comprising the 921st and 923rd Fighter Wings, the 919th Air Transport Wing and the 910th Air Wing. Airfields operated by these units were Gia Lam, Noi Bai, Kep, Hoa Lac, Kien An, Tho Xuan and Vinh.

At this time, fighter pilots numbered 65 and aircraft mechanics 1,686. Commander-in-Chief was Lieutenant Colonel Nguyen Van Tien, with Lieutenant Colonel Dao Dinh Luen as his deputy. Dao Dinh Luen subsequently became Commander-in-Chief, with deputies Lieutenant Colonels Tran Manh and Nguyen Phuc Trac.

April of success

The Vietnamese enjoyed a quadruple victory on 19 April 1967. Two Thunderchiefs and two Skyraiders were shot down by MiG-17s over Suoi Rut, Hoa Binh Province.

On 23 April Kien An airfield, near Haiphong, was struck from the air, the first 'official' bombing of a MiG base. The raid inflicted heavy damage both to the runway and the buildings. In spite of its ploughed condition the airfield was serviceable by the next day, thanks to the assistance of civilians from neigh-

bouring Truong Son and Thai Son.

On 24 April two dozen enemy aircraft attacked Hanoi, to be frustrated by eight MiG-17s of the 923rd Fighter Wing. The flight of Vo Van Man, Nguyen Ba Dich, Nguyen Van Bay and Nguyen The Hon downed two Phantoms. Flight two with pilots Mai Duc Toai, Le Hai, Luu Huy Chao and Hoang Van Ky destroyed another F-4 over Pha Lai, Hai Hung Province.

Later the same day, a flight of four MiG-17s of the 923rd Fighter Wing was ordered to take off from Gia Lam once again. This time flying in radio silence at low level to remain undetected, pilots Nguyen Van Bay, Nguyen The Hon, Ha Bon and Nguyen Ba Dich made for Kien An and landed safely.

Hanoi came under attack again on 25 April. Mai Duc Toai, Le Hai, Luu Huy Chao and Hoang Van Ky engaged the enemy formation and downed an F-105 over Gia Lam. On the same morning, another raid struck the port of Haiphong. While the MiG-17s deployed to Kien An on the previous day stayed away, anti-aircraft fire brought down 10 enemy aircraft.

Haiphong suffered further early that afternoon under the attack of a formation composed of at least 24 carrierborne aircraft. At 13.15 the four MiGs at Kien An were ordered up. On their way to the rendezvous they flew over Voi Mountain and climbed to 1500 m (4,921 ft), heading for Van Uc River. The enemy was completely unaware of the MiG-17s because Kien An was thought to be incapacitated. Furiously engaged by the MiGs, they soon lost two A-4 Skyhawks and one F-8 Crusader. Two more US Navy aircraft were destroyed by anti-aircraft batteries.

When the Vietnamese could disengage, they turned for home with a Crusader pursuing them until they reached Hai Duong. A surface-to-air missile unit based at Kim Thanh succeeded in driving off the pursuer by firing SAMs at it. The relieved MiG pilots landed at Gia Lam.

In spring 1967 seven pilots, including four flying MiG-17s, were awarded by Ho Chi Minh for their distinguished service since the outbreak of the air war. Of Nguyen Van Bay, Luu Huy Chao, Le Hai and Nguyen Dinh Phuc, the latter two had been trained entirely in Vietnam.

Triumph turns to defeat

In May 1967 battles over Hanoi continued with the same intensity. VPAF aircraft flew 30-40 or even 78 sorties daily, with increasing effectiveness.

On 12 May three MiG-17 flights of the 923rd Fighter Wing were involved in destroying five enemy aircraft. Duong Trung Tan and Nguyen Van Tho downed a Thunderchief over Vinh Yen. Successful co-operation between anti-aircraft units and the flight of Cao Thanh Tinh, Le Hai, Ngo Duc Mai and Hoang Van Ky resulted in three F-4C Phantoms mortally hit over Hoa Lac, Ha Tay Province. Establishment of the exact identity to whom these Phantoms could be attributed – anti-aircraft units or MiGs – has been impossible.

One week later Phan Thanh Tai and Nguyen Huu Diet destroyed two F-4s over Xuan Mai, Hoa Binh Province. With these kills the scoreboard of the 923rd Fighter Wing totalled 62 enemy aircraft. The fighter unit received a challenge pennant from Ho Chi Minh, who celebrated his 77th birthday on that day.

In May 1967 85 American aircraft were shot down over North Vietnam: 34 fell to SAMs, 32 to anti-aircraft artillery and 19 to fighter aircraft. From 24 April to 25 May the VPAF flew 469 sorties and successfully blunted 222 enemy air raids.

Owing to these achievements, some pilots became conceited, scornful and careless – for which they paid a heavy price. At the end of May and in the beginning of June, 10 MiG-17 pilots perished in seven air battles. The loss of experienced airmen in rapid succession was detrimental to the morale of the novices. The apprehension felt by some pilots occasionally jeopardised the outcome of the missions.

In addition to human losses, hardware attrition also peaked, due to intensive utilisation, poor maintenance and heavy attacks against

These MiGs show signs of having their previous national insignias painted over, the new markings being applied over crudely sprayed patches. This would suggest that they are ex-Chinese Shenyang J-5s rather than Soviet-built MiG-17Fs.

MiG-17 over Vietnam

MiG bases. The six airfields suitable for operating fighter aircraft – Noi Bai, Gia Lam, Kep, Hoa Lac, Kien An and Tho Xuan – were repeatedly attacked, and except for Noi Bai and Gia Lam were not always quickly repaired. On 19 May the bombing raid on Kep airfield found MiG-17s of the 923rd Fighter Wing left on the flight line instead of having been towed away, and they were slaughtered on the spot. Serious shortages of spare parts led to cannibalisation of grounded aircraft to keep the rest of them operational. Insufficient fuel supply resulted in limitations even of practice flights.

A strenuous summer

Following the defeats early in June 1967, General Van Thien Tung, Chief of the General Staff, visited the fighting units and instructed them not to waste their strength, otherwise they would not be able to keep fighting. The MiGs were settled for a while and sent into combat almost exclusively against EB-66s – albeit without success. The first EB-66 was only shot down on 19 November, by two MiG-21s. The aircraft attrition rate was further reduced by the mobilisation of manpower to aircraft repair units and by the improvement of maintenance.

From the middle of June, meetings were held to disclose the causes that had led to the beatings the VPAF suffered in previous weeks. While the enemy had been developing air combat tactics and had switched to two-level formations, the Vietnamese had continued to employ intercept procedures and manoeuvres that had once been successful, but which by then were outdated. Some pilots still thought that impromptu shots would certainly be followed by quick victories.

With many airmen, mainly experienced ones, dying in combat, by the summer of 1967 the number of fighter pilots serving in the two fighter wings did not exceed the original effective force of one wing. The survivors were overburdened by being on duty and fighting around the clock.

On 11 July 1967 a MiG-17 flight successfully assisted two MiG-21s of the 921st Fighter Wing in the defence of Lai Vu and Phu Luong Bridges of Highway 5, and helped them to shoot down an A-4 Skyhawk.

At 13.45 on 23 August, radar stations reported a 40-strong enemy formation approaching from the direction of Xam Nua, Laos, very

Tran Hanh and Pham Ngoc Lan examine a gun camera film beside a MiG-17 for the benefit of the photographer. Pham Ngoc Lan (right) completed his pilot training in China, and was the first VPAF pilot to land on a North Vietnamese airfield in a jet aircraft. Lieutenant Lan became a flight leader in the 921st Fighter Wing and the first Vietnamese MiG-17 pilot to shoot down an enemy aircraft. Later he was selected for conversion training to the MiG-21. In April 1975 he led the conversion training of the Vietnamese pilots to the captured A-37B Dragonfly light attack aircraft.

likely in an attempt to attack Hanoi. A pair of MiG-21s and two flights each of four MiG-17s were ordered to take off. The MiG-21s struck from behind and the cat-and-mouse chase resulted in the loss of an F-105 Thunderchief and an F-4 Phantom to the MiGs' air-to-air missiles. The MiG-17s joined in by initiating a head-on attack. The flight of Cao Thanh Tinh, Le Van Phong, Nguyen Van Tho and Nguyen Hong Diep shot down two F-105s, and flight two downed an F-4. All the Vietnamese aircraft returned to their bases. First Lieutenant David B. Valdrop, flying an F-105D Thunderchief, was credited with a MiG-17 on that day. This claim seems to be erroneous, in the light of Vietnamese reports.

In the third quarter of 1967 Vietnamese fighters flew 74 missions and were credited with nine enemy aircraft.

MiGs unexpected

The sky over North Vietnam was somewhat bereft of MiGs until the second half of October 1967. The recent achievements had shaken off the lethargy of the pilots, who were relaxing to regain their strength. Vietnamese fighter activity had also been diminished by the devastating air raids against MiG bases. The enemy was apparently concentrating again on the utter destruction of North Vietnamese airfields. Prime target became Noi Bai, which was considered to be vital to the defence of the capital, but Kep, Kien An, Cat Bi and Hoa Lac also suffered repeatedly.

Following the strike on 24 October, Kep was

repaired overnight by army units and local people. On the next day the base regained its operational status, and the 923rd Fighter Wing launched a flight of MiG-17s led by Nguyen Huu Thao to shoot down an F-105 Thunderchief.

US Navy aircraft were similarly waylaid on 19 November. Two days before, the runways of Kien An had been heavily damaged and on 18 November American reconnaissance aircraft still returned with photographs showing heavy cratering. The 28th Engineering Battalion, however, was hard at work repairing the airfield. In the early morning of 19 November, four MiG-17s of the 923rd Fighter Wing from Gia Lam escaped the notice of US radar surveillance and stealthily landed at Kien An.

At 10.00 a 20-ship enemy formation comprising Skyhawks and Phantoms was observed approaching Haiphong. The flight of Ho Van Quy, Le Hai, Nguyen Dinh Phuc and Nguyen Phi Hung departed from Kien An and remained undetected until they ambushed the raiders. The first F-4B fell to Le Hai. A couple of minutes later two other Phantoms (F-4Bs of VF-151 'Vigilantes' from USS Coral Sea) were shot down by Nguyen Dinh Phuc and Nguyen Phi Hung. After disengaging, the Vietnamese flight returned safely to Kien An.

From the middle of November, air operations against Hanoi continued at higher intensity despite the rather heavy enemy losses. The immense raids comprised 15- to 20-aircraft elements separated by 20 to 30 minutes. Some were successfully caught by Vietnamese fighters as this exhausting year of the air war drew to a close.

On 14 December a MiG-17 shot down an F-8 Crusader over Ninh Giang, Hai Hung Province. Three days later a MiG-17 flight assisted three MiG-21s in pouncing on a formation of 32 F-105 Thunderchiefs and F-4 Phantoms heading toward the capital. While the MiG-21s scattered the bombers and brought down three F-105s, the MiG-17s ventured to attack the Phantoms and destroyed two F-4Cs over Ha Hoa, Vinh Phu Province.

On 19 December a mixed force of MiG-17s and MiG-21s clashed with the enemy over Tam Dao, Vinh Phu Province and shot down four of them.

Above: A dozen MiG-17Fs are neatly lined up on the flight line. Four of them are grey while the rest are natural metal. The reason why the national insignia is overpainted is unknown. The aircraft are probably Shenyang J-5s.

Left: A warmly dressed pilot climbs into the cockpit of a MiG-17. The gun camera of the aircraft is positioned over the intake, slightly offset to the starboard.

First battle of 1968

Early on the morning of 3 January 1968, radar stations reported an EB-66 coming from the northwest. At 07.33 the hostile aircraft entered Mai Chau Province. Following two MiG-21s that had taken off a couple of minutes previously, four MiG-17s of the 923rd Fighter Wing left Gia Lam at 07.39. Luu Huy Chao, Nguyen Hong Diep, Bui Van Suu and Le Hai were directed over Thai Nguyen but the haze prevented visual contact and therefore they missed the rendezvous with the enemy.

Following the order to turn back and land, they suddenly spotted eight F-4 Phantoms flying 45° to port at 8 km (5 miles). The MiGs went into action. Luu Huy Chao, escorted by Nguyen Hong Diep, pushed forward on the throttle to pick up speed and began to harry a Phantom, just as his wingman took a hit and ejected from his doomed aircraft. The Vietnamese lead also took a pounding, but managed to keep his tattered aircraft in the air and continue fighting. Veering away and down on the numerous Phantoms that appeared low on his left, he accelerated and soon found himself behind the tail of an F-4. After firing three bursts from 700 m (2,296 ft) but observing no hits, Luu Huy Chao disengaged, set a course for Bac Ninh and landed at Noi Bai.

Two F-4D crews claimed to have shot down one MiG-17 each on this day. According to Vietnamese records, however, only Nguyen Hop Diep's aircraft was hit mortally.

Van Suu pursued another Phantom flight, opened fire, but missed, too. Turning back he sighted more F-4s. Closing to 500 m (1,640 ft) of one, he opened fire and apparently damaged the Phantom.

Le Hai also attacked an F-4, squeezing the trigger from 800 m (2,624 ft), but the Phantom escaped unharmed. The Vietnamese pilot spent the next moments of his life avoiding air-to-air missiles being shot at him. In doing so he became disorientated and, what is more, ran into friendly anti-aircraft fire over Viet Tri. Le Hai composed himself and, finally, flew along the Red River to Gia Lam.

Moving southward

On 31 March 1968 US President Johnson announced that bombing operations would be restricted to a limited area of North Vietnam.

An air offensive of unprecedented ferocity concentrated on the 4th Military Zone began. Its aim was to systematically destroy communication and supply lines running through a narrow corridor between the mountains and the sea from Vinh down to the DMZ. These roads, trails and paths originating in Nghe An Province and passing Truong Son Mountains and western Laos were called Duong Truong Son or Duong Mon Ho Chi Minh (Ho Chi Minh Trail). The VPAF was urged to begin preparations for the defence of this region.

The defenders had to grapple with numerous difficulties. The climate of North Central Vietnam is exasperatingly harsh, with unpredictable weather and frequent typhoons, making it less than ideal for fighter operations, reconstruction of demolished airfields, improvement of the region's air defence system and ensuring that the necessary aircraft were readily available.

Commander-in-Chief Nguyen Van Tien, Chief of the General Staff Tran Manh, his deputy Nguyen Phuc Trac and high-ranking VPAF officers visited the 4th Military Zone to assess the state of airfields, study weather conditions and enemy tactics.

The construction of new airfields in the provinces of the 4th Military Zone was ordered, along with reconstruction of the existing ones. Tho Xuan air base in Thanh Hoa Province was soon to be opened. Its location meant that the strategically important supply routes heading south would be within reach of the defending fighters. Airfields badly damaged by enemy air strikes, like Vinh, Dong Hoi, Cam Thuy, Anh Son, and Gat, were repaired and put back into operation, and underwent developments in their communication systems and runways. Radar stations were operated at Mui Lay, Huong Lap, Ca Roong, Ta Lech, Lum Bum, La Vang, A Luoi and Xe Pon (Laos).

During three years of fighting, corrosion caused by the extreme humidity had taken a heavy toll among aircraft (in addition to operational losses). Repair units were evacuated to remote areas, thus providing relatively undisturbed working conditions. Of even greater concern was the shortage of qualified maintenance personnel. Engineers Truong Khanh Chau and Huynh Ngoc An, together with technicians of the A.33 Aircraft Repair Unit at Bach Mai airfield, Hanoi, repaired 19 aircraft, assembled 24 new ones and changed 12 engines. Shock absorber struts had to be changed on many MiG-17s.

The few serviceable aircraft were regularly subjected to temporary deployments to Noi Bai, Kep, Gia Lam, Kien An, Hoa Lac, Tho Xuan and Vinh, according to operational requirements.

Additional pilots were sent abroad to flying training schools, and courses continued in Vietnam. In the first months of 1968, 14 pilots completed their MiG-17 training at the 910th Air Wing and arrived at the 921st and 923rd Fighter Wings.

Early in April 1968 two MiG-17s were deployed to Vinh with two AAA regiments and four SAM battalions. As soon as the MiGs arrived, devastating air strikes swept in. The remains of the two aircraft were dismantled and the useful parts were transported back to Hanoi by truck.

The two NS-23 and single N-37D cannon of the MiG-17 were mounted on the same tray, together with their ammunition boxes and link ejection ports. The whole system could be lowered and lifted manually by turning a hand crank. This arrangement provided easy and quick access for loading and maintenance.

The removed tail section is inspected from inside. With their relatively small build, the Vietnamese could easily work in the fuselage even of such a small aircraft as the MiG-17.

A turbulent flight to Tho Xuan

Following endeavours with MiG-21s in May 1968, a pair of MiG-17s of the 923rd Fighter Wing was dispatched south again on 14 June. Luu Huy Chao and Le Hai took off from Gia Lam at 14.28 and climbed to 500 m (1,640 ft). Following Highway 15 at 650 km/h (404 mph), they soon reached Nghia Dan where they wound up to 1000 m (3,280 ft). Over Thanh Chuong they were flying at 1500 m (4,921 ft) when ground control warned them of six F-4 Phantoms 10° to port, flying at 3000 m (9,842 ft). The Vietnamese fighters increased their speed to 730 km/h (454 mph), and upon reaching 2000 m (6,561 ft) Le Hai saw the enemy aircraft coasting in at right angles to their direction.

A missile launch indicated that the enemy had spotted them, too. Le Hai jettisoned the external fuel tanks, accelerated to 800 km/h (497 mph), evaded the oncoming missile and climbed to 2700 m (8,858 ft). Luu Huy Chao followed his wingman and gave cover while Le Hai was turning left, and tried to hit a Phantom but with no success. The enemy lead made a steep turn. Le Hai, however, chose the wingman to follow, turned left and dropped the nose of his MiG to lose some height and close up. From 300 m (985 ft) he opened fire. After the second burst, the Phantom caught fire and crashed into the sea.

Le Hai made a left climbing turn to regain his original wingman position. Suddenly, an F-4 popped up 1000 m (3,280 ft) in front of him. He closed in before opening fire, but not enough to hit the Phantom, which escaped.

Luu Huy Chao recognised the enemy's attempt to leave southeasterly, so he turned right, and found an F-4 dead ahead. He fired a burst but was out of range and missed. Turning right, the Vietnamese lead saw another Phantom making for the coast, southward. Accompanied by Le Hai on his wing, Luu Huy Chao positioned himself behind his quarry and gave him three bursts. The Phantom blew up and crashed.

As the rest of the F-4s cleared the coast the Vietnamese flight set course for Tho Xuan. After crossing Highway 7, they flew along Highway 15 and landed at 15.00.

Defending the supply routes

Even the sporadic VPAF air operations in the 4th Military Zone between April and June 1968 resulted in temporary relief for the 559th Army Corps, which was responsible for forwarding supplies south. Taking advantage of the easing of the bombing campaign against the supply routes, movements of troops and material gained additional momentum.

Between 9 and 29 July 1968, seven MiG-17s of the 923rd Fighter Wing deployed to the 4th Military Zone shot down three American aircraft. At the request of 559th Army Corps HQ, the VPAF occasionally also flew weather reconnaissance missions to help in the planning of road repairs and the dispatch of lorry convoys.

On 17 September the Vietnamese attempted to use a mixed force of MiG-17s and MiG-21s over Yen Thanh, Thanh Chuong and Do

MiG-17 variants

MiG-17
The MiG-17 came into life as an attempt to increase the maximum speed of the MiG-15bis solely by aerodynamic improvements. It resulted in a new wing, a lengthened fuselage and larger airbrakes. The wing had thinner airfoils, increased compound sweepback (earning the nickname 'sickle wing'), enlarged area and three fences on each side.

MiG-17F
To increase the performance of the MiG-17, the Mikoyan OKB installed the new VK-1F afterburning turbojet in the MiG-17. The new engine required both internal and external modifications. Cooling air for the afterburner section was ducted from the engine intake. Increased fuel flow was provided by the modification of the fuel system. The new nozzle with its variable exhaust resulted in the redesign of the rear fuselage, including the repositioned and enlarged airbrakes.

MiG-17PF
With the installation of the RP-1 Izumrud radar in the MiG-17F in 1952, the aircraft gained all-weather/night-fighter capabilities. The upper intake lip housed the search radar, while the conical radome on the splitter plate housed the fire control antenna. The avionics bay forward of the windscreen accommodated the radar related electronics. The windscreen was modified according to the larger space required by the CRT display of the radar. An ASP-3N gunsight was also installed.

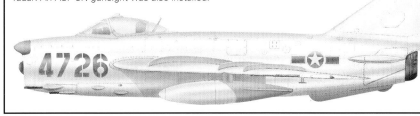

Luong. The only success they met was that all of them returned from the mission.

By October the enemy had increased its air activity along Highways 1 and 15 and enhanced radar surveillance of this region. At 07.35 on 26 October, 11 US radar stations were on the air. Fifteen minutes later three more were activated. Taking previous experiences into account, an enemy air raid was expected against targets along Highway 15 in the vicinity of Nam Dan.

At 08.17, two MiG-17s took off and orbited over Tan Ky awaiting American aircraft. Due to the heavy overcast they could not make visual contact with the enemy flying at the same altitude, so were ordered back. A pair of MiG-21s departed one minute after the MiG-17s, downed one F-4 Phantom and landed safely.

The first 1,305 days

The first major part of the air war came to a close on 31 October 1968, when President Johnson ordered the cessation of the aerial offensive against North Vietnam.

At the beginning of hostilities, the VPAF's sole fighter unit had comprised 36 MiG-17s flown by three dozen freshly trained pilots. Withstanding three and a half years of relentless bombing, North Vietnam – with mainly Soviet and Chinese material support and training, but

In spite of being one of the primary targets of American air operations, and the subject of some intense campaigns, the transport of men and materiel to the South along the communication lines of the Ho Chi Minh Trail was continuously increased. Air defence of this network was based mainly on anti-aircraft forces, but VPAF aircraft were also involved occasionally in the 4th Military Zone to counter enemy air raids. To help the technical units and civilians to repair damaged roads, reconstructing railway lines and bridges, and plan the launch of supply convoys in the unpredictable weather of this region, MiG-17s were sometimes tasked to fly weather reconnaissance sorties.

MiG-17 aces

Right: Nguyen Van Bay was the top-scoring Vietnamese MiG-17 pilot, credited with seven kills while flying with the 923rd Fighter Wing. He was one of the pilots who flew the VPAF's first anti-ship mission on 19 April 1972, and was highly decorated for his achievements.

Left: Luu Huy Chao scored six aerial victories on MiG-17s. He later rose to become deputy commander of the 923rd Fighter Wing. He was decorated by Ho Chi Minh for his successes.

Right: Le Hai was the third VPAF MiG-17 ace, also scoring six victories. He was trained in Vietnam by the 910th Training Wing, before joining the 923rd Fighter Wing.

independent operation – had evolved this small group of inexperienced but dedicated airmen flying unsophisticated aircraft into an effective fighter force.

It is hard to imagine that Vietnam could have resisted without Chinese and Soviet assistance. It must be realised, however, that as a consequence much of Vietnam's foreign debt is owed to the former Soviet Union. Hostilities with China originate to about the 2nd century BC. China's support is summarised in Truong-Chinh's *On Kampuchea* (Foreign Languages Publishing House, Hanoi, 1980): "[The] Chinese...had pursued a policy of maintaining Vietnam between victory and defeat and in a permanent state of partition...permanently weak and dependent on China."

Left: North Vietnam's air defence partially relied on the people's militia, armed with infantry arms and light artillery. These units posed a considerable threat to low flying aircraft, be they enemy or friendly. Here, a militiawoman guards the wreckage of an A-4 Skyhawk, which seems to be either an E or F model. The photograph was probably taken in 1969 during the Oriskany's Westpac cruise with Air Group 16 aboard.

Below: Four pilots of the 923rd Fighter Wing are seen with a MiG-17F behind. First and second from the left are Luu Huy Chao and Le Hai, each of them eventually credited with the destruction six enemy aircraft.

No-one realistically had expected that this air force could gain air superiority over one of the world's major air arms, but it had managed to disrupt USAF activity. It did so on countless occasions by popping up out of the blue and disrupting bomber formations, forcing them to dump their bombs before reaching their targets. Moreover, between 3 April 1965 and 31 October 1968, Vietnamese fighters shot down 218 enemy aircraft of 19 types in 251 air battles. Those figures derived from official VPAF sources, including reconnaissance drones. According to recent information, USAF and USN aircraft shot down 119 Vietnamese aircraft during this period. Both countries' lists contain questionable data of roughly the same proportion.

The VPAF successfully transplanted the traditional way of Vietnamese warfare into the air, and, although sometimes it seemed that it was terminally decimated, the air force survived. It established a second fighter wing, and the number of its pilots doubled and of aircraft quintupled.

The protagonist in the first act of North Vietnam's air war was the MiG-17. Its relative simplicity, robust construction, formidable cannon armament, supreme agility and undemanding handling characteristics made it an ideal mount for pilots with little experience. After the first three years, however, the MiG-17 appeared again only as a supporting character, overshadowed by the MiG-21.

The interval

The bombing halt did not mean the end of all American aerial activity over North Vietnam. In addition to SR-71A strategic reconnaissance aircraft and Ryan Firebee drones, carrierborne and land-based tactical reconnaissance aircraft were sent regularly over the North to gather intelligence data. Besides these 'passive' missions, however, road junctions, ferry boats and airfields were sometimes struck from the air, especially in provinces south of Nghe Anh.

MiG-17 over Vietnam

Left: Technicians install a store of unknown purpose under the port wing of a MiG-17. The lens suggests some kind of optical device, perhaps a reconnaissance camera. The concrete shelter provided undisturbed working conditions.

Below: A pilot and ground personnel pose beside a MiG-17F, apparently celebrating a successful mission. There were periods in the war when scenes like this could be spontaneous and not only made for the media.

In February 1969 the Ministry of Defence and the VPAF decided to form a new fighter unit, which became the 925th Fighter Wing (trung doan khong quan tiem kich 925) consisting of MiG-17 and MiG-19 aircraft. (The Vietnamese do not usually distinguish between MiGs of Soviet and Chinese origin by using their different designations, e.g. MiG-17F/Shenyang J-5 or MiG-19S/Shenyang J-6.) The unit, led by Commander Nguyen Quang Trung, began life at Yen Bai airfield. MiG-17 pilots were supplied by the 910th Air Wing, plus others who had just returned from the Soviet Union after completing MiG-21 training. For a time, the unit also had two bomber battalions equipped with Il-28s piloted by Soviet-trained aircrew.

Although the number of airmen were increasing, differences in their experience and skill began to show. The hard core of combat-proven pilots was hindered in passing their knowledge of fighter tactics to the novices because of limited flying time. Although the fleet of aircraft was also growing, a high attrition rate was caused by the humid climate, poor maintenance, and neglect of technical instructions. Operational aircraft were flown well beyond their theoretical fatigue life. Skilled technicians still numbered only 43 instead of the demanded 120.

Groups involved in airfield reconstruction were also understaffed. Each of them would have required about 80 experts, whose numbers really totalled only 148. In May 1969 Noi Bai was still scarred by at least 230 bomb craters, Gia Lam by 204, Kep by 222, Kien An by 114 and Tho Xuan by 30. The 28th Engineering Battalion, assisted by local people, covered 174 bomb craters and completely repaired the runways of Vinh airfield. That was followed by the lengthening of the runway at Dong Hoi airfield from 1600 to 2000 m (5,249 to 6,651 ft), then the building of the secret Gat airfield. In two years, most of the airfields of North Vietnam were reconstructed. Landing strips were also built near Cam Thuy and Phu Cuy villages.

Aircraft repaired in Vietnam, plus the ones returned from abroad following overhaul, were put into hardened shelters at Kien An, Hoa Lac, Ha Bac and Lang Son. Maintenance began to improve at Yen Bai, Noi Bai and Kep, so flying hours increased somewhat. In 1969 and 1970 fresh pilots were doing cross-country training flights in two- and four-ship formations, and familiarisation sorties to operational airfields. Experienced pilots underwent advanced tactical training in ground attack and maritime attack sorties, and in eight- and 12-ship formations, and practised air defence sorties with simulated interception profiles against B-52 and AC-130 aircraft.

Due to regular enemy reconnaissance flights over North Vietnamese territory, especially north of Thanh Hoa, VPAF fighter units and Anti-Aircraft Forces remained in readiness. The most frequent visitors with the least predictable flight path were the unmanned Ryan Firebee reconnaissance drones. In 1969 MiG-17s of the 923rd Fighter Wing shot down two out of 10. In 1970 the VPAF flew 70 sorties against these pilotless aircraft, engaged them six times and shot bursts on three occasions, but without success. In 1971 MiGs were scrambled six times against drones, but only one pilot could make visual contact. On 9 March Luong Duc Truong from the 923rd Fighter Wing took off in his MiG-17 to intercept an unmanned reconnais-sance aircraft. He spotted the small flying object, closed in and shot it down. Unfortunately, the Vietnamese pilot crashed and died during this mission.

Victories south, misfortune north

On 30 March 1972 People's Liberation Armed Forces launched a full-scale offensive across the DMZ with artillery, armour and infantry units. Fire bases and fortified positions near the 17th Parallel in Quang Tri Province, in the Loc Ninh and An Loc areas and along Highways 14 and 19 in the Central Highlands were taken in a month. On 1 May, Quang Tri City fell to the PLAF.

In response to the spring offensive, bomber operations against North Vietnam resumed. Operation Freedom Train was nominally limited to the region below the 20th Parallel. On 6 April 106 sorties were flown against targets in Quang Binh Province. B-52D Stratofortresses carried out devastating raids against Vinh on 10 April and, three days later, against Thanh Hoa.

Technicians are busy on the flight line as the MiG-17Fs are prepared for the next sortie. The lack of revetments indicate that this photograph was probably taken in the early war years.

113

This photograph illustrates **Le Xuan Di** and **Nguyen Van Bay** recalling their maritime attack mission against the destroyers USS **Highbee** and USS **Oklahoma City** on 19 April 1972.

Major Tranh Hanh climbs down from a MiG-17PF radar-equipped all-weather interceptor. Tran Hanh was one of the first pilots to complete fighter pilot training in China. Considered as having exceptional aeronautical skill, he, then as a captain, became flight leader immediately upon the homecoming of the 921st Fighter Wing. Following service as the deputy of Dao Dinh Luyen, he rose to become the Wing Commander early in 1966. In 1977 he was selected as Deputy Commander in Chief of the VPAF.

VPAF fighters could not engage the enemy in the first 10 days of the renewed air operations. On 16 April Vinh, Than Hoa, Haiphong and the Duc Giang kerosene storage farm was struck by American aircraft. The Vietnamese sent 30 fighters into action, including 10 MiG-21s, six MiG-19s and 14 MiG-17s. The unsuccessful attempt to use a combined force of all three fighter types in VPAF inventory resulted in the loss of three MiG-21s to AIM-7 Sparrows launched from F-4D Phantoms.

Going maritime

In 1971 10 pilots from the 923rd Fighter Wing had been selected for special ground attack training. With the assistance of a pilot advisor (whose name the Vietnamese spelled as 'Et-net-to' – perhaps meaning Ernesto) and ground personnel from Cuba, the Vietnamese began to prepare for anti-shipping strikes. By March 1972 six pilots were capable of flying maritime attack missions. In the meantime, the 28th Engineering Battalion was building the secret Gat airfield down south.

In addition to bombing raids, naval strikes against military and industrial targets and Vietnamese maritime operations had resumed by the beginning of April 1972. The VPAF was ordered to support shore batteries in their fight against US Navy ships.

To command the oncoming mission, Deputy Commander-in-Chief Nguyen Phuc Trach moved to Quang Trach in Quang Binh Province, while Luu Huy Chao, Deputy Commander of the 923rd Fighter Wing, moved to Dong Hoi. Cao Thanh Tinh led the deployment at Gat airfield. The 403rd radar unit, with its aerials installed on the bank of Dinh River opposite to the port of Nhat Le, kept enemy shipping under surveillance.

On 10 April pilots had arrived at Gat and began preparations to be ready for the mission in a week.

On 18 April a pair of MiG-17s of the 923rd Fighter Wing, with Le Hong Diep and Tu De at the controls, took off from Kep at 15.45 and, after making a stopover at Noi Bai, landed at Vinh. They departed Vinh one by one, launching the second MiG only when the first had arrived at Gat. Ground personnel covered the aircraft immediately after engine shut-down and made the necessary post-flight checks.

The appearance of four enemy vessels between 23.00 and 23.50 off the shores of Quang Xa and Ly Nhan villages, 10-15 km (6.2-9.3 miles) from Quang Binh, indicated that the MiGs had arrived undetected.

Looking for ships

At 09.30 on 19 April 1972, the 403rd radar unit reported three or four ships sailing 40 km (25 miles) from Le Thuy and 120 km (75 miles) from Dinh. Another three vessels were picked up 80 km (50 miles) from the mouth of the Sot River. Although Gat was put in readiness, poor flying weather and fog prevented any air activity. At noon, some of the ships were observed to sail south but two remained in the area. Their movements were regularly reported to Gat.

At 15.00 three ships were detected 18 km (11 miles) away, four were approaching 15 km (9.3 miles) from Ly Hoa, and another two were sailing 7 km (4.3 miles) from Quang Trach. One hour later more vessels appeared 16 km (9.9 km) from Nhat Le. This time the MiGs were ordered off.

Known VPAF MiG-17 air-to-air victories

Date	Location	Aircraft	Unit	Crew
03 Apr 65	Thanh Hoa	F-8	921.	Pham Ngoc Lan
03 Apr 65	Thanh Hoa	F-8	921.	Phan Van Tuc
04 Apr 65	Thanh Hoa	F-105D	921.	Tran Hanh
04 Apr 65	Thanh Hoa	F-105D	921.	Le Minh Huan
17 Jun 65	Nho Quan	F-4	921.	?
17 Jun 65	Nho Quan	F-4	921.	?
20 Jun 65	Mai Chau	A-1H	921.	?
20 Jun 65	Mai Chau	A-1H	921.	?
20 Jul 65	Tam Dao	F-4	921.	?
20 Sep 65	Nha Nam	F-4	921.	Nguyen Nhat Chieu
06 Nov 65	Hoa Binh	helicopter	921.	Tran Hanh – Ngo Doan Nhung – Pham Ngoc Lan – Tran Van Phuong
03 Feb 66	Cho Ben	A-1H	921.	Lam Van Lich
03 Feb 66	Cho Ben	A-1H	921.	Lam Van Lich
04 Mar 66	Yen Bai -Phu Tho	F-4	923.	Ngo Duc Mai
26 Apr 66	Bac Son	F-4C	923.	Ho Van Quy
26 Apr 66	Binh Gia	F-4C	923.	Ho Van Quy
05 Jun 66	?	F-8	923.	?
05 Jun 66	?	F-8	923.	?
21 Jun 66	Kep	RF-8A	923.	Phan Thanh Trung – Duong Trung Tan – Nguyen Van Bay – Phan Van Tuc
21 Jun 66	Kep	F-8E	923.	Phan Thanh Trung – Duong Trung Tan – Nguyen Van Bay – Phan Van Tuc
29 Jun 66	Tam Dao	F-105D	923.	Tran Huyen – Vo Van Man – Nguyen Van Bay – Phan Van Tuc
29 Jun 66	Tam Dao	F-105D	923.	Tran Huyen – Vo Van Man – Nguyen Van Bay – Phan Van Tuc
13 Jul 66	An Thi	?	923.	Phan Than Trung
14 Jul 66	An Thi	F-8E	923.	Ngo Duc Mai
19 Jul 66	?	F-4	923.	Nguyen Ba Dich
19 Jul 66	Vinh Phu	F-105	923.	Nguyen Bien
19 Jul 66	Vinh Phu	F-105	923.	Vo Van Man
05 Sep 66	?	F-8E	923.	?
05 Sep 66	?	F-8	923.	?
05 Feb 67	Luong Son	F-4	921.	?
26 Mar 67	Hoa Lac	F-4C	921.	?
19 Apr 67	Suoi Rut	F-105	921.	?
19 Apr 67	Suoi Rut	F-105	921.	?
19 Apr 67	Suoi Rut	A-1H	923.	?
19 Apr 67	Suoi Rut	A-1H	923.	?
24 Apr 67	Hanoi	F-4	923.	Vo Van Man – Nguyen Ba Dich – Nguyen Van Bay – Nguyen The Hon
24 Apr 67	Hanoi	F-4	923.	Vo Van Man – Nguyen Ba Dich – Nguyen Van Bay – Nguyen The Hon
24 Apr 67	Pha Lai-Son Dong	F-4	923.	Mai Duc Toai – Le Hai – Luu Huy Chao – Hoang Van Ky
25 Apr 67	Gia Lam	F-105	923.	Mai Duc Toai – Le Ha – Luu Huy Chao – Hoang Van Ky
25 Apr 67	Hai Phong	A-4C	923.	Nguyen Van Bay – Nguyen The Hon – Ha Bon – Nguyen Ba Dich
25 Apr 67	Hai Phong	A-4E	923.	Nguyen Van Bay – Nguyen The Hon – Ha Bon – Nguyen Ba Dich
25 Apr 67	Hai Phong	F-8	923.	Nguyen Van Bay – Nguyen The Hon – Ha Bon – Nguyen Ba Dich
12 May 67	Hoa Lac	F-4C	923.	Cao Thanh Tinh – Le Hai – Ngo Duc Mai – Hoang Van Ky
12 May 67	Hoa Lac	F-4C	923.	Cao Thanh Tinh – Le Hai – Ngo Duc Mai – Hoang Van Ky
12 May 67	Hoa Lac	F-4C	923.	Cao Thanh Tinh – Le Hai – Ngo Duc Mai – Hoang Van Ky
12 May 67	Vinh Yen	F-105	923.	Duong Trung Tan – Nguyen Van Tho
19 May 67	Xuan Mai	F-4	923.	Phan Thanh Tai
19 May 67	Xuan Mai	F-4	923.	Nguyen Huu Diet
23 Aug 67	Noi Bai	F-105	923.	Cao Thanh Tinh – Le Van Phong – Nguyen Van Tho – Nguyen Hong Diep
23 Aug 67	Noi Bai	F-105	923.	Cao Thanh Tinh – Le Van Phong – Nguyen Van Tho – Nguyen Hong Diep
23 Aug 67	Noi Bai	F-4	923.	
25 Oct 67	Kep	F-105	923.	Nguyen Huu Tao
19 Nov 67	Hai Phong	F-4B	923.	Le Hai
19 Nov 67	Hai Phong	F-4B	923.	Nguyen Dinh Phuc
19 Nov 67	Hai Phong	F-4B	923.	Nguyen Phi Hung
14 Dec 67	Ninh Giang	F-8	?	?
17 Dec 67	Ha Hoa	F-4C	?	?
17 Dec 67	Ha Hoa	F-4C	?	?
19 Dec 67	Tam Dao	?	921.	? (may have been MiG-21)
19 Dec 67	Tam Dao	?	921.	? (may have been MiG-21)
19 Dec 67	Tam Dao	?	921.	? (may have been MiG-21)
03 Jan 68	Thai Nguyen	F-4	923.	Bui Van Suu
14 Jun 68	Thanh Chuong	F-4	923.	Le Hai
14 Jun 68	Thanh Chuong	F-4	923.	Luu Huy Chao
09 Mar 71	?	Firebee	923.	Luong Duc Truong
18 May 72	Kep	F-4	923.	?
11 Jul 72	Pha Lai	F-4J	923.	Han Vinh Tuong

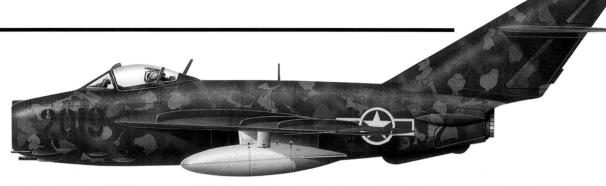

Many MiG-17s were painted in this heavy mottled camouflage. This made them very difficult to see from above, which was not only useful in air combat over the jungle but, more importantly, kept them hidden when on the ground.

Right: Unfortunately, no information is available about the Vietnamese use of the Shenyang JJ-5 aircraft, except this photograph. These two-seater fighter trainers were derivatives of the Shenyang J-5A, the Chinese version of the MiG-17F. They were probably used by the 910th Air Wing for domestic training of future fighter pilots.

At 16.05 the afterburners were lit and Le Xuan Di and Nguyen Van Bay began their take-off run with the bomb-laden MiG-17s. Flying 10 km (6.2 miles) from the coast in the direction of Hill 280, they soon turned left. Dong Hoi control reported ships 15° south and ordered the pilots to embark on an attack. Leaving Ly Hoa, it seemed that smoke was rising from the sea surface, suggesting warships shelling targets inland. It soon turned out to be the wakes left by the vessels.

Le Xuan Di reported visual contact with enemy ships ahead of him at 10-12 km (6.2-7.5 miles). After coasting out, the Vietnamese lead turned left and headed for his target. Increasing his speed to 800 km/h (497 mph) and descending to 50 m (31 ft) above sea level, Le Xuan Di began the bombing approach. He released the two 250-kg (551-lb) bombs, broke left and cleared the target, so he could observe the direct hits. After informing the ground controller, he made for Gat and touched down at 16.18. Due to excessive landing speed the MiG engaged the barrier at the end of the runway, but, fortunately, neither the pilot nor the aircraft was damaged.

While the Vietnamese lead was turning left in the direction of his target, Nguyen Van Bay separated. Turning back, he realised that he had lost the sight of the other MiG. He continued cruising northeast until he reached the Dinh River, but no ships were apparent. Flying further northeast, he suddenly sighted two enemy vessels. The short distance and high closure rate rendered an attack on the first pass impossible. Nguyen Van Bay streaked over his target, turned back and released his bombs from as far away as 750 m (2,460 ft).

"Is it done?" asked Le Xuan Di, his wingman. "Not quite," replied Nguyen Van Bay, who thought his bombs had not hit the destroyer. At 16.22 the second MiG landed at Gat. Upon arriving home he was informed that a smoke column of 30 m (98.4 ft) was observed in the direction of his target, followed by bursts of flames.

A couple of minutes after the MiGs left, a pair of F-4 Phantoms appeared in the area, supposedly to catch the Vietnamese fighters.

The first successful attack of VPAF fighters against US Navy ships lasted 17 minutes. The upper structure of USS *Highbee* was seriously damaged, with the rear guns destroyed, while USS *Oklahoma City* suffered only minor damage.

On 19 April a retaliatory strike was conducted against Dong Hoi and, on the following day, against Vinh. A few days later the enemy discovered Gat airfield and attacked it with 20-30 aircraft. Although the MiGs were camouflaged with protective cover, one was hit and damaged. The other was flown back to Gia Lam.

Signs of fading out

On 8 May 1972 President Nixon announced the mining of North Vietnamese harbours and the launch of a bombing campaign, with increased scope against northern supply and communication lines and military targets. Operation Linebacker began the next day.

On 9 May, US Navy aircraft mined the entrances of seven North Vietnamese ports under Operation Pocket Money. The airfields of Vinh, Tho Xuan, Hoa Lac, Yen Bai and Na San suffered heavy bombing raids. Communication lines between Hanoi and Haiphong were seriously damaged.

The VPAF resolved to concentrate all of its fighter aircraft on the defence of the Hanoi and Haiphong area. The Kep-based 923rd Fighter Wing flying MiG-17s was ordered to operate along the Hanoi-Lang Son railway line and in the areas of the Lai Vu and Phu Long Bridges of Highway 5.

The hectic engagements of the following day made it one of the most memorable in the history of the Vietnam air war. The heyday of the MiG-17s in Vietnamese service was over, but battles of crucial importance were to be fought by the more modern MiG-19s and MiG-21s. The breathing space of the past few years had brought forth a breed of fighter pilots

This completely disassembled MiG-17F is probably being overhauled in a rudimentary hangar. Seeing these field maintenance conditions, one can easily understand the extremely high attrition rate of VPAF aircraft.

With the introduction of g-suits, VPAF pilots could use the MiG-17's extreme manoeuvrability to the full. The aircraft revetments in the background are the consequences of the repeated attacks against the MiG bases.

Vietnamese MiG-17s were sent into combat almost exclusively in flights of four. Initially, they kept rather tight formations with 50-100 m separation between lead and wingman, and 100-200 m between the two pairs. This may have been good for formation display flight, but not for air combat, as it required too much attention to maintain position. Other tactical disadvantages are the lack of possibility for energetic manoeuvring and individual initiative. Digesting the lessons of air battles, the Vietnamese spread the formations out to 600-800 m between aircraft and 800-1200 m between pairs. Later the flights became even more spaced, with 2000 m horizontal and 400-500 m vertical separation between the pairs. This quartet is overflying a post-war military parade.

A pilot is about to embark on a late afternoon mission with a MiG-17PF. The light emphasises the clean cigar-shaped fuselage of the aircraft, devoid of any disturbing protuberances.

acclimatised to the demanding environment of the much more sophisticated MiG-21 then dominating the VPAF fighter forces. The MiG-17 was simply outshone.

Morning air battles on 10 May were fought by MiG-21s and MiG-19s of the 921st and 925th Fighter Wings. The 923rd Fighter Wing joined only when, at 12.25, a mixed force of F-4 Phantoms, A-6 Intruders and A-7 Corsairs attacked Lai Vu and Phu Luong Bridges, and Hai Duong. A flight of four MiG-17s departed Kep and was approaching the target area north of Lai Vu Bridge, when, 15 km (9.3 miles) from Hai Duong flight, lead Nguyen Van Tho spotted enemy aircraft. Followed by his wingman, Ta Dong Trung, he immediately turned into them. Ta Dong Trung fired but missed and, seeing the coastline immediately ahead of him, disengaged. Flying along the Thai Binh River, he returned to Kep.

Nguyen Van Tho followed an A-7 and fired a single burst, but the Corsair escaped unscathed. As the Vietnamese lead looked back, he saw an F-4 in his six o'clock position. He immediately turned back hard, but the Phantom evaded the head-on dash and made for the sea. Discovering that two pairs of Phantoms were stuck on the tails of Nguyen Hang and his wingman, Nguyen Van Tho called to them to turn back. The Vietnamese number four threw off his chasers, but number three was hit by an air-to-air missile. Nguyen Hang ejected safely, but was strafed and shot dead as he descended by parachute. (This scenario was repeated on at least one other occasion. On 19 July four F-4s downed a lone MiG-21 of the 921st Fighter Wing. The Vietnamese pilot ejected but was fired upon several times in his chute by the Phantoms. That time, they missed, but the pilot unfortunately landed on a tree and received fatal injuries.)

Number four soon had another Phantom on his tail. Nguyen Va Tho tried to drive it off by firing at the F-4 three times, but ran out of ammunition and eventually was shot down by a missile. The Vietnamese lead ejected northwest of Tu Ky.

Following the MiG-17s' attempt, MiG-21s were sent up again, this time from the 927th

The MiG-17PF all-weather interceptors were used in relatively small numbers by the VPAF. The dielectric panels of the nose housed the two antennas of the RP-1 Izumrud radar. Instead of the N-37D cannon, the aircraft was equipped with a third NR-23 cannon. Besides the nose section, the windscreen was also reshaped to accommodate the radar's bulky CRT display.

Fighter Wing. By the close of the longest day, wrecks of five American aircraft falling to Vietnamese fighters were scattered around North Vietnam. None of them was credited to MiG-17s.

Of the six Vietnamese fighters known to be lost on that day, four were shot down by enemy aircraft, one MiG-19 exploded in a landing mishap and a MiG-21 was downed by a friendly SAM. The eventual fate of number four of the MiG-17 flight is not clear from available data; perhaps he fell victim to his pursuers.

The last victories

On 18 May 1972 four MiG-17s of the 923rd Fighter Wing, plus a MiG-19 and MiG-21 flight of the 925th and 927th Fighter Wings, mixed it up with enemy aircraft over Kep. The MiG-17s were still climbing when air-to-air missiles were launched at them. Following successful evasive manoeuvres, the Vietnamese lead shot down an F-4 Phantom.

In the second half of 1972 no MiG-17s were credited with enemy aircraft, except on 11 July. Han Vinh Tuong and Hoang Cao Thang from the 923rd Fighter Wing departed for a practice sortie over Kep airfield. When they detected enemy aircraft over Pha Lai, the Vietnamese pilots were ordered to divert and land at Noi Bai. Turning right, Hanh Vinh Tuong spotted two Phantoms flying about 5 km (3 miles) from them. The MiG pilots dropped their wing tanks and asked for clearance to engage the enemy.

Flying at an altitude of 1000 m (3,280 ft), the Vietnamese lead attacked a Phantom, fired three bursts from 500 m (1,640 ft) and sent it crashing into the ground. With Hoang Chao Thang on his wing he began pursuing another F-4, and over Hiep Hoa, Ha Bac Province, closed in to firing range. While Han Vinh Thuong was busy trying to shoot down the American aircraft with a burst from his triple cannon, he failed to see a missile tracking for his MiG. The Vietnamese pilot was killed in the subsequent explosion and crash. This incident was not included in 'MiG-killer' lists, although the Vietnamese have deemed the missile to be an air-to-air one launched by a Phantom.

MiG-17 survivors

At least seven VPAF MiG-17 war veterans survive in Vietnam, most on display. Two are in the VPAF Museum in Hanoi.

Above: This MiG-17F is at Dong Hoi. The original code number, '2019', has been repainted as '2002'.

Below: '2047', now in the VPAF Museum, was one of the two MiG-17Fs sent to Gat for anti-ship operations, and is shown carrying two 250-kg bombs. The aircraft was modified by the A-33 Aircraft Repair Unit with a brake chute.

Above: '2614' is a MiG-17 from the original batch, displaying the early-style airbrakes which distinguished this model from the MiG-17F. The aircraft is on display at Nha Trang.

Right: Hidden away in a courtyard in Haiphong is this MiG-17. Behind the MiG are scattered the engines of crashed aircraft and the wing of an A-7 Corsair II.

Below: MiG-17F '2010' rests in poor condition at Vinh. It is fitted with the early-style ejection seat without a face curtain.

MiG-17F '2011' of the 923rd Fighter Wing is on display at the VPAF Museum in Hanoi. Lt Ngo Duc Mai flew this aircraft in the air battle of 12 May 1967. Two small red stars are barely visible under the cockpit.

This MiG-17F, lacking its rear-view periscope, is on display at Da Nang.

Epilogue

On 27 January 1973 North Vietnam, South Vietnam, the USA and the Viet Cong signed the Paris Agreements. Although the ground war raged on until the fall of South Vietnam in April 1975, with the withdrawal of US combat troops the war for the VPAF MiG-17s was practically over.

The following years of the 923rd Fighter Wing were spent in recovery and practice,

Late in the war, MiG-17 pilots began to wear the hard 'bonedomes' familiar to the MiG-21 airmen. These pilots of the 923rd Fighter Wing seem to be quite relaxed when compared to comrades photographed earlier in the war. The MiG-17Fs are, however, still active, as represented by the gun smoke stains on '2056'.

mostly at Kien An, Tho Xuan, Vinh and Dong Hoi airfields, with special emphasis on ground attack and maritime attack missions. In April 1975 six MiG-17 pilots were selected for training to transition to captured Cessna A-37 Dragonfly light attack aircraft and to take part in

the final offensive against Saigon. The MiG-17s remained north.

Dr Zoltán Buza and Dr István Toperczer

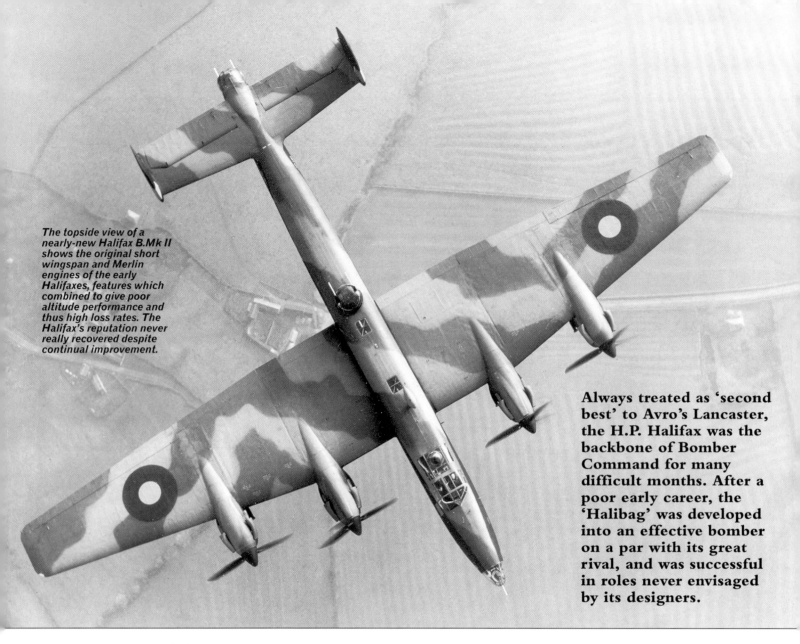

The topside view of a nearly-new Halifax B.Mk II shows the original short wingspan and Merlin engines of the early Halifaxes, features which combined to give poor altitude performance and thus high loss rates. The Halifax's reputation never really recovered despite continual improvement.

Always treated as 'second best' to Avro's Lancaster, the H.P. Halifax was the backbone of Bomber Command for many difficult months. After a poor early career, the 'Halibag' was developed into an effective bomber on a par with its great rival, and was successful in roles never envisaged by its designers.

Handley Page Halifax Variants

It has become fashionable to decry Bomber Command's campaign against the Third Reich as having been brutal, unjustifiable and of limited effectiveness. The popular view seems to be that certain events (like the fire raids on Dresden) were little short of an Allied war crime, which went unprosecuted largely because the RAF was on the winning side. Against such opinions, remembering the aircraft which took part in the campaign seems to be in the poorest possible taste.

Inevitably, a counter-view has been articulated, not least by the survivors of Bomber Command themselves, who point to their sacrifice with pride, and to the enormous contribution they made to bringing the Nazi empire to its knees. The symbol of their story has come to be the Avro Lancaster, the last – and arguably the finest – of the heavy bombers sent against Germany. Although Lancasters did not join the night offensive until 11 March 1942 (and then with only two aircraft), they formed the backbone of the force by 1945, and a handful served long enough for several to find their way into museums, and even to serve as

One of the least known roles of the Halifax was night anti-shipping attack. Here, the crew of a GR.Mk III of either No. 58 or No. 502 Squadron based at Stornoway in early 1945 review the route for another patrol off Norway.

'flying memorials'. The other bombers involved in the offensive were less lucky. Obsolete by 1945, they were simply scrapped and, with no reminders sitting in museums, were quickly forgotten.

Perhaps the most unfortunate victim of this mass aircraft amnesia was the poor old Handley Page Halifax, remembered (when remembered at all) as being second-best to the Lancaster. While it is true that the Halifax was less effective than the 'Lanc' in the pure bomber role, it had other qualities which made it far more suitable for use in other roles. Moreover, having entered operational service in March 1941, the Halifax was, for 12 long and difficult months, the most modern and most effective aircraft in Bomber Command's hands, pending the introduction of the Lancaster in March 1942.

Fall from grace

Once the Lancaster was available, the Halifax fell from grace with astonishing rapidity. It was widely reported that Lancaster crews cheered when they learned that the lower-flying, slower-flying Halifaxes would be accompanying them on this or that raid. The only opportunity the Halifax crews had for similar good cheer and relief was if a raid was also going to include the prehistoric and even more lumbering

Halifax B.Mk II Series I W7676 was typical of many early Halifaxes in that its career was a short one. Arriving on the strength of No. 35 Squadron at Linton-on-Ouse in April 1942, it flew an intense series of missions, including the 1,000-bomber raid on Cologne, before its loss in August over Nuremburg.

Stirling! And if Bomber Command as a whole was dismissive of the Halifax, it was an attitude reflected at the very top.

Air Vice Marshal Don Bennett, the Pathfinders' AOC and himself a former Halifax pilot, was lukewarm about the aircraft, describing it as "not as good as the Lancaster, but it nevertheless did a sound job of work." This faint praise was regarded by many as marking Bennett as one of the aircraft's leading supporters, and he himself reported that the attitude of his C-in-C was very much less tolerant. By December 1943, Arthur Harris ('Bomber' Harris to the press and the public, 'Butch' to his contemporaries and friends), the AOC-in-C Bomber Command, was outspoken in his condemnation of the Halifax, which he bluntly regarded as a waste of production resources.

"I will state categorically, one Lancaster is to be preferred to four Halifaxes. Halifaxes are an embarrassment now, and will be useless for the bomber offensive in six months – if not before. The Halifax suffers about four times the casualties for a given bomb tonnage when compared to the Lancaster. Low ceiling and short range make it an embarrassment when planning attacks with Lancasters."

It is certainly true that the Halifax could rarely stagger above 18,000 ft (5490 m), where it was vulnerable to enemy flak, and was often forced to fly below cloud, silhouetting itself instead of using cloud for cover. The aircraft carried significantly less tonnage than the Lancaster (about 5,000 lb/2270 kg over the same range), and also had a range about 500 miles (805 km) shorter. It was widely believed that, in addition to these drawbacks, the Halifax was slower and more expensive to build, and many felt that factories producing the aircraft and its engines should have halted production and retooled to concentrate on the Lancaster, re-equipping Bomber Command squadrons as they ran out of Halifaxes. This would have been a bold step, but was not taken, and the Halifax remained in production until the war's end.

Perhaps surprisingly, personnel on the Halifax squadrons had a less jaundiced view of their aircraft, even though they had to fly it. Most were fond of their aircraft, and some were even fiercely proud of it. Remarkably, morale on the Halifax force held up every bit as well as it did on the Lancaster force, despite suffering

heavier losses, despite winning less glory, fame and recognition, and despite being widely felt to be the poor relation of Bomber Command. Rivalry between the Lancaster and Halifax communities was powerful, and the Halifax crews derisively nicknamed the Lancaster the 'Daily Mirror Bomber' for its headline-hogging qualities.

'Halibag' vs 'Lanc'

Despite this, the Halifax flew more missions against Germany than any other bomber, excepting the Lancaster. In fact, the Halifax dropped more bombs than all of Bomber Command's other aircraft types put together, again excluding the Lancaster. This was a remarkable feat, giving the Halifax a greater overall contribution than that of the Mosquito, Wellington, Stirling, Hampden, Manchester, Whitley, Blenheim, Battle, Fortress, Mitchell and Ventura – combined. The Halifax flew 36,995 sorties against Germany by night and 10,074 by day, dropping 224,207 tons (227795 tonnes) of bombs (compared to 83,881 and 23,204 sorties and 608,612 tons/618350 tonnes

for the Lancaster). Bomber Command Halifax losses totalled 2,236, compared to 3,936 Lancasters. This gave the RAF a loss rate of one Halifax per 21.05 sorties, and one 'Lanc' per 27.2 sorties. An average Lancaster sortie delivered 5.68 tons (5.77 tonnes) of bombs, while a typical Halifax sortie delivered only 4.76 tons (4.84 tonnes). These figures were surprisingly close, and represented a great improvement over the Stirling, which suffered one loss for every 10.7 sorties, and delivered only 3.38 tons (3.43 tonnes) of bombs per sortie. Moreover, the Halifax figures given reflect the very heavy losses suffered by the early variants. Evidence suggests that the later Hercules-powered variants suffered a lower level of losses than the late-mark Lancasters. At its peak, the Halifax force consisted of 35 front-line squadrons, with 1,500 aircraft including those serving with HCUs.

As the war's end neared and fighter opposition diminished, Bomber Command switched increasingly to daylight raids. This B.Mk VI seen attacking oil targets at Wanne-Eickel in late 1944 displays its longer wings and a well-worn finish.

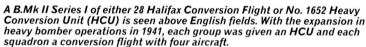

A B.Mk II Series I of either 28 Halifax Conversion Flight or No. 1652 Heavy Conversion Unit (HCU) is seen above English fields. With the expansion in heavy bomber operations in 1941, each group was given an HCU and each squadron a conversion flight with four aircraft.

It is easy to become too focused on figures, and it should be remembered what those figures actually meant. A loss rate of one Halifax every 21.05 sorties meant that the average crew could expect to survive only 21.05 of the 30 missions allocated on their tour – very poor odds even when you took into account the disproportionately high losses in the early years of the war, and among crews fresh from training. In their 21.05-sortie lifetime, our average crew would have delivered just over 100 tons (101.6 tonnes) of bombs, while the average 'Lanc' crew survived a little longer (almost a complete tour), delivering 154 tons (156.5 tonnes) of bombs in the process. Although the Halifax crew was statistically more likely to be shot down, they were also more likely to survive such a shooting down. Twenty-nine per cent of Halifax crews shot down survived the experience, compared to 17 per cent of Stirling crews and a mere 11 per cent of Lancaster men. Having its crew survive as POWs was not Bomber Command's primary aim, and few were aware of those statistics, during the war or after. There can be no doubt which aircraft was the more effective bomber over the whole run of the bomber war. These figures were applicable primarily to main force operations, since, during its brief service with the Pathfinders, the Halifax proved more successful, with a loss rate of 2.5 per cent compared to 3.7 per cent for the Lancaster, 5.4 per cent for the Stirling and an alarming 6 per cent for the Wellington.

General-purpose bomber

In fact, it was a good job that Halifax production did continue, since there was a multiplicity of roles to which the aircraft was better suited than the Lancaster. This was hardly surprising, since the Halifax had been designed from the start as a bomber with general-purpose and out-of-area capabilities, whereas the Lancaster was specifically designed for the bomber role in northern Europe. By the time the Lancaster was developed from the unsuccessful Manchester, Avro could ignore huge swathes of the P13/36 requirement, including the stipulated 100-ft (30.5-m) maximum wingspan, producing an aircraft closely tailored to only one role. The Halifax's more roomy fuselage made it a better choice for the bomber support and airborne forces support roles, with easier access to black boxes, and

better accommodation for any special operators or paratroops. The aircraft was also comfortable enough for long endurance sorties. This made it arguably a better platform for maritime patrol and meteorological reconnaissance work, although the type's adaptation for these roles was partly motivated by Bomber Command's unwillingness to forego deliveries of the precious and all-important Lancasters.

Declining loss rate

Even in the bomber role, the Halifax played a vital part, dropping 23.5 per cent of Bomber Command's total (with the 'Lanc' contributing 63.7 per cent). During daylight operations, which predominated during the latter part of the war, the Halifax actually had a better return rate than the Lancaster, with 0.56 per cent of those Halifaxes dispatched being lost, compared to a figure of 0.74 per cent for the Lancaster. During the last nine months of the war, No. 4 Group regularly enjoyed Bomber Command's lowest loss rates, and bomb tonnage rose inexorably. But the official view, based largely on the results achieved by the early Merlin-engined bombers, prevailed, and the Halifax was ignored, sometimes literally. On 13 January 1945, for example, Bomber Command reported that a force of 234 Lancasters and Mosquitoes

An RAF heavy bomber crew normally consisted of seven men. This aircraft of the 'Royal Australian Air Force operating in the Middle East' had a Scottish pilot, New Zealand bomb-aimer, English flight engineer, rear gunner and navigator, Australian mid-upper gunner and Canadian wireless operator.

had raided Saarbrücken. In fact, the fleet had consisted of 201 Halifaxes, 12 Mosquitoes and 20 Lancasters. Long after the war, the effects of the 'Halifax reputation' were still being felt. When Britain built the V-bombers, it was Avro's Vulcan that was chosen as the primary type. Some maintain that it was the memory of the Lancaster and Halifax which prevented the Victor (which carried a heavier bombload, further, faster and even higher) from ever being more than second best to the Vulcan.

Bomber Command actually finished operations more than a week before the end of hostilities, but large numbers of Halifaxes remained on charge as the war ended. The last Halifax bomber operation was the attack on coastal batteries on the Friesian island of Wangerooge on

Replacement of the Merlin with the Bristol Hercules cured most of the performance failings of the Halifax and dramatically reduced the loss rate compared to the Lancaster. Ironically, LL599 of No. 462 Squadron seen here was lost in a collision with a 'Lanc' in October 1944.

With the increase in daylight missions from mid-1945, distinctive tail markings were introduced to help unit coherence. Halifaxes wore particularly colourful tails such as the red trellis pattern on this No. 346 (Free French) Sqn B.Mk VI.

Top: The Halifax found its niche in supporting the airborne forces. Seen here on the eve of D-Day are over 30 A.Mk V glider tugs of Nos 298 and 644 Squadrons at Tarrant Rushton. The gliders are Horsas (front) and Hamilcars.

The bomb bay of the Halifax was less capacious and less adaptable than that of the Lancaster. Nevertheless, with a bit of ingenuity (and maybe the doors cranked open a bit), outsize loads such as this Spitfire could be carried.

25 April, though No. 100 Group's Halifaxes were still flying on operations on 2/3 May, when two No. 199 Squadron aircraft were shot down. Within Bomber Command, No. 4 Group operated 283 Halifaxes in 11 squadrons (the official establishment was 220 aircraft). Most had a mix of B.Mk IIIs and B.Mk VIs, though Nos 10, 51 and 466 had only B.Mk IIIs, and Nos 77 and 640 had only Halifax B.Mk VIs. No. 6 (RCAF) Group had partly re-equipped with Lancasters, with only one squadron (No. 420) remaining fully equipped with Halifax Mk IIIs (and holding five Halifax B.Mk VIIs). Three more units (Nos 408, 426 and 432 Squadrons) were fully equipped with B.Mk VIIs. Four squadrons converting to Lancasters still had between one and 20 Halifax Mk IIIs on charge, but each also had between 18 and 23 Lancasters.

No. 100 Group's four Halifax squadrons had a total of 93 Halifax B.Mk IIIs on strength. With the airborne forces (No. 38 Group), four squadrons (Nos 296, 297, 298 and 644) operated 101 A.Mk IIIs and 23 Halifax A.Mk VIIs, the latter serving beside A.Mk IIIs with Nos 298 and 644 Squadrons. Two more squadrons (Nos 190 and 620) were re-equipping with Halifaxes as the war ended, but were still primarily equipped with Short Stirlings, which were augmented by just three more Halifax A.Mk IIIs. In Transport Command, a single Halifax C.Mk III served with No. 246 Squadron. The Halifax had disappeared entirely from the shadowy world of the SOE squadrons,

As the sun sets over Yorkshire, Halifax B.Mk IIs of No. 102 Squadron set out for another night raid. The squadron used three main versions of the Halifax from December 1941 to May 1945.

Left: Hundreds of Halifaxes went into storage soon after the war. Some, like these ex-Free French B.Mk VIs, flew on in France or as civil freighters, but the majority were scrapped.

Above: The Halifax proved more suited to the military transport role than the Lancaster and nearly 100 C.Mk VIII conversions with capacity for 8,000 lb (3630 kg) of freight were completed.

whose *raison d'être* had disappeared with the liberation of almost all of the territories seized by the Nazis.

Coastal Command included two home-based Halifax meteorological squadrons (Nos 517 and 518) operating a mix of 22 Halifax Met.Mk Vs and 21 Halifax Met.Mk IIIs on the day the war ended. The Command also had two Halifax long-range reconnaissance squadrons (Nos 58 and 502) operating 23 GR.Mk IIIs and four

GR.Mk IIs. The Halifax was in large-scale service overseas, in the bomber, transport, training and bomber support roles, and in the meteorological role.

The post-war retention of Lancasters for bombing and survey work, and the acquisition of the related York transport and Lincoln bomber, led to their eventual replacement of the Halifax even in the roles for which the latter was arguably better suited, most notably the ASW role with Coastal Command. Even if the Lancaster GR.Mk 3 was inferior to the Halifax GR.Mk VI, it made little sense, from the point of view of logistics and support, to retain the Halifax in service. This was particularly true since neither aircraft was expected to be more than an interim type, pending introduction of Avro Shackletons and Handley Page Hastings aircraft in the ASW/Maritime Patrol and meteorological reconnaissance roles. With this in mind, it was perhaps surprising that all Halifaxes were not replaced by Lancasters at the end of the war.

On the other hand, many believed that standardising on the Lancaster was a mistake, since it left the RAF with an aircraft unsuitable

for 'hot-and-high' or tropical operation, and an aircraft known to be suffering from serious wing defects. When Nos 298 and 617 Squadrons operated side by side at Digri in India, the Lancasters of No. 617 had to obtain take-off clearance before engine start-up, to avoid overheating, while the Halifaxes operated normally, with no problems. But the decision had been made on the basis of operational capability in Europe, two years earlier, and the Halifax bomber was thus doomed.

The last Halifaxes

In fact, the five Coastal Command meteorological squadrons continued operations much as before, until mid-1946, when four of the units disbanded. One unit survived (albeit under a new numberplate, of No. 202 Squadron), but tasking was sufficient for a second squadron, No. 224, to form in March 1948. Both units were based at Aldergrove, but maintained a detachment at Gibraltar. The RAF's last Halifax in squadron use was RG841, a Met.Mk VI, which was flown from Gibraltar for storage at No. 48 MU at Hawarden, Cheshire, on 17 March 1952.

Civil Conversions

With airfields jammed with ex-military aircraft and few civil designs actually available, both aspiring new airlines and established carriers purchased surplus freighters and bombers so as to meet the expected post-war air travel boom. Particularly prized was the Halifax C.Mk VIII with its detachable underfuselage freight pannier and relatively capacious internal space. BOAC (below) acquired 12 aircraft which were fitted with 10 seats and civilian interiors, and renamed as Haltons. G-AHDU Falkirk was the first of them. The French carrier SANA operated several C.Mk VIIIs including F-BESE Ker Goaler (right), which was formerly G-AKGP. London Aero and Motor Service began services with six virtually brand-new aircraft including G-AIWT Port of Sydney (lower right) in 1946. Many of these civil aircraft were involved in the Berlin Airlift, which began in June 1948.

Probably due in part to its inferior reputation compared to the Lancaster, the Halifax had little export success. France took on some of the aircraft flown by the Free French squadrons and Pakistan and Egypt (pictured) acquired handfuls of Halifaxes for bombing, patrol and transport.

In the assault transport role, the unique capabilities of the Halifax were rendered irrelevant by the end of the war. With the outbreak of peace, there was no requirement for the towing of gliders and for the dropping of paratroops, and speed, agility and defensive firepower (all offered by the Halifax A.Mk VII and A.Mk IX) were suddenly of no interest. The airborne forces role shrunk to a shadow of its former glories, ticking over as little more than a field of continuing operational research and limited training, though two squadrons continued until they were re-equipped with the Hastings, and two more squadrons flew A.Mk VIIs and IXs well into 1948, while a handful of units briefly remained active in the Middle East and in India.

It is perhaps appropriate that the last flying Halifax in Britain was operated in the support of the airborne forces role. Although trials Halifaxes remained active at Farnborough into the 1950s (including A.Mk VII PP350 with the universal freight container), the last RAF Halifax was an A.Mk IX, RT936, which was finally struck off charge in August 1954.

Halifax freighters

In the straight transport role, the Halifax was largely replaced by higher-capacity purpose-built transports such as the slower Douglas DC-3 and the Avro York, which carried twice as many passengers, and whose cabin could accommodate bulky items. The two Transport Command Halifax C.Mk VIII squadrons were Polish-manned, and disbanded (with the other Polish units) at the end of 1946. From mid-1946, they had been restricted to flights within the UK, which had limited their usefulness. Their aircraft were withdrawn and sold, forming the core of the civil Halifax fleet, which played a vital, if unsung, part in the Berlin Airlift. Due to this, the Halifax had a

short life on the civil register, with engines rapidly becoming scarce and above all expensive (£1,200 by 1949, from their scrap value, by weight.). The dispensation to operate with a 59,000-lb (26760-kg) landing weight was removed at the end of the airlift, and this further reduced the Halifax's viability, while peak charter rates of £85.00 per hour slumped to £45.00 hour in a price war following the airlift. This was scarcely enough to cover the aircraft's direct operating costs (estimated at £40.00 per hour). Most aircraft were scrapped by the end of 1950.

G-AHDV (actually a Halton) and G-AKEC of the 'Lancashire Aircraft Corporation' were almost certainly the last flying civilian Halifaxes. Both were damaged in a gale at Squires Gate on 17 December 1952 and never flew again, although, in truth, neither had operated for some weeks prior to the gale.

Export bombers

The Halifax survived longest overseas. The Pakistan air force's No. 12 Squadron (operating eight B.Mk VI aircraft in the bomber, transport and maritime reconnaissance roles) finally retired the type in 1954. Probably the last Halifaxes in service were those in Egypt, where a number survived long enough to be destroyed by strafing during the Suez campaign of 1956.

Incredibly, no-one saw fit to preserve a Halifax for posterity, although a single A.Mk VII airframe lingered on trials of radio antennas at Radlett until 1961, and a forward fuselage

was preserved by the Imperial War Museum. Remarkably, there will soon be three Halifaxes on view. An early B.Mk II Series I was fished out of a Norwegian Lake on 30 June 1973 (having force-landed on that lake's frozen surface on 27 April 1942) and subsequently went on display in the RAF Museum at Hendon. A full restoration was planned and then cancelled, and apart from an immaculate front turret the aircraft languishes rather sadly, in a slightly poorer state than it was when it emerged from the water in 1973. In the belief that the Halifax deserved a prouder memorial, a full-scale replica (using large components and assemblies from a number of crashed aircraft) has been built by the Yorkshire Air Museum. This incorporates a new-built rear fuselage manufactured to original drawings, a Hastings centre-section and wings, a dummy undercarriage (non-functioning) cast from original components, and an externally recognisable nose section. Although the major part of the rear fuselage was recovered from a GR.Mk II, the replica has been completed as a B.Mk III. This aircraft is now on display.

More recently, a second Halifax was recovered from a lake in Norway, and is to be fully restored to static display condition in Canada. This aircraft was an A.Mk VII shot down by flak after a Special Operations Executive insertion mission. It can only be hoped that the aircraft will be restored in its original colours, since it represents arguably the Halifax's most successful and important role.

Although it was surpassed by the Lancaster in certain key areas, the Halifax was never outclassed, and deserves to be remembered as something more than second best, not least because in certain key roles it was the best aircraft available, and was truly 'second-to-none'.

Jon Lake

Below: Until 1973, there were said to be 'no Halifaxes left'. In that year B.Mk II W1048 was raised from Lake Hoklingen in Norway and later delivered to the RAF Museum. In 1995 B.Mk VII NA337 was recovered from Lake Mjosa, also in Norway, and is being restored at CFB Trenton.

Below right: The Yorkshire Air Museum at Elvington has done an incredible job in recreating a complete Halifax from the remains of three or more aircraft including HR792, LW687 and JP158, and Hastings TG536. The aircraft is painted to represent LV907 Friday the 13th.

Handley Page Halifax Variants

HP.55

The HP.55 was designed to meet the Air Ministry's Specification B1/35, which called for a bomber with a span of 100 ft (30.5 m) and 20,000 lb (9070 kg) AUW. The HP.55 was to have been powered by a pair of Hercules HE1SM engines, carrying a 2,000-lb (907-kg) bombload over 1,500 miles (2415 km) at 224 mph (360 km/h). The aircraft would have had a tare weight of 16,220 lb (26100 kg), and a normal loaded weight of 26,326 lb (11940 kg). With a wing area of 1,070 sq ft (99 m²) the aircraft had a wing-loading of 24.6 lb/sq ft. The Air Ministry considered placing an order without first ordering prototypes, but one was later ordered under contract 441975/35. In the end, the B1/35 specification was won by the aircraft that became the Vickers Armstrong Warwick, and the HP.55 was simply overtaken by events, and by the HP.56.

HP.56

Air Ministry Specifications P13/36 and B12/36 respectively called for twin- and four-engined medium bombers carrying 4,500-lb (2045-kg) or 5,500 lb (2500-kg) bombloads. The Air Ministry expected a cruising speed of 275 mph (442 km/h), and specified a load of 4,000 lb (1820 kg) over a range of 3,000 miles (4830 km) at 15,000 ft (4575 m) at two-thirds power, following a catapult launch. With an overload of 8,000 lb (3635 kg), the Air Ministry demanded a range of 2,000 miles (3220 km). Both specified designs were intended to be capable of a trade-off between range or payload, and were to be capable of catapult-assisted take-offs. Competing firms were strongly urged to produce a general-purpose aircraft, with the intention of producing specialised versions for other roles during production of the basic bomber.

The Air Ministry specified the use of variable-pitch propellers, and demanded easy field maintenance. It expected that the aircraft would be armed with front and rear powered gun turrets, respectively with two and four 0.303-in Browning machine-guns. Each turret would traverse through 180° in azimuth, and carried 1,000 rounds per gun, with a reserve for both turrets of 6,000 rounds. The aircraft was expected to have a crew of four: two pilots, one of whom also acted as bomb-aimer and navigator, a wireless operator/front gunner, and a dedicated rear gunner. The aircraft's size was determined by Air Ministry specifications for component sizes, dictated by the need to recover and transport damaged aircraft using standard vehicles. These requirements included a centre fuselage length of 35 ft (10.67 m), a height of 9 ft 6 in (2.89 m), and a width of 8 ft (2.44 m), with the other fuselage sections no more than 22 ft (6.71 m) long, 9 ft (2.74 m) high and 7 ft (2.13 m) wide.

Handley Page used its HP.55 as the basis for its revised HP.56 design to meet the two specifications (B1/35 and P13/36), suggesting that two prototypes should be built, one powered by twin Hercules HE15M, the other by Vulture-engined. The aircraft was to have a shorter wing than originally planned, in order to increase cruising speed. Other features included swept leading edges on the outer wing panels (like those on the DC-2), with a two-spar, fully stressed skin construction and integral fuel cells. The aircraft was also to have stainless steel exhausts, sliding bomb doors, combined corrugated and flat sheet stressed skins, and a Messier hydraulic undercarriage. Most of these features (except the sliding bomb doors) were eventually incorporated in the production Halifax. Like many of its contemporaries, the Halifax divided its bombload between separate bomb bays, including six bays in the wing itself. This was to prevent the Halifax from carrying the very large outsize weapons which later became a feature of the bomber war. The Halifax could carry two 2,000-lb (907-kg) bombs and six 1,000-lb (454-kg) bombs in the fuselage, plus six 500-lb bombs in the wings. Handley Page offered to build the two prototypes for £50,000 each.

In January 1937 the Air Ministry cancelled the Handley Page B1/35 aircraft, having instead ordered the Short Stirling as its four-engined bomber. Work on the twin-engined P13/36 aircraft continued unabated. Two prototypes were ordered on 30 April 1937, under contract No. 624972/37, both to be powered by the Vulture engine. They were allocated the serials L7244 and L7245. At the same time, Avro received an order for two Vulture-engined Avro 679s (which subsequently became known as the Manchester).

The Vulture was an unusual engine, combining two Kestrels on a single crankshaft to produce an X-section, 24-cylinder, 21-litre engine. The engine took 50 per cent more man hours to build than the Merlin, and was already suffering problems which foreshadowed the more serious difficulties that would eventually kill the Vulture. At the time, though, the difficulties merely reduced production of the engine. It soon became apparent that Rolls-Royce would be unable to produce enough Vultures for both the Avro 679 and the HP.56, and at the very last minute the decision was taken to re-engine the HP.56 with four Rolls-Royce Merlins. Drawings of the new design were requested in July 1937, to the vociferous objections of Handley Page. Since the HP.56 had been designed as a twin, the changes required would generate extra weight and drag, while also causing delay. There was insufficient space for the necessary extra tanks, controls and mounts required by four Merlins, and the wingspan was increased from 88 ft (26.83 m) to 98 ft 8 in (30.07 m), a mere 4 in (10 cm) shy of the specified maximum, a length dictated by standard hangar dimensions. Nevertheless, the company submitted the requested drawings, and was rewarded with an order for two prototypes of the four-engined version (to Specification 32/37) on 7 January 1938. Empty weight rose to 23,000 lb (7010 m), and AUW rose to 55,000 lb (16770 m). The name Halifax was agreed, but was not immediately divulged.

HP.57 Halifax prototypes

When the twin-Vulture HP.56 was abandoned, the two commissioned prototypes were completed with four 1,145-hp (853-kW) Merlin X engines as HP.57s. The four-engined derivative of the basic twin-Vulture HP.56 was designed to meet the same Air Ministry Specification, becoming a four-engined aircraft because of anticipated Vulture shortages. The Air Ministry reportedly considered using four Napier Daggers or Bristol Taurus engines, or even Hercules radials, as alternatives to the Merlin. The Wright G-200 Cyclone was examined as a possible powerplant, as was the Pratt & Whitney Twin Wasp. Handley Page preferred radial engines, and suggested using 1,500-bhp (1117-kW) Hercules HE-65Ms with 100 Octane fuel, but the lower-powered 87 Octane HE-15M was chosen for comparison with the Merlin; it was found to be inferior to the Merlin in its range performance, though it gave a higher speed. Accordingly, the prototypes were powered by four 1,145-hp (854-kW) Merlin Xs.

Handley Page was also unable to get its own way when it came to the HP.57's defensive armament. The company reportedly wanted mid-upper and 'mid-under' turrets rather than a tail turret, and wanted to use Frazer-Nash turrets. They went to Avro for the Manchester, however, leaving Handley Page with Boulton Paul turrets.

Some requirements were relaxed, including the original need to carry two torpedoes, the need to make 25° dive attacks (already reduced from 70°) and the catapult take-off requirement. The design was changed slightly, with a straight spar and taper of both leading and trailing edges, and with the addition of external fuel jettison pipes to allow dumped fuel to clear the tail unit and static discharge wicks.

The first prototype (L7244) was hand-built at Cricklewood, and was completed without gun turrets. Temporary fuel tanks were installed in the bomb bay, with ballast in the integral wing tanks. The integral tanks were eventually abandoned altogether, in favour of four separate tanks in the wings. The aircraft was powered by Merlin 10s, driving two-position variable-pitch de Havilland propellers with metal (Duralumin) blades. The Merlin installation proved troublesome, having coolant leaks, radiator failures and inadequate flame damping, and the complex double-curvature nacelles were difficult to manufacture.

At one time it was expected that the aircraft would have mid-slung nacelles for minimum drag at high speed, but they were not adopted, although the nacelle design was refined during the course of flight testing. The nacelles used eventually proved very suitable for use with radial engines, a lucky break for Handley Page.

The first prototype was completed in August 1939. Radlett was judged to be too small for the first flight, so the aircraft was dismantled and trucked to RAF Bicester, where it was reassembled and flown on 25 October. Chief test pilot J. L. Cordes was at the controls, with 'Ginger' Wright as flight test observer. Despite great secrecy, the aerodrome's perimeter was lined with cars and onlookers, probably including the German air attaché.

The second prototype had a nose and tail turret fitted, and had floor guns in a well behind the bomb bay. The aircraft had Rotol constant-speed propellers with Schwarz wooden blades. It flew for the first time on 17 August 1940.

The prototypes had a reported span of 98 ft 8 in (30.03 m), a length of 71 ft 7 in (21.82 m), and a height of 22 ft (6.7 m). Maximum all up weight was 51,500 lb (23410 kg). The aircraft had a maximum speed of 260 mph (161 km/h), a range of 3,000 miles (1863 km) and a ceiling of 22,000 ft (6707 m).

The first Halifax, L7244, is seen at Boscombe Down in 1940. Guns were neve[r] fitted to this aircraft, which ended its days as an instructional airframe.

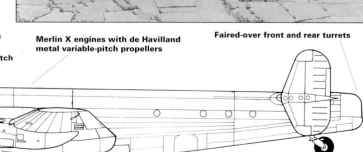

L7245 was the second prototype Halifax and was fitted with representative armament. This included two 'floor' guns.

HP.57 Halifax first prototype

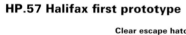

Clear escape hatch

Merlin X engines with de Havilland metal variable-pitch propellers

Faired-over front and rear turrets

Leading-edge slats

Underwing aileron mass balances

Retractable tail wheel

HP.57 Halifax B.Mk I, Series 1

Before production began, there were talks of re-engining the HP.57 with Griffon or Sabre engines, and consideration was given to providing heavier-calibre 0.5-in machine-guns. In fact, the initial production Halifax I differed very little from the prototypes, with leading-edge slats and with 1,280-hp (955-kW) Merlin 10 engines, and Rotol constant-speed propellers with wooden Schwarz blades, although they were replaced by 12-ft 6-in (3.81-m) diameter Rotol RXF5/1 airscrews with magnesium blades. One hundred were ordered on 7 January 1938, and used serials initially set aside for production HP.56s.

The first production HP.57 was L9485, which made its maiden flight on 11 October 1940. Later the same month, the aircraft was evacuated from Radlett to Boscombe Down, where it demonstrated many improvements over the Manchester, which was then undergoing service testing. Boscombe's pilots were especially impressed by the HP.57's superior directional stability, by the easier access to the cockpit (over the low spar), and by the fact that the aircraft was not notably overweight.

The first 50 production HP.57s (L9485-L9534) were designated Halifax I, Series 1s, and had a maximum take-off weight of 55,000 lb (25000 kg). The first 10 aircraft had intermediate inner nacelle fairings. The aircraft had no mid-upper turrets or beam guns, although beam guns had been tested and found satisfactory at speeds of up to 260 mph (160 km). The ventral guns were to have been replaced by a periscopically sighted Boulton Paul K.Mk 1 turret, but in the event were simply deleted. The production Halifax had a 24-V generator on the inboard engines, and aileron mass balances below the wing. The aircraft had their leading-edge slats locked shut, to allow the fitting of barrage balloon cable-cutters. The 13th and subsequent aircraft had new T1154-R1155 radios replacing their T1083-R1082 sets.

The Halifax I Series 1 entered service with No. 35 Squadron at Boscombe Down in early November 1940, quickly moving to the No. 4 Group airfield at Leeming in Yorkshire, with the first Halifax prototype and the second production aircraft (L9486). All crews were led by experienced operational pilots, each of whom already wore a DFM or DFC, compensating for the complete absence of four-engined experience. At Leeming and Linton-on-Ouse where it moved in early December), No. 35 Squadron received more production Halifaxes. There were many problems and

temporary groundings, and a run of accidents, with hydraulics proving a particular weakness and a cause of many belly landings. The squadron flew its first mission (with six aircraft) on 11/12 March 1941 against Le Havre, supported by eight Blenheims. The raid ended in tragedy, when one aircraft was shot down by an RAF night-fighter on its return. The night-fighter pilot had never heard of the still-secret Halifax, and knew that the RAF's 'only' four-engined bomber, the Stirling, had but a single fin. Two nights later, three Halifaxes made their first attack against a German target, as part of an 88-aircraft raid which also marked the 'German debut' of the rival Manchester. The service introduction of the Halifax had occurred before that of the Manchester, and only one month after that of the Stirling. This robbed the aircraft of the glory of becoming the RAF's first four-engined bomber, though it was the first such bomber to operate over Germany. Although operating mainly by night, No. 35 Squadrons Halifaxes did also undertake a number of daylight attacks, particularly against ports, including Kiel, La Pallice and Brest, making the French ports sufficiently uncomfortable for the Germans to withdraw the Scharnhorst, Gneisenau and Prinz Eugen to German ports. Such daylight attacks proved costly, however, and aircraft were lost to both flak and fighters, though the Halifax fared rather better than the Stirling and the Manchester.

No. 35 Squadron's 'C' Flight formed the nucleus for the second unit, No. 76 Squadron, which formed on 1 May 1941. The existence of the Halifax was formally admitted in July, the month during which

Above: L9530 of No. 76 Squadron was from the first batch of B.Mk Is. The overwing mass balances were probably retrofitted in service.

L9485, the first production B.Mk I, was used for trials and fitted with Boulton Paul C.Mk II (dorsal) and Frazer-Nash FN.64 (ventral) turrets.

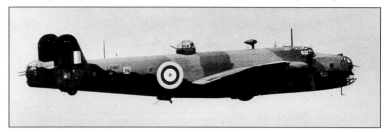

the aircraft bombed Berlin and Turin, attacked the Scharnhorst and shot down two Messerschmitt Bf 109s.

After about three months of operations, the retractable tailwheels were locked down, causing a noticeable drop in speed, but curing a spate of tailwheel failures.

The production B.Mk 1 was slightly shorter than the prototype, at 69 ft 9 in (21.3 m), and its height was measured at 21 ft 4 in (6.5 m). Tare weight was 33,860 lb

(15390 kg), with maximum landing weight of 50,000 lb (22727 kg), and a maximum take-off weight of 55,000 ft (25000 kg). Normal maximum fuel capacity was 1,392 Imp gal (6328 litres), although three bomb bay tanks could each carry 230 Imp gal (1045 litres), and two rest seat tanks could each add another 80 Imp gal (364 litres), bringing total capacity to 2,242 Imp gal (10192 litres).

B.Mk I Srs 1

Boulton-Paul C.Mk II turret with twin 0.303-in Browning machine-guns

Merlin Xs with Rotol constant-speed propellers

ADF loop and aerials for T1083 (later T1154) communications set

Boulton-Paul E.Mk I turret with four 0.303-in Browning guns

Slats locked shut, later deleted

Fuel tank vents

Beam hatches with twin 0.303-in Vickers GO guns on each side

Fixed tailwheel

HP.57 Halifax B.Mk I, Series 2

The next 25 production Halifaxes were Halifax I Series 2s. They had an increased AUW (60,000 lb/27270 kg), but still had no mid-upper gun turret. Vickers K guns were fitted in the beam positions. The aircraft retained the inboard generators, but the

aileron mass balances were repositioned, being fitted above instead of below the wing. The window immediately aft of the front turret was reduced in size, though often covered by a transparent blister fairing, as before.

Left: The above-wing mass balances are clearly visible in this view of L9515 which was retained at Boscombe Down until late 1943.

Prominent here on L9619 of No. 10 Squadron are the fuel tank vents (between the engines) and fuel dumps (on the wing's trailing edge).

HP.57 Halifax B.Mk I, Series 3

The Halifax I Series 3 was introduced with L9600, the 76th aircraft, though L9519 served as the testbed for the new engines and fuel tank arrangements. The new variant introduced a BP Type C mid-upper

turret (the tall, bulbous Hudson-type turret) instead of beam guns. The leading-edge slats (locked shut on Mk I Series 1s and Series 2s) were finally deleted altogether. The new version had a 24-V generator on the Nos 2, 3 and 4 engines. The engines themselves were Merlin XXs, with larger-diameter oil coolers, which necessitated a scallop in the under-spinner intake lip. The new engine also had a fishtail at the end of the exhaust pipe. The Merlin XX represented a remarkable feat of design engineering, with the engine producing 205

hp (153 kW) more take-off power (1,280 hp/955 kW) at 3,000 rpm with no increase in dimensions, and with only an 8.5 per cent weight increase. It also maintained higher power at greater height, with the Merlin XX managing 1,175 hp (876 kW) at 21,000 ft (6400 m), while the Merlin X produced only 1,010 hp (753 kW) at 17,750 ft (5410 m).

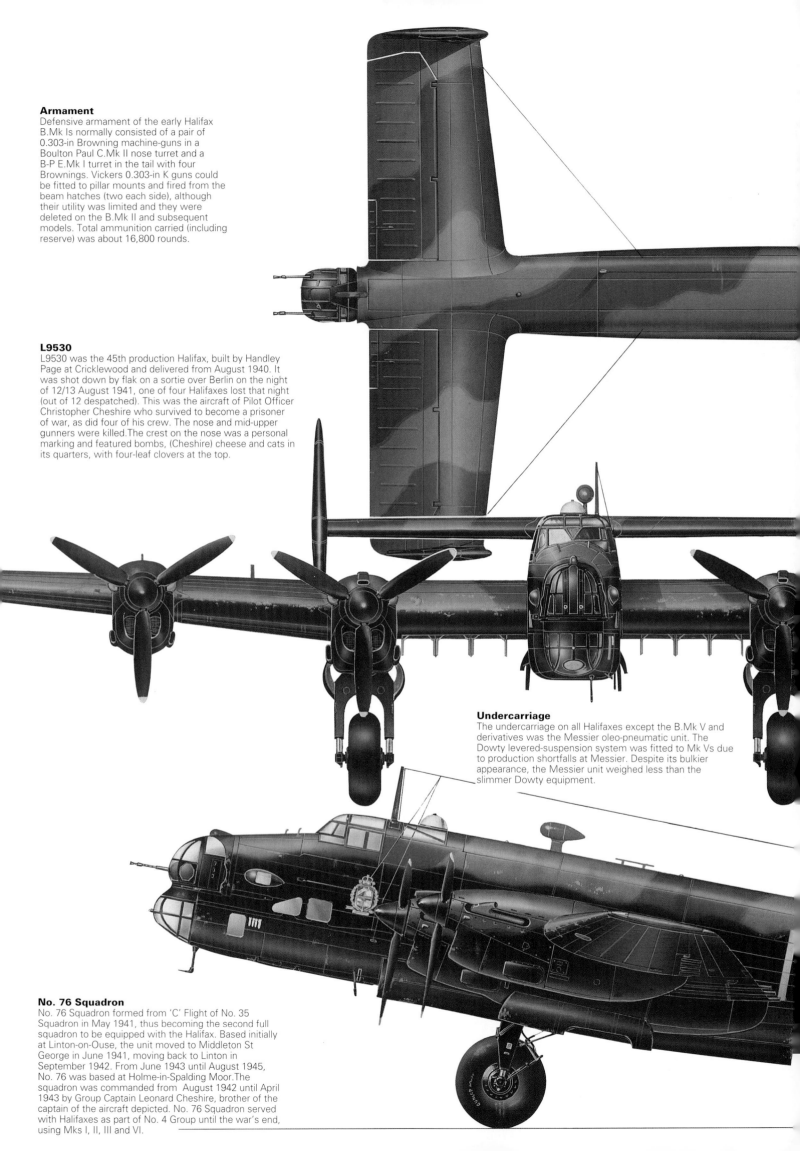

Armament
Defensive armament of the early Halifax
B.Mk Is normally consisted of a pair of
0.303-in Browning machine-guns in a
Boulton Paul C.Mk II nose turret and a
B-P E.Mk I turret in the tail with four
Brownings. Vickers 0.303-in K guns could
be fitted to pillar mounts and fired from the
beam hatches (two each side), although
their utility was limited and they were
deleted on the B.Mk II and subsequent
models. Total ammunition carried (including
reserve) was about 16,800 rounds.

L9530
L9530 was the 45th production Halifax, built by Handley
Page at Cricklewood and delivered from August 1940. It
was shot down by flak on a sortie over Berlin on the night
of 12/13 August 1941, one of four Halifaxes lost that night
(out of 12 despatched). This was the aircraft of Pilot Officer
Christopher Cheshire who survived to become a prisoner
of war, as did four of his crew. The nose and mid-upper
gunners were killed. The crest on the nose was a personal
marking and featured bombs, (Cheshire) cheese and cats in
its quarters, with four-leaf clovers at the top.

Undercarriage
The undercarriage on all Halifaxes except the B.Mk V and
derivatives was the Messier oleo-pneumatic unit. The
Dowty levered-suspension system was fitted to Mk Vs due
to production shortfalls at Messier. Despite its bulkier
appearance, the Messier unit weighed less than the
slimmer Dowty equipment.

No. 76 Squadron
No. 76 Squadron formed from 'C' Flight of No. 35
Squadron in May 1941, thus becoming the second full
squadron to be equipped with the Halifax. Based initially
at Linton-on-Ouse, the unit moved to Middleton St
George in June 1941, moving back to Linton in
September 1942. From June 1943 until August 1945,
No. 76 was based at Holme-in-Spalding Moor. The
squadron was commanded from August 1942 until April
1943 by Group Captain Leonard Cheshire, brother of the
captain of the aircraft depicted. No. 76 Squadron served
with Halifaxes as part of No. 4 Group until the war's end,
using Mks I, II, III and VI.

Powerplant

Like the Lancaster, developed from the unsuccessful Manchester, the Halifax was derived from a design incorporating twin Rolls-Royce Vulture engines. The HP.56 with Vultures was never built and the design was modified to accept four Merlin Xs which were fitted to the Halifax B.Mk I. The nominal rating of the considerably more reliable Merlin X was 1,145 hp (853 kW) compared to 1,800 hp (1341 kW) for the Vulture.

Pre-war Handley Page studies had concentrated on twin-Bristol Hercules configurations and, ironically, it was the Hercules that helped rescue the Halifax from the mediocre performance suffered by the early marks of the type. A direct comparison with the Lancaster I and Halifax II (both fitted with the 1,390-hp/1035-kW Merlin XX) shows that while the unloaded Halifax weighed eight per cent less than the Lancaster, the Handley Page design could achieve only about 90 per cent of the maximum speed and service ceiling reached by Avro's bomber, and a dismal 55 per cent of the range. Some of this disparity was due to the smaller wing area of the Halifax, a hangover from pre-war restrictions on wingspan dictated by the size of RAF hangar doors.

Crew

The complement of a bomber Halifax was usually seven men, as was typical for RAF 'heavies' of the period. A crew consisted of a pilot, flight engineer, navigator, wireless operator and three gunners. A second pilot was sometimes carried on training flights or on mining sorties or other less dangerous raids in order to introduce him to operational flying.

Handley Page Halifax B.Mk I Srs 1 No. 76 Squadron Middleton-St George 1941

Specification
Halifax B.Mk I Series 1

Type: four-engined heavy bomber
Powerplants: four 1,145-hp (853-kW) Rolls-Royce Merlin X V-12 engines
Performance: maximum speed 262 mph (422 km/h) at 18,000 ft (5490 m); initial climb rate 750 ft (229 m) per minute; service ceiling 22,800 ft (6950 m), at maximum weight 18,000 ft (5490 m); range with maximum bomb load 1,000 miles (1609 km), with auxiliary tanks 2,720 miles (4377 km)
Weights: empty 33,860 lb (15370 kg); loaded 58,000 lb (26310 kg)
Dimensions: span 98 ft 10 in (30.12 m); length 70 ft 1 in (21.36 m); height 20 ft 9 in (6.32 m); wing area 1,250 sq ft (116 m²)
Armament: six Browning 0.303-in machine-guns and two to four Vickers 0.303-in machine-guns; normal bombload 13,000 lb (5897 kg)

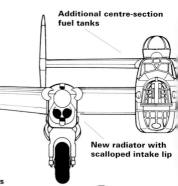

The B.Mk I Series 3 was the first model equipped with a dorsal turret, although only nine were produced. They were built by the parent company at Cricklewood.

contrasted its aims (of putting up houses) with those of the Halifax bomber – "Our interests do not run in the same channels at all." Production of the B.Mk I in its three sub-types was entirely by Handley Page, and reached 84 aircraft. The B.Mk I was declared obsolete in June 1944, and none was left (even in storage) by the war's end.

B.Mk I Srs 3

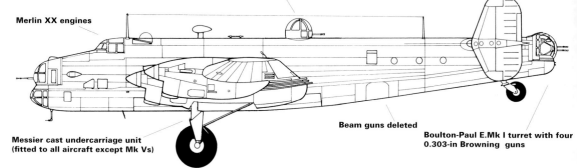

Boulton-Paul C.Mk II turret with twin 0.303-in guns

Merlin XX engines

Messier cast undercarriage unit (fitted to all aircraft except Mk Vs)

Beam guns deleted

Boulton-Paul E.Mk I turret with four 0.303-in Browning guns

The new engines drove 12-ft 9-in (3.88-m) R7/35/34 propellers or the new, slightly wider diameter Rotol R7/35/55 propellers (13 ft/3.96 m instead of 12 ft 9 in). The Series 3 also introduced increased fuel tankage, with new permanent tanks in each mid-wing section replacing Hampden-type tanks fitted in the fuselage rest area, raising total tankage from 2,242 to 2,330 Imp gal (10190 to 10135 litres). The type served with Nos 35 and 76 Squadrons.

It was a Halifax I Series 3 (the ninth and last, L9608) which was officially and formally named Halifax (by Lord Halifax) in a ceremony which included the earnest hope that the Germans would soon be praying for deliverance from "Hull, Hell and Halifax," in the words of the ancient prayer. The ceremony was stage-managed by the Handley Page company, which was never slow to publicise itself and its aircraft. A later attempt to forge a link between the aircraft and the Halifax Building Society foundered when the building society airily

HP.58 Halifax II

The original Halifax II marked a return by Handley Page to its favoured defensive armament layout, with four 20-mm cannon amidships in low-drag BP Type O and H turrets, reminiscent of those used by the Hampden. The aircraft was intended to have a faired tail, with no turret. A mock-up of the new armament layout was built, and Handley Page received a contract to convert L7244 to serve as a prototype, but delays with the turrets led to the cancellation of the project and the variant remained unbuilt, although L9515 was used for development. The HP.58 Halifax II designation was also applied to an aircraft with a twin 0.303-in Browning dorsal turret on a standard Halifax I fuselage, and to projects with various layouts using 0.5-in guns. These versions also remained unbuilt.

Consideration was given to the use of Beaufighter or Mosquito Merlin nacelles on the Mk II Halifax, but they were judged to give insufficient cooling for overseas operation. Avro was under no such constraints when it redesigned the Manchester to become the Merlin-engined Lancaster.

Other features considered for the Mk II Halifax included new lowered nacelles, Merlin 60 engines, enclosed mainwheels, single-leg main undercarriage units and a retractable tailwheel.

HP.59 Halifax B.Mk II Series 1

The Halifax I suffered heavy losses on operations, and by January 1942 only half remained. The Merlin XX-engined Halifax B.Mk I Series 3 had marked a very significant improvement, but was built in tiny numbers only and formed the basis of the B.Mk II. The original B.Mk I aircraft was

By mid-1942 most of No. 35 Squadron's B.Mk Is had been lost, replaced by B.Mk IIs, such as these seen here practising daylight formation flying, a technique soon to be abandoned.

destined to be quickly replaced by the new Halifax II, massive production of which also allowed the formation of a third and several subsequent new squadrons. Nos 10, 78 and 102 converted from the Whitley V, while Nos 158 and 405 transitioned from the Wellington II. This allowed No. 4 Group to rapidly become an all-Halifax force, and eventually an all-Merlin-engined force. The plans for shadow production of the Halifax were implemented in time for production of the Halifax II, whereas the Halifax I had been built only by the parent company. The Halifax had always been intended for split construction and unit assembly, to an even

greater extent than the Hampden which preceded it. As such, the Halifax was designed for assembly from 24 major sub-assemblies. A second production source (which became the Halifax Group) was founded when English Electric was given a sub-contract to manufacture the aircraft in early 1939, even before it had flown.

For the Halifax II, a large number of factories were available. Apart from Handley Page's Cricklewood plant (expanded by the addition of 70,000 sq ft/6500 m² more floor area from the former Nieuport Aircraft works), the Halifax II was built by the English Electric Company at Preston, by Rootes Securities at Speke, by Fairey Aviation, by Nuffield and by the remarkable

new London Aircraft Production Group. The latter consisted of an amalgamation of the London Passenger Transport Board at Leavesden (where centre-sections were produced from sub-assemblies built at Chiswick), Park Royal Coachworks (outer wings, nacelles and cowlings), Express Motor and Body Works (tail units and flaps), Duple Bodies and Motors (forward fuselage sections) and Chrysler Motors (complete rear fuselages). The aircraft were assembled and test flown at Leavesden. In addition to these full-scale aircraft producers, Halifax components were produced by a plethora of companies, few of which had been involved in aviation before the outbreak of hostilities. These

ompanies included the Armstrong Siddeley ervice Station in Colindale, E. Beckett & on of Willesden, Car Mart Ltd of London JW8, Daimler of Hendon, Godfrey Davis of leasden, Kenneth Hill Sandblasting Co. of etchworth, and MGM at Borehamwood.

Maximum all-up weight of the Halifax II ose to 60,000 lb (27270 kg), while fuel ankage rose to 1,882 Imp gal (8555 litres) y the addition of new no. 6 tanks. Tare veight rose from 33,860 lb (15390 kg) for ne Mk I to 34,980 lb (15900 kg) for the Mk . The Mk II was armed with 0.303-in guns hroughout, in the nose, tail and mid-upper urrets. The aircraft was powered by Merlin X engines, which were eventually fitted vith Morris Block radiators with square chin lets. All but the first few had the beam uns replaced by a two-gun C-type Boulton aul mid-upper turret as used in the Mk I eries 3.

Handley Page's first Halifax II (L9485, onverted from a B.Mk I) made its maiden ight on 11 October 1940, with leading- dge slats still fitted and powered by 1,280- p (955-kW) Merlin 10 engines. The first nglish Electric B.Mk II (V9976) flew on 15 ugust 1941. This aircraft beat the first landley Page production Mk II into the air, ince the latter first flew in September 941.

In March 1942 the Halifax was screened rom operations to allow the fitting of the R1335 navigation aid, better known as iee. The Halifax was involved in the bortive missions to find the *Tirpitz*, and perated during the Channel Dash by iermany's trapped battle cruisers. Some 31 Halifaxes participated in the first 1,000- omber raid, against Köln, on 30/31 May 942. One hundred and twenty-seven were espatched against Essen on 2/3 June (with 27 aircraft of other types), and 124 flew gainst Bremen on 25/26 June. The Halifax vas actually outnumbered by Lancasters or the first time in July 1942, and for the est of the year, Halifaxes seldom ccounted for more than 50 aircraft within ach raid.

From July 1942 Nos 10 and 76 quadrons mounted detachments to Aqir to

bomb Tobruk and other targets in North Africa. These detachments marked the first overseas use of an RAF four-engined 'heavy', and later formed No. 462 Squadron. In August No. 35 Squadron transferred (with its Halifaxes) to the newly formed Pathfinder Force. The basic B.Mk II (and its derivatives) were declared obsolete in February 1946.

Official dimensions of the Halifax B.Mk II included a span of 98 ft 10 in (30.12 m), a length of 70 ft 1 in (21.3 m), a height of 20 ft 9 in (6.3 m), and an all-up weight of 60,000 lb (27272 kg).

Right: This B.Mk II seen on a test flight displays asbestos exhaust shrouds and the locked-down landing light particular to the Mk II.

As part of the investigation into declining Halifax performance, 'A-Able' of No. 78 Squadron was sent to Boscombe Down for tests, having completed 10 operations.

HP.59 Halifax B.Mk II Series 1 (Special), SOE

Jo. 138 Squadrons of No. 4 Group began perating Halifaxes in October 1941, flying esupply missions for European resistance novements on behalf of the SOE. The quadron had only three war-weary early lalifax B.Mk IIs, and began operations with hem on 7/8 November, flying mainly in upport of the Polish resistance, at the very mit of the aircraft's range. They retained nose and tail turrets, and had tailwheel uards to prevent static line fouling. That ne unit had Halifaxes at all was remarkable, ince Bomber Command was jealously uarding all four-engined aircraft, and since larris himself had no regard for the rganisation's role or work.

The unit rapidly came to the conclusion nat a lighter, more streamlined aircraft vould be more useful, and the cleaned-up 1k II Series 1 (Special) was produced in esponse. B.Mk I L9515 served as the evelopment aircraft, with new no. 6 tanks nd Merlin 10 engines in reduced-area owlings. It later gained a streamlined nose nd Merlin 22s, with extended inboard acelles and Mod. 451, the Type A.Mk 8 nid-upper gun turret. Handley Page's repair

B.Mk II Srs 1 (Special), SOE   **No exhaust shrouds**   **Dorsal turret deleted**

Tempsford 'Z'-type nose fairing. No forward armament

Fuel vent pipes deleted

depot at Rawcliffe (also known as Clifton) fitted a new streamlined metal nose fairing in place of the nose turret. This was known as the Tempsford, or Z-type nose. Also in the interests of reducing drag, the underwing fuel jettison pipes were deleted, and the flame-damping exhaust shrouds were removed, with the exhaust pipes painted with heat-resistant paint which covered the glow. The dorsal turret was removed, and the aircraft were fitted with a

new paratroop door and associated exit cone, and a retractable tailwheel. They also received extra-long-range fuel tanks. The Series I (Special) was not designed solely for SOE use, although many early aircraft were delivered to No. 138 Squadron at Tempsford, and the first five Specials were modified under Works Order No. 228 specifically for the SOE. Other Special Duties squadrons using the variant later included No. 624 Squadron and No. 148

Squadron. The normal load for SOE Halifaxes was up to 15 containers: nine in the bomb bay, and three in each wing.

The Specials were replaced by Series 1As during early 1944. Examples of SOE B.Mk II Series 1 (Special) aircraft included L9612 L9618, W1002, W1007, W1229, BB281, BB302, BB313, BB318, BB338, BB344, BB378, BB381, BB421, BB441, BB444, DT542, DT543, DT620, DT726, DT727 and HR680.

HP.59 Halifax B.Mk II Series 1 (Special)

he increasing weight of operational quipment (including Gee and H2S) and eavier loads conspired to further reduce alifax operating heights, and losses creased. The introduction of RDM2A pecial night finish also dramatically creased drag, as did the introduction of unnel-like exhaust shroud fairings and the se of large bombs with the bomb doors artly open. Halifaxes frequently found nemselves being hit by bombs from higher- ying Lancasters, some aircraft surviving to ell the tale.

Trials of various drag-reducing modifications were carried out, mainly using a No. 138 Squadron aircraft, W7776. Measures included removal of the fuel jettison pipes, fin leading-edge de-icer boots, barrage balloon cable-cutters, whip aerial, flare chute fairing, upper fuselage hand rail and carburettor intake ice guards, together with the removal of one aerial mast and one (later two) navigation blister. The same aircraft also tested an increased 6-psi (41-kPa) boost setting, raising maximum altitude to 19,000 ft (5790 m) and

increasing top speed by about 20 mph (32 km/h) at the full throttle height of 17,400 ft (5300 m). The trials resulted in the Halifax B.Mk II Series 1 (Special) both for use by the SOE (described above) and for operation by Bomber Command units.

An improved Halifax for Nos 4 and 6 Groups and the PFF had become an urgent necessity. A loss rate which reached 10 per cent in August 1942 prompted questions from Lord Cherwell and Winston Churchill himself, and though it was found that the Halifax had flown a higher proportion of

risky missions than the Lancaster (and had tended to carry bombloads 2,000 lb/910 kg heavier, on average), the losses were unacceptable. The interim answer was the adoption of the Halifax II Series 1, as used by SOE squadrons, with the Tollerton Aircraft Services Z type nose.

The aircraft for Bomber Command were virtually identical to the SOE Mk II Series 1 (Special)s. There was more variation, and the modifications were not always uniformly applied, particularly to aircraft being retrospectively brought to the Special configuration, rather than being completed as B.Mk II Series 1 (Special) bombers on the production line. On existing B.Mk IIs the

Halifax Variants

mid-upper turret was often retained or restored. This was usually a two-gun Boulton Paul C.Mk II turret (the Hudson unit) or the later four-gun A.Mk VIII turret (the squatter Defiant-type turret). The latter was initially mounted on raised decking to allow at least 10° of depression, and contained 550 rounds per gun, yet weighed only 586 lb (266 kg). It was found to significantly increase drag, and the turrets were eventually fitted 'flush' at decking level. A new 1,404-lb (638-kg) two-gun turret mounting a pair of 0.50-in Brownings was tested in R9436, but this turret, the T.Mk 1, did not enter production and was instead sent to the USA for testing and trials. In Bomber Command squadrons, the Mk II Series 1 (Special) was sometimes

colloquially known as the Halifax IIZ.

Some Halifax Mk II Series 1 (Special) aircraft were fitted with Rotol Type R7/14B5/4 propellers, and others flew with a mix of both three- and four-bladed propellers. They were usually (but by no means inevitably) fitted symmetrically, with the four-bladed props mounted outboard for preference. Four-bladed propellers were also retrofitted to Coastal Command Halifaxes, but were rare on bomber B.Mk IIs. Some Halifax II Series 1 (Special) bombers were also fitted with the ventral Preston-Green ventral gun turret, containing a single 0.50-in gun.

Similar modifications applied to the Halifax B.Mk V produced the B.Mk V Series 1 (Special), described separately.

Above: New B.Mk II (Special)s are seen in April 1943 at the English Electric plant at Samlesbury.

Above: Some Halifax B.Mk IIs were converted to Specials at Warton. There was no exact standard for these aircraft. The Halifax at centre, W1173 Xcalabar (sic) of No. 405 (RCAF) Squadron, has the Boulton Paul Type C turret, and the far aircraft the Type A Defiant unit.

Left: Unit-modified aircraft were often of a different standard. This No. 10 Squadron aircraft has no turret to reduce drag, but still has the fixed landing light.

The new nose of the B.Mk II Series 1A can be seen on this aircraft of No. 35 Sqn, as can the Type A dorsal turret and the D-shaped fins which were incorporated or added to many aircraft.

HP.59 Halifax B.Mk II Series 1A

The Tempsford nose of the Series 1 (Special) significantly reduced drag, but did little for forward visibility and was always regarded as an interim modification. The Series 1A introduced a neater solution in the form of a fully transparent nose fairing, which increased overall length by about 18 in (45 cm) and offered more space, light and visibility for the navigator and bomb-aimer. Tested on L9515, the new Mod 452 nose fairing was originally produced in one piece, but battle damage repair considerations led to the adoption of a two-piece design, split horizontally into upper and lower halves. It was lighter than the metal Vollerton fairing and contributed to the lower Tare weight of 35,270 lb (16030 kg).

Although head-on attacks had proved rare, the Mk II Series 1A reintroduced a forward-facing weapon, in the form of a gimbal-mounted Vickers K gun in the nose fairing. Most Mk II Series 1As were fitted with the Defiant-type Boulton Paul Type A Mk VIII four-gun mid-upper turret. Early

Series 1As (from R9534?) were powered by Merlin 22s with the original Gallay radiators, which officially made them Series 1s (even with long noses and Merlin 22s), since the Morris radiator modification was officially essential for an aircraft to rate as a Series 1A. Later aircraft had the more powerful Merlin 22 in low-drag nacelles, with Morris Block radiators, pioneered by HR679, the Series 1A prototype, which incorporated both the Mod 452 nose and Merlin 22s. Use of the Merlin 22 allowed an increase in all-up weight to 65,000 lb (29545 kg), which represented a 4,000-lb (1818-kg) increase in useful load. Unfortunately, a fully laden Halifax B.Mk II Series 1A could not operate with weak mixture and maintain the minimum speed of 155 mph (249 km/h), and thus had to operate with rich mixture and at +6 lb boost, resulting in very heavy fuel consumption.

The bomb bay doors over the wing centre-section bays had proved prone to drooping slightly open (thereby incurring a

drag penalty) and this fault was cured in the Series 1A. Additionally, alternative bomb doors were designed for the main bomb bays, to allow the carriage of larger bombs (two 4,000-lb/1818-kg bombs or a single 8,000-lb/3636-kg bomb). With such weapons the new doors did not close fully, and there was therefore a drag and range penalty, but nonetheless it marked a new capability for the Halifax. When Halifaxes and Lancasters participated in the April 1942 raid against the *Tirpitz*, both types operated with full tanks. The Halifaxes carried a 5,500-lb (2500-kg) load (RN.Mk 19N mines), 500 lb (227 kg) less than the Lancasters, but demonstrated much better take-off performance. The aerodynamic cleaning-up of the Series 1A was extremely effective, with the new variant proving to have about 10 per cent lower drag than even a Series 1 (Special) with no mid-upper turret.

Some Halifax IIs were among the first Bomber Command aircraft to be fitted with H2S navigation and bombing radar, the antenna for this being mounted in a ventral fairing immediately aft of the bomb bay. Two Halifax IIs (V9977 and later W7711) were allocated to the TRE for use as trials aircraft, and another (W7808) by the BDU at Gransden Lodge. H2S was first used operationally in January 1943, when 13 H2S-equipped bombers included six Halifax B.Mk IIs of No. 35 Squadron. No. 35 was one of the first two PFF squadrons

equipped with H2S, the other being the Stirling-equipped No. 7. Once the use of H2S was extended from the Pathfinders to the Main Force, Lancasters were given priority for the new equipment.

Other Halifax IIs served in the Elint and EW roles with No. 192 Squadron, including DT735 and DT737.

Late production HP.59 Halifax II Series 1A aircraft were delivered with rectangular D-type fins and rudders (tested on R9534, the B.Mk III prototype, and on B.Mk V DK145), and other aircraft had them retrofitted (as Mod 814), especially those Series 1A aircraft fitted with Merlin 22s or H2S. A working party of 41 personnel, from No. 13 MU at Henlow, commanded by a warrant officer, travelled from airfield to airfield, modifying 225 Mk II and Mk V Halifaxes in less than four months. Two hundred and seventy-seven more were modified during the next two months, before 60 Coastal Command Halifaxes were refinned at St Davids in March 1944. The new fins cured the Halifax's tendency to 'rudder stall' and enhanced directional stability, allowing more accurate bombing.

This Halifax is possibly an SOE derivative of the B.Mk II Series IA, as evidenced by the tailwheel guard fitted to such parachute-dropping aircraft. Four-bladed propellers were unusual but not unknown.

Some Halifax II Series 1As were fitted with the Preston-Green ventral gun turret, containing a single 0.50-in gun. It was intended to deter attacks from behind and below, but was rarely fitted. Others were delivered to SOE squadrons, with similar modifications to the Series 1 (Special) for their specialised role. Examples included JP181, JP239, JP259, and JP276.

The Merlin-engined Halifax bomber was never really satisfactory, proving unreliable and lacking in performance. Loss rates were always high, and Halifax squadrons frequently had to be suspended from operations for rest and for the training of new crews. Once the radial-engined variants became available in quantity, the Merlin-engined bombers were suspended from operations over Germany itself, flying only against less heavily defended French targets. A raid against Leipzig on 19/20 February 1944 provided the catalyst, since it saw the loss of 34 of the 255 Halifaxes despatched. The type was finally withdrawn from front-line Bomber Command squadrons by the early summer of 1944,

Forward armament was reintroduced on the Series 1A in the form of a single World War I-era Vickers 'scare' gun.

B.Mk II Series 1A

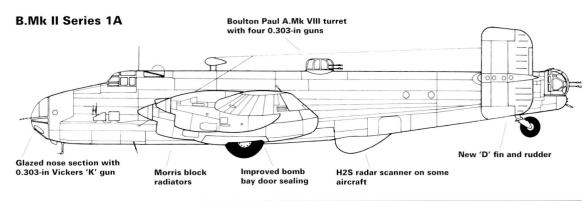

Boulton Paul A.Mk VIII turret with four 0.303-in guns

Glazed nose section with 0.303-in Vickers 'K' gun

Morris block radiators

Improved bomb bay door sealing

H2S radar scanner on some aircraft

New 'D' fin and rudder

though it continued to serve with Heavy Conversion Units. A handful of Merlin-engined Halifaxes were even delivered to the HCUs until mid-1944, before all the Halifax plants switched to the B.Mk III. All surviving Merlin-engined Halifaxes were declared obsolete in February 1946, but this hardly affected the B.Mk II, 114 of which had remained in store at the end of 1945, earmarked for scrapping.

HP.59 Halifax B.Mk II Series 2

The first Halifax B.Mk II Series 1A (HR679) demonstrated a significant improvement over the basic B.Mk II, but further refinements were clearly possible, and HR756 was set aside to test these further modifications. This aircraft had Merlin 22s with Morris block radiators and thermostatically controlled radiator flaps in lowered, extended inboard nacelles, with three-bladed Rotol Type XHF53/W propellers (R7/35/54s modified with Beaufighter-type spinners). The aircraft also had six-way ejector exhausts without shrouds, and a fully-enclosed undercarriage when retracted. On HR756 the cabin heat airscoops were repositioned from above the cowlings to below the wingroot. The various improvements were accompanied by increased boost, and cruising ceiling was improved to over 19,000 ft (5790 m), although the speed gain was only 9 mph (14 km/h) – insufficient to justify production, when the Hercules-powered B.Mk III was already showing even greater

HR756 was the sole B.Mk II Series 2 . This view shows the deeper nacelles, Beaufighter spinners and six-stack exhausts.

promise. HR756 was subsequently converted with Merlin 85 engines, and then with Merlin 65s. They were better, but the B.Mk III was by then well on the way and introduction of new Merlins was neither practical nor even desirable. The Series 2 prototype remained a one-off, though some of its features were expected to be incorporated into the B.Mk IV. Had the Halifax B.Mk II become a reality, another potential powerplant might have been the Merlin 24. It was tested on a very early B.Mk III (V9985) with full turrets (except mid-upper), beam gun hatches, wireless masts, navigation blisters and early fins, which compared very favourably with a fully-streamlined, Merlin XX-powered, rectangular-ruddered B.Mk V (DK145), especially on take-off and climb-out.

HP.59 Halifax B.Mk II Series 1 Freighter

A handful of SOE Halifaxes were temporarily attached to No. 511 Squadron for freighting duties in December 1942, but these aircraft were unmodified. In the Middle East, a number of time-expired B.Mk IIs (including W7671, W7845, W7847 and W7849) were converted by No. 144 MU at Maison Blanche, Algeria to serve as freighters, with crude metal fairings allowing semi-conformal carriage of engines or Spitfire fuselages.

HP.59 Halifax A.Mk II

Some sources suggest that a handful of the first airborne forces Halifaxes were converted B.Mk IIs. If so, they may have been designated as A.Mk IIs, or may have been interim aircraft which retained their bomber designations.

Twin tug towing of gliders (a Hamilcar is seen here) was trialled at Farnborough in 1943. After take-off, one Halifax would release to return and assist another tow.

HP.59 Halifax GR.Mk II Series 1

Only a handful of B.Mk II Series 1s or Series 1 (Special)s were actually converted to GR.Mk II configuration by Cunliffe-Owen Aircraft at Eastleigh. These aircraft almost certainly retained the early fin shape and

This Halifax GR. Mk II Series 1A, HR686, belonging to No. 502 Squadron, was reported missing on patrol from Stornoway on 3 October 1944.

carried ASV Mk 3 radar in an H2S type fairing. Unusually, despite the solid nose, a 0.50-in 'scare' gun was sometimes mounted. The Series 1A was undoubtedly the most important early Coastal Command Halifax.

HP.59 Halifax GR.Mk II Series 1A

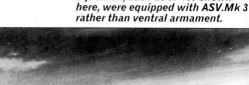

The GR. Mk II Series 1As of No. 58 Squadron, such as JP165 shown here, were equipped with ASV.Mk 3 rather than ventral armament.

The excellent ditching characteristics of the Halifax, coupled with its long endurance and capacious fuselage, made it top of Coastal Command's wish list, though the Command preferred the Hercules-engined Halifax III to the Merlin-engined Halifax II. Coastal Command actually gained its first experience of the aircraft when No. 405 Squadron temporarily transferred to the Command between 25 October 1942 and 1 March 1943, moving from Topcliffe in Yorkshire to Beaulieu in Hampshire where it mounted 365 patrols, resulting in 11 contacts and three attacks against German U-boats. This might sound modest, but it was sufficient to prompt the Germans to form a dedicated Ju 88 fighter unit, specifically tasked with protecting U-boats from Bordeaux, Lorient, St Nazaire and La Pallice as they transitted the Bay of Biscay. During one daylight mission a Halifax of No. 405 downed two of three Ju 88s which attacked it, and drove off the third. No. 158 Squadron also mounted detachments to Coastal Command. The Halifax proved a more useful tool than had the Lancaster (a squadron of which had been detached during mid-1942) and the decision was made to procure a dedicated version of the aircraft for ASW work, to replace the ageing Whitley.

The definitive GR.Mk II was converted by Cunliffe-Owen Aircraft at Eastleigh, and equipped Nos 58 and 502 Squadrons at Holmsley South and St Eval for operations over the Bay of Biscay. The type was also used by No. 1674 HCU at Aldergrove.

Some aircraft were transferred direct from Bomber Command, with No. 58 Squadron, retaining H2S and other role equipment, and being equipped with ASV Mk.3 radar and 'Boozer' in service, at station level. Most GR.Mk IIs were converted from aircraft delivered straight from the factory to Cunliffe-Owen and had an FN.64 ventral turret or single 0.5-in Browning in a ventral Preston Green mounting, with another 0.5-in gun replacing the Vickers K VGO 0.303-in gun in the nose. This was intended to allow the aircraft to suppress hostile fire from surfaced U-boats, but also gave an added measure of protection against enemy fighters. On one occasion a No. 58 Squadron aircraft was attacked by seven Ju 88s for 47 minutes,

yet returned to base with minor damage, having inflicted far worse on its assailants. The GR.Mk II was fitted with 690-Imp gal (3136-litre) tanks in the bomb bay, which increased range, albeit at the cost of reduced bombload. The aircraft generally carried Torpex depth charges for use in the ASW role, or 600-lb (272-kg) anti-submarine bombs. The two squadrons sank five U-boats during 1943 and 1944, restricted U-boat operations over a wide area, and led other forces to make additional U-boat kills. The aircraft were also tasked with anti-shipping attacks, and from 1944 began night ASW patrols, using flares to illuminate any contact, as fighter defences and U-boat defensive armament increased in potency. Some GR.Mk IIs were fitted with four bladed airscrews. In August 1943, Cunliffe-Owen converted JD212 with rocket projectile launchers under the centre-section, but the modification (though successful) was not adopted. Tare weight was 36,030 lb (16377 kg).

Four GR.Mk IIs remained in service with No. 58 Squadron at Stornoway as the war ended, but three were categorised as being unserviceable, and the squadron was primarily equipped with the radial-engined GR.Mk III. The GR.Mk II was officially declared obsolete in February 1946.

Conversions included BB312, BB314,

DT636, DT692, HR675, HR683, HR686, HR688, HR689, HR693, HR741, HR744, HR746, HR774, HR782, HR792, HR815, HR983, HX152, HX177, HX178, HX222, HX223, HX224, HX225, JB895, JB901, JD176, JD178, JD212, JD218, JD245,

JD376, JP163, JP164, JP165, JP167, JP169, JP172, JP173, JP238, JP255, JP257, JP271, JP297, JP298, JP299, JP300, JP319, JP320, JP328, JP329, JP330, JP333, JP336 and JP339.

GR.Mk II Series 1A

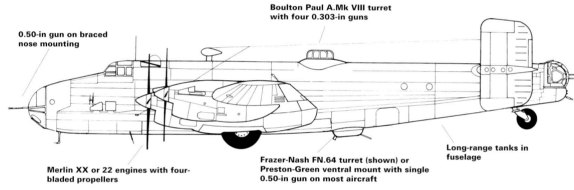

0.50-in gun on braced nose mounting

Boulton Paul A.Mk VIII turret with four 0.303-in guns

Merlin XX or 22 engines with four-bladed propellers

Frazer-Nash FN.64 turret (shown) or Preston-Green ventral mount with single 0.50-in gun on most aircraft

Long-range tanks in fuselage

HP.59 Halifax Met.Mk II

There have been reports that the Met.Mk II existed, but this seems unlikely. Post-war Handley Page records quoted a Tare weight of 35,370 lb (16077 kg) for a Met.Mk II, however. In service, the B.Mk V formed the basis of virtually all the early meteorological Halifaxes, and there may have been no conversions from the basic B.Mk II.

All surviving Merlin-engined Halifaxes (B.Mk II, GR.Mk II, Met.Mk II, B.Mk V, A.Mk V, GR.Mk V, and Met.Mk V) were declared obsolete in February 1946, by which time the survivors were in long-term storage.

HP.61 Halifax III prototype

The Halifax III prototype, R9534, had a variety of fins and dorsal turrets during its career. The H2S radome has been cleverly censored here.

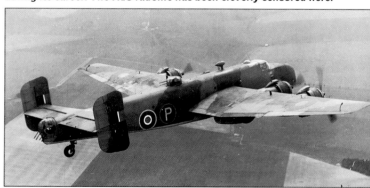

The Halifax III was intended as an interim type, though the cancellation of the Mk IV left it as the main production version. Fortuitously, Handley Page's dissatisfaction with the Merlin as a Halifax powerplant ran alongside massive demand for the engine for use on other aircraft types, including the rival Lancaster. The company had long wanted to fit radial engines to the Halifax, and the Mk III was the eventual result. The prototype (R9534), a converted B.Mk II Series 1 (Special) with a Tempsford nose, was powered by Hercules VI engines. The aircraft's Boulton Paul C.Mk II-type turret was later replaced by an A-type turret, and a retractable tailwheel was fitted.

The B.Mk III prototype took shape as

Handley Page was struggling to find a definitive fin and rudder shape which would solve the aircraft's rudder overbalance at low airspeeds. The aircraft was fitted with F-type fins and rudders (which looked like the original units) but, in the end, the distinctive rectangular D-type fin was selected for production B.Mk IIIs and for retrofit to late B.Mk IIs and B.Mk Vs. The Halifax's fin problems were no worse than those suffered by many of its contemporaries, though the solution of providing a redesigned fin of entirely new shape did draw attention to it. In fact, the Lancaster probably suffered more severe problems, with fin failures and a marked reluctance to pull out of a fast dive.

HP.61 Halifax B.Mk III

The production Halifax B.Mk III was based on the fuselage of the B.Mk II Series 1A, with the late clear nosecone. The variant was powered by Hercules XVI engines, which were similar to the Hercules VI, but with fully automatic carburettors. The variant featured DH airscrews, and (after the first two aircraft) a retractable tailwheel.

Most B.Mk IIIs also had either a ventral H2S antenna fairing or a ventral gun. Flame dampers, engine rear armour, an astrograph, a DF loop, glider towing capability, increased electrical generation, and fittings for 4,000-lb and 8,000-lb bombs were featured as standard. With its powerful engines and new tailfins, the new

variant flew and handled well, and morale on the Halifax squadrons improved immeasurably.

The Halifax III had strengthened structure, with some spar webs doubled in thickness, increased bolt sizes, a stronger undercarriage, and the strengthened floor designed for the Halifax Mk IV. Fuel tankage was increased to 2,688 Imp gal (12220 litres) (with a reserve of 142 Imp gal/645 litres), giving the aircraft an

endurance of about 10.3 hours, with its average fuel burn of 168 Imp gal (763 litres) per hour. The no. 2 tanks were transferred to the centre-section (total wing tank capacity was 1,806 Imp gal/8210 litres), and provision was made for two extra 96-Imp gal (436-litre) long-range tanks in the outer bomb cells in the centre wing panels, as Mod 673. Three 230-Imp gal (1045-litre) tanks could be carried in the fuselage, raising maximum fuel capacity to 2,688 Imp

gal (12219 litres). Cruising at 178 mph (110 km/h), the new variant had a range of 1,600 nm (1840 miles; 2960 km). With a representative 8,220-lb (3736-kg) bombload, the Halifax III had an endurance of 8.5 hours, and a range of 1,280 nm (1470 miles; 2360 km).

Once the strengthened undercarriage components were introduced, the Halifax III had a maximum AUW of 65,000 lb (29545 kg), though early examples were limited to 63,000 lb (28636 kg). Other early changes included the addition of H2S (a working party visited the first four squadrons and fitted sets at the rate of one per day) and the use of new Vokes Modified Internal Tunnel type air filters in place of the Bristol

B.Mk III

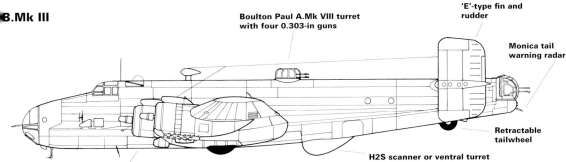

Boulton Paul A.Mk VIII turret with four 0.303-in guns

'E'-type fin and rudder

Monica tail warning radar

Retractable tailwheel

H2S scanner or ventral turret

Bristol Hercules XVI 14-cylinder radial engines with de Havilland three-bladed propellers

Strengthened structure and undercarriage

Increased wing tankage

Wingtips extended from 99 ft 2 in (30.2 m) to 104 ft 2 in (31.7 m) on late aircraft

Fittings for 4,000-lb and 8,000-lb bombs

Boulton Paul E.Mk I turret with four 0.303-in Browning guns

The Hercules engines restored the performance of the Halifax, which had degraded progressively with the addition of more and more operational equipment. The new wingtips and fins improved altitude performance and stability.

Open Scoop type. The oil coolers proved too efficient in service, and blanks were designed to stop oil from congealing, which would in turn have raised engine temperatures. Four squadrons received the first batch of Halifax B.Mk IIIs from November 1943, including No. 35, the RAF's first Halifax unit, and Nos 51, 433 and 466. The type began flying operations in December 1943.

Many Halifax IIIs were fitted with extended wingtips (first flown on R9534 and HR845 and tested at Boscombe Down in January 1944) which increased span to 103 ft 8 in (31.59 m), as Mods 862/863. They increased the climb rate by between 70 and 120 ft/min (21 and 36 m/min), increasing cruise ceiling by 1,700 ft (518 m), and absolute ceiling by 800 ft (243 m). Bulbous nose ailerons were often fitted as Mod 929.

The improved Halifax III cruised 3 mph (1.86 km/h) faster than a contemporary Lancaster (at 241 mph/149 km/h) and was 4 mph (2.5 km/h) faster (at 282 mph/175 km/h) flat out. It reached 20,000 ft (6097 m) two minutes quicker (in 42 minutes) but had a ceiling 3,000 ft (914 m) lower.

There were many one-off and squadron-level modifications to the Halifax. No. 77 Squadron, for instance, designed a rebalanced ventral gun mounting for a single 0.5-in machine-gun. Massive losses (94 aircraft) during the 30/31 March 1944 raid against Nuremberg prompted a more official modification, trialled on JD380 at Park Street and later adopted by front-line

squadrons, initially those serving with No. 6 Group. This saw the addition of a ventral 0.5-in Browning in the Preston-Green turret. This installation was made possible by the slow delivery of H2S radar sets, which produced a shortage of H2S equipment and left the ventral position empty in some new Halifax B.Mk IIIs. Many Halifaxes had prominent window chutes, and some had a clear Perspex fairing below the bomb-aimer's position.

By the last quarter of 1944, the Halifax B.Mk III was playing a major part in the Bomber Command offensive, and on many nights Halifaxes actually outnumbered Lancasters. At the end of the year, daylight attacks (some of which targeted German airfields) were even mounted. By this time, the Halifax B.Mk III was suffering lower losses than the Lancaster, though the 'Brass' seemed to fail to notice the change.

During 1945, some B.Mk IIIs (probably configured for transport duties) were converted for service in the Far East, with extra fuel tankage to give extended range, and with extensive use of 'termite-proof materials'. Examples included SNAKE NA644.

Coastal Command showed great interest in the Mk III Halifax even as it was taking shape, preferring the Hercules 7 or 17 to the unreliable Merlin, and admiring the capacious fuselage of the Halifax. The Command wanted an aircraft which could carry four 18-in (45-cm) torpedoes, or two 21-in (53-cm) torpedoes, and the Halifax promised to fit the bill. The Halifax had also

already demonstrated excellent ditching characteristics, with 41 aircrew (of 64) rescued from nine ditchings in the first months of 1943. Unfortunately, radial-engined Halifaxes could not be spared by Bomber Command, and Coastal Command found itself receiving Mk II Series 1As which were converted as GR.Mk II Series 1As, most with ASV.Mk 3 radar. Some Halifax IIIs were used to test equipment and weapons for Coastal Command, but the type did not initially form the basis of any dedicated maritime variants.

The B.Mk III was declared obsolete in August 1946, at the same time as the GR.Mk III and Met.Mk 3, although 18 B.Mk IIIs formed the main equipment of the Empire Air Navigation School until August 1947, and one more B.Mk III, ST814 *Sirius*, remained in use for trials until January 1948.

The Mk III was the most numerous Halifax sub-type, and a total of 2,091 was built. Of these, 325 were built by Handley Page, these being HX226-247, HX265-296, HX311-357, LV771-775, LV777-799, LV813-842, LV857-883, LV898-923, LV985-999, LW113-143, LW157-179, and LW191-195. Nine hundred were built by English Electric, these being serialled LW346-348, 361-397, 412-446, 459-481, 495-522, 537-559, 572-598, 613-658, 671-696, 713-724, MZ500-544, 556-604, 617-660, 672-717, 730-775, 787-831, 844-883, 895-939, NP930-976, 988-999, NR113-156, 169-211, 225-258, 271-290, RG345-390, and 413-446. Fairey produced 325 Mk IIIs, consisting of LK747-766, 779-812, 826-850, 863-887, NA492-531, 543-587, 599-644, 656-704, and PN167-207. Rootes built 281 B.Mk IIIs, these being LL543-559, 573-615, MZ945-989, NA102-150, 162-205, 218-263, 275-309, 428 and 452. The London Passenger Transport Board built the remaining 260 B.Mk IIIs. These were MZ282-321, 334-378, 390-435, 447-495, PN365-406, and 423-460.

Above: The new planform provided by the extended wingtips can be seen on MZ359, an aircraft of No. 77 Squadron in 1944.

Left: Colourful tail markings began to appear on No. 4 Group Halifaxes in late 1944. Yellow bands identified No. 158 Squadron.

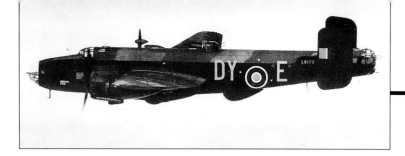

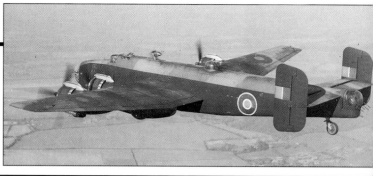

LW179 was a Handley Page-built B.Mk III which was lost on a mission to Magdeburg in January 1945 when serving with No. 102 Squadron at Pocklington.

Right: The first production B.Mk III, HX227, shows its fixed tailwheel (retractable on subsequent aircraft). This aircraft was used for trials of Vokes engine air scoops.

HP.61 Halifax B.Mk III (BS) 'Elint'

Elint operations by Bomber Command in Europe have now become well known. Less attention has been paid to the radar-snooping role of units such as No. 1341 Flight, which operated out of Digri, India from May 1945. Note the ADF-like fairing under the rear fuselage.

Halifaxes used by No. 100 Group (and in the Far East) in the bomber support role retained their bomber designations, though unofficial BS suffixes were sometimes applied. The Halifax was used in the Elint role by No. 192 Squadron and by Nos 1341 and 1473 Flights. The aircraft were used to identify and locate enemy radars and fighter control centres, and also gained considerable raw intelligence from German RT and radar transmissions, identifying and classifying new AI radars to allow the development of effective countermeasures. The Elint aircraft were basically standard bombers, with two Special Operators facing to port, between the two wing spars. The aircraft carried a number of search receivers, with cylinder dictaphones or wire recorders to record the signals, and with a 35-mm camera to record the visual CRT display. A paper tape recorder known as 'Bagful' was carried by some aircraft, which detailed wavelength, duration and time of an intercepted signal. Blonde was an automatic camera which continuously

recorded signals within a specified band on the CRT. One receiver, known as Coal Scuttle, was simply a modified H2S connected to a recorder, this giving a bearing on a signal under investigation.

Externally, the Elint Halifaxes could be distinguished by an array of small antennas. A half-wave horizontally polarised dipole search antenna was carried on each side of the nose, in front of and above the usual Rebecca aerial, with a half-wave vertically polarised dipole search antenna just ahead of and below the Rebecca aerial. A quarter-wave capped cone antenna was carried below the tail turret, with additional dipoles below the fuselage, immediately in front of the H2S radome and slightly further aft. Some aircraft also carried large whip antennas below the nose. Elint Halifax IIs included DT735, and DT737, with Mk Vs DK244 and DK246 while Elint Halifax IIIs included LK780, LK781, LK782, LV255, LV955, LW613, LW621, LW623, LW624, LW625, LW626, MZ501, MZ564, MZ638, MZ706, MZ795, MZ806, MZ817, MZ929,

MZ932, NA187, NA242, NR187, NR272, PN369, PN370, PN371, PN381, PN382, PN431, and PN446. Some aircraft were fitted with Mandrel, most had Monica tail warning equipment, and all carried Window.

HP.61 Halifax B.Mk III (BS) Mandrel

The Lancaster's capacious bomb bay and superior performance allowed it to supplant the Halifax in the bomber role, but, by contrast, the Halifax's roomier fuselage made it a better choice for the bomber support role, with easier access to black boxes and better accommodation for any special operators. No. 100 Group therefore preferred the Halifax to the Lancaster, and began to standardise on the Handley Page type, a process well underway when the war ended. Two Halifax squadrons (Nos 171 and 199) converted from Stirlings equipped with Mandrel to similarly equipped Halifaxes. Mandrel was an offensive jammer aimed against German Freya early warning radar. The aircraft carrying it were also used for Window dropping. Mandrel's first operational success was in screening airborne forces on D-Day.

B.Mk III Mandrel

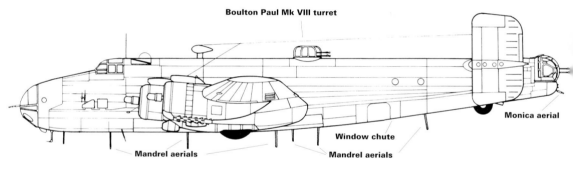

Boulton Paul Mk VIII turret

Monica aerial

Window chute

Mandrel aerials   Mandrel aerials

The Mandrel Halifax carried a single special operator to look after the eight Mandrel sets (six Mandrel Is or American Mandrels and two Mandrel IIIs), this crewman also manning the rear Window chute, while the bomb-aimer manned the front chute. Late in the war, a semi-automatic dispenser was fitted, which

regulated dispensing to a constant, pre-set rate. The Mandrel suite was served by eight blade and rod antennas below the fuselage, with a fan of three wire antennas from the rear fuselage to the tailplane leading edge serving a third Mandrel III set introduced from January 1945. The beam approach antenna was moved to starboard.

Mandrel-equipped Halifaxes included LK868, LK874, LK875, LW471, MZ491, MZ971, NA106, NA107, NA109, NA110, NA164, NA275, NA674, NA690, NA694, NR243, NR244, PN192, PN372, PN374, PN375, RG373, and RG375.

HP.61 Halifax B.Mk III (BS) 'Airborne Cigar'

No. 462 Squadron, RAAF, used Halifaxes equipped with three 'Airborne Cigar' jamming transmitters, together with Carpet II and Piperack jammers and (naturally) Window. Two massive ABC Type 313 antenna masts were carried above the fuselage, with one below the nose. ABC receiver antennas took the form of four whips above the rear fuselage, between the mid-upper turret and the tail. Carpet II antennas were carried below the fuselage, behind the H2S radome, while Piperack whip antennas were mounted in pairs above and below the wingtips of about 11 aircraft. ABC was aimed against Luftwaffe RT fighter control channels and against certain fighter navaids, and depended on a German-speaking operator for effective employment. Window was often used in its own right, particularly for spoofing enemy fighters into believing that tiny diversionary raids were the 'real thing'; enemy fighters were often lured into areas where they could be engaged by Mosquito intruders,

and away from the Main Force bombers.

ABC-equipped Halifaxes included MZ913, PN168/G, PN423/G, PN433/G, PN442/G and PN451/G.

B.Mk III (ABC)

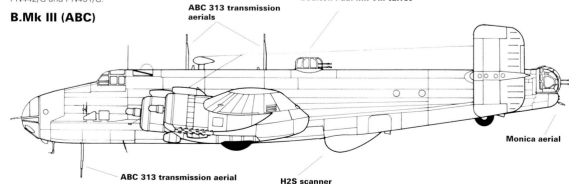

ABC 313 transmission aerials

Boulton Paul Mk VIII turret

Monica aerial

ABC 313 transmission aerial   H2S scanner

HP.61 Halifax A.Mk III

The priority for Hercules-engined Halifax deliveries was given to Bomber Command, and little importance was attached to the development of a Hercules-powered Airborne Forces variant. The A.Mk III was primarily a new-build version for No. 38 Group, and was intended for interim support of the airborne forces, pending introduction of the dedicated A.Mk IX. Thirty A.Mk IIIs were built by Rootes, the first

being delivered in October 1943. Aircraft had their dorsal turrets deleted, while glider towing hooks, seats and strops for 12 paratroops were provided, using the existing paratroop exit cone and static line support bar designed for the A.Mk V. The aircraft usually had Rebecca and Gee incorporated as Mods 856 and 1359, and could be fitted with seats for eight passengers under Mods 862/863/929. Its

Tare weight was 37,630 lb (17104 kg). Although it has been suggested that there were only 30 A.Mk IIIs, the following 43 aircraft have all been quoted as being A.Mk IIIs. LK848, LK988, LV691, LW385, LW446, LW467, MZ558, MZ569, MZ637, MZ650, MZ668, MZ688, MZ745, MZ955, MZ966, MZ970, MZ973, MZ976, MZ979, MZ989, NA103, NA104, NA116, NA128, NA129, NA135, NA139, NA141, NA146, NA163,

NA290, NA294, NA296, NA568, NA613, NA614, NA657, NA667, NA673, NA684, NA686, NA688, and NA700.
The Halifax A.Mk III replaced the A.Mk V quite rapidly after the Arnhem operation, in October 1944, but was itself largely replaced by the A.Mk VII and C.Mk VIII as the war ended. The A.Mk III was withdrawn from HCU use in May 1946 and was finally declared obsolete in January 1947.

HP.61 Halifax C.Mk III

The Halifax C.Mk III was a stripped converted bomber incorporating Mod 1105 with nine stretchers or eight passenger seats, in addition to the normal crew rest bunks, which could seat six. All guns (normally except those in the tail), the dorsal turret, the H2S and its radome, Monica and the tri-cell chute were removed, resulting in a Tare weight of 37,700 lb (17136 kg). The aircraft had a flush-fitting 3,000-lb (1363-kg) freight container and was not normally compatible with the ventral pannier, although some trials C.Mk IIIs did carry it.
The first four C.Mk IIIs (including LW547,

LW548, and NA683) were delivered to No. 246 Squadron (which also operated C-87 Liberators and Avro Yorks) from November 1944 for trials, carrying passengers and freight. No. 187 Squadron formed on 1 February 1945 with 25 Halifax C.Mk IIIs, and later gained No. 246 Squadron's Halifax flight. No. 96 Squadron never fully equipped with Halifaxes, before both units re-equipped with Dakotas from March 1945.
The C.Mk III was declared obsolete in January 1947.

The C.Mk III normally retained the tail armament of the B.Mk III but lost the other defensive positions. Up to 14 seated passengers could be carried.

HP.61 Halifax GR.Mk III

The first Halifax GR.Mk IIIs were delivered to Nos 58 and 502 Squadrons in February 1945, rapidly replacing Merlin-engined GR.Mk IIs. The aircraft had a Tare weight of 39,000 lb (17727 kg), and was similar to the B.Mk III, with much the same modifications as the GR.Mk II and GR.Mk V. The new variant allowed the carriage of nine 500-lb (227-kg) bombs, and proved very effective

in the anti-shipping role, though its service life was destined to be very short. The GR.Mk III was declared obsolete in August 1946, at the same time as the B.Mk III and Met.Mk III. Known GR.Mk IIIs included NA226, NA235, PN183, PN202, PN205, PN399, PN402, RG363, RG364, RG369 and RG395.

The GR.Mk III was delivered in February 1945 to two Coastal Command units, which sank 18 enemy-operated vessels between them before the war ended. Many Coastal Command Halifaxes retained night bomber camouflage.

HP.61 Halifax Met.Mk III

Meteorological conversions of the B.Mk III (with long- or short-span wings) replaced Met.Mk Vs from March 1945, though they were destined to enjoy only a short service life. They had a Tare weight of 38,340 lb

(17427 kg). Met.Mk III aircraft included LV170, LV876, NA231, NA247, NA248, PN190 and RG414. The Met.Mk III was declared obsolete in August 1946, at the same time as the GR.Mk III and B.Mk III.

HP.60A Halifax Mk IV

The Halifax Mk IV was originally intended as a Hercules-s or Griffon-engined variant, with two mainwheels per side on a single oleo leg, and with a redesigned tail unit. Various undercarriage configurations were explored, including a side-retracting single oleo, an aft-retracting single oleo with a twisting mainwheel and even a tricycle undercarriage. The aircraft was subsequently redesigned as a Merlin 60-series powered version of the Halifax. Handley Page could have simply used existing Lancaster-type nacelles, but felt that they gave inadequate cooling and opted for new lowered and refined nacelles. A single aircraft (HR756, a B.Mk II) was set

aside to serve as a prototype for the new version. This aircraft was fitted with the long-tailed inner nacelles, but still retained Merlin XX engines. It eventually became the Mk II Series 2, described above. Plans for strengthened bomb bay and enlarged doors would have allowed carriage of 4,000-lb (1818-kg) and 8,000-lb (3636-kg) bombs. Planned extended wingspan was 104 ft (31.71 m). The aircraft had E-type rudders.

Left and below: Two views of a B.Mk V taken in September 1942. This was one of the first Mk Vs delivered by Rootes Securities, following directly on from Mk II production. Apart from the new Dowty undercarriage, the basic Mks II and V were little different.

HP.63 Halifax B.Mk V

With the Halifax Group's new factories coming 'on-line', production of the aircraft soon threatened to outstrip the availability of the Messier main undercarriage units. Instead of building more Halifax IIs, Rootes Securities and Fairey produced the Halifax V and its sub-variants. Some 246 aircraft were built by Fairey, and 658 were built by Rootes. Rootes actually also built 12 B.Mk IIs, one of which was lost before delivery. It was basically identical to the Halifax II, but featured a redesigned Dowty levered-suspension undercarriage and a revised new hydraulic system which used DTD 44. The new undercarriage retracted faster than the original, giving notably better take-off

and climb-out performance and smoother running on bumpy ground. The new undercarriage was tested on B.Mk I L9520. Unfortunately, the threat of manufacturing delays led to the incorporation of cast components instead of forgings, and they proved to have weaknesses at high stress levels. It was too late to substitute forged parts, and thereafter the Halifax V was handicapped by a 40,000-lb (18181-kg) maximum landing weight. This defect led to the cancellation of planned production of the Halifax V in Canada. That programme got as far as despatching a Rootes-built Mk V, DG399, to Canada as a pattern aircraft. Interestingly, the flimsier-

looking Dowty undercarriage was significantly heavier than the Messier original, and the basic B.Mk V had a Tare weight of 36,570 lb (16622 kg). Most sources gloss over the B.Mk V, suggesting (erroneously) that the type was used almost entirely in the meteorological

reconnaissance, general reconnaissance, Airborne Forces and glider-towing roles. Large numbers of Mk Vs were converted to other marks to fulfil other roles, but the type did see service as a bomber. Despite the weight restrictions on the aircraft, nine squadrons flew the B.Mk V with Bomber

Command, and Mk Vs were actually the last Merlin-engined bombers in service. B.Mk Vs underwent much the same modifications as the Mk II in service, rapidly resulting in the B.Mk V aircraft and a Series 1A. The retirement of the B.Mk V and the Merlin-Halifax was not mourned; Sir Arthur Harris

rejoiced that the Halifax could now "hold its own against the formidable fighter defences of the Reich."

HP.63 Halifax B.Mk V Series 1 (Special)

B.Mk V Series 1 (Special)s are seen undergoing servicing at night. The nearest aircraft is one of the few with Rotol four-bladed propellers.

No. 161 Squadron used the Mk V Series 1 (Special) in the special operations role, its aircraft being similar to the B.Mk II Series 1 (Special) aircraft used by No. 138 Squadron. The type was also used by No. 1575 (SD) Flight, which became No. 624 Squadron; by No. 301 (Special Duties) Flight, which subsequently became No. 1586 (SD) Flight; and later by No. 301 Squadron. No. 138 Squadron eventually re-equipped with similar B.Mk Vs. The aircraft were stripped of most armament in the same way as the SOE B.Mk II Series 1 (Special) Halifaxes, and had a new paratroop hatch with a blast deflector exit cone. SOE B.Mk V Series 1 (Special) aircraft included DG244, DG245, DG252, DG253, D283, DG286, DG406, DJ996, DK119, EB140, EB141, EB142,

EB143, EB147, EB154, EB196, EB197, LK695, LK738, LK742, LK743, LL118, LL120, LL187, LL249, LL250, LL251, LL254, LL279, LL282, LL290, LL306, LL308, LL354, LL358, LL364, LI367, LL381, LL385, LL387, LL388, LL390, LL392, LL409, LL416, LL453, LL465, LL466, LL467, LL468 and LL521. The aircraft were sometimes known as the B.Mk V (Special Duties).

Some B.Mk V Series 1 (Special) bombers were delivered to squadrons of Nos 4 and 6 Groups, and to HCCUs. A handful went to Coastal Command, some of them (including DG250) gaining rectangular D-type fins and four-bladed propellers. The B.Mk V Series 1 (Special) had a Tare weight of 36,290 lb (16495 kg).

HP.63 Halifax B.Mk V Series 1A

The Mk V Series 1A was broadly equivalent to the Mk II Series 1A, albeit with the Dowty undercarriage and built by Rootes Securities or Fairey. The variant was powered by the Merlin 22, and most new-build aircraft were completed with the rectangular D-type fin/rudders. Some Halifax V Series 1As were fitted with the Preston-Green ventral gun turret, containing a single 0.50-in gun. The Series 1A had a Tare weight of 35,390 lb (16086 kg).

As the Rootes- and Fairey-built version of the basic Merlin-engined B.Mk II, the B.Mk

V's career paralleled that of the more numerous variant. Many were refined with rectangular fins and rudders (Mod 814). Unlike the B.Mk II, the B.Mk V often had four-bladed propellers retrofitted. The B.Mk V Series 1As of Nos 346 and 347 Squadrons were actually the last Merlin-engined Halifaxes in front-line Bomber Command service, giving way to B.Mk IIIs in July 1944. Late B.Mk V Series 1A aircraft were converted for glider towing and were used by Nos 298 and 644 Squadrons as Halifax A.Mk Vs.

Some B.Mk V Series 1As were delivered to SOE squadrons, with similar modifications to the Series 1 (Special) for their specialised role. Examples included LL119, LL385, LL484 and LW280. Others went to No. 192 Squadron for Elint duties (DK244, DK246, and LL132). Production of the B.Mk V totalled 904. Some 658 were built by Rootes, these being DG231-253, DG270-317, DG338-363, DG384-424, EB127-160, EB178-220, EB239-258, EB274-276, LK890-932, LK945-976, LK988-999, LL112-153, LL167-198.

LL213-258, LL270-312, LL325-367, LL380-423, LL437-469, LL481-521, LL534-542 (LL122 may have been built as a GR.Mk V). The remaining 246 B.Mk Vs were built by Fairey, these being DJ980-999, DK114-151, DK165-207, DK223-271, LK626-667, LK680-711, LK725-746.

All surviving Merlin-engined Halifaxes (B.Mk II, GR.Mk II, Met.Mk II, B.Mk V, A.Mk V, GR.Mk V, and Met.Mk V) were declared obsolete in February 1946, by which time the survivors were in long-term storage. The mass scrapping of B.Mk IIs and B.Mk Vs at No. 29 MU, High Ercall, began in January 1946.

HP.63 Halifax A.Mk V

The weight limitations applied to the Mk V made it a natural choice for conversion to other roles, and the type formed the basis of the first 'A for Airborne' version, the A.Mk V. In fact, use of the Halifax in support of airborne forces began long before the provision of a dedicated version. On 19 June 1940, with an invasion of Britain apparently a very real possibility, Britain established a Central Landing School (later Establishment) at Manchester's Ringway airport to prepare an airborne force for an eventual airborne invasion of mainland Europe. This was intended to have a strength of 5,000 paratroops, with another 5,000 soldiers who would be landed by glider. No. 4 Bomber Group tasked its Whitleys with the secondary role of glider towing, and when Whitleys were eventually replaced by Halifaxes, they also adopted the same secondary role. Whitleys replaced in the bomber role were passed to dedicated No. 38 Group squadrons, but Bomber Command continued to provide aircraft and aircrew, even after No. 38 Wing (later No. 38 Group) was formed in June 1942. The Halifax was of critical importance, since it was judged to be the best available aircraft capable of towing the new heavyweight Hamilcar, after a study of the Manchester, Lancaster, Liberator, Stirling and Halifax.

The Central Landing Establishment gained a small cadre of its own aircraft for training in October 1940 with the formation of the Airborne Forces Development Unit. Halifaxes joined the AFDU from October 1941, R9435 being the first. They were primarily used for towing trials with Horsa and Hamilcar gliders. Halifax glider tugs were used 'in anger' for the first time on 9 November 1942, when a pair of aircraft towed two Horsas to Norway for an attack

on German heavy water production facilities. One tug was lost, and both gliders crash landed. The surviving sappers were captured by the Germans and executed by the Gestapo, some being poisoned in hospital and the rest simply shot.

The first dedicated Halifax glider tugs were converted from baseline B.Mk V Series 1 (Special)s, and received the new designation A.Mk V, although they were sometimes erroneously referred to as GT.Mk V at the time (GT for Glider Transport, or Glider Tug). There was no change of designation when similar aircraft were produced through the conversion of later B.Mk V Series 1As, however. The Series 1 (Special) and Series 1A designations were simply not used by No. 38 Group.

The A.Mk V had no H2S or Tricell flare chutes, though Rebecca and Gee were fitted as standard. The front and mid-upper gun turrets were also deleted, and the ammunition tracks to the rear turret were shortened. The fuselage was fitted out to carry 12 paratroops, with a circular hatch in the bottom of the fuselage. From this projected an exit cone, a circular windshield which acted as a blast deflector. The aircraft

were fitted with a No. 6A glider tow hook on a short outrigger under the tail. The cable release handle was fitted on the right-hand edge of the throttle box. The first A.Mk Vs went to one flight of No. 295 Squadron at Netheravon in February 1943, for bombing, leaflet dropping, paratroop training and glider towing trials. These trials culminated in a 10.5-hour tow of a Horsa, proving that it was theoretically possible to tow a glider to

Above: An A.Mk V with D-Day stripes is seen here towing a Horsa, probably from Tarrant Rushton. Weight limitations on the Messier undercarriage limited the Mk V's utility as a bomber but made it a suitable tug and parachute aircraft.

The towing rig fitted behind the tailwheel of the Airborne Forces versions of the Halifax is prominent in this view of A.Mk V LK665.

Africa, where Horsas were required for the invasion of Sicily.

After these tests 30 Horsas were towed to North Africa: a handful were lost en route, one ditched after its tow line broke and another ditched after its tug was shot down by enemy fighters. In late 1943, the Halifax Vs were re-engined with Merlin 22 engines, and were fitted with rectangular D-type tailfins and rudders. This was necessary to allow the enormous and heavyweight Hamilcar to be safely towed. By D-Day there were two squadrons of Halifax A.Mk Vs (Nos 298 and 644 at Tarrant Rushton), and they were used almost exclusively for the towing of heavy Hamilcar gliders. The same two squadrons were in action for the Arnhem operation, towing Horsas and Hamilcars. Prior to the

Arnhem operation, the Halifax was modified to allow the carriage of a Jeep and 'six-pounder' gun, slung from a heavy duty beam in the bomb bay and dropped by parachute. This load was primarily dropped as part of SAS operations, along with supply containers in the wing bomb bays. The first use of the parachuted Jeep was made just prior to D-Day.

The aircraft eventually equipped No. 298 Squadron (formed from the Halifax element of No. 295) and No. 644 Squadron, and also Nos 296, and 297 Squadrons. Although the first Hercules-engined Halifax A.Mk IIIs entered squadron service in October 1943, Halifax A.Mk Vs were used for the bulk of the glider towing and paratroop dropping sorties on D-Day and during the Arnhem operation. A handful may have remained

active by March 1945 for use in the massive push across the Rhine, although by then the A.Mk III was in large-scale service, and virtually all A.Mk Vs had vanished by February 1945. At Arnhem, the main glider force, towed primarily by Halifaxes, delivered 4,500 men, 95 guns and 544 Jeeps.

Examples of the A.Mk V included DG384, DG388, DG391, DG396, DJ989, DJ993, DJ994, DK124, DK131, DK197, DK199, EB130, EB139, EB153, EB159, KG654, LK641, LK651, LK655, LK665, LK966, LK988, LL129, LL147, LL148, LL149, LL198, LL217, LL218, LL219, LL224, LL256, LL270, LL271, LL273, LL274, LL275, LL277, LL278, LL281, LL291, LL292, LL293, LL295, LL299, LL301, LL302, LL303, LL304, LL305,

LL309, LL310, LL311, LL312, LL325, LL326, LL327, LL328, LL329, LL330, LL331, LL332, LL333, LL334, LL335, LL336, LL337, LL338, LL340, LL342, LL343, LL344, LL345, LL347, LL348, LL349, LL350, LL351, LL352, LL353, LL354, LL355, LL357, LL361, LL382, LL384, LL399, LL400, LL401, LL402, LL403, LL404, LL405, LL406, LL407, LL411, LL412, LL441 and LL469.

All remaining Merlin-engined Halifaxes (B.Mk II, GR.Mk II, Met.Mk II, B.Mk V, A.Mk V, GR.Mk V, and Met.Mk V) were officially declared obsolete in February 1946, by which time the survivors were already in long-term storage.

HP.63 Halifax Met.Mk V

Coastal Command wanted Hercules-engined Halifax IIIs, but it actually received Merlin-engined B.Mk IIs and B.Mk Vs, almost exclusively late Series 1As. The Mk IIs were used primarily in the ASW and ASV roles as GR.Mk IIs, while the B.Mk Vs were assigned to meteorological reconnaissance duties as Met.Mk Vs. The meteorological reconnaissance role was of critical importance, taking the barometric pressure, humidity, temperature, wind and cloud readings vital for the preparation of the accurate weather forecasts needed by Bomber Command. The Met.Mk Vs were converted by Cunliffe-Owen Aircraft at Eastleigh.

Coastal Command and Bomber Command operations were extremely weather dependent, and great reliance was placed on meteorological reconnaissance by specially equipped Hampdens. They became increasingly vulnerable to enemy action, and it was decided to produce a meteorological version of the Halifax. The first meteorological Halifax was LL186, allocated as a trials aircraft. It was decided that Cunliffe-Owen Aircraft would incorporate Mod 1020 to turn the aircraft into a meteorological reconnaissance platform, with radio altimeters and a dedicated meteorological observer's station. The aircraft (equipped with Gee, LORAN and API) was flown from the factory to Marwell Hall where it was converted, before being sent to St Athan for installation of the ASV.Mk 2 radar.

The first Met.Mk Vs used Gee for navigation, but later aircraft also added LORAN. Radio altimeters ensured accurate height-keeping on long missions over the sea, where pressure altimeters could become unreliable. A psychrometer, for measuring temperature and humidity, projected from the navigator's compartment, in front of a new window, and the aircraft was fitted with a B3 drift meter. The Met.Mk V had a Tare weight of 35,490 lb (16131 kg). The meteorological reconnaissance sorties flown by the Met.Mk Vs frequently consisted of a run of about 700 miles (434 km) on a fixed heading from base, incorporating steep climbs and descents, crossing specific pressure levels at particular points, and taking sea level pressure readings every 100 miles (62 km). The run would finish with a circular climb to 20,000 ft (6097 m). Meteorological information was transmitted back to base half-hourly, in five five-figure coded groups.

Merlin-engined Halifaxes were never ideally suited to the meteorological role, which entailed prolonged running at high boost and low revs, culminating in a rapid climb. Boost surges were routine and engine failures were common.

On 8 January 1943, an order was issued to the effect that all Coastal Command Halifaxes would have extra dark sea grey topsides, and on 9 February a second order stipulated that undersides would be in white.

Twenty-three Halifax Met.Mk Vs were in

service with Nos 517 and 518 Squadrons on the day war ended, and they were probably the last Merlin-engined Halifaxes in service. Met.Mk V aircraft included DG250, DG288, DG304, DG316, DG344, DK256, DT642, LK707, LK682, LK745, LL117, LL144, LL186, LL188, LL216, LL220, LL221, LL295, LL296, LL297, LL298, LL299, LL393, LL469, LL485, LL506, LL517, LL518, LK688, LK692, LK706, LK906, LK960, LK962, LK966 and LK997. Their replacement (by Met.Mk IIIs) had begun in March 1945, at a modest rate.

All remaining Merlin-engined Halifaxes (B.Mk II, GR.Mk II, Met.Mk II, B.Mk V, A.Mk V, GR.Mk V, and Met.Mk V) were

The Halifaxes used on meteorological duties carried full armament in the event that they encountered enemy aircraft on their long patrols. LK966 was serving with No. 518 Squadron at Tiree when it was photographed in 1945.

officially declared obsolete in February 1946, by when the survivors were already in long-term storage.

HP.63 Halifax GR.Mk V

It seems that a handful of B.Mk Vs were converted by Cunliffe-Owen Aircraft at Eastleigh to serve with Coastal Command GR squadrons, though the Mk II was always more common, with Mk Vs normally

going to the meteorological squadrons. Handley Page quoted the variant's Tare weight as being 36,150 lb (16431 kg). Examples of the GR.Mk V Series I reportedly included DG250, LK966, LL299,

and LL469.

As with other Merlin Halifaxes, the GR.Mk Vs were officially declared obsolete in February 1946.

A B.Mk VI with a relatively subtle example of nose art runs up at an airfield 'somewhere in England'. The piping for the Graveley cabin heating system can be seen at the rear of the engine exhaust. All but the port outer engine exhausted to the starboard side.

HP.61 Halifax B.Mk VI

The ability of the Halifax to operate successfully in hot conditions was one of the main advantages it enjoyed over the Lancaster. A pair of Halifax B.Mk IIs (DK254 and DK263) accompanied a pair of Lancasters to India, where they underwent trials with No. 1577 Flight of No. 221 Group. The unit's CO was a long-time Lancaster pilot but, despite this, the Merlin Halifax shone through and the Lancasters were sent home and replaced by a pair of B.Mk IIs (NA642 and NA644), which proved to be even better-suited to operations in the Far East. Trials with these aircraft led to front-line service in the Far East theatre, and eventually to the development of a specific tropical variant.

The Halifax VI was intended from the start for hot-and-high and tropical operations, and was intended primarily for Tiger Force. As such, it was powered by four self-contained Hercules 100 'power egg' engines, using 100 Octane fuel and fitted with RAE Hobson injector carburettors. The new engines retained the exhaust arrangement of the B.Mk III, with the port outer engine exhausting to the right and all others exhausting to the left. The

engine nacelles of the B.Mk VI did differ slightly from those of the B.Mk III, with a fixed section on the trailing edge breaking the cooling gills which occupied the circumference of the trailing edge.

The use of injector carburettors necessitated the provision of a high-pressure fuel supply. The fuel system was completely revised, not just pressurised, with seven flexible bag-type tanks in wings and a nitrogen protection system. The new fuel system was tested on HR875. The new engines delivered 1,675 hp (1249 kW) on take-off and 1,630 hp (1215 kW) at 20,000 ft (6097 m), and were fitted with large Gallay oil coolers and tropical carburettor filters; they also allowed a maximum all-up weight of 68,000 lb (30909 kg), which in turn allowed increased fuel tankage and extended range. Tankage of the B.Mk VI rose to 2,190 Imp gal (9955 litres), plus 690 Imp gal (3136 litres) in fuselage bomb cell tanks. Total overload capacity was 2,880 Imp gal (13092 litres). A 150-Imp gal (681-litre) tank finally replaced the outboard wing bomb cell, and the no. 6 tank was enlarged and redesignated as the no. 7 tank. The tanks were grouped for each engine. A

Halifax B.Mk VIs were optimised for hot-and-high conditions, but saw relatively little service with front-line units before the war ended. This is the prototype, LV838, undergoing service trials at Boscombe Down in early 1944.

Below: No. 1 Radio School at Cranwell operated four modified B.Mk VIs in 1946 including PP214, TC-AB. The aircraft were fitted with a C.Mk VIII tailcone and a faired-over nose which contained Air Intercept (AI) radar.

Graveley cabin heating system was fitted, as Mod 999, and used four exhaust heaters. The B.Mk VI could cruise at 272 mph (168 km), and had a maximum speed of 312 mph (193 km). It had a ceiling of 24,000 ft (7317 m) with a 14,500-lb (6590-kg) load, and its range was 1,260 miles (782 km) with maximum bombload, or 2,400 miles (1490 km) with a reduced load.

The aircraft was designed to incorporate an H2S scanner as standard, and had the extended-span wing of 103 ft 8 in (31.59 m). Geared rudder tabs were used to alleviate the tendency to swing if an engine failed on take-off.

The prototype B.Mk VI (LV838, a converted B.Mk III) made its maiden flight on 19 December 1943, and was delivered to Boscombe Down on 5 February 1944. The aircraft used three-bladed de Havilland Type 55/18 13-ft (3.96-m) diameter semi-flared propellers, and later tested experimental Type 55/10 propellers, but they produced no real improvement. It was soon joined by a second converted B.Mk III (LV776). The first production B.Mk VI (NP715) initially flew on 10 October 1944.

The first B.Mk VIs retained short wings and a shortage of VG recorders gave a reduced AUW of only 65,000 lb (29545 kg). The definitive B.Mk VI was more of a heavyweight, with a Tare weight of 38,900 lb (17681 kg), a maximum landing weight of 57,000 lb (25909 kg) and a maximum take-off weight of 68,000 lb (30909 kg).

Service introduction of the B.Mk VI was painfully slow, and the type was never available in large numbers during the war. No. 102 Squadron began conversion in February 1945, followed by the Free French squadrons, Nos 346 and 347, and No. 158 Squadron during April 1945. The end of the war led to a rapid run-down in the Halifax force, and the squadrons spent the last weeks of their existence dumping unwanted bombs into the North Sea, repatriating PoWs and flying sightseeing missions over the Reich.

Sixty-four Halifax B.Mk VIs were transferred to France between 31 October 1945 and 21 August 1947. Six (RG736, 779,

B.Mk VI

Extended (104 ft 2 in/31.7 m) wingtips

Hercules 100 'power egg' engines with sand filters

Redesigned pressurised fuel system

H2S standard, no ventral gun

781, 783, 784 and 785) were sold to Pakistan.

Production of the Mk VI totalled 473 aircraft, most of which were completed as B.Mk VI bombers. Some 148 were built by Handley Page, these being LV776, NP715, NP752-753, NP821-836, NP849-895, NP908-927, PP142-164 (reserialled as

TW774-796), PP165-187, PP203-216 and PP225. Another 325 were built by English Electric, some of which were delivered as Met.Mk VIs. The English Electric B.Mk VIs included RG480-513, RG527-568, RG583-625, RG639-679, RG693-736, RG749-779, RG781-790, RG813-832, RG836, RG838, RG842, RG844-847, RG849-872, RG874-

879, ST795, ST797, ST799, ST800, ST805, ST806, ST808, ST814 and ST817.

The RAF declared the B.Mk VI obsolete in October 1950.

HP.61 Halifax B.Mk VI 'Supersonic Halifax'

The Halifax was extensively used as a trials and test aircraft. One of the most interesting was a B.Mk VI (NP715) modified

with early model short-span wings, which in turn had much-reduced ailerons fitted with separate trim and balance tabs, an auxiliary

flap, and which were linked to a line of semi-circular cross-section spoilers. The aircraft was intended to be used to develop

control systems for future heavy supersonic aircraft, but the experiments were abandoned because of inadequate controllability at the stall.

HP.61 Halifax C.Mk VI

Although the Halifax C.Mk III only fully equipped a single squadron, and had a career lasting just five months, the transport Halifax lasted longer. The C.Mk VIs were converted stripped bombers incorporating Mod 1105 with nine stretchers or eight passenger seats, in addition to the normal crew rest bunks, which could seat six. All guns, the dorsal turret, the H2S and its radome, Monica and the tri-cell chute were removed. The C.Mk VI had a relocated rudder trim wheel for the pilot, and rudder tab gearing was increased. Most obviously, a 272-cu ft (7.7-m3) freight pannier was fitted into the former bomb bay, projecting down and giving the aircraft a distinctively pot-bellied appearance. The Tare weight was 38,360 lb (17436 kg).

The development of the more radically modified C.Mk VIII left the C.Mk VI as something of a rarity, and no units were fully equipped with the type. LV838 served

as the prototype. Only a handful of C.Mk VIs were converted (including ST801), and the variant was declared obsolete (along with the C.Mk VII) in April 1949.

Right and below: The prototype C.Mk VI is seen at Boscombe Down in June 1945. This was the first version with the ventral freight pannier.

HALIFAX C

HERCULE

HP.61 Halifax GR.Mk VI

Hercules-engined aircraft had already replaced most Coastal Command Halifaxes by the end of the war, but the interim GR.Mk IIIs and remaining Met.Mk Vs soon gave way to similarly modified aircraft based on the B.Mk VI.

The new variant (initially known as the Met.Mk 6) was produced in a basic form that was compatible with both meteorological reconnaissance and general reconnaissance/anti-shipping duties. The type was built new by English Electric, and the first was issued to No. 1361 Met. Flight in June 1945. The type equipped a number of squadrons, usually very briefly, since the meteorological units were disbanding as the force rapidly contracted. Eventually the situation stabilised, and a mix of Met.Mk IIIs and Met.Mk VIs equipped No. 202 Squadron and No. 224 Squadron, which eventually took up station at Gibraltar. Some 35 Met.Mk VIs were issued, including two to the Meteorological Research Flight. As far as can be ascertained, all Met.Mk VIs were built by English Electric as part of that company's last two orders. The first production Met.Mk VI was RG778, and the second was RG787. Other Met.Mk VIs in the batch included RG780, 830, 833, 834, 835, 836, 837, 839, 840, 841, 843, 848, 851 and 873. Sixteen of the last 25 English Electric-built Halifax VIs were completed as Met.Mk VIs. They were ST794, 796, 798, 801, 802, 803, 804, 807, 809, 810, 811, 812, 813, 815, 816 and 818.

No. 202 Squadron converted to the Hastings in January 1951, leaving No. 224 Squadron to soldier on until March 1952, when the last sortie was flown.

Plans to use inflight refuelling for Tiger Force operations were rendered unnecessary when the USAF dropped atomic bombs on Hiroshima and Nagasaki. Work on inflight refuelling continued for the Met. (later GR.) Mk VI, however, with plans for 10 Halifax GR.Mk VI receivers and three Lancaster tankers. One aircraft (possibly RG839) was delivered to Staverton for a trial installation, but the programme was cancelled soon after trials began.

The Halifax flew its last sortie in RAF Squadron service on 17 March 1952, when the last GR.Mk VI of No. 224 Squadron (RG841) returned home from Gibraltar. The type was declared obsolete during that same year.

GR. Mk VI RG778 was one of the last operational Halifaxes, flying its last sorties in early 1952 with No. 224 Squadron.

HP.61 Halifax B.Mk VII

The Halifax B.Mk VII was produced because production of the B.Mk VI airframe outstripped production of the Hercules 100 engine. The aircraft was thus similar to the B.Mk VI but with Hercules XVI engines, a Tare weight of 38,330 lb (17422 kg), and AUW reduced to 65,000 lb (29545 kg). A simple recognition feature was that all engines (including the port outer) exhausted to the left.

The interim B.Mk VII re-equipped No. 426 Squadron from 15 June 1944, followed by No. 432 Squadron and then by No. 408 (which converted from Lancasters!), and a few aircraft were eventually taken on

charge by No. 415 Squadron. The last 15 of Handley Page's B.Mk III batch (LW196-210) were completed as B.Mk VIIs and delivered to No. 426 Squadron.

Handley Page built 114 more B.Mk VIIs (NP681-714, NP716-723, NP736-751, NP754-781 and NP793-820), and the variant was also built by Fairey (21 aircraft – PN208, and PN223-242) and English Electric (20 aircraft, RG447-458 and RG472-479). The total was thus only 160 aircraft. The type was declared obsolete in February 1946.

The B.Mk VII was a Mk VI airframe mated to the earlier Hercules XVI powerplant. This came about due to low supply of the Hercules 100.

HP.61 Halifax A.Mk VII

The Halifax A.Mk VII was a new-build version for No. 38 Group, for interim support of Airborne Forces, pending introduction of dedicated A.Mk IX. More than half of the total number of Mk VIIs produced were actually A.Mk VIIs, which outnumbered the B.Mk VII and outlasted it in service. Some 69 A.Mk VIIs were built by

Fairey (PN243-267, PN285-327 and PN343), 49 were built by Handley Page (PP277, PP339-350, PP362-389 and RT753-757), and 120 by Rootes (NA310-320, NA336-367, NA369-380, NA392-427, NA429-431, NA444-451, NA453-468). Eight were said to have been built by English Electric, but no serials are known.

The Halifax A.Mk VIIs of No. 21 Heavy Glider Conversion Unit (HGCU) were used alongside A.Mk IIIs for training in operations with large gliders until the end of 1947. The triangular object under the fuselage is the parachute exit cone.

The aircraft had their dorsal turrets deleted, but a glider towing hook was provided, together with seats and straps for 12 paratroops, using the existing paratroop exit cone and static line support bar. The Halifax A.Mk VII could easily be converted back to the bombing role, and three No. 298 Squadron aircraft in India were so modified following a mutiny by Indian seamen on British warships in Bombay harbour. Fortunately, they did not have to be called into action. With a Tare weight of 37,720 lb (17145 kg), the A.Mk VII was similar to the earlier A.Mk III, with much the same Mods. Late A.Mk VIIs had ARI.5686 in place of Rebecca and Gee, under Mod 1378.

One Halifax A.Mk VII (PP350) tested the Universal Freight Container, a ventral pannier with three integral shock absorbers, designed to be dropped using eight 47-ft (14.33-m) diameter parachutes. A.Mk VIIs replaced A.Mk IIIs in No. 38 Group squadrons as the war ended, and were deployed to the Middle East with Nos 620

and 644 Squadrons (later renumbered as Nos 113 and 47) and, in tropicalised form, to India with No. 298 Squadron. The A.Mk VII first saw action in Operation Varsity in March 1945 with No. 298 Squadron, but was destined to be short-lived. The last A.Mk VIIs in regular service were retired from the ATTDU and TCDU in December 1946. The type was finally declared obsolete in February 1948, and was briefly replaced by the A.Mk IX, and then by the new Hastings transport. At least one A.Mk VII (PP350) remained active with the RAE into the 1950s, engaged mainly in dropping trials, particularly of the Universal Freight Container; this aircraft had a Frazer-Nash Lancaster-type rear turret to allow easier rearward-looking photography. The aircraft also had bulged camera fairings under the wingtips. A handful of B.Mk VIIs were converted as glider tugs, and some were used by the Airborne Forces Experimental Establishment at Beaulieu, designated as GT.Mk VIIs (e.g., TW780).

HP.61 Halifax C.Mk VII

The Halifax C.Mk VII was a converted and stripped bomber incorporating Mod 1105 in the same way as the C.Mk III and C.Mk VI.

The aircraft was fitted with nine stretchers or eight passenger seats, in addition to the normal crew rest bunks, which could seat

six. All guns, the dorsal turret, the H2S and its radome, Monica and the tri-cell chute were removed. The variant weighed 37,790 lb (17177 kg) empty, and was normally

compatible with ventral pannier. Only a handful of C.Mk VIIs were produced, and the variant was declared obsolete in April 1949.

HP.64 Freighter-Bomber

The original P13/36 specification had dictated that "consideration shall be given in the design for the provision of light removable seating for the accommodation of the maximum number of personnel in the fuselage," intending that the aircraft should have a secondary transport role, like some previous Handley Page bombers. British Airways enquired about the possibility of acquiring a civil version of the original HP.57, to be powered by four Perseus, Pegasus or Dagger engines, hoping that

such an aircraft would be able to carry 25 passengers over a 1,000-mile (621-km) stage length (London-Copenhagen) or 1,600 lb (727 kg) of mail over 2,500 miles (1552 km) (London-Bathurst). Handley Page estimated that this would be possible, but that at a gross weight of 38,000 lb (17272 kg) it would give an unacceptably high wing loading for operation from typical civilian grass strips.

In 1942, Handley Page returned to examining dedicated transport derivatives of

the Halifax and drew up a version with the standard 99-ft (61-km) bomber wing, D-type rectangular tail unit, and the normal undercarriage. Powered either by Merlin XXs or Hercules VIs, the new aircraft had a new circular section fuselage 9 ft 6 in (2.9 m) in diameter, with a 26-ft (7.93-m) constant section. Intended as a freighter, fuel transporter (using three large underfloor tanks with a total capacity of 1,880 Imp gal/8546 litres) or troop transport, the aircraft could mount a four-gun mid-upper turret. Bomber versions were also

sketched, one pressurised for high-altitude . As a dedicated civil transport, the wing was moved to a low position, the new circular-section fuselage was pressurised, the cross-section was increased to 11 ft (3.35 m) diameter and the type number HP.64 was allocated. Flight Refuelling Limited built a rear fuselage section for tests. Efforts to produce the type for the RAF bore no fruit, however, and the aircraft was eventually abandoned (as the Transport C) in favour of using stripped Halifax bombers in the transport role.

HP.70 Halifax C.Mk VIII

Following cancellation of the HP.64, an unarmed production transport version of the Halifax B.Mk VI was designed, initially known as Transport B. Transport A referred to the C.Mk III, C.Mk VI and C.Mk VII variants, while the HP.64 had been Transport C. In the Transport B the dorsal and tail turrets were removed and faired over, leaving no military or defensive equipment whatever. Even the tail turret was replaced by a streamlined fairing which increased overall length to 73 ft 7 in (22.4 m), and which necessitated a 0.5° reduction in tailplane incidence. Elevator trim tab movement was reduced, and the elevator was reset, with 2° less downward movement and 2° more upward movement.

A detachable underfuselage pannier for up to 8,000 lb (3636 kg) of freight was designed by the Transport Command Development Unit to replace the bomb doors, as Mod 1377. Some 160 panniers were ordered from Handley Page, which sub-contracted 60 to Evans Bellhouse, and 144 more were ordered by the Ministry of Aircraft for production by D. M. Davies Ltd.

Mod 1192 allowed for the carriage of freight or stretchers, and the aircraft could also accommodate 11 passengers (plus six on the rest bunks). Alternatively, the aircraft could be fitted with the eight-seat Mod 862/863/929. The A.Mk VII-style paratroop

Very few Halifaxes ever wore RAF insignia over bare metal. This C.Mk VIII was in fact retained by the manufacturer for trials use.

door was retained, with an exit cone fairing. As a derivative of the Halifax B.Mk VI, the C.Mk VIII was powered by Hercules 100s. It had a Tare weight of 37,250 lb (16931 kg). Mod 1401 provided for the installation of new radio and radar equipment.

A B.Mk VI, PP225, was converted to serve as the prototype C.Mk VIII, and began its initial trials at Boscombe Down on 4 April 1945. Production of the C.Mk VIII began with PP217, which was delivered to the ATTDU on 9 June 1945. Production eventually reached 98 aircraft, all of them produced by Handley Page. They were PP217-224, PP226-247, PP259-276, PP278-296 and PP308-338.

The Polish Nos 301 and 304 Squadrons exchanged their Warwick Mk IIIs and Wellington Mk XIVs, respectively, for Halifaxes from January 1946 and May 1946. Unfortunately, the Poles became a political 'hot potato' and flying by the squadron outside the UK was stopped from 17 April. The squadrons ceased flying on 21 November, and disbanded on 10 December 1946.

Three aircraft were loaned to BOAC in June 1945 for West African route development. The first to be sold to a civil operator was PP336, which was registered to the Maharajah Gaekwar of Baroda, a noted horse-racing enthusiast who needed rapid transport between India and Newmarket. The aircraft was registered as G-AGZP.

The RAF declared the C.Mk VIII obsolete in January 1947.

HP.70 Civil Halifax VIII

Although its RAF career had been cut short by the enforced disbandment of the Polish squadrons which operated it, the C.Mk VIII was destined to have a longer life as a civilian transport aircraft. Some 94 civilianised Halifax VIIIs were converted from ex-RAF C.Mk VIIIs; two more were converted to the same standard from A.Mk IXs, and one from a B.Mk VI. Many more Mk VIs and Mk IXs were broken up for spares, and a handful may have been simply civilianised to their original standards, and not as HP.70s.

Most HP.70s had the standard C.Mk VIII type of underfuselage freight pannier, but a handful had larger squared-off panniers, with cruder, squared-off fairings fore and aft. These larger fairings were used, for instance, by British American Air Services for the transport of cars. Many of the aircraft converted to HP.70 standards were almost brand new, but serviceability was affected by a shortage of spares, which progressively worsened. Spares shortages were so acute that even during the Berlin Airlift, aircraft damaged in minor accidents were often scrapped for spares rather than repaired, and nine aircraft were written off in such circumstances during the airlift.

The Halifaxes were remarkably serviceable, and the type had the highest utilisation figures of any civil aircraft used in the airlift. The aircraft completed 22,576 hours in 4,653 freight and 3,509 fuel flights, delivering an average of 311 tons per day. The Lancashire Aircraft Corporation (with a fleet of 10 aircraft) made 26 round trips to Berlin in one 14-hour period, and on another occasion one single aircraft clocked up 96 hours and seven minutes flying time in a single week. Aircraft on the airlift were fitted with Rebecca as a mandatory homing and approach aid. Due to this high utilisation and the shortage of spares, the Halifax had a short life on the civil register, with engines rapidly becoming scarce and above all expensive (£1,200 by 1949). The dispensation to operate with a 59,000-lb (26818-kg) landing weight was removed at the end of the airlift, which further reduced the Halifax's viability, and peak charter rates of £85 per hour slumped to £45 per hour in a price war following the airlift. This scarcely covered the aircraft's direct operating costs (estimated at £40 per hour). Most aircraft were scrapped by the end of 1950, and the last aircraft in use was damaged beyond repair in a gale in December 1952.

At its peak, the civil Halifax was operated by a number of companies, several of which employed large fleets of aircraft. London Aero & Motor Service (LAMS) had a peak strength of 14 aircraft, while other operators included the Lancashire Aircraft Corporation (which operated six tankers, and another six freighter aircraft configured as milk tankers), Bond Air Services, Eagle Aviation, World Air Freight, Scottish Airlines, Westminster Airways and Skyflights. A small number were operated by overseas airlines and charter companies. Seventeen of 41 civilian Halifaxes and Haltons engaged in Operation Plainfare were fitted with special tanks for the vital 'Wet Lift' element of the Berlin Airlift, allowing them to transport diesel

G-AKEC, formerly PP282, of the Lancashire Aircraft Corporation took part in the Daily Express circuit race of 1950. It was wrecked in a storm in December 1952.

fuel, and other aircraft were specially anodised to allow the carriage of corrosive cargoes of salt.

The civilian Halifax VIII did see military service, with three former Pak-Air aircraft (themselves ex-RAF C.Mk VIIIs PP279, PP312 and PP322) passing to the Pakistan air force to augment its six B.Mk VIs. Five more were delivered to the Royal Egyptian air force, augmenting Mk IXs.

HP.70 Civil Halifax VIII tanker

The Lancashire Aircraft Corporation operated six Halifaxes as tankers even before the Berlin Airlift, but the aircraft required extra modifications to meet civil licensing requirements. They soon proved their value on the airlift, and LAC requested to modify all of its aircraft to the same configuration. Airtech Ltd devised an improved tanker conversion during the Berlin Airlift, and this was fitted to about nine aircraft. The conversion involved the

fitting of a single 1,350-Imp gal (6137-litre) lorry tank in the belly, with metal fairings fore and aft, with three 250-Imp gal (1136-litre) tanks inside the fuselage. All four tanks were interconnected, providing a usable capacity of 2,050 Imp gal (9319 litres). Two 2.5-in (6.4-cm) drain cocks allowed pressure filling of the tanks in about 14 minutes, with a similar discharge time 'at the other end'. Tankers included G-AHWN, G-AJZZ and G-AKBJ.

HP.70 Halton

BOAC was a major operator of the Halifax, mainly using standard HP.70s for hauling freight. However, experience with borrowed RAF C.Mk VIIIs for route-proving to West Africa, coupled with delays in the delivery of the Avro Tudor, led to a requirement for a small number of more highly specified Halifax transports. Accordingly, 12 of its aircraft were more extensively modified before they entered service, receiving the new name Halton. All

ex-RAF C.Mk VIIIs, the 12 aircraft were structurally modified by Handley Page at Radlett with larger rectangular passenger windows, a solid nose fairing (with a small door to port) covering a new extra baggage hold (the main hold being in the ventral pannier), and an outward-opening cabin door to starboard near the tailplane.

The aircraft were then fitted out and furnished by Short Brothers and Harland to carry 10 passengers in some comfort. Ten Rumbold (IP) seats were fitted, eight on the starboard side, and two more (again one behind the other) on the port side; all were forward-facing. The aircraft had a well-equipped pantry in what had been the midships rest bay, accessed by swinging doors. The fuselage walls were in two shades of beige, and the seats and carpet were in BOAC's usual blue. Each seat was provided with oxygen and a stewardess call button, and there were three electric roof lights. A small vestibule separated the cabin from the entrance door and from the toilet facilities at the aft end of the fuselage.

While awaiting delivery of the Haltons, BOAC used eight Halifaxes loaned to the company by the Air Ministry (G-AHYH, G-AYHI, G-AIAN, G-AIAO, G-AIAP, G-AIAR, G-AIAS and G-AIID). All operated without a formal Certificate of Airworthiness and were subsequently returned to the RAF when the Haltons were delivered.

The first Halton to be delivered was G-AHDU, which was formally named *Falkirk* by Lady Winster at Radlett on 18 July 1947. The first six aircraft were returned to Handley Page for the fitting of de-icing equipment and hydraulic system modifications, after only six weeks. They were G-AHDL *Fitzroy*, G-AHDM *Falmouth*, G-AHDS *Freemantle*, G-AHDU *Falkirk*, G-AHDV *Finnesterre* and G-AHDW *Falaise*. The Haltons replaced Yorks and Dakotas, and were augmented by six additional aircraft, G-AHDN *Flamborough*, G-AHDO *Forfar*, G-AHDP *Fleetwood*, G-AHDR *Foreland*, G-AHDT *Fife*, and G-AHDX *Folkestone*. They flew primarily to Africa, but also briefly took over the route to Karachi and Colombo. The aircraft were withdrawn in May 1948 and were sold.

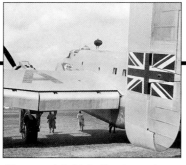

Above and right: In the days when Britain's national flag carrier felt it worthwhile to actually carry the flag, Haltons of BOAC helped re-establish civil air links to the Empire. G-AHDU, seen here over the pyramids, was scrapped in 1950 after further service with Aviation Traders and Bond Air Services.

Halton

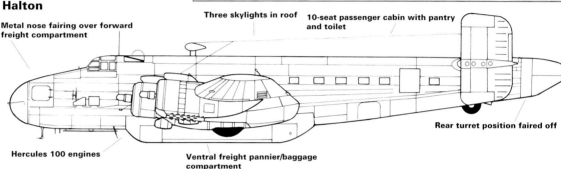

Metal nose fairing over forward freight compartment

Three skylights in roof

10-seat passenger cabin with pantry and toilet

Rear turret position faired off

Hercules 100 engines

Ventral freight pannier/baggage compartment

HP.71 Halifax A.Mk IX

A.Mk IX

The Halifax A.Mk IX was the definitive No. 38 Group Airborne Forces version. It was an Airborne Forces derivative of the B.Mk VI, with further improvements over the A.Mk VII, though it retained the Hercules 16 engines of the Mk III and Mk VII and not the Hercules 100s of the Mk VI. Design work on the A.Mk IX was sub-contracted to Boulton Paul in February 1945. The existing port side entrance door and underfuselage paratroop hatch were replaced by a large (33 x 59 in/83 x 150 cm), rectangular, inward/upward-opening paratroop exit door set into a strengthened floor aft of the bomb bay. This was then tested on an A.Mk VII, RT758, which was thus completed as the prototype A.Mk IX.

The new variant had the usual signalling panel to allow the bomb-aimer to signal to the dispatcher. There were two roof-mounted rails for static lines, and a winch for retrieving the lines after the drop. Two inward-facing, folding, metal bench-type seats were provided per side, aft of the spar, for up to 16 paratroops.

The A.Mk IX was fitted with Boulton Paul Type D, Mk I tail turret with two 0.50-in machine guns (as fitted to late Mk VIs), and later aircraft had the Mk II turret with provision for automatic gun laying. Throughout 1944 trials with an automatic gun-laying turret had been conducted on a succession of Halifax B.Mks IIs, IIIs and VIs, finding a degree of success by January 1945.

There was no dorsal turret, which was replaced by an extra escape hatch. The Mk XIV bombsight and nose-mounted 0.50-in scare gun were retained. The A.Mk IX had a slight reduction in fuel capacity compared to B.Mk VI, with the no. 2 replenishment tank (in the wing bomb cells) being reduced from 150 to 90 Imp gal (681 to 409 litres). The new version had a Tare weight of 39,750 lb (18068 kg), and fuel tankage of 2,772 Imp gal (12600 litres). Mod 1277 provided for the installation of new radar and radio equipment, but was not incorporated. Some 145 A.Mk IXs were delivered, and 50 more were cancelled. The completed aircraft were RT758-799, RT814-856, RT868-908 and RT920-938. Like many late Halifaxes, the A.Mk IXs usually wore treaded tyres.

The A.Mk IX did not usually carry a bomb bay pannier but could often be seen carrying a Jeep and/or a light artillery piece for air-dropping, usually on a crash pannier.

The new variant partly equipped No. 297

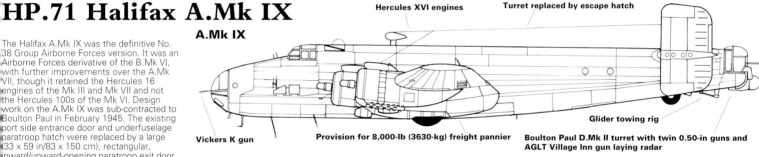

Hercules XVI engines

Turret replaced by escape hatch

Vickers K gun

Provision for 8,000-lb (3630-kg) freight pannier

Glider towing rig

Boulton Paul D.Mk II turret with twin 0.50-in guns and AGLT Village Inn gun laying radar

The last British military Halifaxes were the A.Mk IXs of No. 1 Parachute Training School. RT841, seen here, was sold for scrap in 1949.

Squadron, and fully equipped Nos 620 and 644 Squadrons from July 1946, although these units renumbered as Nos 113 and 47 Squadrons on 1 September 1946. The type then equipped the Fairford Flying Wing which, from October 1946, parented four six-aircraft squadrons, Nos 47, 113, 295 and 297. Strength at Fairford reduced to 12 aircraft in August 1947, and No. 113 Squadron disbanded while No. 47 moved out for conversion to the Hastings. In October 1947, the Halifax A.Mk IX was retired from squadron service, with No. 295 disbanding and No. 297 converting to the Hasting. The A.Mk IX remained in use with No. 1 Parachute and Glider Training School at Upper Heyford, which had received 10 new A.Mk IXs. Gliders were withdrawn from general service in 1948, and the unit scaled down as No. 1 Parachute Training School, moving to Henlow where it maintained two A.Mk IXs, the last of which (RT396) was finally written off following an accident on 21 April 1953. This was almost certainly the last Halifax in British military service. The variant had already been declared obsolete in March 1951.

Although delivered to Egypt stripped of armament, the nine A.Mk IXs which reached the REAF were hastily rearmed with Brownings taken from damaged Spitfire Vs and were used in the transport and bombing roles. Some 22 aircraft were ordered from Aviation Traders, but an arms

Armament on the A.Mk IX was reduced to a single nose gun and a two-gun rear turret. The AGLT gun laying radar is not fitted to this aircraft, seen in November 1945.

embargo resulted in only nine actually being delivered. The aircraft involved were serialled between 1155 and 1163 and were respectively RT846, 793, 888, 787, 852, 901, 938, 907 and 788. They served until about 1956, but spares shortages had reduced the number in use to three by as early as 1955.

At least three Halifax A.Mk IXs (RT786, 798 and 923) were transferred to No. 202 Squadron for meteorological reconnaissance duties (and so became Met.Mk IXs) when No. 297 Squadron

disbanded. The three aircraft were modified with role equipment at station level. One (RT798) served until No. 202 re-equipped with the Hastings, and the other two were written off after minor accidents.

As far as civil use of the Mk IX went, two A.Mk IXs (G-ALON and G-ALOS) were operated in civil guise during the Berlin Airlift, both by Bond Air Services. Thirty more were registered to Aviation Traders at Southend and 12 were exported to the Egyptian air force, but most were broken up during 1951.

Fleet Air Arm 1950-59

Like many air forces, the Fleet Air Arm underwent dramatic changes during the 1950s. It entered the decade flying World War II-vintage aircraft such as the Seafire and Firefly, yet ended it as the proud operator of powerful all-weather jet fighters. Along the way the helicopter was to revolutionise the assault and ASW roles.

The 1950s were to see great changes in the Fleet Air Arm. At the beginning of the decade, over four years had elapsed since the end of World War II, but the hard-won peace had turned out to be an uneasy one, with fascism conquered, only to be replaced by Communism in both east and west.

Things came to a head at 04.00 on 25 June 1950, when North Korean forces launched a large-scale attack across the 38th Parallel, which had been established as a demarcation line with non-Communist South Korea. The United Nations quickly voted to come to the aid of the defenders, and in the ensuing conflict the Fleet Air Arm was to play a small but invaluable role.

HMS *Triumph* was among a number of British warships in Japanese waters that summer, all being placed immediately at the disposal of Vice-Admiral Joy, USN, the Flag-Officer Commanding, Far East (or COMNAVFE). Aboard the British carrier was the 13th Carrier Air Group, comprising No. 800 Squadron with 12 Seafires and No. 827 Squadron with the same number of Fireflies. Operational equipment was, therefore, little advanced from that used in World War II, when both types had been in use in the later stages. The Seafires were the final F.Mk 47 version, but the Fireflies were still the FR.Mk 1 variant.

The Seafire F.Mk 47 was the very last of all versions of Spitfire/Seafire, yet in its ultimate form as used in Korea it hardly appears in standard textbooks. External features included a frameless bubble canopy, cut-down rear fuselage (housing a side-looking reconnaissance camera in the FR.Mk 47 sub-type), a large and very powerful rudder with 'sting-type' arrester hook fixed to the downward-hinged lower part, a chin inlet to the Rolls-Royce injection system for the 2,350-hp Griffon 88 engine driving 11-ft contra-rotating propellers, and 22.5-Imp gal combat tanks scabbed against the underside of the outer wings. Other external loads could include a 90-Imp gal drop tank on the centreline, three 500-lb bombs or eight rockets, and the gun armament was four 20-mm Hispano cannon. It was a delight to fly, and in the Korean context able to do useful

work without feeling inferior, though of course it could not reach the heights and speeds of swept-wing jets.

Remarkably, as noted later, a Sea Fury pilot did shoot down a MiG-15 which was foolish enough to engage in close turning combat. This aircraft again was the end of a long line of piston-engined fighters which started with the Hawker Hurricane. Powered by the 2,550-hp Bristol Centaurus XVIII sleeve-valve radial (which being air-cooled should have been better suited to carrier operations than the vulnerable liquid-cooled engines), the Sea Fury FB.Mk 11 was again the pinnacle of the piston-engined fighter art. Like the Seafire Mk 47 it at last introduced power-folding for the elliptical outer wings, in which were the four short-barrel Hispano Mk V cannon and racks for up to 12 rockets or two bombs of 1,000 lb each. At around 460 mph at medium heights it was fractionally faster than any other piston-engined aircraft in the theatre, and the Sea Furies certainly had more range and endurance than any of the contemporary jets.

Firefly variants

On the other hand, the Firefly FR.Mk 1 was getting long in the tooth. The wartime requirement to carry a backseater, as an observer and navigator, resulted in an aircraft insufficiently fast or agile to tangle in close combat with single-seaters, and its armament was no better than that of the Seafire and Sea Fury. The only plus was that some were fitted with ASH radar, which conferred limited ability to find targets at night, especially ships and (at least in theory) submarines. Far more important were the much faster and more agile Firefly Mks 4, 5 and 6, which had more powerful Griffon engines with two-stage superchargers, wingroot radiators and power-folding outer wings with clipped tips. Nearly 600 were delivered, carrying four 20-mm guns and no fewer than 22 different types of external store in day fighter/attack, night fighter, fighter reconnaissance, anti-submarine and training roles.

The British carrier was placed under the command of Rear Admiral Hoskins, USN,

At the start of the 1950s the Hawker Sea Fury FB.Mk 11 was the principal FAA fighter-bomber. These were serving with 898 Sqn in HMS Theseus in the Mediterranean during 1952/53.

The unpopular Blackburn Firebrand TF.Mk 5 served briefly in the early 1950s as a torpedo-strike platform. 813 Sqn (aboard Indomitable) was one of only two front-line units to fly the type.

The other front-line Firebrand TF.Mk 5 user was 813 Sqn, which operated the type from the decks of Eagle during 1952. The squadron was disbanded at the end of the year, reforming in 1954 with Wyverns.

commanding the 3rd US Carrier Division from the American carrier USS *Valley Forge*, both of which were to carry out strikes against enemy targets from the Yellow Sea. The first strikes were flown off by the two carriers on the morning of 3 July, but the British aircraft soon proved inferior to their American counterparts. Fully loaded, the Fireflies had a range of only 120 to 130 miles, whereas the Skyraiders and Corsairs could be catapulted off with bombs

---

FAA Chronology 1950-1959

1950

4 January 1950 773 (Fleet Requirements Unit) Squadron reformed at Lee-on-Solent with 5 Martinet, 6 Seafire F.15 and 2 Mosquito FB.6, to be based at Gibraltar for the Home Fleet's Spring Cruise.
17 January 1950 727 (Air Courses Training) Squadron disbanded at Gosport.
31 March 1950 773 Squadron disbanded at Lee-on-Solent on return from Gibraltar.
1 May 1950 738 Squadron reformed at

Culdrose as part of the Naval Air Fighter School with Seafire F.17s and Sea Furies.
14 June 1950 719 Squadron reformed at Eglinton as a Naval Air Anti-Submarine Training squadron with Firefly AS.5, being part of the 53rd Training Air Group.
25 June 1950 North Korean forces crossed the 38th Parallel, and the Korean War began. HMS *Triumph* with 13th Carrier Air Group, comprising 12 Seafire FR.47s of No. 800 Squadron and 12 Firefly FR.1s of No. 827 Squadron and Black Flight of 4 Firefly NF.1, placed at disposal of Vice-

Admiral C.T. Joy, USN (COMNAVFE).
2 July 1950 First strikes from *Triumph* by 12 Fireflies and 9 Seafires on Haeju airfield.
12 July 1950 739 Squadron disbanded at Culham to become the Photographic Flight of 703 Squadron.
28 July 1950 Seafire VP473 shot down in error by B-29, Commissioned Pilot White picked up by US destroyer.
16 August 1950 792 Squadron, the Night Fighter Training Unit at Culdrose disbanded.
1 September 1950 (Fleet Requirements Unit) Squadron reformed at Lee-on-Solent with Martinet, to be based at Gibraltar for the Home Fleet's Autumn and Spring Cruises.

5 October 1950 HMS *Theseus* took over from *Triumph*, with 17th Carrier Air Group, consisting of 807 Squadron with 21 Sea Fury FB.11 and 810 Squadron with 12 Firefly AS.5. Later awarded annual Boyd Trophy for its activities.
10 October 1950 17th CAG made its first attack, in Changyan area. Lt S. Leonard of 807 Squadron shot down, rescued 5 miles from target by USAF helicopter despite opposition.
19 November 1950 814 Squadron (12 Firefly 5) disbanded at Culdrose after two years in HMS *Vengeance*.
22 November 1950 814 Squadron reformed at Culdrose with 12 Firefly 5 (later

Early Fleet Air Arm helicopters are represented here by (from bottom to top) the Hoverfly Mk I, Hoverfly Mk II and Dragonfly HR.Mk I. The two Hoverflies are from 705 Sqn at Gosport.

Sea Fury training was undertaken by the Naval Air Fighter School at Culdrose, initially by 736 Sqn. In 1952 the aircraft were passed to 738 Sqn to continue the task.

Above: The Sea Fury FB.Mk 11 is best known for its exploits during the Korean War. Here an 804 Sqn example launches from HMS Glory. For most of the time the type was employed on fighter-bomber duties, armed with bombs and underwing rockets.

Left: The Sea Furies of 802 Sqn crowd the deck of Ocean in 1952. The squadron accounted for one officially credited MiG-15 kill on 9 August.

Above: Seafires were in widespread use during the early years of the decade. 781 Sqn at Lee-on-Solent flew this Mk 17 on general duties.

The Seafire had an important second life in the RN Volunteer Reserve. This FR.Mk 47 flew with 1833 Sqn at Bramcote.

This Seafire F.Mk 17 was assigned to 1832 Sqn, RNVR at Culham. This was controlled by the Southern Air Division from 1 June 1952.

Seafire FR.Mk 47s of 800 Sqn line the deck of HMS Triumph in 1950. This unit saw action in the opening months of the Korean War.

and rockets, their drop tanks giving them a better radius of action, more suited for launching well out to sea. As a consequence the Seafires were largely confined to combat air patrols and the Fireflies to anti-submarine patrols.

Early combats showed that American forces often confused Seafire F.Mk 47s and Yak-9s, and it was probably this that led to a Seafire

being shot down by USAF B-29 on 28 July, the pilot being fortunately picked up by a US destroyer. To lessen such risks, black and white stripes were painted on all FAA aircraft, similar to those used during the Normandy invasion.

In September HMS *Triumph* was withdrawn, to be replaced by HMS *Theseus* carrying the 17th Carrier Air Group. This had more suitable equipment, in the shape of No. 807 Squadron with 21 Sea Fury FB.Mk 11s and No. 810 Squadron with 12 Firefly Mk 5s, both with

greater range and load-carrying capacity. These two types were to be standard equipment throughout the remainder of the campaign. By November the UN ground forces were advancing rapidly, but in early December Chinese forces arrived in the north and the advance turned to a hasty retreat, followed by evacuation by sea from the east coast.

HMS *Glory* took over from HMS *Theseus* in April, the 14th Carrier Air Group being similarly equipped with the 21 Sea Fury FB.Mk 11s

AS.6) for HMS *Vengeance* (later HMS *Theseus*, then HMS *Eagle*).
22 November 1950 827 Squadron disbanded at Lee-on-Solent after disembarking from HMS *Triumph* on its return from Korean waters.
1 December 1950 1830 RNVR Squadron in Scottish Air Division detached to Donibristle during runway reconstruction at Abbotsinch, until 1 November 1952.
13 December 1950 827 Squadron reform at Ford with 12 Firebrand TF.5 to become the second first-line squadron with this type.

1951

7 January 1951 17th CAG in *Theseus* began 10 days as Air Support Element, providing close support for US 25th Division on west coast of Korea, under control of airborne controllers in USAF Texans. First such support by FAA.
February 1951 804 Squadron in HMS *Glory* increased from 12 to 21 Sea Fury FB.11 before leaving Hal Far for Korean Waters.
10 March 1951 801 Squadron at Lee-on-Solent exchanged its obsolescent Sea Hornets for 12 Sea Fury FB.11.

31 March 1951 773 Squadron disbanded at Lee-on-Solent on return from Gibraltar.
14 April 1951 1840 Squadron reformed as an RNVR unit at Culham with 6 Firefly FR.4.
25 April 1951 HMS *Theseus* sailed for home with a reduced complement of 12 Sea Furies and 5 Fireflies. Replaced in Korean waters by HMS *Glory* carrying the 14th CAG comprising 21 Sea Fury FB.11 of 804 Squadron and 12 Firefly 5 of 812 Squadron, plus a Dragonfly rescue helicopter.
15 May 1951 826 Squadron reformed at Ford with 8 Firefly AS.6.
11 June 1951 HMS *Glory* withdrawn from operations due to heavily contaminated

aviation fuel. Sabotage suspected initially, but fault found in internal supply pipe which had not been used for several years in supply ship RFA *Wave Premier*.
12 June 1951 825 Squadron reformed at Eglinton in the 15th CAG with 8 Firefly 5 for service in HMS *Ocean* in the Far East.
25 June 1951 Four plainly marked Sea Furies of 804 Squadron attacked by USAF P-80s, but escaped unscathed after evasive action.
30 June 1951 1840 RNVR Squadron moved from Culham to Ford, re-equipping with 9 Firefly AS.6.
3 July 1951 820 Squadron reformed at Eglinton with 8 Firefly AS.5 (later AS.6) for

Fleet Air Arm Order of Battle, 1 January 1950

First-Line Squadrons

UNIT	SHIP ASSIGNMENT	AIRCRAFT	BASE
800 Squadron	HMS *Triumph* (13th Carrier Air Group).	13 Seafire F.47	Sembawang
801 Squadron	HMS *Implacable* (1st Carrier Group)	20 Sea Hornet F.20	Lee-on-Solent
802 Squadron	HMS *Vengeance* (15th Carrier Air Group)	12 Sea Fury FB.11	Culdrose
804 Squadron	HMS *Glory* (14th Carrier Air Group)	13 Sea Fury FB.11	aboard ship in the Mediterranean
807 Squadron	HMS *Theseus* (17th Carrier Air Group)	13 Sea Fury FB.11	St Merryn
809 Squadron		8 Sea Hornet NF.21	Culdrose
810 Squadron	HMS *Theseus* (17th Carrier Air Group)	12 Firefly FR.4 and AS.5	St Merryn
812 Squadron	HMS *Glory* (14th Carrier Air Group)	12 Firefly 5; Black Flight 4 Firefly NF.1	aboard ship in the Mediterranean
813 Squadron	HMS *Implacable* (1st Carrier Group)	12 Firebrand TF.5	Lee-on-Solent
814 Squadron	HMS *Vengeance* (15th Carrier Air Group)	13 Firefly 5	Culdrose
815 Squadron		12 Barracuda TR.3	Eglinton
827 Squadron	HMS *Triumph* (13th Carrier Air Group)	12 Firefly FR.1; Black Flight 4 Firefly NF.1	Sembawang

RNVR Squadrons

UNIT	AIRCRAFT	BASE
1830 Squadron	7 Firefly FR.1, 3 Harvard T.2B/T.3	Abbotsinch
1831 Squadron	7 Seafire F.17, 3 Harvard T.2B/T.3, 1 Auster 5	Stretton
1832 Squadron	8 Seafire F.15/F.17, 6 Seafire FR.46, 4 Harvard T.2B/T.3, 1 Anson 1, 1 Auster 5	Culham
1833 Squadron	7 Seafire F.15/F.17, 3 Harvard T.2B/T.3, 1 Anson 1	Bramcote

Second-Line Squadrons

UNIT	AIRCRAFT	BASE
702 Squadron (Naval Jet Evaluation and Development Unit)	4 Sea Vampire F.20, 3 Meteor T.7	Culdrose
703 Squadron (Naval Air Sea Warfare Development Unit and Carrier Trials Unit)	Avenger 3, Mosquito FB.6, Sea Mosquito TR.33, Sea Mosquito TR.37, Sea Hornet F.20, Sea Hornet NF.21, Firefly 5, Sea Fury FB.11, Firebrand TF.5, Sea Vampire F.20, Meteor 3	Lee-on-Solent
705 Squadron (Fleet Requirements Unit)	8 Hoverfly	Gosport
727 Squadron (Sub-Lieutenants and Royal Marine Officers Air Course)	30 Tiger Moth T.2, 2 Harvard T.2b/T.3	Gosport
728 Squadron (Fleet Requirements Unit)	4 Mosquito TT.39, 2 Martinet TT.1, 4 Seafire F.17, 3 Mosquito PR.16, 1 Expeditor C.2, 2 Sea Otter	Hal Far
736 Squadron (Naval Air Fighter School)	Sea Fury FB.11, Martinet TT.1, Firefly FR.1, Firefly T.2	Culdrose
737 Squadron (Operational Flying School Part II)	18 Firefly FR.4, 18 Firefly AS.5, 4 Firefly 1(TT), 7 Firefly T.2, 18 Seafire F.17	Eglinton
739 Squadron (Strategic Reconnaissance Photographic Development Unit)	Dominie, Sea Hornet F.20, Sea Hornet PR.22, Sea Mosquito TR.33	Culham
766 Squadron (Operational Flying School Part I)	Firefly FR.1, Firefly T.1, Seafire F.15, Seafire F.17	Lossiemouth
767 Squadron (Deck Landing Control Officer Training)	Firefly FR.1, Firefly T.1, Firefly FR.4, Seafire F.15, Seafire F.17, Sea Fury F.10, Harvard T.2B & T.3	Yeovilton
771 Squadron (Fleet Requirements Unit)	7 Martinet TT.1, 12 Seafire F.45, 4 Mosquito PR.16, 8 Mosquito TR.33	Lee-on-Solent
781 Squadron (Southern Communications Squadron)	Dominie, Expeditor C.2, Sea Otter, Oxford, Seafire F.15, Firefly FR.1, Firefly T.1, Harvard T.2B	Lee-on-Solent
782 Squadron (Northern Communications Squadron)	Dominie, Oxford, Expeditor C.2, Firefly FR.1, Firefly FR.4	Donibristle
787 Squadron (Naval Air Firing Development Unit)	Vampire F.1, Vampire FB.5, Sea Vampire F.20, Oxford, Sea Hornet FR.20, Sea Hornet NF.21, Sea Fury FB.11	Attached to Central Fighter Establishment at RAF West Raynham
792 Squadron (Night Fighter Training Unit)	Firefly NF.1, Anson 1	Culdrose
796 Squadron (Air Navigation Training for Aircrewmen)	Firefly FR1, Barracuda 3	St Merryn
799 Squadron (Flying Check and Conversion Refresher)	Seafire F.15, Seafire F.17, Harvard T.2B, Firefly FR.1, Firefly FR.4, Firefly T.1, Sea Fury FB.11, Firebrand TF.5	Yeovilton

Various Mosquito versions survived into the 1950s on second-line duties. This is a Sea Mosquito TR.Mk 33, employed by 771 Sqn on fleet requirement duties, including operations in support of the Fighter Director School.

A Navy special variant was the Sea Mosquito TT.Mk 39, developed as a high-speed target-tug from the B.Mk XVI with a large glazed nose, observation turret and winch gear.

Over 60 de Havilland Dominies entered RN service during World War II, and the last did not retire until 1958. Used primarily for communications, many were operated by Station Flights, such as this example from Stretton.

of No. 804 Squadron and 12 Firefly Mk 5s of No. 812 Squadron, with the welcome addition of a Dragonfly rescue helicopter. Their black and white markings did not always prove effective against American attack, four of the Sea Furies being very fortunate to escape without damage when they were attacked on 25 June by four F-80 jets. *Glory* was replaced in July by HMAS *Sydney*, also carrying Sea Furies and Firefly 5s. Numerous attacks were made on road and rail targets, and in a clear spell on 20

HMS *Eagle*.
4 July 1951 898 Squadron reformed at Arbroath in the 17th CAG with 8 Sea Fury FB.11 for HMS *Ocean*.
14 July 1951 HMS *Ocean* sailed for the Mediterranean with the 17th CAG comprising 807 and 898 Squadrons with 8 Sea Furies each and 810 Squadron with 8 Firefly 5s.
20 July 1951 744 Squadron reformed at Eglinton as a Trials and Development squadron with Fireflies, Barracudas and Ansons for the development of search receivers to detect submarine radar.
August 1951 1831 RNVR Squadron at Stretton re-equipped from 9 Seafire F.17 to 9 Sea Fury FB.11.
16 August 1951 759 Squadron reformed at Culdrose as No.1 Operational Flying School with Seafire and Firebrand, and later a Jet Conversion Course with Meteor T.7 and Sea Vampire.
21 August 1951 800 Squadron reformed at Ford with 8 Attacker F.1 (later FB.1 then

FB.2) to become the first naval jet squadron, for service in HMS *Eagle*.
18 September 1951 821 Squadron reformed at Arbroath with 9 Firefly AS.6 (to FR.5 in 1952).
October 1951 After completing 2,892 sorties, HMS *Glory* sailed for Australia. Replaced by HMAS *Sydney* carrying Sea Furies of 805 and 808 Squadrons, and Fireflies of 817 Squadron.
November 1951 1832 RNVR Squadron at Culham re-equipped from 9 Seafire F.17 to 9 Sea Fury FB.11.
November 1951 778 Squadron reformed at Culdrose as an airborne early warning squadron with 4 Skyraider AEW.1.
26 November 1951 803 Squadron reformed at Ford with 8 Attacker F.1 (later FB.2) for HMS *Eagle*.
3 December 1951 751 Squadron reformed at Watton as the radio warfare unit with Sea Fury, Firefly, Mosquito and Avenger.

1952

January 1952 The first major use of helicopters in the search and rescue task by the FAA, when a Dragonfly refuelled at Culdrose in an unsuccessful attempt to rescue the captain and mate of the freighter *Flying Enterprise*, adrift in the Western Approaches.
7 January 1952 HMAS *Sydney* departed after 64 days in the battle area, having flown 2,366 sorties. Replaced by HMS *Glory* with the 14th CAG for a further tour, still comprising 804 Squadron with 21 Sea Fury FB.11 and 812 Squadron with 12 Firefly 5.
18 February 1952 824 Squadron reformed at Eglinton with 8 Firefly AS.6 for HMS *Illustrious*.
1 March 1952 HMS *Eagle* commissioned to become the Royal Navy's first carrier to carry jet aircraft.
2 April 1952 890 Squadron

recommissioned at Ford with 8 Attacker FB.1 for HMS *Eagle*.
17 April 1952 750 Squadron reformed at St Merryn as part of the Observer School with Barracuda.
May 1952 803 Squadron at Ford increased from 8 to 12 Attacker F.1.
29 May 1952 HMS *Ocean* took over from HMS *Glory* in Korean Waters, with the 17th CAG comprising 802 Squadron with 21 Sea Fury FB.11 and 825 Squadron with 12 Firefly 5.
1 June 1952 RNVR squadrons re-grouped into Air Divisions, allowing for expansion. The Scottish Air Division controlled 1830 Squadron, the Northern Air Division controlled 1831 Squadron, the Southern Air Division controlled 1832 Squadron, the Midland Air Division controlled 1833 Squadron and the Channel Air Division controlled 1840 Squadron.
July 1952 1833 RNVR Squadron at Bramcote re-equipped from 11 Seafire F.17 to 10 Seafire FR.47.

1

From March 1950 the ancient Fairey Barracuda TR.Mk 3s of 796 Sqn at St Merryn were occupied in training observers. In April 1952 this task was assumed by 750 Sqn, although the Barracudas lasted little over a year.

The day-fighter Sea Hornet F.Mk 20 had largely left FAA service at the start of the 1950s, but the NF.Mk 21 (illustrated) was the main night-fighter of the early part of the decade. It only served with one front-line unit, however, flying with 809 Sqn from 1949 to 1954. This aircraft wears the codes of Eagle, one of three carriers in which the squadron was embarked.

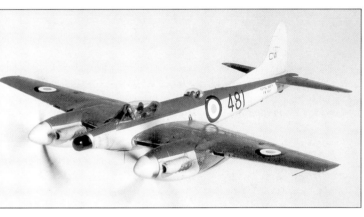

Above: Between 1947 and 1953 815 Sqn at Eglinton used Barracuda TR.Mk 3s on anti-submarine work. This was mostly undertaken from shore bases, but there were occasional shipborne deployments.

Left: When ashore, 809 Sqn was based at Culdrose. Its Sea Hornet NF.Mk 21s were augmented by a few single-seat PR.Mk 22s.

and 21 November 113 sorties were flown against targets in the Hungman area during Operation Athenaeum.

In January 1952, HMS *Glory* returned to the scene, still with the 14th CAG. Despite bitterly cold weather flying was usually possible, the Sea Furies often carrying two 500-lb bombs to act as very accurate dive-bombers, the alternative 60-lb rockets having been found less effective against available targets. The 15th CAG arrived in *Ocean* in May, comprising Nos 802 and 825

Squadrons, with Sea Furies and Firefly 5s respectively. By this time the Chinese were using MiG-15s, and on 9 August one of these was shot down by Lt P. Carmichael RN of No. 802 Squadron. *Glory* took over for its third and last Korean tour in November, now with No. 801 Sea Fury Squadron and No. 821 Firefly Squadron.

Poor weather handicapped activities in the New Year, and attacks against bridges were somewhat ineffective as the frozen ground and

rivers enabled the enemy to drive round any damage. Switching to attacks on rail communications proved more effective, 33 cuts being made on inaccessible sections of the routes. *Ocean* returned in May with Nos 807 and 810 Squadrons, respectively Sea Furies and Fireflies, and 560 sorties were flown on the carrier's first patrol. By the this time armistice discussions were in progress and hostilities finally ended on 27 July 1953.

Korea round-up

During the conflict the five British carriers involved had steamed 279,000 miles, and their 10 squadrons had flown almost 23,000 operational sorties with the loss of 22 lives in action and another 13 in accidents. The arrival of the helicopter on the scene had proved its worth, both for short-range rescue over land and sea, and as an efficient and economical planeguard able to quickly pick up aircrew from accidents near the carrier.

The Korean War now being over, it became possible for a complete reorganisation and modernisation of the equipment and working methods. The days of the light fleet carrier were numbered with the advent of jet aircraft.

7 July 1952 849 Squadron reformed at Culdrose from the disbanding 778 Squadron with 20 Skyraider AEW.1, comprising a Headquarters Flights, plus 'A', 'B', 'C' and 'D' Flights for service in carriers as required, each flight having four aircraft.
9 August 1952 4 Sea Furies of 802 Squadron led by Lt P. Carmichael in WJ232 '114/O' attacked north of Chinnampo by 8 MiG-15s, one of which was shot down.
12 August 1952 799 (Refresher Flying Training) Squadron disbanded at Machrihanish.
18 August 1952 1841 Squadron reformed as RNVR at Stretton as part of the Northern Air Division with 6 Firefly FR.1 (later 6 AS.6).
25 August 1952 736 Squadron disbanded at Culdrose.
26 August 1952 736 Squadron reformed as an Advanced Jet Flying School at Lossiemouth with Attacker F.1 and Meteor T.7.
29 October 1952 848 Squadron reformed

at Gosport with 10 Whirlwind HAR.21 for service in Malaya.
November 1952 HMS *Glory* returned to Korean waters to take over from HMS *Ocean*, carrying 21 Sea Fury FB.11 of 801 Squadron and 12 Firefly 5 of 821 Squadron.
3 December 1952 827 Squadron disbanded at Ford after disembarking HMS *Eagle*.
3 December 1952 890 Squadron disbanded aboard HMS *Eagle*, its aircraft being disposed to 800 and 803 Squadrons.
10 December 1952 802 Squadron disbanded at Lee after a spell in HMS *Theseus* in the Mediterranean.

1953

1 January 1953 898 Squadron disbanded into 807 in HMS *Ocean*.
8 January 1953 848 Squadron arrived at Singapore in the ferry carrier *Perseus* to provide helicopter support against Malayan

Communist guerrillas, becoming operational on 24 January.
February 1953 705 Squadron Dragonflies performed invaluable rescue work during flooding of much of the east coast of England and large areas of Holland.
2 February 1953 802 Squadron reformed at Arbroath with 12 Sea Fury FB.11 for service in HMS *Theseus*.
2 March 1953 806 Squadron reformed at Brawdy with 8 Sea Hawk F.1 for service in HMS *Eagle* (later HMS *Centaur* with FB.3 then FGA.4).
2 March 1953 825 Squadron reformed at Lee-on-Solent with 8 Firefly AS.5 for service in HMS *Eagle*.
28 March 1953 1835 and 1836 Squadron reformed as RNVR at Culham as part of the Southern Air Division with Sea Fury FB.11.
28 March 1953 1842 Squadron reformed as RNVR at Ford as part of the Channel Air Division sharing Firefly AS.6 with 1840 Squadron.
28 March 1953 1843 Squadron reformed

as RNVR at Abbotsinch in the Scottish Air Division sharing aircraft with 1830 Squadron.
May 1953 813 Squadron re-equipped at Ford from 12 Firebrand TF.5 to 12 Wyvern S.4 for HMS *Albion* (later HMS *Eagle*).
May 1953 815 Squadron, the resident shore-based UK anti-submarine squadron, re-equipped at Eglinton from 10 Barracuda 3 to 8 Avenger TBM-3E (later AS.4, then AS.5).
17 May 1953 HMS *Ocean* arrived at Sasebo to take over from *Glory* for its last Korean tour, with 21 Sea Fury FB.11 of 807 Squadron and 12 Firefly 5 of 810 Squadron.
18 May 1953 764 Squadron reformed for Advanced Training at Lossiemouth with Seafire F.17 and Firefly.
9 June 1953 First production Gannet AS.1 had its maiden flight.
15 June 1953 Coronation Review at Spithead. 9 carriers comprised HMS *Eagle*, HMS *Illustrious*, HMS *Implacable*, HMS *Indefatigable*, HMS *Indomitable*, HMCS

A Decade of Air Power

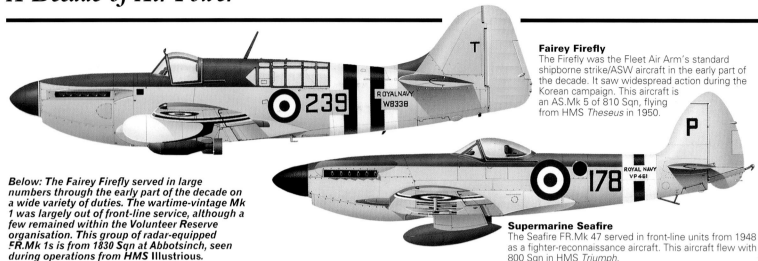

Fairey Firefly
The Firefly was the Fleet Air Arm's standard shipborne strike/ASW aircraft in the early part of the decade. It saw widespread action during the Korean campaign. This aircraft is an AS.Mk 5 of 810 Sqn, flying from HMS *Theseus* in 1950.

Supermarine Seafire
The Seafire FR.Mk 47 served in front-line units from 1948 as a fighter-reconnaissance aircraft. This aircraft flew with 800 Sqn in HMS *Triumph*.

Below: The Fairey Firefly served in large numbers through the early part of the decade on a wide variety of duties. The wartime-vintage Mk 1 was largely out of front-line service, although a few remained within the Volunteer Reserve organisation. This group of radar-equipped FR.Mk 1s is from 1830 Sqn at Abbotsinch, seen during operations from HMS Illustrious.

Below: Target-towing was an important function for the Firefly, performed primarily by the TT.Mk 4 with fuselage-mounted winch gear. This example is from Ford-based 771 Sqn, the Southern Fleet Requirements Unit.

During 1952 825 Sqn was aboard HMS Ocean for a combat cruise, using Firefly FR.Mk 5s on strike duties. Here one of the aircraft cruises along the Korean coastline.

During the Korean War Fireflies undertook intensive strike operations armed with bombs and rockets, demonstrating exceptional serviceability. This armed pair is from 810 Sqn.

The Supermarine Attacker, designed specifically for carrier use, became the first to join an operational unit when it reached No. 800 Squadron at Ford in August 1951. The squadron joined the new fleet carrier HMS *Eagle* soon after she commissioned in March 1952, as part of the 13th CAG, which also included the Firebrands of No. 827 Squadron. This group was later expanded to include another Attacker squadron, No. 803, and also No. 849A Flight with Douglas Skyraider AEW.Mk 1s.

Early warning

Designed extremely quickly by brilliant Ed Heinemann in 1944, the Skyraider was an outstanding all-can-do aircraft, which flew from carrier decks carrying enormous loads of bombs, mines, torpedoes, rockets, anti-submarine weapons and even troops or electronic countermeasures. Under the Mutual Defense Assistance Program the Royal Navy received 50 Skyraiders of the specialised AD-4W type, receiving British designation Skyraider AEW.Mk 1. They carried powerful APS-20 surveillance radar, with the two operators in the rear fuselage and the scanner rotating inside a huge pregnant 'guppy' radome under the fuselage. Like most US equipment they proved efficient and very popular in service.

Though these aircraft reached Britain in 1951 they did not become operational with 849 Sqn until 1953, the year of Her Majesty's coronation. It was a good year for the FAA, because four other types became available: the Hawker Sea Hawk, Grumman Avenger AS.Mk 4, Westland Wyvern and Westland Whirlwind, and in addition the Fairey Gannet completed carrier trials.

The British designs in this group had been many years coming, reflecting the relaxed atmosphere in the post-war procurement machine. The Hawker P.1040 had been

737 Sqn at Eglinton formed half of the Naval Anti-Submarine School. It used a variety of Fireflies, including this AS.Mk 4.

The Mk 7 was the last production Firefly variant – an unarmed ASW aircraft. This T.Mk 7 was used by Eglinton-based 719 Sqn for ASW training.

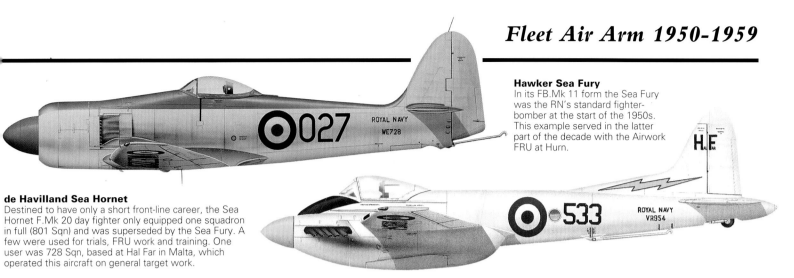

Hawker Sea Fury
In its FB.Mk 11 form the Sea Fury was the RN's standard fighter-bomber at the start of the 1950s. This example served in the latter part of the decade with the Airwork FRU at Hurn.

de Havilland Sea Hornet
Destined to have only a short front-line career, the Sea Hornet F.Mk 20 day fighter only equipped one squadron in full (801 Sqn) and was superseded by the Sea Fury. A few were used for trials, FRU work and training. One user was 728 Sqn, based at Hal Far in Malta, which operated this aircraft on general target work.

The Firefly AS.Mk 6 was a dedicated anti-submarine version, equipped with search radar. RNVR unit 1840 Sqn operated this aircraft from Ford as part of the Channel Air Division.

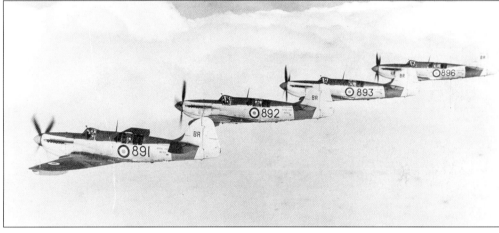

The AS.Mk 6 was the last of the Firefly variants in operational service, giving way in the ASW role to Avengers in 1956. One of the last operators was RNVR ASW unit 1844 Sqn, part of the Midland Air Division at Bramcote, which kept its aircraft just long enough to see them recoded in the new system introduced in 1956.

At Culdrose 796 Sqn flew Firefly T.Mk 7s on observer training duties. They served until late 1957 and were replaced by Gannets.

The Firefly U.Mk 8 was based on the Mk 7, and was a new-build pilotless drone for missile development work. Forty Mk 5s were also converted as drones to become U.Mk 9s. Both variants were used by 728B Sqn at Hal Far.

designed during the war and flown on 2 September 1947. A year earlier the naval N.7/46 version had been ordered, leading to the prototype of the carrier-based Sea Hawk which flew in 1948. It was perhaps the most graceful of all jet fighters, because the fuselage looked almost perfectly streamlined, the 5,000-lb (later 5,400-lb) thrust Rolls-Royce Nene engine having a unique bifurcated jetpipe with two half-size nozzles behind the wingroots. This enabled an extra fuel tank to be installed behind the engine. Armed with four Hispano 20-mm guns, the Hawk could carry bombs, rockets or drop tanks, and in clean condition could reach 630 mph.

In contrast, the Wyvern was powered by a huge 4,110-hp Armstrong Siddeley Python turboprop, driving a formidable eight-bladed contra-rotating propeller. It took seven years to bring to operational service, and even then had

a chequered record of dangerous failures of the propulsion system. It was much bigger than it looked, more than 10 ft longer than a Seafire, and weighing up to 24,500 lb (as much as a loaded Dakota). With a speed of 383 mph, it had four 20-mm guns and could carry a torpedo, three bombs of 1,000 lb or 16 rockets.

MDAP Avengers

Though developed primarily as an anti-submarine aircraft (hence the designation), the Grumman Avenger AS.Mk 4 was used mainly as a multi-role strike aircraft replacing the Barracuda. Like the Skyraider, the 100 of this type were supplied from the USA under the MDAP, chiefly to fill the gap left by the delayed entry to service of the Gannet. They had a crew of three and rather limited sensors for detecting submarines, as well as the Avenger's large internal weapon bay and racks

---

Magnificent, HMS *Perseus*, HMAS *Sydney* and HMS *Theseus*. A flypast of 300 aircraft from 37 squadrons included Attackers, Avengers, Dragonflies, Fireflies, Gannets, Meteors, Seafires, Sea Furies, Sea Hawks, Sea Hornets, Sea Vampires, Sea Venoms, Skyraiders, Vampires, and Wyverns.
July 1953 824 Squadron re-equipped at Lee-on-Solent with 8 Avenger TBM-3 (later AS.4). It was to have had Firefly AS.7, but this variant was deemed unsuitable for the anti-submarine task, and was instead relegated to training duties.
18 July 1953 1832, 1835 and 1836 RNVR Squadrons moved from Culham to Benson, where they operated Sea Furies on a pooled basis.
23 July 1953 HMS *Ocean* aircraft completed their last operation in Korean waters, having made a record 1,197

accident-free landings during this patrol.
27 July 1953 Korean armistice signed at Panmunjom. The five British carriers involved had between them steamed 279,000 miles and flown nearly 23,000 operational sorties, for the loss of 35 aircraft, including 13 in accidents.
17 August 1953 811 Squadron reformed with 9 Sea Fury FB.11 at Arbroath for service in HMS *Warrior* in the Mediterranean and the Far East.
24 August 1953 898 Squadron reformed at Brawdy with 12 Sea Hawk F.1 (later FB.3) for service in HMS *Albion* in the Mediterranean.
7 September 1953 706 Squadron reformed at Gosport as an anti-submarine helicopter squadron with 8 Whirlwind HAS.22 and 2 Hiller HT.1.
9 October 1953 782 (Northern

Communications) Squadron disbanded at Donibristle, its Dominies and task being taken over by the Airwork-operated Northern Communications Squadron.
10 October 1953 1834 Squadron reformed as RNVR at Benson as part of the Southern Air Division with Sea Fury FB. 11 .
20 October 1953 812 Squadron disbanded at Eglinton after service in HMS *Theseus* and HMS *Eagle* in Home Waters.
November 1953 804 Squadron re-equipped at Lossiemouth from 9 Sea Fury FB.11 to 12 Sea Hawk F.1
9 November 1953 738 Squadron moved from Culdrose to Lossiemouth, where it re-equipped with Sea Hawks and Sea Vampire T.22.
17 December 1953 810 Squadron disbanded at Culdrose after service in HMS *Ocean* in Korean waters.

1954

16 January 1954 1834 RNVR Squadron moved from Benson to Yeovilton.
February 1954 1833 RNVR Sqn at Bramcote re-equipped 9 Sea Fury FB.11.
15 February 1954 1844 Squadron reformed as RNVR at Bramcote in Midland Air Division with 6 Firefly FR.5 (later AS.6).
March 1954 802 Squadron converted at Lossiemouth to Sea Hawk F.1 (later F.2 then FGA.4). The first Sea Hawk squadron.
March 1954 814 Squadron re-equipped at Eglinton with Avenger AS.4 and AS.5 for service in HMS *Centaur*.
March 1954 820 Squadron re-equipped at Eglinton with 8 Avenger AS.4 for service in HMS *Centaur*.
1 March 1954 810 Squadron reformed at

A Decade of Air Power

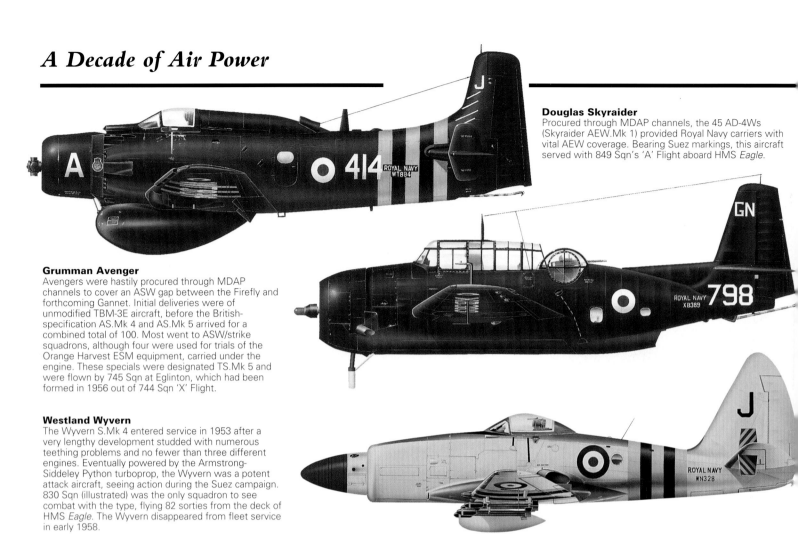

Douglas Skyraider
Procured through MDAP channels, the 45 AD-4Ws (Skyraider AEW.Mk 1) provided Royal Navy carriers with vital AEW coverage. Bearing Suez markings, this aircraft served with 849 Sqn's 'A' Flight aboard HMS *Eagle*.

Grumman Avenger
Avengers were hastily procured through MDAP channels to cover an ASW gap between the Firefly and forthcoming Gannet. Initial deliveries were of unmodified TBM-3E aircraft, before the British-specification AS.Mk 4 and AS.Mk 5 arrived for a combined total of 100. Most went to ASW/strike squadrons, although four were used for trials of the Orange Harvest ESM equipment, carried under the engine. These specials were designated TS.Mk 5 and were flown by 745 Sqn at Eglinton, which had been formed in 1956 out of 744 Sqn 'X' Flight.

Westland Wyvern
The Wyvern S.Mk 4 entered service in 1953 after a very lengthy development studded with numerous teething problems and no fewer than three different engines. Eventually powered by the Armstrong-Siddeley Python turboprop, the Wyvern was a potent attack aircraft, seeing action during the Suez campaign. 830 Sqn (illustrated) was the only squadron to see combat with the type, flying 82 sorties from the deck of HMS *Eagle*. The Wyvern disappeared from fleet service in early 1958.

Above: 815 Sqn was one of the fleet ASW units which re-equipped with the Avenger. Here AS.Mk 4s are seen during a Mediterranean cruise in HMS Eagle.

Above: Although primarily procured for the ASW role, the Grumman Avenger was used for general strike duties as well. This TBM-3E wears the codes of 703 Sqn, the Ford-based Service Trials Unit.

Right: This is one of 745 Sqn's Avenger TS.Mk 5s used for trials of ESM equipment (note the empty mast below the engine). The test work took the aircraft to St Mawgan, Ballykelly and Culdrose, and aboard Bulwark and Albion.

for eight rockets. Like the Skyraiders, these aircraft were painted in US Navy 'midnight blue'.

On 15 June 1953, headed by HMS *Eagle*, an array of nine British carriers participating in the Coronation Review of the Fleet before Her Majesty Queen Elizabeth II at Spithead. In the air, a flypast of 300 naval aircraft from 37 first-and second-line squadrons was led by a Sea Vampire piloted by the Flag Officer Flying Training. The 14 different types of aircraft flown included several of the new ones. The Westland Wyvern would replace the Firebrand as a torpedo fighter, while the Attacker would be superseded by the Hawker Sea Hawk. The

Fairey Gannet had only just started to leave the production lines, but a later AEW.Mk 3 variant would eventually replace the Skyraider.

Further new carriers were now coming into commission, and their wartime predecessors either sold or scrapped, except for HMS *Victorious* which was being extensively modernised. The new 737-ft long 'Centaur'-class of light fleet carriers comprised the HMS *Albion*, HMS *Bulwark* and HMS *Centaur*, all completed during 1953 and 1954. Somewhat larger than the wartime fleet carriers, they had much improved facilities for the crew. The new 803-ft long HMS *Ark Royal* incorporated many new

ideas, including two steam catapults, a partially angled deck, a port-side deck lift and a mirror landing device to replace the batsman. For the crew, it had its own television network, and when within range of shore transmitters could show current BBC and ITV programmes or the overseas counterparts.

For aircrew, Cromwell helmets, nicknamed 'bone-domes', provided better protection in the event of an accident, rubberised fabric immersion suits gave protection in the event of a ditching, being particularly invaluable in low sea temperatures. Martin-Baker ejector seats became standard when fitted to later production

Hawker Sea Hawk
Large-scale re-equipment with jets came in the form of the simple yet sturdy and effective Sea Hawk. It was built in several variants, this being an FGA.Mk 4, the first equipped for the close support role. 810 Sqn flew the aircraft from *Albion* during the November 1956 raids on Egypt.

de Havilland Sea Venom
Radar-equipped for the night-fighter role, the Sea Venom served for the latter half of the decade in this primary function, also undertaking attack sorties. The attack capability was employed by this aircraft of 809 Sqn (from *Albion*) during the Suez raids.

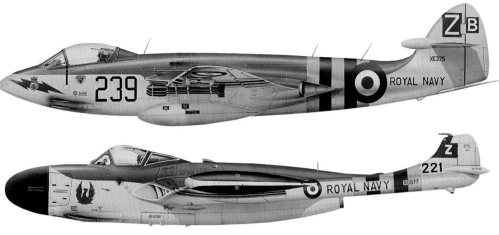

Three front-line squadrons flew the Attacker, although 890 Sqn (FB.Mk 1 illustrated) was mainly used to provide a pool of pilots for the other two units (800 and 803 Sqns).

In addition to the front-line units, Attackers were also assigned to 736 Sqn, the Advanced Jet Flying School at Lossiemouth. These are some of the squadron's FB.Mk 2s.

Supermarine Attacker
The FAA's first fleet jet fighter, the Attacker flew on both fighter and attack duties. This FB.Mk 2 flew with 1831 Sqn at Stretton, part of the Northern Air Division. This was the first RNVR unit to receive jet equipment, in May 1955.

Above: The initial Attacker version was the F.Mk 1, identified by an unframed one-piece canopy. The similar FB.Mk 1 introduced the capability to carry eight rockets or two 1,000-lb (454-kg) bombs.

Right: With their front-line days over, the surviving Attackers (mostly FB.Mk 2s – note the framed canopy) flew with three RNVR squadrons in 1955-57. This aircraft is from 1832 Sqn at Benson, part of the Southern Air Division.

de Havilland Sea Venoms.

Helicopters in the shape of Westland Dragonflies, an Anglicised version of the American Sikorsky S-51, were now a practical proposition, pioneered by No. 705 Squadron at Gosport. In January 1952 squadron aircraft refuelled at Culdrose for a gallant but unsuccessful attempt to rescue the captain and mate of the freighter *Flying Enterprise*, which had broken down and gone adrift in the Western Approaches. Just over a year later the squadron performed magnificent rescue work when the North Sea flooded much of eastern England and large areas of Holland.

Despite its successes, the Dragonfly was inadequate for many purposes. A larger machine

was now required, and Sikorsky technology was again turned to, this time in the shape of the S-55. An initial 25 were provided under the MDAP, the US Marines HRS-2 variant being designated the Whirlwind HAR.Mk 21, while the HAS.Mk 22 anti-submarine version was basically the US Navy HO4S-3. A licence for

UK production was again granted to Westland. A notable feature of these helicopters was that the engine was in the nose, installed at an angle to drive the main gearbox via a shaft which sloped up diagonally between the seats in the high cockpit. This enabled an unobstructed cabin for the load to be under the main rotor

Ford with 12 Sea Fury FB.11 for service in HMS *Centaur*.
1 March 1954 744 Squadron disbanded at Eglinton.
1 March 1954 744 Squadron reformed with Firefly AS.6 at Culdrose as the Naval Air-Sea Warfare Development Unit, to work in conjunction with the RAF's ASWDU at nearby St Mawgan.
15 March 1954 845 Squadron reformed by redesignating 706 Squadron with 8 Whirlwind HAS.22 for the Mediterranean.
20 March 1954 890 Squadron reformed at Yeovilton with 9 Sea Venom FAW.20 for service in HMS *Albion*.
10 May 1954 809 Squadron disbanded at Culdrose.
10 May 1954 809 Squadron reformed at Yeovilton with 9 Sea Venom FAW.20 (not fully equipped until October) for service in

HMS *Ark Royal* in the Mediterranean.
27 May 1954 HMS *Albion* commissioned with interim angled deck and deck landing mirror sight.
11 June 1954 800 Squadron disbanded at Ford.
August 1954 803 began to rearm with 12 Sea Hawk FB.3.
12 October 1954 759 Squadron disbanded at Lossiemouth.
1 November 1954 827 Squadron reformed at Ford with 9 Wyvern S.4 for service in HMS *Eagle*.
8 November 1954 800 Squadron reformed at Brawdy with 12 Sea Hawk FB.3 for service in HMS *Ark Royal* (re-equipped with FB.4 in June 1955 before embarking).
8 November 1954 891 Squadron reformed at Yeovilton with 9 Sea Venom

FAW.20.
23 November 1954 764 Squadron disbanded at Lossiemouth.
December 1954 804 Squadron rearmed at Lossiemouth with 12 Sea Hawk FGA.4 (later FGA.6), initially for service in HMS *Eagle*.
30 December 1954 811 and 825 Squadrons disbanded at Lee-on-Solent after disembarking from HMS *Warrior* on return from the Far East.

1955

January 1955 826 Squadron re-equipped at Lee-on-Solent with 8 Gannet AS.1 for service in HMS *Eagle*.
31 January 1955 801 Squadron disbanded at Ford.

February 1955 824 Squadron rearmed at Eglinton with 8 Gannet AS.1.
1 February 1955 764 Squadron reformed at Ford as a fighter pilot holding unit or jet fighter pool with 10 Sea Hawk and 10 Sea Vampire.
7 February 1955 765 (Piston Engine Pilot Pool) Squadron reformed at Culdrose with Firefly T.2 and T.7.
22 February 1955 HMS *Ark Royal* commissioned, fitted with two steam catapults, a partially angled deck, a port-side deck lift and a mirror landing sight.
March 1955 820 Squadron re-equipped at Eglinton with 9 Gannet AS.1.
1 March 1955 891X Squadron formed at Yeovilton to train Australian crews pending formation of 808 RAN Squadron there in August.
14 March 1955 801 Squadron reformed at

A Decade of Air Power

The Hawker Sea Hawk was the most widespread fleet aircraft of the mid-1950s, equipping 13 front-line units, three Reserve squadrons and five second-line units. This F.Mk 1 line-up is from 898 Sqn, shore-based at Brawdy.

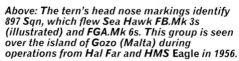

Above: The tern's head nose markings identify 897 Sqn, which flew Sea Hawk FB.Mk 3s (illustrated) and FGA.Mk 6s. This group is seen over the island of Gozo (Malta) during operations from Hal Far and HMS Eagle in 1956.

Left: Six Sea Hawk squadrons saw action during the Suez campaign, including 800 Sqn here, which flew from HMS Albion. With the exception of 802 Sqn, which retained FB.Mk 3s, all flew the FGA.Mk 6 version.

Photographed aboard HMS Ark Royal in 1957 are a Sea Hawk FGA.Mk 4 of 898 Sqn (foreground) and FGA.Mk 6s from 804 Sqn, the latter retaining their Suez campaign identification stripes.

Demonstrating a near-simultaneous cartridge start are the Sea Hawk FB.Mk 3s of 806 Sqn. Operating mainly between Hal Far and HMS Centaur, the unit was instrumental in developing Sea Hawk carrierborne operations during 1954-55.

Right: A Sea Hawk FGA.Mk 4 of 898 Sqn lands on Ark Royal, displaying the long 'sting'-type arrester hook. For about two years in the 1955/57 period the squadron operated both FGA.Mk 4s and 6s, flying from three carriers.

Sea Hawks had a brief career in the Reserve, F.Mk 1s flying with 1832 Sqn at Benson between January 1956 and March 1957.

hub, evenly disposed about the centre of gravity. Like the Sikorsky-built machines, early versions of Westland-built Whirlwinds were powered by either the 600-hp Wasp or 700-hp Cyclone, and were used mainly as SAR (search and rescue) and general liaison vehicles. In 1955, however, the Whirlwind HAS.Mk 7 entered service, powered by the 750-hp Alvis Leonides Major and equipped as a limited anti-submarine platform, using dipping sonar similar to that of the HAS.Mk 22.

At the beginning of 1953, the ferry carrier *Perseus* arrived at Singapore with the 10 Whirlwind HAR.Mk 21s of No. 848 Sqn, tasked with providing helicopter support in Malaya, where Communist guerrilla troops and terrorists had been trying since 1948 to take over the country. In addition to casualty evacuation duties, they were able to carry troops and supplies quickly and accurately to remote locations, often in a matter of minutes, instead of the previous days and sometimes weeks of hacking through the jungle. Among the many tasks, tracker dogs could be lowered down,

---

Lossiemouth with 12 Sea Hawk FGA.4
16 March 1955 811 Squadron reformed at Lossiemouth with 8 Sea Hawk FB.3.
22 March 1955 810 Squadron disbanded at UK ex Hal Far.
31 March 1955 767 (Landing Signal Officers Training) Squadron disbanded at Stretton.
25 April 1955 718 Squadron reformed at Stretton with Attackers and Sea Vampire T.22s to give jet conversion training to RNVR piston-engined pilots.
30 April 1955 1834 RNVR Squadron disbanded at Yeovilton.
May 1955 1831 RNVR Squadron at Stretton re-equipped with 7 Attacker FB.2.
June 1955 898 Squadron re-equipped with 12 Sea Hawk FGA.6 for service in HMS Ark Royal.
4 July 1955 810 Squadron reformed at

Lossiemouth with 10 Sea Hawk FGA.4 (later FGA.6) for service in Albion.
4 July 1955 825 Squadron reformed at Culdrose with 8 Gannet AS. 1 for service in Albion in the Mediterranean and the Far East.
4 July 1955 892 Squadron reformed at Yeovilton with 8 Sea Venom FAW.21 for service in Albion (later HMS Eagle).
August 1955 1832 RNVR Squadron at Benson re-equipped with 8 Attacker FB.2.
18 August 1955 700 (Trials and Requirements) Unit formed at Ford to replace the disbanding 703 and 771 Squadrons, with 2 Sea Vampire F.20, 2 Anson, 2 Sea Hawk, 2 Wyvern and 2 Gannet.
10 October 1955 845 Squadron disbanded at Lee-on-Solent.
13 October 1955 815 Squadron

disbanded at Abbotsinch after disembarking from HMS Albion.
18 October 1955 890 Squadron redesignated 766 Squadron at Yeovilton as an all-weather fighter pool with 8 Sea Venom FAW.20.
23 October 1955 1833 RNVR Squadron moved from Bramcote to RAF Honiley on re-equipping with 7 Attacker FB.2.
November 1955 1830/1843 RNVR Squadrons re-equipped from 9 Firefly AS.6 to 8 Avenger AS .5.
1 November 1955 705 (Helicopter Training) Squadron moved from Gosport to Lee-on-Solent.
4 November 1955 803, 806 and 814 Squadrons disbanded on arrival at Portsmouth after service in HMS Centaur.
4 November 1955 807 Squadron disbanded after service in HMS Albion.

7 November 1955 812 Squadron reformed at Eglinton with 8 Gannet AS.1 for service in HMS Eagle.
7 November 1955 897 Squadron reformed at Brawdy with 12 Sea Hawk FB.3 for service in HMS Eagle in the Mediterranean.
7 November 1955 899 Squadron reformed at Brawdy with 12 Sea Hawk FGA.6 for service in HMS Eagle in the Mediterranean.
14 November 1955 845 Squadron reformed at Lee-on-Solent with 8 Whirlwind HAS.22.
17 November 1955 804 Squadron disbanded at Devonport after service in HMS Eagle on return from the Mediterranean.
19 November 1955 827 Squadron disbanded at Ford after service in HMS

Westland Dragonfly
Seventy-two Dragonflies were procured for the Navy, mostly for rescue duties and communications work. This HR.Mk 3 was assigned to *Ark Royal*'s Ship's Flight.

Sikorsky HRS Whirlwind
The Whirlwind was used initially for assault transport duties. This machine was a HAR.Mk 21 of 848 Sqn, as used in Malaya.

Above: The Skyraider AEW.Mk 1 was first issued to 778 Sqn at Culdrose. This evolved into 849 Sqn in July 1952. Headquarters flight aircraft, like this one, wore Culdrose shore codes.

Right: Skyraiders saw action during the Suez campaign, this aircraft from 849 Sqn 'A' Flt aboard Eagle being photographed during the fighting.

Below: HMS Albion rests in Grand Harbour, Malta in 1955. The Sea Hawks of 898 Sqn are dwarfed by the bulk of 849 Sqn 'C' Flight's Skyraider AEW.Mk 1.

Fairey Gannet
Entering service in 1955, the Gannet AS.Mk 1 combined the ASW hunter and killer roles in one airframe. This machine flew from the deck of *Ark Royal* with 815 Sqn.

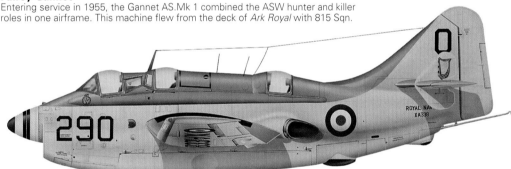

supplies and personnel dropped by parachute, leaflets dropped and prisoners taken to base. They were also able to demonstrate the practicability of commando drops. By the end of 1953 the squadron had flown 6,000 operational hours, during which it transported 18,000 men and 363,000 lb of stores and ammunition. The squadron was eventually disbanded at the end of 1956, being awarded by the Malayan government a suitably inscribed silver *kris*, this curved dagger being the national symbol.

Meanwhile, events in the Middle East had taken a turn for the worse. President Nasser of Egypt nationalised the Suez Canal in July 1956.

Important French and British interests were at stake, including the supply of oil from the Persian Gulf. Supertankers did not exist at that time, and in fact they were only conceived as a means of circumventing the need for the canal. It was decided to mount a joint attack, also involving the Israelis, under the codename Operation Musketeer. However, the nearest RAF land bases were in Cyprus and Malta, so the Fleet Air Arm was called upon to undertake a vital part. As in the Korean War, British, and also French, aircraft were painted up with identification stripes, this time black and yellow. On 1 November aircraft took off from HMS

Albion, HMS *Eagle* and HMS *Bulwark* for an early morning pre-emptive strike on Egyptian air force airfields. These attacks continued, and by next day the defending air force was virtually wiped out. HMS *Bulwark*'s aircraft alone claimed to have disposed of over 100 Egyptian aircraft. Destruction of other targets continued, and on 5 November, British and French ground and parachute troops were landed. A shuttle-service of helicopters from *Ocean* and HMS *Theseus* brought ashore food and ammunition, and next day No. 845 Squadron and the Joint (Experimental) Helicopter Unit transported ashore 500 commandos and their equip-

---

Eagle in the Mediterranean.
21 November 1955 830 and 831 Squadrons reformed at Ford, each with 9 Wyvern S.4 for service in HMS *Eagle*.
21 November 1955 813 Squadron disbanded at Ford after service in HMS *Eagle* in the Mediterranean.
22 November 1955 802 and 826 Squadrons disbanded at Lee-on-Solent after service in HMS *Eagle* in the Mediterranean.
December 1955 1841 RNVR Squadron re-equipped with 6 Avenger AS.5.
31 December 1955 718 Squadron disbanded at Honiley.

1956

January 1956 1832 RNVR Squadron at Benson with re-equipped 13 Sea Hawk F.1.

4 January 1956 727 Squadron reformed at Brawdy as the Dartmouth Cadet Air Training Squadron with 3 Sea Balliol, 3 Sea Vampire T.22 and a Sea Prince T.1.
16 January 1956 787 Squadron, the Naval Air Fighting Development Unit, disbanded at West Raynham.
February 1956 1840/1842 RNVR Squadrons re-equipped with 8 Gannet AS.1.
1 February 1956 890 Squadron reformed at Yeovilton with 6 Sea Venom FAW.21.
6 February 1956 802 Squadron reformed at Lossiemouth with 11 Sea Hawk FB.3 for service in HMS *Bulwark*.
6 February 1956 804 Squadron reformed at Lossiemouth with 11 Sea Hawk FGA.6 for service in HMS *Bulwark* (later HMS *Ark Royal*).
6 February 1956 815 Squadron reformed at Eglinton with 8 Gannet AS.1 for service

in HMS *Ark Royal*.
6 February 1956 893 Squadron reformed at Yeovilton with 6 (later 12) Sea Venom FAW.21 for service in HMS *Eagle* (later HMS *Ark Royal*).
March 1956 1835/1836 RNVR Squadrons re-equipped with Sea Hawk F.1.
March 1956 1844 RNVR Squadron re-equipped with 6 Avenger AS.5.
1 March 1956 767 Squadron reformed as a fighter pilot pool squadron at Ford with Sea Hawk.
17 March 1956 847 Squadron reformed at Eglinton with 3 Gannet AS.1 (later AS.4) for Cyprus.
20 March 1956 809 Squadron disbanded at Yeovilton after service in HMS *Ark Royal* in the Mediterranean.
17 April 1956 824 Squadron disbanded at Ford after service in HMS *Ark Royal*.

17 April 1956 891 Squadron disbanded at Yeovilton after service in *Ark Royal* in the Mediterranean.
19 April 1956 898 Squadron disbanded at Brawdy after service in HMS *Ark Royal* (the Mediterranean) .
23 April 1956 895 Squadron reformed at Brawdy with 12 Sea Hawk FGA.6 for service in HMS *Bulwark*.
23 April 1956 745 Squadron reformed at Eglinton as a radar jamming trials unit with 4 Avenger TS.5 for tactical evaluation of Orange Harvest equipment.
7 May 1956 809 Squadron reformed at Yeovilton with 6 Sea Venom FAW.21 for *Albion* in the Mediterranean.
7 May 1956 824 Squadron reformed at Culdrose with 8 Gannet AS.1 (later AS.4) for *Albion*.
15 May 1956 820 Squadron disbanded in

A Decade of Air Power

703 Sqn at Ford was a Service Trials Unit, and operated a few Wyvern S.Mk 4s in 1954/55. This example is undertaking catapult trials from HMS Ark Royal.

827 Sqn formed on Wyverns out of 703W Flt in November 1954, adorning its aircraft with a wyvern badge. It flew briefly from Eagle before disbanding in December 1955.

The 'Dennis the Menace' badge was worn by 813 Sqn's Wyverns during 1957/58 operations from Eagle. The squadron operated the type for two separate periods, lying dormant in between.

Right: Suez-striped Wyverns of 830 Sqn are seen aboard Eagle just after the fighting. The main targets during the air strikes were Egyptian airfields.

For most of 1956 830 Sqn was either at Hal Far or aboard Eagle. This dramatic photograph was taken in September during exercises off Malta. Two months later the Wyverns would be rocketing targets for real over Egypt.

Twenty Hiller HT.Mk 1s were supplied under MDAP, being used primarily for rotary-wing training with 705 Sqn at Gosport, Lee-on-Solent and Culdrose. Here one makes a landing on HMS Vidal, the first helicopter-capable survey ship.

ment. By nightfall on 6 November Port Said had been captured and good progress made with capturing the Suez Canal, but international politics then brought a sudden end to the conflict with a ceasefire at midnight that night. The first full-scale operation by the Fleet Air Arm since the end of World War II had been carried out with precision and competence, and had proved the practicability of the helicopter for this type of operation, but it was destined to be the last major operation by a large British carrier force.

Disbandment of the Reserve

The carriers remained in the Mediterranean until the following March, but then returned home. This turned out to be a sad month for the Fleet Air Arm, recent defence cuts having led to a disbandment of all the RNVR squadrons, which had grown from four to 11 over the previous decade, the original equipment of Seafires and Fireflies having given way gradually to Sea Furies, Sea Hawks, Attackers, Avengers and Gannets.

The Gannet had at last entered service in January 1955, its place having been temporarily filled by the Avenger AS.Mk 4 and also the

three-seat Fairey Firefly AS.Mk 7. Part of the delay had been caused by the belated recognition that a crew of three was needed, but the main reason was the sheer newness and complexity of the whole aircraft. Its portly fuselage housed a unique engine at the front, a capacious weapon bay under the mid-mounted wing, a row of three cockpits spaced on top and a retractable radar under the rear. The engine, the Armstrong Siddeley Double Mamba, was really two completely separate 1,500-hp turboprops joined only by the casing of the reduction gear to two four-bladed propellers. The two jetpipes emerged from the sides of the rear fuselage. The Gannet took off on 3,000 hp, but once in the air one of its engines could be shut down and its propeller feathered, the other remaining at quite high power to give good fuel economy for the necessary range and endurance. Other unusual features were tricycle landing gear and wings which power-folded along two hinges on each

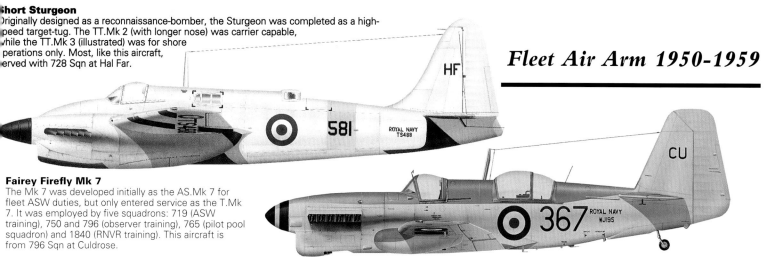

Short Sturgeon
Originally designed as a reconnaissance-bomber, the Sturgeon was completed as a high-speed target-tug. The TT.Mk 2 (with longer nose) was carrier capable, while the TT.Mk 3 (illustrated) was for shore operations only. Most, like this aircraft, served with 728 Sqn at Hal Far.

Fairey Firefly Mk 7
The Mk 7 was developed initially as the AS.Mk 7 for fleet ASW duties, but only entered service as the T.Mk 7. It was employed by five squadrons: 719 (ASW training), 750 and 796 (observer training), 765 (pilot pool squadron) and 1840 (RNVR training). This aircraft is from 796 Sqn at Culdrose.

Gloster Meteor
The Navy employed several Meteor variants, including the hooked Mk III for trials, T.Mk 7 for jet training and the TT.Mk 20 for target-towing. This T.Mk 7 was assigned to the Lossiemouth Station Flight as a hack.

Westland-built Sikorsky Dragonflies were assigned in small numbers to most Navy shore bases for SAR duties. Here a HAR.Mk 3 from the Culdrose Station Flight practises a casevac from HMS Thule, a 'T'-class submarine.

A transport-configured Sikorsky-built Whirlwind HAS.Mk 22 lands with a Special Boat Section canoe carried underneath. In both Malaya and at Suez the Whirlwind demonstrated the capabilities of the helicopter as an assault vehicle.

815 Sqn was reformed in 1958 as the Naval Air Anti-Submarine School (Rotary Wing), equipped with the Whirlwind HAS.Mk 7 at its Eglinton base. The success of the HAS.Mk 7 and its dipping sonar, and the impending introduction of the Wessex HAS.Mk 1, spelled the end for the Gannet ASW aircraft.

845 Sqn was the first to introduce the Whirlwind for ASW duties with dipping ASDIC (sonar). From 1957 the squadron embarked its HAS.Mk 7s in HMS Bulwark. In the foreground is a 701 Sqn HAR.Mk 3, used for transport and rescue.

side to keep down the folded height to 13 ft.

Another completely new aircraft for the FAA was the de Havilland Sea Venom, though outwardly it bore a family resemblance to the Sea Vampire which from 1948 had been used as a fighter trainer to familiarise naval pilots with jet flying. In contrast, the Sea Venom was a two-seat radar-equipped all-weather and night fighter, also able to fly ground attack missions. Though hardly any bigger than the Vampire, it was a quart in a pint pot. All versions were powered by a de Havilland Ghost turbojet of 4,850-5,150 lb thrust at the rear of the short central nacelle. The first FAA sub-type was the

FAW.Mk 20, which began to replace the Sea Hornet NF.Mk 21 in 1954. The FAW.Mk 21 introduced a more modern Westinghouse radar supplied under MDAP and given the British designation AI.21, as well as hydraulically powered ailerons. With the FAW.Mk 22 these aircraft were at last fitted with Martin-Baker ejection seats, ending an outrageous situation in which money (and easily overcome technical difficulty) had counted for more than lives. The FAW.Mk 22 had an even better US-supplied radar, designated AI.22. By 1958 the FAW.Mk 22 was the first FAA aircraft to be armed with guided missiles, a heat-homing Firestreak being

---

HMS *Bulwark* during the Suez campaign.
26 December 1956 892 Squadron disbanded into 893 in HMS *Eagle* after Suez operations.

1957

5 January 1957 830 Squadron disbanded on disembarking from a spell in HMS *Eagle* in the Mediterranean.
5 January 1957 897 Squadron disbanded at Lee-on-Solent after service in HMS *Eagle* in the Mediterranean.
5 January 1957 899 Squadron disbanded at Brawdy after service in HMS *Eagle* in the Mediterranean.

14 January 1957 803 Squadron reformed at Lossiemouth with 11 Sea Hawk FGA.6
14 January 1957 806 Squadron reformed at Lossiemouth with 10 Sea Hawk FB.5 (later FGA.6) for service in HMS *Eagle*.
14 January 1957 814 Squadron reformed at Culdrose with 9 Gannet AS.4 for service in HMS *Eagle*.
14 January 1957 894 Squadron reformed at Merryfield with 12 Sea Venom FAW.22 for service in HMS *Eagle*.
10 March 1957 All RNVR squadrons disbanded as part of the 1957 defence cuts.
18 March 1957 700H Whirlwind HAS.7 IFTU formed at Lee-on-Solent.
25 March 1957 765 Squadron disbanded at Culdrose.

1 April 1957 767 Squadron disbanded at Brawdy.
4 May 1957 801 Squadron reformed at Brawdy with 10 Sea Hawk FGA.6 for service in HMS *Bulwark* (later 16 aircraft in HMS *Centaur* in the Far East).
6 May 1957 825 Squadron reformed at Culdrose with 8 Gannet AS.4.
June 1957 845 Squadron re-equipped at Lee-on-Solent with 8 Whirlwind HAS.7
27 August 1957 700X Scimitar IFTU formed at Ford with 7 Scimitar F.1
6 September 1957 700H Whirlwind HAS.7 IFTU disbanded at Lee-on-Solent.
31 October 1957 701 Squadron reformed as a Helicopter Fleet Requirements Unit at Lee-on-Solent with Whirlwinds and

Dragonflies. It had detached flights on various carriers.
1 November 1957 824 Squadron disbanded at Culdrose after service in HMS *Albion*.
1 November 1957 745 Squadron disbanded at Eglinton.
22 November 1957 737 Squadron disbanded at Eglinton.
December 1957 891 Squadron re-equipped with Sea Venom FAW.22 at Merryfield.
2 December 1957 820 Squadron disbanded at Ford after service in HMS *Bulwark*.
10 December 1957 831 Squadron disbanded at Ford.

The 74 de Havilland Sea Vampire T.Mk 22s received by the FAA were very valuable in training jet pilots, and as hacks. This example served with 781 Sqn for the Junior Officers Air Course (JOAC).

Until September 1957 the JOAC training function had been handled by a flight of 781 Sqn, but for a year afterwards was entrusted to 702 Sqn, which moved to Ford. Sea Vampire T.Mk 22s served alongside the Sea Balliol and Sea Prince.

736 Sqn formed part of the Naval Air Fighter School at Lossiemouth. Its Sea Vampire T.Mk 22s were used for a variety of tasks, including continuation training, especially in instrument flying, and instructor training.

The Fairey Gannet was employed in the latter half of the 1950s to re-equip the ASW squadrons. AS.Mk 1s gave way to AS.Mk 4s (with increased power), an example of which is seen here taking off from HMS Albion. It served with 824 Sqn, which flew the type until Whirlwinds arrived in 1957.

The Southern Air Division of the RNVR at Benson consisted of 1832, 1835 and 1836 Sqns, sharing a pool of aircraft. Among the SAD complement were two Sea Vampire T.Mk 22s for training purposes.

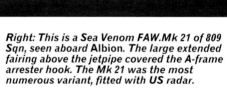

The Gannet was an effective hunter-killer, equipped with search radar for detection and various weapon options (including torpedoes) for the hard kill. 815 Sqn operated this AS.Mk 1, shore based at Culdrose and deployed in Ark Royal.

This Gannet AS.Mk 1 is seen with its retractable search radar 'dustbin' deployed from the rear fuselage. The aircraft is from 812 Sqn which, like most early squadrons, had a T.Mk 2 trainer assigned alongside the mission equipment.

Right: This is a Sea Venom FAW.Mk 21 of 809 Sqn, seen aboard Albion. The large extended fairing above the jetpipe covered the A-frame arrester hook. The Mk 21 was the most numerous variant, fitted with US radar.

fired from under each wing.

1958 saw further involvement in the Middle East. On 1 February, Egypt, Sudan and Syria combined as the United Arab Republic, followed on 14 February by Iraq and Jordan forming the Arab Federation. However, a military *coup* in Iraq on 14 July saw King Feisal II and his young son murdered. King Hussein of Jordan was declared head of state, and two weeks later he dissolved the federation and asked Britain for help under a defence treaty. HMS *Eagle* was at Malta at the time, and two days later it arrived at Cyprus to afford protection for an airlift from Cyprus to Amman. The Sea Venoms of No. 894 Squadron were aboard,

and they were soon joined by the Sea Hawks of No. 802 Squadron which flew out from Ford in stages. The Gannets of No. 814 Squadron undertook A/S patrols around the carrier and its escorts, while the Skyraiders of No. 849A Squadron carried out early warning patrols to warn of possible attacks by low-flying aircraft or motor torpedo boats. HMS *Bulwark* later arrived at Aden from a South African cruise, and *Albion* became a temporary troop transport. By the time the airlift ended on 23 July around 500 sorties had been flown by HMS *Eagle*'s aircraft, a number of United Arab Republic aircraft having been intercepted and escorted away from the force.

Meanwhile Fleet Air Arm helicopters had been active in the area, the four Whirlwinds of No. 728C Flight being sent from Malta to Cyprus in June 1958, with No. 45 Royal Marine Commando to combat terrorist activities. On 13 July an attack took place across mountainous country against suspected terrorists, but they were never found. The flight returned to Malta on 26 July, having gained useful experience but little else.

In 1959 the wartime fleet carrier HMS *Victorious* returned to service after a protracted eight-year refit. It was now virtually a new ship, with fully angled deck, two steam catapults, mirror landing sights and Type 984 radar

*Landing on **Ark Royal** is a **Sea Venom** FAW.Mk 21 from 891 Sqn. The unit had earlier formed 891X Flight to train Australian Sea Venom crews.*

Having been hit by flak over Almaza airfield on 2 November 1956, this lucky 893 Sqn FAW.Mk 21 crew managed to get back aboard the carrier. The slumped observer was unconscious, having been hit in the leg.

The FAW.Mk 22 was the last Sea Venom variant, featuring new radar, ejection seats, uprated engine and, from 1958, the ability to launch Firestreak air-to-air missiles.

Above: The famous badge of a witch riding a broom belonged to 890 Sqn, which had been the first front-line recipient of the Sea Venom (with FAW.Mk 20s) in 1954. The squadron converted to this, the Mk 21, before going to sea.

*Below: Wyverns, Sea Hawks and a Skyraider join the Sea Venom FAW.Mk 21s of 892 Sqn on the deck of **Eagle** during the Suez campaign. The all-weather fighters were mainly employed in their secondary attack task during the fighting.*

linked to what was then the most advanced operations room in the world. The new carrier *Hermes* came into service late in the year, also with a fully angled deck and Type 984 radar, and HMS *Bulwark* departed from service to be converted to a helicopter-equipped commando carrier. New equipment coming into service included the Supermarine Scimitar to replace the Sea Hawk, the de Havilland Sea Vixen to take over from the Sea Venom and the Gannet AEW.3 in place of the Skyraider.

The first two aircraft were large transonic carrier-based fighters with sweptback wings, powered by two Rolls-Royce Avon turbojets each rated at 11,250 lb thrust. Both had also taken many years to develop through a series of interim prototypes. There the similarities ended. The Supermarine programme began in 1945 with the Type 505, to be powered by two Avons of 7,000 lb each and designed to belly-land on a flexible flight deck. After the flexible deck was found to be a bad idea the order was changed to the Type 508, with conventional landing gear, thin unswept wings and a V-type

'butterfly tail'; this flew in August 1951. This led to the Type 525 with swept wings and a conventional tail, flown in April 1954. Various refinements led to the Type 544 of January 1956, and so to the Scimitar F.Mk 1 of which 76 were built, entering squadron service in June 1958. They were used mainly as day visual attack aircraft, with four pylons each rated at up to 2,000 lb, plus four 30-mm guns. A few carried Sidewinder air-to-air missiles before being withdrawn in 1966.

In contrast, the de Havilland Sea Vixen was a

1958

January 1958 HMS *Victorious* recommissioned after an extensive refit, with fully angled deck, two steam catapults, mirror landing sight, Type 984 radar and the most advanced operations room in the world.
7 January 1958 705 (Helicopter Training) Squadron moved from Lee-on-Solent to Culdrose.
13 January 1958 728B (Fleet Requirements) Squadron formed at Stretton for service in Malta with Firefly U.9 and later Meteor U.15 drones for Seaslug missile trials.
21 January 1958 820 Squadron reformed at Eglinton with Whirlwind HAS.7, as the first ex-Gannet anti-submarine squadron

under new AS policy.
27 January 1958 800 Squadron embarked in HMS *Ark Royal* for the Mediterranean.
31 March 1958 803 Squadron disbanded at Lossiemouth after service in HMS *Eagle*.
21 April 1958 824 Squadron reformed at Eglinton with 8 Whirlwind HAS.7 for service in HMS *Victorious*.
22 April 1958 813 Squadron disbanded at Ford after service in HMS *Eagle*.
29 April 1958 825 Squadron disbanded at Culdrose.
1 May 1958 831 Squadron reformed at Culdrose by renumbering 751 Squadron as an electronic warfare squadron with Avenger AS.6 (later Gannet ECM.6) and Sea Venom 21ECM (later 22ECM).
29 May 1958 700X Scimitar IFTU disbanded at Ford to form the nucleus of 803 Squadron.

3 June 1958 803 Squadron reformed at Lossiemouth with 8 Scimitar F.1.
19 June 1958 The four Whirlwind HAS.22 of 728C Flight arrived in Cyprus from Malta to provide help for 45 Royal Marine Commando against terrorists.
13 July 1958 728C Flight assisted in an abortive attack against terrorists believed to be hiding in northern Cyprus.
15 July 1958 815 Squadron disbanded at Culdrose after service in HMS *Ark Royal*.
16 July 1958 HMS *Eagle* arrived at Cyprus from Malta to help provide support for King Hussein of Jordan after a military *coup* in Iraq.
18 July 1958 802 Squadron Sea Hawks arrived in Cyprus after staging from the UK.
20 September 1958 701 Squadron disbanded at Lee-on-Solent.
1 October 1958 807 Squadron reformed

at Lossiemouth with 8 Scimitar F.1 for service in HMS *Ark Royal*.
1 October 1958 815 Squadron reformed at Eglinton with 12 Whirlwind HAR.3 and HAS.9.
1 October 1958 796 (Observer Training) Squadron disbanded at Culdrose.
14 October 1958 848 Squadron reformed at Hal Far ex 728C Flt as Amphibious Warfare Trials Unit with 5 Whirlwind HAS.22.
4 November 1958 700Y Sea Vixen IFTU formed at Yeovilton with 10 Sea Vixen FAW.1.
December 1958 The Airwork-operated Northern Communications Squadron closed, its task being taken over by 781 Squadron at Lee-on-Solent.

Flying past Mount Etna is a Short Sturgeon TT.Mk 2 of 728 Sqn, based at Hal Far in Malta. The Mk 2 was readily identified by its lengthened nose incorporating a glazed position. Sturgeons were used by the unit as high-speed target-tugs from 1951 to 1958, by which time the much faster Meteor TT.Mk 20 was available.

Thirty of the Merlin-powered Sea Balliol T.Mk 21s were acquired by the Fleet Air Arm, used for basic training purposes, including deck landing training. This is a JOAC aircraft (781 or 702 Sqns).

A handful of Sea Balliol T.Mk 21s were distributed to the RNVR squadrons as hacks and trainers. This aircraft was assigned to the Channel Air Division's 1840 Sqn at Ford.

Hunting Percival Sea Prince C.Mk 1s and 2s were procured as staff transports, including one which flew in support of the Joint Services Mission in Washington. This C.Mk 2 'Admiral's Barge' was initially assigned to Vice Admiral Sir John Eccles.

The Sea Prince T.Mk 1 was procured as a 'flying classroom', and most were given to training units. However, several were assigned to the RNVR squadrons. 1840 Sqn at Ford operated the type between 1953 and 1956.

The Sea Prince T.Mk 1 was fitted out with three stations for observer pupils. Wireless and ASW-type systems were installed. In this role 750 Sqn was the principal user, the type serving from February 1953 to May 1979.

night and all-weather fighter from the start. Like the Vampire and Sea Venom it had its tail carried on twin booms, the central nacelle being short. The pilot sat on the left, under an offset canopy, and the large nose radar was managed by an observer seated in 'the coal hole' inside the nacelle on the right. The DH.110 prototype flew on 26 September 1951 and soon exceeded the speed of sound in a dive, but tragically broke up in the air at the 1952 Farnborough air show. Virtually no action was taken for six months, but gradually the project was restarted for the Fleet Air Arm. A modified prototype flew in June 1955, and after further redesign with AI.18 radar, folding wings and four

Firestreak missiles the first Sea Vixen FAW.Mk 1 flew on 20 March 1957, the first squadron forming two years later. After building 114 of these useful machines production switched to the FAW.Mk 2 with greater internal fuel and more deadly Red Top missiles. Only 29 of this mark were built, but 67 FAW.Mk 1 Vixens were converted.

Throughout much of the 1950s Bristol had been trying to develop helicopters with tandem rotors (like today's Chinook). After many years this work led to the Type 191 with two Napier Gazelle engines, used in the anti-submarine role. Wisely, the FAA abandoned this (it led to the RAF's Belvedere transport) and again went

to Sikorsky, with the S-58. By May 1957 this had flown in Anglicised form as the Westland Wessex, powered by a single Gazelle and designed for anti-submarine operations from the outset. The Wessex HAS.Mk 1 entered FAA service in April 1960, followed by the HAS.Mk 3, dubbed the 'Camel' because of its hump-backed radome.

The decade ended on a somewhat lighter note, with Fleet Air Arm participation in the Bleriot Air Race from the Arc de Triomphe to Marble Arch. An entry involving a Scimitar and Whirlwind and two motorcycle rides achieved an overall time of 47 minutes, but only came sixth in the race. **Ray Sturtivant**

1959

3 March 1959 800 Squadron disbanded at Brawdy.
17 March 1959 719 Squadron disbanded at Eglinton.
10 April 1959 802 Squadron disbanded at Lossiemouth after service in HMS *Eagle* in the Mediterranean.
14 April 1959 815 Squadron to Portland.
20 April 1959 810 Squadron reformed at Culdrose with 6 Gannet AS.4 for service in HMS *Centaur*.
20 April 1959 824 Squadron disbanded at Culdrose after service in HMS *Eagle*.
20 April 1959 845 Squadron disbanded at Culdrose after service in HMS *Centaur* in the Mediterranean.
30 April 1959 898 Squadron disbanded at

Brawdy after service in HMS *Eagle*.
May 1959 820 Squadron disbanded at Sembawang after service in *Albion*.
1 June 1959 700H Whirlwind HAS.7 IFTU reformed at Culdrose with 7 Whirlwind HAS.7.
July 1959 HMS *Bulwark* paid off for conversion to commando carrier.
1 July 1959 800 Squadron reformed at Lossiemouth with 6 Scimitar F. I for service in HMS *Ark Royal*.
1 July 1959 892 Squadron reformed at Yeovilton ex 700Y Flt with 12 Sea Vixen FAW.1 for service in HMS *Ark Royal*.
15 July 1959 Scimitar piloted by Cdr I.H.F. Martin RN came sixth in Bleriot Race from Arc de Triomphe to Marble Arch.
17 August 1959 809 Squadron disbanded at Yeovilton after service in *Albion* in Far East.

17 August 1959 700G Gannet AEW.3 IFTU formed at Culdrose with 3 Gannet AEW.3.
27 August 1959 700H Whirlwind HAS.7 IFTU disbanded at Culdrose.
28 August 1959 815 Squadron at Portland became an Anti-Submarine Operational Flying School as 737 Squadron with Whirlwind HAR.3 and HAS.7.
30 September 1959 804 Squadron disbanded at Brawdy after service in *Albion* in Far East.
30 September 1959 814 Squadron disbanded at Culdrose after service in HMS *Eagle* in the Mediterranean.
October 1959 700X Wasp P.531 IFTU formed at Yeovilton with 3 P.531.
13 October 1959 750 Squadron moved from Culdrose to Hal Far with 9 Sea Prince.
November 1959 848 Squadron re-

equipped at Worthy Down with 8 Whirlwind HAS.7 for service in HMS *Bulwark* in the Far East.
2 November 1959 892B Flt formed with 4 aircraft out of 892 Squadron for Firestreak IFTU evaluation.
3 November 1959 820 Squadron reformed at Culdrose with 6 Whirlwind HAS.7 for service in HMS *Ark Royal*.
3 November 1959 824 Squadron reformed at Culdrose with 9 Whirlwind HAS.7 for service in HMS *Ark Royal*.
18 November 1959 The new carrier HMS *Hermes* commissioned, with fully angled deck, twin catapults and Type 984 radar.
1 December 1959 847 Squadron disbanded at Yeovilton on return from Cyprus.

For the introduction of new types into service, 700 Sqn was responsible for establishing Intensive Flying Trials Units. For the Scimitar F.Mk 1, 700X Sqn was formed at Ford, receiving its first aircraft in August 1957.

Above: 803 Sqn was the first front-line unit to receive the Scimitar F.Mk 1, acquiring its first aircraft in June 1958. The initial cruises were made in Victorious, the first in September 1958. Here two of the powerful fighters share the deck with the Skyraider AEW.Mk 1s of 849B Flt and Sea Venom FAW.Mk 21s of 893 Sqn.

The Scimitar was launched with the nosewheel in the air, the tail being held down by a cable restraint system. Here a pair of 803 Sqn aircraft prepares to launch from HMS Victorious.

Right at the end of the decade the FAA welcomed the de Havilland Sea Vixen FAW.Mk 1 as a potent all-weather fighter replacement for the Sea Venom. The new fighter lacked guns, but did carry four Firestreak missiles or unguided rockets. This line-up of aircraft is at Yeovilton in July 1959 for the commissioning of the first squadron: 892 Sqn.

A total of 28 Meteor T.Mk 7s were procured by the RN, including 11 ex-RAF aircraft. This machine was on the strength of the Brawdy Station Flight.

In 1955 Ford-based 700 Sqn replaced 703 and 771 Sqns as the Trials and Requirements Unit. This Meteor TT.Mk 20 target tug served briefly at the end of the 1950s. Most of the TT.Mk 20s served with 728 Sqn and the Airwork FRU.

Thirteen de Havilland Sea Devon C.Mk 20s were bought by the Navy for transport tasks, in which they served for many years. 781 Sqn at Lee-on-Solent operated this example.

Fleet Air Arm Order of Battle, 1 January 1960

First-Line Squadrons

UNIT	SHIP ASSIGNMENT	AIRCRAFT	BASE
800 Squadron	HMS *Ark Royal*	6 Scimitar F.1	Lossiemouth
801 Squadron	HMS *Centaur*	14 Sea Hawk FGA.6	aboard ship in the Far East
803 Squadron	HMS *Victorious*	12 Scimitar F.1	Lossiemouth
806 Squadron	HMS *Eagle*	14 Sea Hawk FGA.6	Brawdy.
807 Squadron	HMS *Ark Royal*	8 Scimitar F.1	Lossiemouth
810 Squadron	HMS *Centaur*	6 Gannet AS.4	aboard ship in the Far East
815 Squadron	HMS *Albion*	8 Whirlwind HAS.7	Culdrose
820 Squadron	HMS *Ark Royal*	6 Whirlwind HAS.7	Portland
824 Squadron	HMS *Ark Royal*	8 Whirlwind HAS.7	Portland
831 Squadron 'A' Flight	HMS *Victorious*	4 Gannet ECM.6	Culdrose
'B' Flight	HMS *Victorious*	4 Sea Venom 21 (ECM)	
848 Squadron	HMS *Bulwark*	13 Whirlwind HAS.7	Worthy Down
849 Squadron	Headquarters	6 Skyraider AEW.1	Culdrose
'B' Flight	HMS *Victorious*	4 Gannet AEW.3	Culdrose
'C' Flight	HMS *Albion*	4 Gannet AEW.3	Culdrose
'D' Flight	HMS *Centaur*	4 Skyraider AEW.1	Culdrose
892 Squadron	HMS *Ark Royal*	8 Sea Vixen FAW.1	Yeovilton
892B Flight	(Firestreak evaluation)	4 Sea Vixen FAW.1	Yeovilton
893 Squadron	HMS *Victorious*	14 Sea Venom FAW.22	Yeovilton
894 Squadron	HMS *Albion*	12 Sea Venom FAW.22	Yeovilton

Second-Line Squadrons

UNIT	AIRCRAFT	BASE
700 Squadron (Trials and Requirements Unit)	3 Sea Venom FAW.21, 2 Gannet AS.1, 1 Meteor TT.20, 2 Whirlwind HAR.3/HAS.7	Yeovilton
700G (Gannet AEW.3 Intensive Flying Trials Unit)	4 Gannet AEW.3	Culdrose
700X (P.531 Intensive Flying Trials Unit)	3 P.531 (Wasp)	Yeovilton
705 Squadron (Helicopter Training Unit)	6 Hiller HT.1, 7 Dragonfly HR.3/HR.5, 13(?) Whirlwind HAR.1/HAS.3	Culdrose
727 Squadron (Dartmouth Air Cadets Training)	4 Sea Prince T.1, 9 Sea Vampire T.22, 2 Dragonfly HR.5, 1 Sea Devon C.20	Brawdy
728 Squadron (Fleet Requirements Unit)	2 Sea Devon C.20, 4 Meteor T.7, 5 Meteor TT.20	Hal Far
728B Squadron (Fleet Requirements Unit target drones)	9 Firefly U.9, 5 Meteor U.15	Hal Far
736 Squadron (ID Flight, Operational Flying School)	14 Sea Hawk FGA.6, 4 Scimitar F.Mk 1	Lossiemouth
737 Squadron (Air Anti-Submarine School)	12 Whirlwind HAS.7	Portland
738 Squadron (All-weather, Flight Operational Flying School)	12 Sea Venom FAW.21, 4 Venom T.22	Lossiemouth
750 Squadron (Observer and Air Signal School)	13 Sea Prince T.1	Hal Far
764 Squadron (Air Warfare Instructor Training Squadron)	5 Hunter T.8	Lossiemouth
766 Squadron (All-weather Flying Training Squadron)	14 Sea Venom FAW.21, 2 Sea Vixen FAW.1	Yeovilton
781 Squadron (Communications Squadron)	8 Sea Devon C.20, 1 Whirlwind HAS.22, 1 Dominie	Lee-on-Solent

INDEX

Picture acknowledgments

Front cover: Lockheed. **4:** via Harry Gann, Harry Gann. **5:** Grumman via Harry Gann, via Harry S. Gann, Cecil B. Ogles via Robert L. Lawson via Harry S. Gann. **6:** Grumman via Harry S. Gann (two), National Museum of Naval Aviation via Harry S. Gann, via Harry S. Gann. **7:** via Harry S. Gann (five). **8:** via Harry S. Gann (two), G.S. Williams via Harry S. Gann (two), J.D. Lane via Robert L. Lawson via Harry S. Gann. **10:** Grumman via Harry S. Gann (three), US Navy. **11:** Vought Aircraft via Paul Bower (two), National Museum of Naval Aviation via Harry S. Gann (three). **12:** Harry Gann (two), Jelle Sjoerdsma, via Harry S. Gann, William Swisher via Harry S. Gann. **14:** Nick Williams via Harry S. Gann, via Harry S. Gann, Aerospace, Al Hansen via Harry S. Gann, Clay Jansson via Harry S. Gann. **15:** US Navy, via Harry S. Gann. **16:** via Harry S. Gann, Harry S. Gann. **17:** Harry S. Gann (three), via Harry S. Gann. **18:** Harry S. Gann (three). **19:** Harry S. Gann (four), US Navy. **20:** US Navy, Harry S. Gann (three), Jim Preston via Harry S. Gann. **21:** C. Ziebold via Harry S. Gann, via Harry S. Gann (two), Harry S. Gann, US Navy. **22:** Dassault via Salvador Mafé Huertas (two), Salvador Mafé Huertas. **23:** 2ª Eslla via Salvador Mafé Huertas, via Salvador Mafé Huertas (four). **24:** via Salvador Mafé Huertas (two). **25:** via Salvador Mafé Huertas (two), MoD via Salvador Mafé Huertas. **26:** via Salvador Mafé Huertas (three). **27:** via Salvador Mafé Huertas, MoD via Salvador Mafé Huertas. **28-29:** via Salvador Mafé Huertas. **30-31:** Lockheed, Paul F. Crickmore. **32:** Paul F. Crickmore (two). **33:** Lockheed via Jay Miller via Paul F. Crickmore (five), James C. Goodall Collection (two). **34:** Lockheed via Jay Miller via Paul F. Crickmore, James C. Goodall Collection (four). **35:** Paul F. Crickmore, James C. Goodall Collection (two). **36:** Lockheed via Jay Miller via Paul F. Crickmore, James C. Goodall Collection, Paul F. Crickmore (three). **37:** James C. Goodall Collection (two), Lockheed, Paul F. Crickmore. **38:** Paul F. Crickmore (two), USAF via James C. Goodall Collection. **39:** Lockheed via Paul F. Crickmore (four). **40:** Lockheed via Paul F. Crickmore (three), Lockheed via Jay Miller via Paul F. Crickmore. **42:** James C. Goodall Collection (four), Lockheed via Jay Miller via Paul F. Crickmore (two). **43:** Jim Eastham via Paul F. Crickmore, Lockheed via Paul F. Crickmore, Lockheed, USAF, James C. Goodall Collection. **44:** Jim Eastham via Paul F. Crickmore, Hughes via Paul F. Crickmore, Paul F. Crickmore (two), Norm E. Taylor via Paul F. Crickmore, James C. Goodall Collection, Lockheed via Jay Miller via Paul F. Crickmore. **45:** James C. Goodall Collection (four). **46:** Lockheed (four). **47:** Lockheed, USAF, James C. Goodall Collection. **48:** Lockheed (three), James C. Goodall Collection. **49:** NASA (two), James C. Goodall Collection, NASA via Paul F. Crickmore. **50:** James C. Goodall Collection (two), Lockheed, USAF. **53:** Lockheed, USAF, Paul F. Crickmore. **54:** B. Bailey via David Donald (three), Lockheed via Paul F. Crickmore, USAF via James C. Goodall. **55:** Lockheed (four). **56:** Lockheed, USAF. **57:** James C. Goodall Collection (two), Paul F. Crickmore. **58:** D.M. Brown via Paul F. Crickmore, Lockheed (three), David Donald. **59:** Lockheed (two), David Donald. **60:** USAF, Tom Pugh via Paul F. Crickmore, Lockheed, James C. Goodall Collection. **61:** USAF (two), GIFAS, Aerospace, Lockheed. **62:** Lockheed via Paul F. Crickmore, USAF, Paul F. Crickmore. **63:** James C. Goodall Collection (three). **64:** Paul F. Crickmore, USAF. **65:** Paul F. Crickmore (two), USAF via Paul F. Crickmore. **66:** Paul F. Crickmore, USAF, Lockheed. **67:** David Donald, Paul F. Crickmore, MoD via Paul F. Crickmore, via David Donald. **68:** James C. Goodall (six), James C. Goodall Collection (three), Lockheed. **69:** David Donald, James C. Goodall (four), James C. Goodall Collection (three), Paul F. Crickmore. **75:** Paul F. Crickmore (three). **76:** Pratt & Whitney, Paul F. Crickmore (five), David Donald (two). **77:** via Paul F. Crickmore (five). **78:** Paul F. Crickmore, USAF (two), DoD via Paul F. Crickmore (two). **79:** Lockheed (two), USAF, Paul F. Crickmore (four). **80:** Lockheed, Paul F. Crickmore. **81:** Lockheed via Paul F. Crickmore (tw[o]), Paul F. Crickmore (two). **82:** NASA via Paul F. Crickmore, NASA (three). **83:** NASA via Paul F. Crickmore, NASA (three). **84:** Lockheed, USAF, NASA via Paul F. Crickmore (two). **85:** James C. Goodall, David Don[ald] (two), Lockheed (two), USAF, Ted Carlson. **86:** Lockheed, David Donald (two). **87:** Don Emmons via Pau[l] Crickmore (two), Lockheed (two). **88:** Paul F. Crickmore (eight), Lindsay Peacock via Paul F. Crickmore. **8[9]:** Jim Winchester (two), Paul F. Crickmore (three), Ted Carlson, NASA. **90:** Paul F. Crickmore (two), NASA. **91:** Lockheed (three), NASA, Lockheed via Paul F. Crickmore, USAF via Paul F. Crickmore, USAF (two), Marysville Appeal-Democrat via Paul F. Crickmore, James C. Goodall Collection. **92:** David Donald (two), Lockheed (three), L. Peacock via Paul F. Crickmore, USAF via Paul F. Crickmore, James C. Goodall Collection (two). **93:** Chris Ryan (two), Paul F. Crickmore (two), Lockheed (three), USAF (two), Marysville Appeal-Democrat via Paul F. Crickmore, David Donald, James C. Goodall Collection. **94:** Aerospace, via Robert F. Dorr. **95:** Boeing, via Nick Veronico via Robert F. Dorr, Aerospace, Republic. **96:** Boeing via Robert F. Dorr (two), Aerospace. **97:** Boeing (two), Boeing via Robert F. Dorr, Norm Taylor Collection via Robert F. Dorr. **98:** Boeing via Warren M. Bodie (two). **99:** via Robert F. Dorr (two), Hal Andrews Collection via Robert F. Dorr. **100:** VPAF via Dr Zoltán Buza. **101:** VPAF, VPAF via Dr Zoltán Bu[za] (two). **102:** Colonel Ferenc Varga via Dr Zoltán Buza (two), VPAF via Dr Zoltán Buza. **103-104:** VPAF via Dr Zoltán Buza. **105:** VPAF via Dr Zoltán Buza (three), USAF. **106:** VPAF via Dr Zoltán Buza (three), USAF, [1??] VPAF via Dr Zoltán Buza (two), Dr Zoltán Buza (four). **108-116:** VPAF via Dr Zoltán Buza. **117:** Dr Zoltán Buza (six), Dr István Toperczer, VPAF via Dr Zoltán Buza. **118:** Aerospace (two). **119:** Charles E. Brown Collection/RAF Museum, Imperial War Museum. **120:** Charles E. Brown Collection/RAF Museum, Aerospace, Imperial War Museum. **121:** Imperial War Museum (four). **122:** Charles E. Brown Collection/RAF Museum, Aerospace (two), British Airways, Handley Page. **123:** Aerospace (two), Michae[l] Stroud. **124:** Aerospace, Rolls-Royce. **125:** via Roy C. Nesbit, Aerospace (two). **128:** via Roy C. Nesbit, RAF Museum. **129:** via Mike Hooks, Aerospace. **130:** BAe via Mike Hooks (tw[o]) Aerospace (two), via Patrick Laureau. **131:** Aerospace (three), RAE via Dr. Alfred Price. **132:** via Ray C. Sturtivant, Aerospace. **133:** Aerospace (two), via Andrew Thomas. **134:** via Andrew Thomas (two), Aerospace. **135:** Aerospace (four). **136:** via Roy C. Nesbit, via Mike Hooks, Aerospace. **137:** via Ray C. Sturtivant, Aerospace. **138:** Aerospace (four). **139:** Charles E. Brown, Aerospace, via Andrew Thomas. **1[??]:** RAF Museum, Aerospace. **141:** Aerospace (two), via Mike Hooks, via Bruce Robertson. **142:** Imperial W[ar Museum], Brown, MoD MAP via Ray C. Sturtivant. **145:** Aerospace (two), MoD (two). **146:** MoD (six). **147:** MoD, MAP via Ray C. Sturtivant, Ray C. Sturtivant, Aerospace. **148:** MoD (two), Aerospace. **149:** Aerospace, C. Sturtivant, RAF Museum, MAP via Ray C. Sturtivant. **150:** MoD (two), Bruce Robertson (two), MoD via Ray C. Sturtivant, Ray C. Sturtivant, MAP via Ray C. Sturtivant. **151:** Bruce Robertson, MoD. **152:** MoD, MAP via Ray C. Sturtivant (two), Ray C. Sturtivant, Bruce Robertson (two). **153:** Bruce Robertson (two), MoD (two). **154:** MAP via Ray C. Sturtivant (two), MAP via Grant Race, Aerospace, Bruce Robertso[n] (two), Ray C. Sturtivant, Fleet Air Arm Museum via Grant Race. **155:** Ray C. Sturtivant, Fleet Air Arm Museum via Grant Race (two), Aerospace, Bruce Robertson. **156:** Bruce Robertson, Ray C. Sturtivant (tw[o]) Aerospace, MAP via Ray C. Sturtivant, MoD. **157:** RAF Museum, Aerospace (three), MoD, Ray C. Sturtiv[ant] MAP via Ray C. Sturtivant.